# LIBERALISM: OLD AND NEW

# LIBERALISM: OLD AND NEW

*Edited by*

**Ellen Frankel Paul, Fred D. Miller, Jr.,
and Jeffrey Paul**

**CAMBRIDGE**
UNIVERSITY PRESS

PUBLISHED BY THE PRESS SYNDICATE OF THE UNIVERSITY OF CAMBRIDGE
The Pitt Building, Trumpington Street, Cambridge, United Kingdom

CAMBRIDGE UNIVERSITY PRESS
The Edinburgh Building, Cambridge CB2 2RU, UK
32 Avenue of the Americas, New York, NY 10013-2473, USA
477 Williamstown Road, Port Melbourne, VIC 3207, Australia
Ruiz de Alarcón 13, 28014 Madrid, Spain
Dock House, The Waterfront, Cape Town 8001, South Africa

http://www.cambridge.org

First published 2007

Printed in the United States of America

*Typeface* Palacio 10/12 pt.

*A catalog record for this book is available from the British Library*

*Library of Congress Cataloging-in-Publication Data*
Liberalism: Old and New /
edited by Ellen Frankel Paul, Fred D. Miller, Jr., and Jeffrey Paul.    p.    cm.
Includes bibliographical references and index.
ISBN 0-521-70305-0 (pbk.)
1. Liberalism. *10 0 6 7 8 6 4 5 X*
I. Paul, Ellen Frankel.   II. Miller, Fred Dycus, 1944   III. Paul, Jeffrey.   IV. Title.
JC574.L5199   2007
320.51–dc22      2006038526

The essays in this book have also been published,
without introduction and index, in the semiannual journal
*Social Philosophy & Policy*, Volume 24, Number 1,
which is available by subscription.

# CONTENTS

# INTRODUCTION

As a political tradition, liberalism has had a profound influence on public policy and jurisprudence. Yet throughout its history liberalism has taken different forms, and the character of liberalism has long been a subject of contentious debate. On the one hand, classical liberalism emphasizes individual freedom, strong rights to private property, and limited government. On the other hand, welfare (or egalitarian) liberalism allows for a more prominent role for government intervention in the market in order to reduce inequality and regulate economic activity.

Historically, the American variant of the controversy over the nature of liberalism began in the latter part of the nineteenth century with the Progressive movement, when Progressive historians, political scientists, philosophers, and lawyers criticized the Lockean and natural-rights framework of the founding. This debate originated in philosophical or historical criticisms of the founders and their professed principles by figures such as Woodrow Wilson (writing as an academic rather than as a politician), John Dewey, Charles Beard, and many others. The debate also manifested itself in competing views of the United States Constitution.

This debate over the very soul of liberalism is very much alive today, as the thirteen essays in this volume attest. Written by prominent philosophers and political scientists, these essays address the nature of liberalism, its origins, and its meaning and proper interpretation. Some of the essays examine the writings of liberalism's earliest defenders, such as John Locke and Adam Smith, or the influence of classical liberalism on the American founders. Some focus on the Progressive movement and the rise of the administrative state, while others defend particular conceptions of liberalism or examine liberal theories of justice, including those of John Rawls and Robert Nozick. Several essays discuss the U.S. Constitution, seeking to determine whether it is best viewed as empowering the federal government to achieve certain ends, including the promotion of the general welfare, or as strictly limiting its power in order to ensure the broadest freedom for individuals to pursue their own ends. Other essays address the limits of economic freedom or focus on the nature and extent of property rights and the government's power of eminent domain.

The collection opens with a trio of essays on the history of liberalism. In "Newer Than What? Older Than What?" Alan Ryan explores liberalism's origins, beginning with the question of whether liberalism existed in antiquity. He contends that it did not, even though many ancient Greek thinkers exhibited qualities that modern liberals rightly admire, such as an appreciation of human diversity and a cosmopolitan tolerance of the beliefs and customs of people in foreign lands. Ryan maintains that genuine liberalism, with its belief in moral individualism and the right of private judgment, emerged only after the Protestant Reformation of the sixteenth century. Two factors were crucial to liberalism's emergence: the Protestant belief that each individual must be responsible for giving an account of himself and his actions to his Creator; and the increasing acceptance of a scientific, non-teleological view of nature, which meant that hierarchical systems of political power could no longer be justified as part of the natural order. In the remainder of his essay, Ryan turns from liberalism's origins to a discussion of its various contemporary forms. One of the most prominent forms is the political liberalism of John Rawls, which advocates the establishment of social institutions that people with different conceptions of the good can all agree upon, because those institutions embody a concern for the moral value of the individual. Rawls contrasted his political liberalism with various "comprehensive" liberalisms—detailed theories of human nature and the human good that include controversial moral claims and commitments. Ryan concludes his essay by arguing, against Rawls, that only a comprehensive form of liberalism can provide the foundation for the sort of liberal political order that Rawls advocates. Specifically, Ryan defends an "autonomist" conception of liberalism which holds that individuals are in some sense self-creating, that they are able to examine and reevaluate their beliefs about the world, and that they are capable of charting the course of their own lives, while allowing others the freedom to do the same.

The next two historical essays deal with the Progressive era in the United States. In "The Progressive Origins of the Administrative State: Wilson, Goodnow, and Landis," Ronald J. Pestritto examines the development of the modern American administrative state, the collection of federal agencies that exercise broad powers to regulate and manage the national economy with the aim of promoting the public interest. The existence of this administrative state, Pestritto notes, is largely at odds with the liberalism of America's founding era. America's founders held that one of the primary purposes of government was to limit the power of majorities to infringe on the rights of individuals. One means of achieving this purpose was the U.S. Constitution's strict separation of powers, but the modern administrative system undercuts the separation-of-powers principle. Under this system, Congress delegates significant legislative power to bureaucratic agencies. These agencies exercise a combination of legislative, executive, and judicial functions; they are charged with developing regulations, enforcing them, and adjudicating disputes that arise over their enforcement. Pestritto shows that the animating idea behind the administrative state is the separation of politics and administration: underlying this idea is the belief that administrators, distinguished by their objectivity and expertise, should be allowed to do their work without undue political influence. This idea was later championed by James Landis, the New Deal architect of the administrative state, but the idea did not originate with Landis or the New Deal. Instead, it originated with the Progressives who had come a generation earlier. Pestritto shows that both Woodrow Wilson and the political scientist Frank Goodnow were pioneers in advocating the separation of politics and administration, and made it the centerpiece of their broad arguments for constitutional reform.

Like Pestritto, Eldon J. Eisenach seeks to explore how the Progressive movement influenced the development of governmental and social institutions in the United States. In "Progressivism as a National Narrative in Biblical-Hegelian Time," Eisenach begins with the observation that Progressive intellectuals at the turn of the twentieth century founded the modern American university system, created its academic disciplines, and edited the journals that codified academic thought. They also exercised a profound influence on national journalism and in national professional organizations, and played a crucial role in the establishment of the administrative and regulatory state. By examining the writings of some of these intellectuals—especially Lyman Abbott, Albion Small, and Simon Patten—Eisenach seeks to underline three main features of Progressive thought. The first of these was the idea of a shared national narrative, a common history and destiny that provided the moral and institutional basis for political mobilization. The second feature was the Progressives' hostility to principled or abstract-philosophical forms of political and social thought, which were viewed as barriers to necessary political reform. The third feature was the Progressives' confidence that historical modes of social inquiry would produce "laws" of progress that would guide political practice and anchor a set of values designed to integrate the individual and society on a democratic basis. After looking at each of these features in detail, Eisenach concludes by examining recent calls by contemporary liberal theorists for a rebirth of Progressivism.

The next three essays explore or defend specific versions of liberalism. Gerald F. Gaus defends a version of classical liberalism in his essay, "On Justifying the Moral Rights of the Moderns: A Case of Old Wine in New Bottles." He begins with the assumption that principles of public morality must be publicly justified, that is, justified to all members of a society as free and equal moral persons. He acknowledges that there will be disagreements over the proper standards for evaluating proposed principles; individuals will differ in their judgments, and these differences will make public justification difficult. Some theorists have attempted to overcome this evaluative diversity by seeking some way to aggregate individual judgments. Others have attempted to abstract away from individual circumstances in order to arrive at a shared evaluative perspective (e.g., John Rawls's original position, in which individuals choose principles of justice from behind a veil of ignorance that prevents them from knowing their specific circumstances). Gaus argues, however, that it is possible to overcome evaluative diversity by instituting a system of classical liberal rights, including rights to private property and freedom of contract as well as freedoms of expression, religion, and association, privacy rights, rights against unreasonable search and seizure, and so on. Classical liberal rights provide a way of addressing the problem of public justification by devolving moral authority to individuals, giving them the authority to decide what evaluative standards to apply in specific situations. The value of such a system of rights, Gaus concludes, is that it defines limited spheres in which the evaluative standards of individuals are given a special standing: within his own sphere, each individual's judgments are taken to be publicly justified.

Debra Satz's essay, "Liberalism, Economic Freedom, and the Limits of Markets," explores a neglected strand of argument in the writings of liberalism's earliest defenders. Satz attempts to show that some classical liberal theorists recognized that market freedom was not always compatible with individual liberty. She acknowledges the many ways that markets enhance the ability of individuals to exercise their capacities as free agents: markets foster cooperation; they provide agents with a wide array of choices; they decentralize decision making; they undermine ethnic and religious discrimination; and they place limits on the viability of coercive social relationships by providing avenues for exit. Yet markets can also have disadvantages: agents who engage in market transactions often lack relevant information; their transactions sometimes negatively affect third parties; and market relationships are sometimes distorted by monopolies or other forms of unequal bargaining power. Satz argues that classical liberals recognized the limits of markets more than is commonly supposed. She focuses on the writings of Adam Smith, noting that Smith viewed market freedom as a form of liberation from the oppressive relationships that existed under the feudal system that capitalism replaced. The undermining of servile relationships between peasants/laborers and feudal landowners was one of the great achievements of markets. Expanding on Smith's analysis, Satz contends that properly functioning labor markets (and credit markets) require certain kinds of intervention and regulation if workers are not to be subjugated to the power of their employers. Specifically, the existence of these markets requires the prohibition of certain market choices—including, for example, bonded labor contracts, child labor, and the charging of excessive rates of interest. Without these restraints on freedom of contract, she argues, we would not have a properly functioning capitalist system.

In his essay, "Populist Perfectionism: The Other American Liberalism," Thomas A. Spragens, Jr. argues that contemporary debates over American liberalism have largely ignored one of the most influential versions of liberalism: populist perfectionism. This normative conception of democracy, Spragens notes, was inspired by philosophical ideas found in the writings of thinkers such as John Stuart Mill and G. W. F. Hegel, and its notable adherents included Walt Whitman and John Dewey. Advocates of populist perfectionism held that one of the goals of a democratic society should be to promote the ability of all its members to pursue lives of their own, choosing their own purposes and developing their talents and capacities as human beings. Once Spragens has sketched out populist perfectionism's basic tenets, he goes on to consider its relevance to contemporary cultural criticism. He examines the philosopher Richard Rorty's recent argument that American liberals would be well advised to recover and reclaim the heritage of Whitman and Dewey, since it can provide a rallying point for contemporary political struggles on behalf of greater inclusion, equality, and social justice. In the course of his discussion, Spragens touches on a number of aspects of the thought of Whitman and Dewey, including their secularism, their accounts of human nature and the human good, and their views on the relationship between social justice and individual freedom. Spragens concludes that populist perfectionism has much to offer for those on the cultural left who would seek to reform liberalism.

The collection continues with a group of essays that focus on liberal views of justice. In "Procedural Versus Substantive Justice: Rawls and Nozick," David Lewis Schaefer critically assesses the procedural accounts of justice set forth by John Rawls in *A Theory of Justice* (1971) and by Robert Nozick in *Anarchy, State, and Utopia* (1974). Schaefer argues that the areas of agreement between Rawls and Nozick are more significant than their disagreements: both theorists maintain that the justice of a given distribution of wealth or resources depends on the justice of the procedure that generates it, rather than on substantive considerations, such as differences in moral desert among individuals. Nozick offers trenchant criticisms of Rawls's argument for economic redistribution (embodied in Rawls's "difference principle," which states that inequalities are permissible only to the extent that they benefit the least-advantaged members of society), yet Nozick's own economic libertarianism is undermined by his principle of "rectification" for past injustices, which could itself lead to widespread redistribution. Schaefer maintains that both Rawls's and Nozick's accounts of justice fail because of their abstraction from human nature as a ground of justice. He contends, moreover, that the libertarianism on which Rawls and Nozick agree in the noneconomic sphere would deprive a free society of its necessary moral underpinnings. As an alternative to Rawls's and Nozick's accounts of justice, Schaefer advocates the kind of Lockean liberalism embodied in the American Declaration of Independence and the U.S. Constitution, a liberalism that leaves room for the adjustment of policies to particular circumstances based on statesmen's prudential judgment and the consent of the governed.

In "Libertarianism and the State," Peter Vallentyne considers whether a government can be considered just even if it does not arise from the mutual consent of its citizens. Vallentyne's conception of justice is grounded in left-libertarianism, a view that combines classical liberalism's concern for individual liberty with contemporary liberalism's concern for material equality. On this view, a government is considered just if it respects the rights of its citizens and if it prohibits only those activities that violate someone's rights. Vallentyne argues that such a government could be financed without coercive taxation if those who violated rights were forced to bear the costs of law enforcement. He also argues, however, that it is possible to provide a libertarian justification of taxation for the sake of redistributing resources to the poor. According to the left-libertarian view that Vallentyne defends, those who appropriate natural resources for their own use have an obligation to use a portion of their gains to promote the well-being of others. In practice, those who hold rights over natural resources would be required to pay a tax for those rights, based on what the value of the rights would be in a hypothetical auction or market. The state would collect the funds and use them to promote equality of opportunity for well-being among the poor. Vallentyne contends that these funds could be invested in education, transportation, communications, research and development, health care, and similar endeavors, since all of these tend to promote individual well-being in the long run. Thus, he concludes, left-libertarian theory can justify a fairly robust state that engages in a wide range of activities.

Loren E. Lomasky considers issues of international justice in his contribution to this collection, "Liberalism Beyond Borders." The citizens of developed countries enjoy lives of unmatched affluence, he notes, while many of the world's poor struggle to subsist on incomes of less than a dollar a day. The poverty of citizens of Third World countries is often viewed as a glaring injustice, and the proposed solution is generally some form of international redistribution. Lomasky maintains, however, that a lack of redistribution is not the problem. The poverty of the underdeveloped world is indeed a matter of injustice, but it cannot be remedied with foreign aid. The responsibility for the injustice lies with corrupt Third World governments that violate the rights of their citizens, as well as with governments in developed countries that erect barriers to trade between foreign nationals and their own citizens, subsidize domestic industries, and prevent innocent movement across borders by would-be workers. In addressing these issues, Lomasky endorses a classical liberal view of international justice, in which individuals have strong rights to exercise their liberty and to control their property without interference from governments or other individuals. In the course of his essay, he sketches several guiding principles of this view. These include the free movement of goods and services across borders and the elimination of tariffs, quotas, and subsidies; the liberalization of immigration policies; the cessation of loans and other aid to Third World leaders who oppress their citizens; and the possibility of humanitarian military intervention in some limited cases where oppression takes the form of open violence against citizens. These measures, Lomasky concludes, are consistent with a classical liberal account of justice, and would go a long way toward relieving poverty and lessening international inequality.

The collection concludes with four essays that explore constitutional interpretation within the liberal tradition. In "Liberalism and the Constitution," Sotirios A. Barber challenges the view that the primary purpose of liberal government is to protect negative rights, rights that secure individuals' freedom of action and require that others refrain from interfering with that freedom. He argues that liberal governments can also have a constitutional obligation to secure positive rights or welfare rights, rights that require the positive provision of benefits such as housing, education, or medical care. On Barber's view, the text of the U.S. Constitution describes a government devoted to the provision of the goods listed in the document's preamble, including the promotion of the general welfare. Barber considers the arguments of conservative writers who hold that the Constitution is chiefly designed to secure negative liberties, but he maintains that these writers are in error, since they ignore the positive nature of the goods (life, liberty, property) that negative liberties protect. The logic of the Constitution is instrumentalist: government is granted specific powers in order to achieve specific ends, chief among which are national security and prosperity. Barber goes on to defend his position in detail, examining specific constitutional provisions as well as the views of the founders as expressed in *The Federalist Papers*. He concludes his essay by addressing the concerns of critics who fear that a welfarist view of the Constitution threatens democracy, since it opens the door to the recognition, by activist judges, of an array of new positive rights that would require an expansion of governmental power and spending that voters and their elected representatives might not support. This fear of judicial activism is overdrawn, he suggests, since there is no necessary connection between welfare constitutionalism and enhanced judicial power.

Michael P. Zuckert's contribution to this volume, "On Constitutional Welfare Liberalism: An Old-Liberal Perspective," offers a critique of Barber and other theorists who advocate a welfarist view of the U.S. Constitution. Zuckert begins by sketching the origins of liberalism in the seventeenth century in the writings of John Locke. This original liberalism emphasized individuals' equality before the law and their right to be left free from coercion; the power of government was strictly limited and its primary purpose was the defense of individual rights. Zuckert goes on to trace the late-nineteenth-century emergence of welfare liberalism, which emphasized the regulation of private economic activity and the redistribution of wealth to achieve greater equality. This new version of liberalism found expression in the Progressive movement in the U.S., as well as in Franklin Roosevelt's New Deal and Lyndon Johnson's Great Society. In its most recent version, Zuckert observes, welfare liberalism claims to be solidly grounded in the fundamentals of the liberal tradition and of the Constitution. Advocates of this "constitutional welfare liberalism," including Barber and theorists such as Stephen Holmes and Cass Sunstein, seek to replace the negative-rights model of the American constitutional order with a positive-rights model. They rest their case on an analysis of rights that denies the meaningfulness of the common distinction between negative and positive rights. In response, Zuckert analyzes this distinction in order to show that it is indeed meaningful when properly understood. He also argues that neither the general character of the Constitution as an empowerment of government nor the particular goals stated in the preamble support the positive-rights model that constitutional welfare liberals seek to advance.

William A. Galston examines the shift from classical liberalism to welfare liberalism in constitutional jurisprudence in his essay, "Why the New Liberalism Isn't All That New, and Why the Old Liberalism Isn't What We Thought It Was." Galston notes that the New Deal is often taken to mark the dividing line between the era of classical liberal governance, with its robust conception of private property and limited role for government in the economy, and the era of welfare liberal governance, which permits government to override individual property rights in pursuit of the general welfare. Galston sets out to challenge this conventional view by focusing on the history of Fifth Amendment takings clause jurisprudence. When we examine Supreme Court decisions regarding property rights, he contends, we find that the movement away from strong property rights begins not with the New Deal but in the late nineteenth century, at what is normally taken to be the peak of constitutionally protected private property. Turning to more recent Supreme Court decisions on eminent domain, Galston discusses the much-criticized 2005 decision in *Kelo v. New London*, in which the Court ruled that the city of New London, Connecticut, could seize the property of a number of homeowners, not for "public use" (as traditionally understood) but in pursuit of a "public purpose," namely, the city's economic development. Under this approach, a kind of consequentialist calculus guides takings clause jurisprudence, as the rights of individual property-holders are traded off against benefits to the community. Galston argues that this approach is difficult to justify in nonemergency situations. As an alternative, he recommends a two-tiered approach: limiting the government's power of eminent domain in ordinary circumstances to cases where property is taken for public use, while allowing for more expanded power (and consequentialist trade-offs) in circumstances of emergency, when the lives or basic well-being of citizens are at stake.

The transition from classical liberalism to welfare liberalism in the United States is also the subject of Jacob T. Levy's essay, "Federalism and the Old and New Liberalisms." This transition has often been identified with the historical shift from a relatively federal to a relatively centralized constitutional structure in the U.S., but Levy challenges this view. He argues that the federal system established by America's founders was supportive of individual freedom only approximately and contingently. Under that system, the states could protect the freedom of their citizens by organizing resistance against potential encroachments by the central government. The central government, in turn, could enhance freedom within the states by guaranteeing each state a republican form of government (as the Constitution provided), but not by supervising the content of state laws (since judicial review of state laws by federal courts only became a common practice many decades after the founding). Indeed, the federal system failed notoriously to protect freedom in the slaveholding Southern states, and Levy notes that the centralization of government that took place in the decades after the Civil War still did not bring an end to the era of Jim Crow restrictions on liberty. Even the centralization of governmental power that took place under Woodrow Wilson and Franklin Roosevelt did not bring about significant advances in civil rights for blacks. Those advances only started to take place in the 1950s, when the federal judiciary began to intervene systematically within the states to strike down racial discrimination, vigorously enforcing the Fourteenth Amendment's guarantee of equal protection of the laws. Levy's essay explores the history of federalism in detail and concludes that a more federalist constitution is not automatically a freer one on classical liberal understandings of freedom, nor is a more centralized constitution automatically a better match with the ideals of welfare liberalism.

Liberalism has a rich and varied history, from its early, classical version to contemporary egalitarian and welfarist versions. The essays in this volume offer important contributions to the ongoing debate over the best rendition of the liberal tradition and its implications for constitutional interpretation and public policy.

## ACKNOWLEDGMENTS

The editors wish to acknowledge several individuals at the Social Philosophy and Policy Center, Bowling Green State University, who provided invaluable assistance in the preparation of this volume. They include Program Manager Nicolás Maloberti, Mary Dilsaver, and Terrie Weaver.

The editors also extend special thanks to Administrative Editor Tamara Sharp, for her patient attention to detail, and to Managing Editor Harry Dolan, for providing editorial assistance above and beyond the call of duty.

# CONTRIBUTORS

**Alan Ryan** is Warden of New College, Oxford University. He has written extensively on liberal political thought for many years, and his Penguin Classics edition of *Mill's On Liberty and The Subjection of Women* was published in 2006. He is also the author of *Property* (1987), *Russell: A Political Life* (1993), *John Dewey and the High Tide of American Liberalism* (1995), and *Liberal Anxieties and Liberal Education* (1998).

**Ronald J. Pestritto** is Charles and Lucia Shipley Associate Professor of the American Constitution at Hillsdale College. He is also a Senior Fellow of the Claremont Institute for the Study of Statesmanship and Political Philosophy. He has published six books, including the recently released *Woodrow Wilson and the Roots of Modern Liberalism* (2005). Among his other books are an edited collection of Wilson's speeches and writings titled *Woodrow Wilson: The Essential Political Writings* (2005) and *Founding the Criminal Law: Punishment and Political Thought in the Origins of America* (2000). He earned his Ph.D. from the Claremont Graduate University in 1996.

**Eldon J. Eisenach** is Professor of Political Science at the University of Tulsa. He received his undergraduate degree from Harvard University and his graduate degrees from the University of California at Berkeley, and he has taught previously at Cornell University and Penn State. He is the author of numerous books, including *The Lost Promise of Progressivism* (1994), *The Next Religious Establishment: National Identity and Political Theology in Post-Protestant America* (2000), and *Narrative Power and Liberal Truth: Hobbes, Locke, Bentham, and Mill* (2002). He is the editor of *Mill and the Moral Character of Liberalism* (1999) and *The Social and Political Thought of American Progressivism* (2006).

**Gerald F. Gaus** is James E. Rogers Professor of Philosophy at the University of Arizona. During 2005–2006, he was Distinguished Visiting Professor of Philosophy at the University of North Carolina at Chapel Hill. His books include *On Philosophy and Economics* (forthcoming, 2007), *Contemporary Theories of Liberalism: Public Reason as a Post-Enlightenment Project* (2003), and *Justificatory Liberalism: An Essay on Epistemology and Political Theory* (1996). He is the editor (with Chandran Kukathas) of *The Handbook of Political Theory* (2004) and a founding editor (with Jonathan Riley) of *Politics, Philosophy, and Economics.*

**Debra Satz** is Associate Professor of Philosophy and Director of the Ethics in Society Program at Stanford University. She has published articles on child labor, prostitution, and commercial surrogacy, as well as on global justice, the family, rational choice theory, and democratic theory. Her work has appeared in journals such as *Philosophy and Public Affairs, Ethics, World Bank Economic Review*, and *The Journal of Philosophy*. She is currently completing a book on the limits of markets.

**Thomas A. Spragens, Jr.** is Professor of Political Science at Duke University. He has written widely on topics of modern political philosophy and contemporary democratic theory. His books include *The Politics of Motion: The World of Thomas Hobbes* (1973), *The Irony of Liberal Reason* (1982), *Reason and Democracy* (1990), and *Civic Liberalism: Reflections on Our Democratic Ideals* (1999).

**David Lewis Schaefer** is Professor of Political Science at College of the Holy Cross in Worcester, Massachusetts, where he teaches courses on political philosophy. Among his books are *The Political Philosophy of Montaigne* (1990) and *Illiberal Justice: John Rawls vs. the American Political Tradition* (forthcoming, 2007). He has published more than forty scholarly articles and sixty book reviews, and is a three-time fellow of the National Endowment for the Humanities. He has also held research fellowships from the Earhart Foundation and the Institute for Educational Affairs. He holds a B.A. from Cornell University and an M.A. and Ph.D. in political science from the University of Chicago.

**Peter Vallentyne** is Florence G. Kline Professor of Philosophy at the University of Missouri–Columbia. He is the editor of *Equality and Justice* (six volumes, 2003) and *Contractarianism and Rational Choice: Essays on David Gauthier's "Morals by Agreement"* (1991). He is also the coeditor (with Hillel Steiner) of *The Origins of Left Libertarianism: An Anthology of Historical Writings* (2001) and *Left Libertarianism and Its Critics: The Contemporary Debate* (2001).

**Loren E. Lomasky** is Cory Professor of Political Philosophy, Policy, and Law, and Director of the Political Philosophy, Policy, and Law Program at the University of Virginia. He has published numerous articles in moral and political philosophy, and is the author of *Persons, Rights, and the Moral Community* (1987) and *Democracy and Decision: The Pure Theory of Electoral Preference* (with Geoffrey Brennan, 1993). He has held research appointments sponsored by the National Endowment for the Humanities, the Center for Study of Public Choice, and the Australian National University.

**Sotirios A. Barber** is Professor of Political Science at the University of Notre Dame. He received his B.A. from the University of Illinois in 1964 and his Ph.D. from the University of Chicago in 1972. He has taught at the University of South Florida and as a visiting professor at Princeton University and the University of Michigan, and he has held fellowships from the National Endowment for the Humanities and the American Council of Learned Societies. His works include *On What the Constitution Means* (1984), *The Constitution of Judicial Power* (1993), and *Welfare and the Constitution* (2003). He has recently completed a book manuscript with James E. Fleming on constitutional interpretation, and his current project is a book on theories of American federalism.

**Michael P. Zuckert** is Nancy R. Dreux III Professor of Political Science at the University of Notre Dame. He has written extensively on the liberal tradition, especially on the philosophy of John Locke. His books include *Natural Rights and the New Republicanism* (1994) and *Launching Liberalism: On Lockean Political Philosophy* (2002). He is the coauthor (with Catherine H. Zuckert) of *The Truth about Leo Strauss: Political Philosophy and American Democracy* (2006), and he is currently finishing a book on the Fourteenth Amendment titled *Completing the Constitution*.

**William A. Galston** is a Senior Fellow in the Governance Studies Program of the Brookings Institution. Prior to January 2006, he was Saul Stern Professor at the School of Public Policy, University of Maryland; Director of the Institute for Philosophy and Public Policy; and Founding Director of the Center for Information and Research on Civic Learning and Engagement (CIRCLE). From 1993 until 1995, he served as Deputy Assistant to President Clinton for Domestic Policy. He is the author of eight books and more than one hundred articles in the fields of political theory, public policy, and American politics. His most recent books are *Liberal Pluralism* (2002), *The Practice of Liberal Pluralism* (2004), and *Public Matters* (2005).

**Jacob T. Levy** is Tomlinson Professor of Political Theory at McGill University, and has taught previously at the University of Chicago. He received his Ph.D. in politics from Princeton University and his LL.M. from the University of Chicago Law School. He has been a Fulbright Scholar and has held fellowships from the National Science Foundation, the Mellon Foundation, and the Earhart Foundation. He is the author of *The Multiculturalism of Fear* (2000) and of numerous essays on multiculturalism, minority rights, federalism, and the history of liberal thought.

# NEWER THAN WHAT? OLDER THAN WHAT?

By Alan Ryan

## I. Introduction

The body of this essay divides into three roughly equal sections. Section II offers a sketch of the origins of liberalism; it is intended to be perfectly banal, historiographically speaking, but to illustrate the fact that the histories we write are less constrained by the historical facts than by our present-day understanding of what liberalism is—or should be. Nonetheless, history provides some useful embarrassments to over-hasty analyses of liberalism. Section III discusses ways of dividing acceptable forms of liberalism from unacceptable forms: political versus comprehensive, minimalist versus perfectionist, and rights-based versus teleological are the three distinctions focused on here. Section IV argues for an "autonomist" view of liberal freedom and for an open-ended view of what liberalism may eventually turn out to be. I try throughout to leave room for reasonable people to reject liberalism; whatever else liberalism may be, it is not in this essay understood as the political doctrine on which mankind is fated to agree. (With apologies to C. S. Peirce's account of truth as the doctrine on which we are fated to agree.)[1]

## II. Was There Liberalism in Antiquity?

Were there liberals in the ancient world? The facile answer is to say that there were not, because the term "liberal" in its modern political sense dates from no earlier than 1800. This is perhaps not a wholly facile answer; words are coined when they are needed, and if the word "liberal"—which had been used for centuries to praise a man's character, to distinguish the liberal professions from the servile trades, and to characterize the education a gentleman ought to receive—was now turned to political uses, it must be because only now was there a felt need for the term.[2] That is, liberalism needed a label only when it came into existence, and we should regard the absence of the label as a near-definitive indicator of the absence

---

[1] This seems to me to be the danger inherent in contractualist theories such as that of John Rawls, *A Theory of Justice* (Cambridge, MA: Harvard University Press, 1971). See C. S. Peirce, "The Fixation of Belief," *Popular Science Monthly* 12 (1877): 1–15.

[2] Its earliest use in English seems to have been in reference to "the liberal arts" in the late fourteenth century; in English politics, the friends of the French Revolution were accused of being liberals in 1801. The conventional dating of self-ascribed liberal politics is 1809 with the rise of Spanish anti-clericalism.

of the thing labeled: *nullum nomen, nullum nominandum,* as some may be tempted to say. That is not a wholly inept response, but it is surely inadequate. Imagine a country whose people were deeply attached to, say, the right to worship whatever deity they chose within the limits of decency and law, the right to be employed by whomever they chose and to employ whomever they chose, the right to reside wherever they chose, the right to buy and sell property of all kinds, both movable and immovable, the right to be tried before impartial judges and the ancillary rights that this implied, such as being tried only for a known offense according to a clear indictment, and so on. I deliberately omit the right to vote for the moment.

Suppose further that this country chose its rulers on the hereditary principle, that these rulers scrupulously operated on constitutional principles that could be adjusted, although rarely and by a process akin to referendum, and that these "kings" had an immemorial tradition of governing with the assistance of a council of statesmen whose advice was rarely ignored and always with reasons stated when it was. Let us imagine further that there was no word in their language that remotely resembled "liberalism." Now we can ask two questions. Are they liberals? And *must* there be a word in their language that should be translated as "liberalism"? My answers are "probably" and "no." That is, if they were asked about their legal and political system, they might go on at great length about the *mos maiorum*[3] and the peculiar political genius of their *ethnos* that has secured to them the rights of movement, worship, trade, and the rest that none of their neighbors enjoy. If they did so, it would be implausible to suggest that they must have a word equivalent to "liberalism" in their vocabulary, because it would be implausible to insist that they *really* saw all aspects of their social, legal, and political arrangements as flowing from their commitment to anything so abstract as the values of liberalism. They are grateful for their inheritance and determined to secure it.

But is the scenario I have sketched a coherent one? I have said, deliberately, that these people are deeply committed to these rights; and I have, deliberately, cheated by supposing that there is no difficulty about calling them "rights," as distinct from customs, habits, or practices. I could have made life harder for the reader and myself by calling them by these latter names, and interposing the further argument that customs maintained and defended in definably appropriate ways are *rights*. Let us, rather, edge forward by asking why the people in this scenario are so attached to these rights. This is where I justify the answer of "probably" to the question of whether these people are liberals. If we ask in what ways it would

---

[3] "The custom of our ancestors"—Cicero's great standby in explaining the nature of the republican freedom that Rome had enjoyed in its most successful years. See Cicero, *On Duties,* ed. M. T. Griffin (Cambridge: Cambridge University Press, 1991).

make a difference to talk only of habits, we see the difference between being a liberal and simply taking a laissez-faire attitude toward each other's religious beliefs. People who took a laissez-faire attitude would do out of habit what ("true," "real," "proper") liberals do out of conviction. They would leave their neighbors to worship as they chose, but would not wonder what they were entitled to do should they decide that they disliked their neighbors' religious practices. This would be true if their habits were so engrained that it never occurred to them that they might feel intolerant, or if divergent practices had never given anyone any anxiety. Only if they wanted to restrict their neighbors' liberty, but sought a reason for not doing so, would they need a synonym for "right" to indicate what their neighbors possessed that they must not violate, or a synonym for "tolerant" or "liberal" to indicate what trait of character in themselves ought to inhibit any inclination to interfere.[4]

If we have good reason to describe these de facto immunities as rights, we should also describe these people as liberals without the word; if there is no pressure to describe their immunities as rights, then we should not describe them as liberals. Turning our attention back to the ancients, there are several points to be made swiftly. The first is that within the Greek world, there are many writers who exhibit a wry acceptance of the sheer variousness of humanity that the political philosopher Isaiah Berlin would have us believe is one of the basic ingredients of liberalism. Herodotus, for instance, reports with pleasure on the famous encounter between Greeks and Indians at the court of the Persian king Darius. Darius asks the Greeks how much they would have to be paid to eat their dead grandparents; they are aghast. He asks the Indians how much they would have to be paid to burn their dead grandparents; they are aghast. The Greeks know they must cremate the dead, and the Indians know they must eat their ancestors. Does this suggest that Herodotus could have made sense of the thought that Greeks and Indians had the right to act as they did? Almost certainly not. What he evinces is skepticism about there being a single right answer to the question of how best to dispose of the dead; and he evinces a conservative and not wholly skeptical commitment to a metaethical—or perhaps an ethical—principle, which is that whatever our own mores are is best for us. "If anyone, no matter who, were given the opportunity of choosing from amongst all the nations in the world the set of beliefs which he thought best, he would inevitably—after careful considerations of their relative merits—choose that of his own country." It is not a skeptical position, because Herodotus regards

---

[4] Robin Lane Fox, *Pagans and Christians* (London: Penguin Books, 1988), suggests that pagan belief was untheological, and therefore provided no basis for principled intolerance; but because cities and states feared to provoke the anger of the local gods by slighting their rituals, there was a great deal of antipathy to Jews and Christians who refused to accept those rituals.

the fact that all of us do in practice think our own mores best as a reason for regarding them as genuinely best—for us.[5]

The set-piece around which the discussion of Greek liberalism appropriately takes place is Pericles' funeral speech.[6] It says many things that modern liberals find deeply attractive. Liberals would like to live in a country that could, with some justification, describe itself as the school of Hellas; they would like to live in a country that believed it was possible to maintain social discipline without everyone interfering with their neighbors' business. Pericles was not engaging in sociology but making a funeral speech, and given the identity of the opponents in the Peloponnesian War, it is not surprising that he praises Athens for qualities that form the mirror image of the Spartans' oppressive, superstitious, and old-fashioned way of life. Nonetheless, even if we think that it would have been more agreeable to live in Athens than in Sparta, we are no nearer an answer to the question of whether Athens was a liberal society. It seems clear that it was not, and that the concept of "classical liberalism"—not the liberalism of Adam Smith and the classical economists, but "classical" in the sense of "ancient"—is almost a contradiction in terms.

The existence of slavery in Athens is not the decisive consideration; one might value the liberal freedoms and do so for liberal reasons—whose nature is yet to be set out—but conclude that the price of anyone enjoying those freedoms was that others must work as slaves. This is not an incoherent view, but it is somewhat unstable, since it forces us to ask difficult questions about who is to be a slave and on what basis they are to be assigned to that status. Aristotle's anxiety over whether slavery is just according to "nature" must cause acute problems for anyone writing in a more liberal perspective than Aristotle's;[7] John Stuart Mill's view that ancient slavery was a condition of political and intellectual progress does not help to defuse such anxieties, because it assumes that a slave-owning society is not a liberal society, but at best a step on the road to such a society; and G. W. F. Hegel's uncomfortable thought that slavery belonged to a time when absolute wrong had a relative rightness is Mill's thought, expressed in a more tortured fashion.[8] There is an implicit universalism in (almost all) liberal accounts of liberal values that makes it difficult to imagine slavery as a long-term feature of a liberal society. It is not absolutely impossible, because there are many ways of defeating universalism: the claim that slavery reflects racial inferiority is the most obvious,

---

[5] Herodotus, *The Histories*, book 3, chap. 38, trans. Aubrey de Selincourt (London: Penguin, 1972), 257–58.

[6] Thucydides, *The Peloponnesian War*, book 2, chaps. 34–46, ed. and trans. Steven Lattimore (Indianapolis, IN: Hackett, 1998), 90–97.

[7] Aristotle, *Politics*, ed. Stephen Everson (Cambridge: Cambridge University Press, 1996), book I, chaps. 3–7.

[8] G. W. F. Hegel, *Philosophy of Right*, ed. Allen Wood (Cambridge: Cambridge University Press, 1991), addition to section 57; John Stuart Mill, *Considerations on Representative Government* (1861; reprint, Amherst, NY: Prometheus Books, 1991), chap. 18.

reached for by Aristotle on more than one occasion. That is a fact with an obvious bearing on the question of whether the United States before the Emancipation Proclamation was a liberal society that practiced slavery, or not a liberal society precisely because it practiced slavery. Somewhat hesitantly, I think the former: there were liberals who thought that economic necessity demanded slavery, and others who thought liberalism could be practiced only by white men. Greek attitudes in the classical period evince no such discomfort. Slavery was treated as a fact of life, along with the fact that prisoners from the losing side in battle could expect to be butchered if they were unlucky and sold into servitude if they were more fortunate. Humanitarian universalism has to be dug for in infertile soil until at least the rise of Stoicism in the third century B.C.E.; and it is notoriously the case that Stoicism's cosmopolitanism is not liberalism's outgoing, progressive, optimistic cosmopolitanism but a self-centered emphasis on the possibility of self-determination in an oppressive world.

In the first century B.C.E., Cicero attached Stoicism to a rather conventional classical republicanism, and a glance at that combination will serve not only to remind us of the political and intellectual allegiances of our eighteenth-century predecessors, but to sharpen our sense of the varieties of liberalism before us. It is arguable that the political analysis that Cicero developed from an eclectic mixture of Stoic, Platonic, and Polybian resources offers the modern world more than liberalism does. Polybius's account of a mixed constitution with characteristics not unlike those of the U.S. Constitution, set within Cicero's account of the good life for a decently educated and prosperous gentleman, can with some tweaking for modern tastes look very attractive. The tweaking required is too obvious to belabor, but includes the abolition of slavery, the equality of the sexes, and a less restrictive version of *la carrière ouverte aux talents*[9] than Cicero imagined possible. What Benjamin Constant described as "modern liberty,"[10] both in its laissez-faire and its "do your own thing" aspects, gets short shrift as moral theory but reappears in practice as a result of the tolerant acceptance of each other's foibles that persons of liberal sentiments find natural to them.

What this historical sketch is intended to suggest is that any liberalism worth arguing about is essentially modern. Much of what liberals value is not distinctively modern because it is what is valued by almost anyone. It is the worldview into which liberalism fits, and the considerations adduced to explain why liberals value what they do, that are modern. My view, for which I only sketch some arguments here, is that liberalism is

---

[9] "Career open to talent"—or meritocracy.

[10] Constant's "The Liberty of the Moderns Compared with That of the Ancients" is the sacred text, and "modern liberty," which is to say the liberty of the individual as distinct from that of the citizen, may come in many varieties. See Benjamin Constant, *Political Writings*, ed. Biancamaria Fontana (Cambridge: Cambridge University Press, 1988), 309–28.

intelligible only as the offspring of the Protestant Reformation, on the one hand, and the collapse of Aristotelian natural science, on the other. The Protestant contribution is the claim that as individuals every one of us is under an obligation to consider our place in the world, and our relationship to God, and to be ready at every moment to give an account of ourselves and our deeds to the Creator. Because we are obliged to render an honest account, we must think for ourselves and say plainly what we think; this yields what the English political philosopher William Godwin termed "the unspeakably beautiful doctrine" of the right of private judgment and therefore a genuine moral individualism.[11] The other aspect is the destruction of the teleological conception of the universe. It did what Shakespeare feared it might, which was to undermine the naturalness of rank and order. No longer could a hereditary and hierarchical system of ranks gain validity by claiming to be inscribed in the natural order. The death of Aristotle casts us adrift, and the political results are unpredictable. Liberalism is by no means the only option; a more probable outcome is a will-based politics such as that of Thomas Hobbes's *Leviathan* (1651) or divine-right absolutisms based on divine fiat. Liberalism emerged as a historical matter only awkwardly and incompletely from a search for alternative bases of social hierarchy and political authority.

### III. MODERN LIBERALISMS

The question of *what* emerged awkwardly and incompletely can no longer be evaded. What follows is intended to carry only as much conviction as is needed to launch the final section of this essay. John Rawls elaborated over a period of forty years what he termed a "political" conception of liberalism; this was founded on a conception of the person that he described as "political not metaphysical," and the kind of liberalism this conception supported was contrasted with "comprehensive" liberalisms. "Comprehensive" liberalism is a moral doctrine, equipped with a conception of human nature and its needs, and therefore controversial in its commitments; Mill's *On Liberty* (1859) sets out a comprehensive liberalism, for instance. Rawls's liberalism provides something closer to a principled defense of the terms of social and political peace of post-Reformation society. What motivated these distinctions was explained somewhat late in the day in the preface to the second edition of Rawls's *Political Liberalism* (1996), and the explanation is, interestingly, one that makes Rawls's version of political liberalism more distinctive and in many respects more exposed than ever to political theorist John Gray's defense of *modus vivendi* liberalism against all contenders.[12]

---

[11] William Godwin, *Political Justice* (London: C&J Robinson, 1798), 182.
[12] John Rawls, *Political Liberalism*, 2d ed. (New York: Columbia University Press, 1996); John Gray, *Two Faces of Liberalism* (Cambridge: Polity Press, 2000).

Rawls rooted his defense of political liberalism within the history of the religious wars that followed the European Reformation of the sixteenth century. Like many other writers, Rawls thought that the virtues of liberalism had become easier to see after a century of faith-based bloodletting. Certainly, some notable English thinkers, of whom John Locke was one, were converted to a belief in religious toleration after traveling on the Continent and discovering the peace and prosperity that toleration brought in its wake. Two small points need to be made, however. The first is a matter of history. The agreement that *cuius regio, eius religio*—the doctrine that a head of state was entitled to establish in his realm whatever variety of Christianity he chose—put an end to European wars of religion; yet it was not itself a liberal doctrine. It gave each nation-state immunity against religiously motivated attacks by other states, but it did not give the individual freedom to practice his own faith by his own lights. Some states became tolerant when they felt secure, some did not. The second point to be made is that the natural outcome of a war fought to the point of universal exhaustion, in which all sides come to think that the costs of imposing their own brand of Christianity on their neighbors are too high, is what John Gray terms *"modus vivendi* liberalism." We do not respect our neighbor's faith, nor do we regard his religious convictions as a matter of deep importance to him and therefore as something to be treated with concern by ourselves. We simply think that the way to get along with each other is to ignore each other's deepest convictions. We might continue to wish that we could make our neighbors see the light. But "live and let live" is better than the only alternative: "proselytize and die."

Rawls wanted something more than a *modus vivendi,* and his explanation of what he wanted let in a flood of light on otherwise obscure parts of his theory. He wanted the "overlapping consensus" within which we could practice a rational politics to be a consensus on deep principle. The ultimate grounds on which we based political principles might be anchored in any number of different comprehensive worldviews, but what was anchored was not an agreement to live and let live, but a concern for the moral value of the individual.

Rawls's concern was with the way in which different religious—or secular but comprehensive—conceptions of the individual could all sustain a respect for moral personality, and thus provide principled support for the system of rights, opportunities, and immunities that constitute the liberal political order. This concern left Rawls dependent on contestable assumptions about the way in which *modern* faiths would, as a matter of fact, incorporate respect for moral individuality; but the idea that a variety of religious and other "comprehensive" convictions can underpin an agreed-upon, nonmetaphysical view of the entitlements of citizens in modern society is itself attractive. There is much to be said about the ways in which different faiths have acquired that conception of the citizen's rights and duties from having to adapt to life in a modern liberal democracy; all we need note is Rawls's claim that political liberalism need not rest on comprehensive liberalism, and that political liberalism is neither comprehensive nor *modus vivendi*.

I shall argue for the impossibility of resting a liberal politics on anything other than comprehensive liberalism below. The first problem for Rawlsians, however, is that *modus vivendi* liberalism is a much more natural operating commitment of citizens of diverse faiths than is political liberalism. The former wears its attractions as a peace treaty on its face. It is equally plausible that any advance beyond *modus vivendi* that was equally impressed with the demands of peaceful coexistence would get no further than the liberal pluralism to which political philosopher William Galston is committed. This is a *modus vivendi* liberalism of communities in which the emancipation of individuals takes second place to a politics that respects collective attachments to ways of life, moral outlooks, ritual practices, and the like, and allows communities a great deal of unofficial authority over their members.[13] Again, the fact that political liberalism is intended to rest upon an "overlapping consensus" of principles founded on different comprehensive doctrines renders it vulnerable to John Gray's critique of liberalism, precisely because Gray presses so hard the question of what kinds of politics we can practice without a moral consensus. *Modus vivendi* is surely what Hobbesians and everyone impressed by human destructiveness would settle for; and not all *modi vivendi* will be liberal ones. *Pace* Gray himself, the millet system of the Ottoman Empire, which allowed a degree of autonomy to recognized religious minorities, was less a form of liberal pluralism than pluralism *simpliciter*.[14] It rested on Islamic principles for the treatment of non-Muslims, not on the rights of the minority. Thus, if the question is what a thought-experiment reveals about the terms of social cooperation between either individuals or communities with dramatically different worldviews who have to get along with each other, Gray seems to have the better of the argument. That is not to say that Gray either establishes or attempts to establish the *moral* superiority of *modus vivendi* to a consensus on "political" liberalism. In a normative sense, the ambitiousness of Rawls's construction makes it very attractive as well as very vulnerable. However, I wish to attack Rawls's account of political liberalism from the opposite direction to that from which Gray does so. I shall argue that, on the one hand, Rawls was not ambitious enough, and that, on the other hand, he was overly optimistic about the prospects for political liberalism without a strong commitment to comprehensive liberalism on the part of at least a substantial minority of the politically active members of society.

---

[13] William Galston, *Liberal Pluralism* (Cambridge: Cambridge University Press, 2002).
[14] Gray, *Two Faces*, 47.

Accepting Rawls's claim that modern forms of the major world religions find room for a conception of the rights of personality that is adequate to sustain political liberalism, we should ask ourselves two questions: whence did this conception come, and what happens when there is a tension between the demands of the underlying faith and those of political liberalism? Rawls thought the right of women to seek an abortion without facing criminal sanctions was an element in liberalism; but Catholic teaching is that abortion is murder, and the Catholic Church has always tried to ensure that abortion is criminalized. It is an open question whether one can derive abortion rights from all forms of comprehensive liberalism—as distinct from more broadly utilitarian premises—but setting that to one side, it seems implausible that there *cannot* be a tension between the demands of political liberalism and the demands of modern Catholicism. What goes for that tension goes for much of Judaism, Islam, and so on; one only has to think of issues around the rights of husbands and wives in a marriage. A liberal state cannot accept the Orthodox Jewish view that a woman is not lawfully divorced until her husband has given her a *get*, nor Sharia law's view that a woman's testimony in court is worthless when contradicted by a man's. The tension is obvious enough: either the liberal state subcontracts its authority to nonliberal religious minorities or these minorities relate to the state on *modus vivendi* terms.

The versions of the major faiths that are at ease with the liberal political order are, I would argue, those that have been adjusted to the demands of comprehensive liberalism. That is, their views of their own religious commitments have been adjusted to a politics that insists that *we have no right* to have the assistance of the state in promoting our faith, that the religious convictions of others are *none of our business,* and that what we may demand of each other is only the right to practice our faith with others of the same persuasion on terms that persons of all faiths and none could assent to. Even then, there may be tensions at the margins. For instance, the Amish are an introspective, unaggressive, unproselytizing sect, who ask little more than to be allowed to continue their traditional way of life in rural America. Yet even they have come into conflict with the American state where their conception of what they owe their children has been at odds with the state's view of the duties of parents. (The Amish have, of course, come into mild conflict with the state over such matters as the lights to be carried by their horse-drawn carts, but for the liberal political theorist, it is only when the right of parents to practice their faith comes into conflict with the state's wish to promote the autonomy of their children that interesting issues arise.) *Wisconsin v. Yoder* was the landmark 1972 Supreme Court decision in which a divided and anxious Court decided that the Yoder family's right to religious freedom overrode Wisconsin's right to require its young people to attend high

school.[15] The Court decided, plausibly enough, that the young Yoder at
the center of the case would not be unemployable and a drain on
Wisconsin's resources; this evaded the question that only Justice William O. Douglas raised: whether the young man himself had an interest in growing up fully informed about all that the modern world
could offer him.

I have argued that Rawls was too optimistic in thinking that all "modern" faiths would provide principled support from within their "comprehensive" worldviews for the political liberalism that Rawls defended in
*Political Liberalism*. If we ask once again what principles lie behind the
liberal state's refusal to accord any special privilege to faith, we find
ourselves once more in the company of Thomas Hobbes, David Hume,
and John Gray: the evident undesirability of religious warfare tells us that
in a religiously divided society, the best *modus vivendi* is to allow free
exercise of religion to all and special privileges to none. The alternative
must be to appeal to the liberal principle that we are entitled to pursue
our own conception of the good life in our own way, so long as we do not
get in the way of others doing the same thing, and so long as we perform
those minimal social duties—paying taxes, serving on juries, performing
military service when required—that are required to keep society operating efficiently. It is that overarching principle, together with whatever
sociological, historical, and psychological considerations come with it,
that constitutes (a substantial part of) comprehensive liberalism. If, as I
suspect, the liberal allegiances of what Rawls regarded as modern forms
of religion result from the impact on them of liberal political systems and
liberal secular thought, this suggests that a sufficient number of citizens
must base their political liberalism on comprehensive liberalism for there
to be an attachment to the search for the principled resolution of conflict,
and solid support for a liberal constitutional order.

If we are to be comprehensive liberals—and I reiterate that for anything
I say here, rational people may choose not to be—the remaining questions
concern where the advantage lies between perfectionist and minimalist
liberalisms, and similarly between teleological and rights-based liberalisms. On the face of it, a person who espouses a rights-based liberalism
must be committed to a minimalist liberalism; but there is more than one
thought here. Someone who thinks that the task of liberalism is to establish what rights we possess, and what rights a state should protect us in,
may also think that this is an essentially political question. The comprehensive liberal answers the political question by first answering the moral
question: What rights do we possess as members of the kingdom of ends
rather than as citizens of earthly states? I evade the issue of the status of
the right that both Kant and Rawls took very seriously, which is to say the
right of a people to constitute itself as a people and establish a state. That

---

[15] *Wisconsin v. Yoder*, 406 U.S. 205 (1972).

right must certainly be prelegal and extralegal, even if it becomes embedded in such documents as the United Nations Charter.[16] However, it is not exactly a moral right in the sense in which I am using the term.

Here I shall proceed on the basis that a rights-based liberalism affirms the moral right of all individuals—of full age and sound mind—to conduct their lives in their own way, subject to their respecting the same right in others. This provides a minimalist and negative liberalism, and implies nothing about the ends individuals should pursue. The grounding of that right, however, is bound to affirm something about us. Thus, on the libertarian view, each of us is "self-owning," and free to dispose of her or his life, capacities, and resources in the same manner as any other freehold owner of resources, while, on the bleaker and more agonistic view, each of us is thrown into the world as the director of this one life, not so much the owner of a life as the bearer of existential burdens. What theory of the human condition is best adapted to liberalism is another question evaded here, but one reason for accepting that a rational person may choose not to be a liberal of any sort is that when we seek the foundations of a comprehensive liberalism, the Lockean view that we are sent into the world about God's business and should attend to it with care becomes increasingly attractive as the kind of moral framework we need.[17] And the belief in Locke's God is not a dictate of reason.

The right to pursue our own good in our own way on the condition that we do not impede others in their pursuit will provide for a minimalist liberalism by prescinding from questions about what that good may be. Let us turn to the alternative of a teleological and perfectionist liberalism. This is currently unpopular, but perhaps wrongly; and just as nonliberal but tolerant societies may be hard to distinguish from committedly liberal and tolerant societies, so we should expect more convergence in the practical commitments of different varieties of liberal than in their foundational convictions. Once again, we must make distinctions within distinctions, and in particular between one and another sort of perfectionism. Mill's essay *On Liberty* is sometimes said to be antiperfectionist because it permits the state and public opinion to coerce us only to prevent damage to other people, and not to make us better people.

This is obviously right. However, the sense in which Mill's version of liberalism is perfectionist is that its focus is on an ideal of *individuality*; and this is a perfectionist principle because it is not the doctrine of "do your own thing" but the doctrine of "discover what is the best you have within you, and make it your own by doing it." The point of experiments in living is to discover what that best may be. We are not to interfere

[16] John Rawls, "The Law of Peoples," in Rawls, *Collected Papers*, ed. Samuel Freeman (Cambridge, MA: Harvard University Press, 1999), 529–64.

[17] Jeremy Waldron, *God, Locke, and Equality* (Cambridge: Cambridge University Press, 2002).

coercively with other people except in self-defense; but the point of that self-abnegating principle is to provide room for the search for individual excellence. Thus, one reason why one might hanker after Locke's confidence that God has put us in the world to go about His business is that such a vision of what we are called on to do answers the question *why* we have to engage in perfecting ourselves to the extent it is possible here below, and gives us guidance on where we should look for standards of excellence.

Just as we must separate one kind of perfectionism from another to become clearer about the ways in which liberalism is and is not perfectionist, so we must distinguish varieties of teleology. There are at least three distinct ideas to be kept in mind. One is very close to perfectionism: it is that human beings have an end or ends toward which they are naturally drawn and whose realization brings happiness and perfects their lives: *finis coronat opus*.[18] Mill officially disbelieved in that Aristotelian vision, but in practice subscribed to it. His official disbelief was the empiricist's disbelief in final causes. His practical acceptance of the view was a matter of acknowledging the fact that individuals find themselves drawn toward thinking in Aristotelian terms about their goals and their ideals. This was the point that Mill made against Bentham in the 1830s and never retreated from. Secondly, and simpler to describe, Mill subscribed to a teleological, goal-directed moral theory when he refused to appeal to a doctrine of right as a thing independent of utility. Rights must rest on utility, which is to say that rights are grounded on teleological considerations. This is the standard contrast. Thirdly, Mill also believed that the particular rights that liberals defended were warranted by their tendency to bring about a particular sort of progress. Teleology is not simply a matter of an instrumental theory of rights, but a distinctive view of what they are instrumental to. Many of Mill's critics have thought that he also subscribed to a historical teleology, almost as though he were an empiricist Hegel. This must be wrong, unless Mill did not know his own mind, given the number of occasions on which he insisted that decay and retrogression were the natural order of things, and that progress was achieved by fighting an uphill battle against human failings.

## IV. One (Only One) Form of Comprehensive Liberalism

There are innumerable good lives; and there are innumerable ways of living *a* good life, and perhaps of living *the* good life. Liberalism offers a vision of *some parts of* the good life, but even at its most comprehensive, liberalism cannot offer a view of all sorts of value. There is no liberal theory of stamp collecting, for instance, although there is certainly a liberal view of the reasons for not interfering with people who wish to

---

[18] "The conclusion crowns the work."

engage in philately—unless they steal the stamps from someone else. There is, by the same token, no conservative theory of stamp collecting, although there could be conservative reasons for approving of people having harmless hobbies; and there is no Marxist theory of stamp collecting, although there might be Marxist accounts of the role of hobbies in distracting the proletariat from a proper understanding of its oppressed condition. Arguments for the virtues of philately are best made by stamp collectors who can point out the particular interest that stamps provide to their collectors and the particular pleasure people derive from completing their holdings of one or another kind of stamp or from hunting down rarities. Liberalism is not obliged to take sides on the value of philately in a full and rich human life, only on the value of the full and rich human life itself.

Having thus far insisted that a rational person might be no sort of a liberal, and that a rational liberal might be doubtful about espousing comprehensive liberalism, and that someone who espoused comprehensive liberalism might well settle for a minimalist and rights-based liberalism, I now change tack. I have no conclusive argument that a perfectionist, teleological, comprehensive liberalism is more plausible than any alternative; but I do wish to lay out what I would want to defend, were there space to do it at the length it needs.[19] It is, unsurprisingly, difficult to describe such a liberalism because—as is true of most forms of liberalism— much of it is couched in negatives; and it is difficult to describe because much of it must be shaded, qualified, and nuanced in ways that can easily seem to be shifty. With those hesitations in place, my view is this: *Pace* Locke, human beings are not born free, nor are they born equal. They are manifestly born into subjection to their parents and their parents in turn to an existing state. As for equality, they vary greatly in intelligence, strength, health, and much else; and, crucially, they vary in their tastes and passions. They can become free, and they can learn to treat each other as equals in crucial respects, summed up in the Kantian demand to treat one another as ends and never as means only. The liberal will find this demand easier because he or she will be deeply conscious of the fact that the world looks very different from different perspectives and that each of us sees the world only through one set of eyes. This is the "autonomist" view. The question is then what the autonomy at which individuals can aim looks like. This is where shiftiness threatens. If the ideal of autonomy is construed as the requirement that we always start from scratch, so that every belief and every value is held only after deep scrutiny, we shall never believe or value anything at all, not least because we shall become neurotic about the status of the logic on the basis of which we make inferences and about the data from which we make them.

[19] Kwame Anthony Appiah, *The Ethics of Identity* (Princeton, NJ: Princeton University Press, 2005), makes the kind of case that is needed.

For the purposes of liberal theory, "autonomy" means, as it literally does, being one's own master, or setting the rules by which we live for ourselves. We will always find ourselves with all manner of beliefs and wishes that at any particular moment constitute us as the persons we are, with the history we happen to have. Autonomy here means having the capacity to endorse and reject those beliefs and wishes without undue anxiety or difficulty. The negativity involved is that the key value in question is the *absence of fear*, not in the Stoic sense that we have so controlled our emotions that nothing can seriously perturb us, but in a much simpler sense; we must be able to contemplate the idea that the world may be quite other than we think, and that it should be quite other than we have hitherto thought, without panicking. Some people seem to have much of this enviable fearlessness almost as a natural gift; but almost anyone can acquire it, with the right education and imagination and practice. I believe that this ability to revise our sense of who we are, and of what we want out of life and from ourselves, is at the core of the liberal conception of the self, although this idea needs more argument than it will receive here. It makes for an open-ended and almost existentialist perfectionism. It may be rooted in an appreciation of straightforward utilitarian values, but it plainly goes beyond them in its conception of an ideal way of life. Mill's attempt to root this ideal in the utility of man as a progressive being has never carried very much conviction with Mill's critics.

This obviously rests on a modern conception of the individual as in some sense and to some degree self-creating. Mill's account of individuality in *On Liberty* is justly famous; but when John Dewey said that he wished he had said more about the individual's ability to be his own creator, and apologized for exaggerating the social quality of individual personality, it was Mill's vision of individuality that he was espousing.[20] Indeed, Dewey's pragmatism is in many ways a more congenial philosophical partner to such a vision than Mill's simpler naturalism. Mill's empiricist naturalism emphasizes the natural endowment of humanity, as though the greater part of what we become in later life is determined by this original endowment; and yet it cannot be, since he emphasizes so strongly our powers of self-creation. It is a familiar difficulty, and one that Mill had struggled with as a young man wrestling to render free will compatible with the psychological determinism he had been brought up to believe in. Dewey, in contrast, dismissed the idea of a fixed human nature as needlessly constraining; "growth" was the underlying principle of his educational theory and his social and political philosophy. If we now ask what is new about new liberalism, one answer is that it is self-consciously rooted in this open-ended, self-creating conception of the

---

[20] John Dewey, "I Believe," in Dewey, *Collected Works, Later Works*, vol. 14, ed. Jo Ann Boydston (Carbondale: Southern Illinois University Press, 1991), 90.

individual. As that suggests, it is more interested in the self than older forms of liberalism were.

A liberalism founded on a contentious view of human nature and embracing a far-reaching ideal of life plainly meets Rawls's conditions for "comprehensive" status. Does that mean it is inimical to Rawls's "political" liberalism? Plainly not, even in terms of Rawls's own theoretical construction. If "political" liberalism can be defended in terms of an overlapping consensus, then one contributor to that consensus is certainly comprehensive liberalism, along with the various religious worldviews that Rawls mentions. The argument of this essay has been that comprehensive liberalism is the *best* of these supports. Someone who begins with the comprehensive view so lightly sketched here will not wish to interfere with the freedoms of his or her fellow-citizens, or if he or she so wishes, will not wish to have that wish acted on. To put it more simply, he or she will think of everyone as possessing *as rights* just those immunities and powers that all liberal theories of politics converge on. What the comprehensive view will not do in the economic arena is side decisively with a libertarianism that sees all rights as possessions whose nature is modeled on freehold property. The role of property rights as usually understood in promoting the larger liberal goals that a comprehensive liberalism aims at is an empirical question of great difficulty, not a matter of principle. But the last sentence of a short essay is not the place to recapitulate the intellectual history of the last two centuries, except to say that if the question had been simple, we would surely by now have agreed on the answer.

*Politics, New College, University of Oxford*

# THE PROGRESSIVE ORIGINS OF THE ADMINISTRATIVE STATE: WILSON, GOODNOW, AND LANDIS

By Ronald J. Pestritto

## I. Introduction

The administrative state in America today—both its legal framework and the manner in which it makes policy—coexists uneasily and often incoherently with the principles of constitutional government upon which the nation was founded and under which, at least in form, it continues to operate.[1] This is by no means a novel observation; within the literature on constitutional and administrative law, many on both the right and the left have pointed to such a development.[2] This state of affairs is also evident from the tortured logic of federal court opinions, as judges must regularly bow to the reality of the administrative state while doing so within the formal framework of a legal or constitutional order that seems to provide little place for that reality. The aim of this essay is not, therefore, to point to the reality of the administrative state or to describe the manner in which it operates in administrative and constitutional law. My aim, instead, is to examine the political ideas that gave rise to the contemporary situation in administrative law and policymaking, and especially to uncover the foundations of these ideas in the political thought of the Progressive era. Some introduction, however, to the current situation and its relationship to the principles of original constitutionalism is in order, and will show how the growth of the modern administrative state is tied to the movement in the United States from the old liberalism to the new.

[1] By "administrative state," I refer to the situation in contemporary American government, created largely although not entirely by Franklin Roosevelt's New Deal, whereby a large bureaucracy is empowered with significant governing authority. Nominally, the agencies comprising the bureaucracy reside within the executive branch, but their powers transcend the traditional boundaries of executive power to include both legislative and judicial functions; these powers are often exercised in a manner largely independent of presidential control and of political control altogether. Given the vast array of activities in which the national government has involved itself in the post–New Deal era, the political branches of government have come to rely heavily on the expertise of bureaucratic agencies, often ceding to them significant responsibility to set, execute, and adjudicate national policy.

[2] From the point of view of criticizing this development, see Gary Lawson, "The Rise and Rise of the Administrative State," *Harvard Law Review* 107 (1994): 1231–54; from the point of view of celebrating it, see Cass R. Sunstein, "Constitutionalism after the New Deal," *Harvard Law Review* 101 (1987): 421–510. For another insightful account, see Eric R. Claeys, "The National Regulatory State in Progressive Political Theory and Twentieth-Century Constitutional Law," in Ronald J. Pestritto and Thomas G. West, eds., *Modern America and the Legacy of the Founding* (Lanham, MD: Lexington Books, 2006).

## II. Founding Principles and Administration Today

The development of American political thought, of the ideas that animate American government and politics, is indeed a story of two liberalisms. The older understanding of liberalism, in which government is based upon the theory of social compact and is dedicated to securing individual natural rights, is the one that dominated the thought of the American founding era. A different, newer version of liberalism, in which government is based upon historicism and its ends adjust to fit the new demands of each historical epoch, began to replace the founding version in the second half of the nineteenth century, and culminated in the Progressive and New Deal recasting of American national government. The national administrative apparatus that is such an integral part of American government today—one that gives a significant role to administrative agencies in national policymaking—grew out of this movement in American political thought from the old liberalism to the new.

There is, of course, much scholarly debate about the characteristics of the old liberalism in America, and even about whether there was enough continuity of thought during the founding era to enable us to describe it under the umbrella of a single concept or theory such as "social compact." There are also those who would question the distinction between "old" and "new" liberalisms, suggesting instead that there is little about modern American politics and culture that does not have its roots in the principles of the founding.[3] But it is not the task of this essay to treat the various nuances of these important debates. Rather, for the purpose of inquiring about the roots of today's administrative state, I will examine those tenets of early American republicanism that the fathers of today's administrative state *themselves* identified as fundamental to the older liberalism, and as the primary obstacles to be overcome if their vision of national administration was to become a reality.

### A. Liberalism: Old

It is not an accident that the fathers of the new liberalism, such as John Dewey and Herbert Croly, and especially those of them who were most responsible for the role of administration today, such as Woodrow Wilson and Frank Goodnow,[4] all found it necessary to focus attention on the American Declaration of Independence, the Constitution, and the theory

---

[3] For just one example, see Peter Augustine Lawler, "Putting Locke in a Locke Box: Natural Law, Our Constitution, and Our Democracy," in Pestritto and West, eds., *Modern America and the Legacy of the Founding.*

[4] Dewey and Croly helped to launch *The New Republic,* the leading American journal of liberal-progressive opinion in the twentieth century. Wilson served as the twenty-sixth president of the United States, and was a leading academic advocate of Progressive ideas long before his entry into politics. Goodnow was the founding president of the American Political Science Association and a pioneer in the field of administrative law.

of social compact represented in these documents.[5] From the point of view of these men, the theory animating the founding documents was responsible for limiting government in the very ways that would make it impossible to realize their vision of the modern state. Particularly troubling was the transhistorical and limited account of the ends of government laid out in the Declaration, which the fathers of the new liberalism correctly identified as grounded in the language of John Locke's *Second Treatise of Government*.[6] The purpose and role of government, according to the Declaration, is the same for all men by virtue of their common nature, and does not change from one generation to the next. The purpose of government, in the words of the Declaration, is to secure "certain unalienable Rights," which the individual has according to "the Laws of Nature and of Nature's God," and which are not granted by government but by his "Creator." Government exists, therefore, for the very purpose of protecting these individual rights, as individuals would not otherwise consent to it.

The task of protecting individual natural rights in a democratic system of government was the primary challenge to the framers of the Constitution. This is why the authors of *The Federalist* focused on the problem of majority faction—on the possibility, or even likelihood, that a government empowered by a passionate majority would continually threaten the natural rights of the minority if its jurisdiction was not limited in extent and its powers were not channeled by a prudent design of national institutions. While the extent of national territory was cited by James Madison in *Federalist No. 10* as a key means of controlling the effects of faction, *federalism* and the *separation of powers* served as the two primary, organizational features of the constitutional order. Both features were predicated, at least partly, on the notion that dividing power made it more likely that it would be exercised in a rational manner more conducive to the securing of rights. In the case of federalism, the national government would be "limited to certain enumerated objects,"[7] thus sharing power with state and local authorities.

---

[5] There is also significant debate over the continuity between the Declaration and the Constitution. To a limited extent, I explain this debate in *Woodrow Wilson and the Roots of Modern Liberalism* (Lanham, MD: Rowman and Littlefield, 2005), 3–5, 26–27 n. 10.

[6] See, for example, Woodrow Wilson, *The State* (Boston: D. C. Heath, 1889), 11–12; John Dewey, *Liberalism and Social Action* (New York: Capricorn Books, 1963), 4–6. See also John Locke, *Second Treatise of Government,* ed. Peter Laslett (Cambridge: Cambridge University Press, 1988), especially chapters 2 ("Of the State of Nature), 3 ("Of the State of War"), 8 ("Of the Beginning of Political Societies"), and 9 ("Of the Ends of Political Society and Government"). On the connection between Locke and the principles of the Declaration, see Peter C. Myers, "Locke on the Social Compact: An Overview," in Ronald J. Pestritto and Thomas G. West, eds., *The American Founding and the Social Compact* (Lanham, MD: Lexington Books, 2003), 1–35.

[7] Publius, *The Federalist,* ed. Jacob E. Cooke (Middletown, CT: Wesleyan University Press, 1961), No. 14: 86. All citations to *The Federalist* will cite the paper number, followed by the page number in the Cooke edition.

In the case of separation of powers, the legitimate authority of the union would be exercised by three coequal departments of government, each making sure that the others remained within the confines of their proper constitutional places.[8] The fundamental aim of the separation of powers—which, as the fathers of progressive liberalism again correctly understood, came not only from Locke's *Second Treatise* but more directly from Montesquieu's *Spirit of the Laws*—was to safeguard rights against the possibility of arbitrary government.[9] Indeed, Madison in *Federalist No. 47*, echoing Thomas Jefferson, redefined "tyranny" to mean the absence in government of the separation of powers.[10] It is from this fundamental aim of separation of powers that we can discern three important tenets of American constitutionalism that bear directly on the administrative state, although this is by no means an exhaustive list. The first is the principle of nondelegation. If the separation of powers means anything at all, it means that one branch of government may not permit its powers to be substantially exercised by another branch.[11] The second tenet is a corollary of the first: there may be no combination of functions within a single branch. Madison, quoting Jefferson in the passage from *Federalist No. 47* mentioned above, elaborates on this point: "The accumulation of all powers legislative, executive and judiciary in the same hands . . . may justly be pronounced the very definition of tyranny."[12] Under this second tenet of

---

[8] See *Federalist No. 51*: 347–49.

[9] See Locke, *Second Treatise,* chapter 12 ("Of the Legislative, Executive, and Federative Power of the Commonwealth"); and Montesquieu, *Spirit of the Laws* (1748), ed. Anne M. Cohler, Basia C. Miller, and Harold S. Stone (Cambridge: Cambridge University Press, 1989), part 2, book 11, chapter 6 ("On the Constitution of England").

[10] *Federalist No. 47*: 324; Thomas Jefferson, *Notes on the State of Virginia,* in *The Portable Thomas Jefferson,* ed. Merrill D. Peterson (New York: Penguin Books, 1977), query XIII: "The Constitution of the State, and Its Several Charters," paragraph 4.

[11] See *Federalist No. 48*: 332. Lawson elaborates on this principle by showing the logic of nondelegation contained in the Constitution's "vesting" clauses, whereby legislative power is granted almost wholly to Congress, the executive power to the president, and the judicial power to the Supreme Court and lower courts. Lawson, "The Rise and Rise," 1237. See also David Schoenbrod, *Power Without Responsibility: How Congress Abuses the People Through Delegation* (New Haven, CT: Yale University Press, 1993), for a comprehensive explanation of the constitutional and political defects of delegation.

[12] *Federalist No. 47*: 324. John A. Rohr attempts to use Madison's subsequent statement in this paper—that an injustice occurs only when "the *whole* power of one department is exercised by the same hands which possess the *whole* power of another department" (ibid., 325–26)—to contend that the separation-of-powers principle cannot be used as an effective critique of the combination of functions in the modern administrative state. Rohr even claims that by this statement "Publius has defined any likely violation of separation of powers out of existence for the entire government as well as for any administrative agency that we know today." While it may be the case that Rohr's defense of the administrative state would be made much easier if *The Federalist* were as unconcerned about the separation of powers as he contends, his interpretation nonetheless contradicts the very purpose of *Federalist No. 47*. Madison's point in the paper is to respond to critics who were claiming that the various checks and balances (presidential veto of legislation, Senate confirmation of executive appointments, etc.), where one branch exercises some small portion of the powers of another branch, violated the separation-of-powers principle. He follows up this point in the subsequent paper, number 48, by explaining how checks and balances keep the separation-

the separation of powers, those making the law would also have to be subject to its being enforced upon them by an independent authority; those involved in execution could not make up the law as they went along, but would instead have to enforce laws that had been previously established by a separate authority; and those on whom the law was enforced could have their cases judged by an authority entirely separate from the one that had brought prosecution. The third tenet of the separation of powers is the responsibility of administration to the republican executive. The government remains "wholly popular," in the words of *Federalist No. 14*, because those who carry out the law (administrators, under the traditional meaning of the term) are directly answerable to the president, who is elected.[13] The Constitution grants all of "the executive power" to the president and requires him to "take care that the laws be faithfully executed."[14] Administration—as vigorous as some of the founders surely envisioned it—was thereby placed wholly within a single branch of government, and a clear line of political accountability for administrators was established.[15]

## B. Liberalism: New

For the American pioneers in the new liberalism, this older, limited understanding of government stood in the way of the policy aims they believed the state ought to pursue in a world that had undergone significant evolution since the time of the founding. They believed that the role of government, contrary to the ahistorical notion of the earlier liberalism, ought to continually adjust to meet the new demands of a new age. As Wilson wrote in *The State*, "*Government does now whatever experience permits or the times demand.*"[16] A carefully limited government may have been appropriate for the founding era, when the primary concern was throwing off central-government tyranny, but in order for government to handle the demands placed upon it by modern times, the founding-era restrictions on its powers and organization would have to be eased and the scope of government expanded. This is why Dewey criticized the founders for believing that their notions about government transcended their own age; they "lacked," he explained, "historic sense and inter-

---

of-powers provisions from becoming mere "parchment barriers" (48:333). The whole point here is to explicate checks and balances as a defense mechanism *against* the combination of powers; Rohr would, instead, have us believe that *Federalist No. 47* is Publius's way of facilitating such a combination. John A. Rohr, *To Run a Constitution* (Lawrence: University Press of Kansas, 1986), 18–19.

[13] *Federalist No. 14*: 84.

[14] U.S. Constitution, Article II, Sections 1, 3.

[15] One of the best explications of this principle is found in Justice Antonin Scalia's dissent in *Morrison v. Olson*, 487 U.S. 654 (1988), at 697–734.

[16] Wilson, *The State*, 651; emphasis in original.

est."[17] At the most fundamental level, therefore, the separation of powers was a deadly obstacle to the new liberalism, since it was an institutional system intended to keep the national government directed toward the relatively limited ends enumerated in the Constitution and the Declaration of Independence.

Beyond this fundamental difference on the very purpose of government, the three tenets of the separation of powers that I have described posed a particular problem for the new liberals' vision for national administration at the outset of the twentieth century. The range of activities they wanted the government to regulate was far too broad for Congress to handle under the original vision of legislative power. Instead, to varying degrees, the fathers of progressive liberalism envisioned a congressional delegation of regulatory power to an enlarged national administrative apparatus, which would be much more capable of managing the intricacies of a modern, complex economy because of its expertise and its ability to specialize. And because of the complexities involved with regulating a modern economy, it would be much more efficient for a single agency, with its expertise, to be made responsible within its area of competence for setting specific policies, investigating violations of those policies, and adjudicating disputes. The fulfillment of progressive liberalism's administrative vision, therefore, required the evisceration of the nondelegation doctrine and the adoption of combination of functions as an operating principle for administrative agencies. Furthermore, the new liberals believed that administrative agencies would never be up to the mission they had in mind if those agencies remained subservient to national political institutions. Since modern regulation was to be based on expertise—which was, its founders argued, objective and politically neutral—administrators should be freed from political influence. Thus, the constitutional placement of administration within the executive branch and under the control of the president was a problem, as the new liberals looked to insulate administrators not only from the chief executive but from politics altogether.

The achievement of these aims for national administration in the course of the twentieth century, at the expense of separation-of-powers constitutionalism, has been described in the legal literature and elsewhere, especially in Gary Lawson's seminal essay "The Rise and Rise of the Administrative State." As Lawson explains, the Supreme Court ceased applying the nondelegation principle after 1935, and allowed to stand a whole body of statutes that enact the new vision of administrative power.[18] These statutes, to varying degrees, lay out Congress's broad policy aims in vague and undefined terms, and delegate to administrative agencies

---

[17] Dewey, *Liberalism and Social Action*, 32.

[18] Lawson, "The Rise and Rise," 1240. Lawson cites two cases as the last instances of the Court applying the nondelegation doctrine: *Schechter Poultry v. United States*, 295 U.S. 495 (1935); and *Panama Refining Co. v. Ryan*, 293 U.S. 388 (1935).

the task of coming up with specific rules and regulations giving them real meaning. Lawson cites, for example, securities legislation giving to the Securities and Exchange Commission (SEC) the power to proscribe the use of "any manipulative or deceptive device or contrivance in contravention of such rules and regulations as the Commission may prescribe as necessary or appropriate in the public interest or for the protection of investors." The agency, on the basis of its expertise, and not Congress, on the basis of its electoral connection, is charged with determining the policy that best serves the public interest. In another example, legislation on broadcast licenses directs that the Federal Communications Commission (FCC) shall grant licenses "if public convenience, interest, or necessity will be served thereby." [19] More recently, the Supreme Court, under Chief Justice William Rehnquist, made clear that there would be no revisiting the abandonment of nondelegation. In the case of *Mistretta v. United States* (1989), the Court upheld the statute which delegated to the U.S. Sentencing Commission the power to set sentences (or sentencing guidelines) for most federal crimes. If any case were going to constitute grounds for nondelegation review, it would have been this one. Congress created the Sentencing Commission as, essentially, a temporary legislature with no purpose other than to establish criminal penalties and then to go out of existence.[20] But *Mistretta* simply served as confirmation that the federal courts were not going to bring the legitimacy of the administrative state into question by resurrecting the separation of powers.

The second tenet of separation of powers—the prohibition on combining functions—has fared no better in modern constitutional and administrative law. As Lawson explains, "the destruction of this principle of separation of powers is perhaps the crowning jewel of the modern administrative revolution. Administrative agencies routinely combine all three governmental functions in the same body, and even in the same people within that body." His example here is the Federal Trade Commission (FTC):

> The Commission promulgates substantive rules of conduct. The Commission then considers whether to authorize investigations into whether the Commission's rules have been violated. If the Commission authorizes an investigation, the investigation is conducted by the Commission, which reports its findings to the Commission. If the Commission thinks that the Commission's findings warrant an enforcement action, the Commission issues a complaint. The Commission's complaint that a Commission rule has been violated is then prosecuted by the Commission and adjudicated by the Commission. The

[19] Lawson, "The Rise and Rise," 1240. Lawson cites here these sections of U.S. code: 15 U.S.C. Sec. 78j(b); 47 U.S.C. Sec. 307(a).
[20] *Mistretta v. United States*, 488 U.S. 361 (1989).

Commission adjudication can either take place before the full Commission or before a semi-autonomous administrative law judge. If the Commission chooses to adjudicate before an administrative law judge rather than before the Commission and the decision is adverse to the Commission, the Commission can appeal to the Commission.[21]

The FTC is a particularly apt example, since it was the "quasi legislative" and "quasi judicial" character of the FTC that was upheld in 1935, in the landmark Supreme Court case of *Humphrey's Executor v. United States*—the first time that the Court so clearly acknowledged that agencies technically within the executive branch could exercise substantially nonexecutive functions.[22]

The new liberalism has also succeeded, at least partly, in defeating the third tenet of the separation-of-powers framework, by weakening the political accountability of administrators and shielding a large subset of agencies from most political controls. While the independence of so-called "independent regulatory commissions" and other "neutral" agencies is not as clearly established as delegation and combination of functions, the federal courts have certainly recognized the power of Congress to create agencies that are presumably part of the executive branch (where else, constitutionally, could they be?) but are nonetheless shielded from direct presidential control. Normally, this shielding is accomplished by limiting the president's freedom to remove agency personnel. The *Humphrey's* case, for example, overturned the president's removal of an FTC commissioner by reasoning that the Commission was more legislative and judicial than it was executive.[23] More recently, the Supreme Court upheld the independent counsel provisions of the Ethics in Government Act of 1978 (the provisions were subsequently repealed), concluding that even an office as obviously executive in nature as a prosecutor could be shielded from presidential control.[24] These rulings reflect the acceptance of a key tenet of the modern administrative state: that many areas of administration are based upon expertise and neutral principles, and must therefore be freed from the influence of politics. That such a notion has become ingrained in the American political mind-set was evidenced by the near universal outrage expressed over the Supreme Court's 2000 decision in *FDA v. Brown and Williamson*. In this surprising exception to its standard deference for agencies, the Court ruled that before the Food and Drug

---

[21] Lawson, "The Rise and Rise," 1248.

[22] *Humphrey's Executor v. United States*, 295 U.S. 602 (1935). See also the more recent case of *Withrow v. Larkin*, 421 U.S. 35 (1975), which upholds and confirms the combination of functions in the administrative state.

[23] *Humphrey's Executor v. United States*. See also Nolan Clark, "The Headless Fourth Branch," in *The Imperial Congress*, ed. Gordon S. Jones and John A. Marini (New York: Pharos Books, 1988), 268–92.

[24] *Morrison v. Olson*, 487 U.S. 654 (1988).

Administration (FDA) could promulgate and enforce regulations on tobacco, Congress first had to pass a law actually giving the agency the authority to do so.[25] The decision was denounced because it would subject tobacco regulation to the control of the people's elected representatives in Congress (where tobacco-state legislators might derail it), instead of giving carte blanche to FDA scientists to regulate in accord with their own expertise.

The acquiescence in the realms of law, politics, and culture to the concepts of delegation, combination of functions, and insulating administration from political control is explained by what legal scholars call the victory of "functionalism" over "formalism," or what political theorists might loosely translate as "pragmatism" over "originalism." Simply defined, a functionalist or pragmatic approach begins not with the forms of the Constitution, but with the necessities of the current age, thereby freeing government from the restraints of the Constitution so that the exigencies of today can be met. As Peter L. Strauss argues, "Respect for 'framers' intent' is only workable in the context of the actual present, and may require some selectivity in just what it is we choose to respect."[26] This sentiment elevating expedience and efficiency over the separation of powers was expressed very clearly by Justice Harry Blackmun in his opinion for the Court in *Mistretta*: "Our jurisprudence has been driven by a practical understanding that in our increasingly complex society, replete with ever changing and more technical problems, Congress simply cannot do its job absent an ability to delegate power under broad general directives."[27]

The rise of the administrative state that is such an integral feature of the new liberalism thus required the defeat of the separation of powers as a governing principle, at least as it was originally understood, and its replacement by a system that allows delegations of power, combination of functions, and the insulation of administration from the full measure of political control. The remainder of this essay will examine the origins of modern administrative law and policymaking in the critique of the constitutional separation-of-powers system that was made by the fathers of progressive liberalism. In actual practice, the biggest steps toward defeating separation-of-powers constitutionalism took place during the New Deal, which was

---

[25] *FDA v. Brown & Williamson Tobacco Corp.*, 529 U.S. 120 (2000). This is, strictly speaking, a statutory case as opposed to a nondelegation (i.e., constitutional law) case, and the Court does not, in its opinion, indicate any reversal of its long-established delegation jurisprudence. Rather, the significance of the case comes from the Court's refusal, in a high-profile controversy, to read into the law a deference to agency expertise that was not there in the first place.

[26] Peter L. Strauss, "Formal and Functional Approaches to Separation-of-Powers Questions: A Foolish Inconsistency?" *Cornell Law Review* 72 (1987): 493. See also Strauss, "The Place of Agencies in Government: Separation of Powers and the Fourth Branch," *Columbia Law Review* 84 (1984): 573–669.

[27] *Mistretta v. United States*, 488 U.S. 361 (1989), at 372.

animated by a strong optimism about the capabilities, public-spiritedness, and objectivity of administrators. Nowhere was this optimism embodied more fully than in James Landis, the New Deal architect of the administrative state, who is the topic of the essay's next section. I proceed in reverse chronological order, beginning with Landis, in order first to identify the central premise of the modern administrative state before investigating where this premise might have originated. While Landis himself was not part of the Progressive era, his optimism reflected the Progressive political theory that had come at least a generation earlier; it was a manifestation of the idea of separating politics and administration, originated in America by Woodrow Wilson and Frank Goodnow. The final sections of the essay address the Progressive vision of replacing the separation of powers with the separation of politics and administration, and thus look to the role of Wilson and Goodnow as founders of administrative law and policymaking today.[28]

When speaking of Wilson and Goodnow as founders of the administrative state, or of Landis as a New Deal facilitator of the growth of administration, I do not suggest that we see in the modern administrative state the complete fulfillment of the ideas of these men. The primary features of administration today—delegation, combination of functions, limited presidential control—are grounded in the notion of separating administration from politics. Like most political phenomena, however, this separation does not go quite as far in practice as it did in theory. In spite of the dramatic push toward establishing significant administrative discretion over policymaking, it still matters very much, for example, what happens in Congress and the presidency. The point of this essay is to explore the *animating ideas* behind the growth of the administrative state in the twentieth century, and to suggest the ways in which such ideas developed out of opposition to the animating ideas of founding-era

---

[28] The premise of this essay runs counter to Rohr's *To Run a Constitution,* a major work on the origins of the administrative state that also delves into the writings of Wilson and Goodnow, among others. While I argue that today's administrative state is illegitimate in the eyes of the founders' constitutionalism, Rohr attempts to demonstrate a continuity between the two. Rohr's work does, however, offer a mixed view on the role of Wilson and Goodnow. At some points, Rohr suggests that Wilson and Goodnow contradicted the Constitution in their vision for administration, but that in doing so they gave administration a bad name. While Wilson and Goodnow's particular form of administration contradicted the constitutional tradition, the modern administrative state does not. See Rohr, *To Run a Constitution,* esp. 4–5, 111–12; see also John A. Rohr, "The Administrative State and Constitutional Principle," in Ralph Clark Chandler, ed., *A Centennial History of the American Administrative State* (New York: The Free Press, 1987), 116–120, 124. Elsewhere, however, Rohr argues on behalf of the continuity between Wilson's thinking and that of the founders; see Rohr, "The Constitutional World of Woodrow Wilson," in Jack Rabin and James S. Bowman, eds., *Politics and Administration: Woodrow Wilson and American Public Administration* (New York: Marcel Dekker, 1984), 43–44. While Rohr contends that the modern administrative state does not necessarily adopt the principles of Wilson and Goodnow, I endeavor to show here that the ideas of Wilson and Goodnow are quite influential in the later thinking of Landis and in the principles of the administrative state today.

liberalism. The principles of Wilson and Goodnow, later adopted by Landis, are in this way central to the very premise of the modern administrative state.

### III. James Landis and the Objectivity of the Administrative Class

*A. Background*

When Franklin Roosevelt assumed the presidency in 1933, he embarked on a mission to enlarge vastly the scope of national government. This mission was not simply a response to the economic circumstances of the day, but was instead a conscious effort to put into practice the vision of a centralized, regulatory government that had been conceived by the Progressives a generation earlier. Such a mission was made clear by Roosevelt in the 1932 presidential campaign, where he identified Wilson as a key source of New Deal principles.[29] Roosevelt's advisor Felix Frankfurter looked to assemble a team to assist the new administration in crafting a plan to implement the goals on which Roosevelt had campaigned. Among others, Frankfurter called on his junior colleague at Harvard Law School, James Landis. Commissioned to work on securities legislation, Landis believed that the only way for the national government to manage capably the scope of affairs outlined in the New Deal program was to establish and empower a variety of regulatory agencies, whose expert staffs would be given significant discretion to implement Roosevelt's broad goals. It was through his work on securities legislation, and his subsequent service on the FTC and SEC, that Landis became the animating force behind the growth of modern administration as we know it today.[30]

Landis wrote two substantial works of interest on the principles of the administrative state. The first was his seminal work *The Administrative Process*, which was based upon lectures Landis delivered after leaving the SEC in 1937 to become dean of Harvard Law School. As Harvard administrative law scholar Louis L. Jaffe has written, "his lectures in 1938 became inevitably a celebration, a defense, and a rationalization of the magnificent accomplishment in which he had played so brilliant a part."[31] Landis left Harvard in 1946 to return to public service as chairman of the Civil

---

[29] Franklin D. Roosevelt, "Campaign Address on Progressive Government," September 23, 1932, in Samuel I. Rosenman, ed., *Public Papers and Addresses of Franklin D. Roosevelt*, vol. 1 (New York: Random House, 1938), 742–56, esp. 749–51.

[30] For biographical information on Landis, see Thomas K. McGraw, *Prophets of Regulation* (Cambridge, MA: Belknap Press of Harvard University Press, 1984), 153–209. See also Donald A. Ritchie, *James M. Landis: Dean of the Regulators* (Cambridge, MA: Harvard University Press, 1980).

[31] Louis L. Jaffe, "James Landis and the Administrative Process," *Harvard Law Review* 78 (December 1964): 320.

Aeronautics Board, but his experience there was disappointing, as President Truman did not reappoint him at the end of his term. Landis ended up working for the Kennedy family and thus was an advisor to John F. Kennedy during his presidential campaign and the early part of his presidency. It was in this capacity that Landis wrote his *Report on Regulatory Agencies to the President-Elect* in 1960, which contains some very useful reflections on the status of the administrative state that he had helped to form.

## B. The evolutionary critique of constitutional formalism

In both of Landis's major works, the traditional forms of the Constitution are critiqued from an evolutionary point of view. Landis contended that there can be no fixed understanding of the ends and scope of government; rather, the role and even the structure of government must be constantly adjusted so that it can deal with the exigencies of the present. The growth of modern administration, which Landis fully conceded does not fit within the form of American constitutionalism, is a manifestation of this evolutionary critique. "In terms of political theory," Landis explained, "the administrative process springs from the inadequacy of a simple tripartite form of government to deal with modern problems."[32] In an entirely functionalist or pragmatic mode, the ultimate standard for Landis was *efficiency*. Government ought not do what the Constitution prescribes; rather, it ought to do that which enables it to deal most efficiently with the problems of the present. "There is no doubt," Landis reasoned, "but that our age must tolerate much more lightly inefficiencies in the art of government."[33]

Landis was fully aware that with the advent of national administration as he envisioned it, the very understanding of the ends of government in the United States had changed. Under the old liberalism, he knew, government was erected for the sake of securing individual rights. The framers of the Constitution thus acted correctly when they implemented the separation-of-powers framework; this was a framework, Landis agreed, that would keep the national government focused on rights protection as its fundamental end. Nonetheless, modern government had to move beyond the separation of powers, since the end of government had changed from rights protection to what Landis called the "promotion of the welfare of the governed" or, more generally, "well-being." For Landis, the establishment of the Interstate Commerce Commission (ICC) in 1887 marked the key turning point in America's self-understanding of the ends and scope of government. "What was

---

[32] James M. Landis, *The Administrative Process* (New Haven, CT: Yale University Press, 1938), 1–2.
[33] Ibid., 46.

important" about the ICC, Landis explained, "was the deliberate organization of a governmental unit whose single concern was the well-
being, in a broad public sense, of a vital and national industry." As for
the understanding of the old government that the end of government
was rights protection, Landis simply explained that "concessions to
rectify social maladjustments thus had to be made."[34]

One of the major concessions to which Landis referred is that the new
vision of national administration does not comport with the separation-
of-powers structure of the Constitution. As I have noted, the original view
of administration placed it wholly within the executive branch of government, subject to the superintendence of an elected president vested
with "the executive power."[35] For Landis, however, administration cannot be confined to exercising solely executive powers. In order for an
agency to operate with maximum efficiency in its regulation of an industry for the purpose of promoting "well-being," rulemaking, investigatory,
prosecutorial, and adjudicatory powers need to be combined and placed
at the agency's disposal.[36] This kind of combination is precisely what
Landis liked about the ICC, where "a government had to be provided to
direct and control an industry, and governance as a practical matter implied
not merely legislative power or simply executive power, but whatever
power might be required to achieve the desired results."[37] "The resort to
administrative process," he subsequently explained, "is not, as some suppose, simply an extension of executive power."[38] Thus, Landis reasoned
that the Constitution cannot be read to require strict adherence to the
separation of powers. Instead, the organization of the government's powers must be determined by the facts on the ground, and therefore he
urged that interpreters look to "constitutional history"—that is, how the
Constitution had been interpreted to accommodate historical changes—as
opposed to the forms of the Constitution itself.[39] This new reading of the
Constitution amounts to an admission that there exist legitimate powers
of the national government that are not directly granted by the Constitution. Landis lamented that some critics insisted on finding a place for
administration within the existing constitutional structure. This lament is
what characterizes his response to the Brownlow Commission, which had
been appointed by President Roosevelt in 1936 for the purpose of exerting
executive supremacy in national government. Its membership consisted
of Luther Gulick, Charles Merriam, and Louis Brownlow, who served as

---

[34] Ibid., 8–10.

[35] U.S. Constitution, Article II, Section 1.

[36] Landis explains that he would like for administrators to have the power to make
modifications to legislation, and also explains that administration cannot work unless agencies have the authority to impose their own sanctions. See Landis, *The Administrative Process*,
52, 89.

[37] Ibid., 10.

[38] Ibid., 15.

[39] Ibid., 47–48.

its chairman.[40] The Commission had been critical, to a degree, of administrative discretion. For Landis, the Commission had responded "hysterically" to the administrative process, and he mocked its labeling of administration as a "fourth branch." Such criticism, he explained, came from too strong a fixation on the number "three" in thinking about the organization of government.[41]

## C. The nature and extent of administrative power

The most significant reason that Landis's vision of administration could not be reconciled with original American constitutionalism was that he could not tolerate any notion of limiting the discretionary authority of administrators. Not only would administrators need to have at their disposal the combination of legislative, executive, and judicial powers, but Landis did not like talk of placing general limits on the extent to which administrators could employ these powers. Such talk, Landis reasoned, would violate the functionalist tenet of using necessity to determine the scope of state power. "Generalization as to the allowable limits of administrative discretion is dangerous," he argued. He pointed to the Securities and Exchange Act of 1934, which he had helped to draft, as an example of how to create an agency with powers flexible enough to meet unforeseen exigencies. The discretionary language with which the act empowered the SEC was a vast improvement, Landis contended, over the 1933 Securities Act, which had placed authority for securities regulation in the FTC and limited the ways in which commissioners could operate.[42]

Landis conceded that his vision of administration had to overcome a substantial objection: that it threatened rights by combining prosecutorial and adjudicatory powers in the same set of hands. Recognizing the need to answer this objection, Landis suggested that his lectures on the administrative process would offer a response to it. His response, however, simply falls back on the functionalist tenet of necessity or efficiency. He defended the combination of functions within agencies by describing the history of how such a combination came about—by explaining that necessity thrust such a change upon government. Furthermore, Landis believed that there are more than sufficient safeguards within agencies to guard against potential abuses; these safeguards, he contended, may not be "traditional," but they are adequate.[43]

[40] See "Report of the President's Committee on Administrative Management," 74th Congress, 2d Session (Washington, DC: Government Printing Office, 1937). See also Donald R. Brand, "Progressivism, the Brownlow Commission, and the Origins of the American Administrative State," in Pestritto and West, eds., *Modern America and the Legacy of the Founding*.

[41] Landis, *The Administrative Process*, 25, 47.

[42] Ibid., 52–55.

[43] Ibid., 91–101.

Ultimately, the main requirement Landis seems to have had for ensuring competence in administration is the shielding of administrators from political influence. Since administration was politically neutral and based on the administrator's expertise in a particular area, political control could only corrupt the quality of administrative decision making. Administrators should, therefore, have the discretion to apply their expertise and to make their own determination of how best to serve the public interest in particular cases within their jurisdiction, free from the specific guidance of those elected by the people to serve their interests. In what has to be one of the clearest expressions of this sentiment that one is likely to see anywhere, Landis stated:

> One of the ablest administrators that it was my good fortune to know, I believe, never read, at least more than casually, the statutes that he translated into reality. He assumed that they gave him power to deal with the broad problems of an industry and, upon that understanding, he sought his own solutions.[44]

Landis's *The Administrative Process* catalogues the virtues that he believed are generated by securing maximum independence for administrators from political influence. In addition to the rule of expertise, Landis also emphasized consistency in administration as a primary virtue.[45] As a rule, administrators should have long tenure, which would both insulate them from political control and ensure consistency even across periods of political change.[46]

This drive to separate administration from politics made Landis a strong admirer of the Supreme Court's *Humphrey's* decision in 1935. As I have noted, this decision limited the president's ability to remove commissioners of the FTC, thus creating an important precedent for shielding administrators from political influence. "The real significance of the Humphrey doctrine," Landis observed, "lies in its endorsement of administrative freedom of movement." [47] Landis himself was involved in this case in two ways. First, he was serving as a clerk for Justice Louis Brandeis when the Supreme Court, in the 1926 case of *Myers v. United States*,[48] handed down the precedent that *Humphrey's* subsequently overturned. Writing for the Court in *Myers*, Chief Justice William Howard Taft laid out a broad precedent requiring presidential control over executive branch officers (and thus the ability of the president to remove them at will). Both Landis and Brandeis recognized the threat that this ruling posed to the development of a modern administrative apparatus with significant discretion-

---

[44] Ibid., 75.
[45] Ibid., 113.
[46] Ibid., 23.
[47] Ibid., 115.
[48] *Myers v. United States*, 272 U.S. 52 (1926).

ary powers and independence from the realm of politics, and thus Landis worked closely with Brandeis on his *Myers* dissent. Landis and Brandeis were particularly alarmed that Taft had gone out of his way to include independent commissions among the executive entities over which the Constitution required direct presidential control. In the second instance of Landis's involvement, the individual whose estate brought suit for back wages in the *Humphrey's* case was William E. Humphrey, who was a member of the Federal Trade Commission when Landis himself was appointed to the FTC by Franklin Roosevelt. Humphrey was a holdover on the FTC, and thus a continuous thorn in the side of New Dealers like Landis. Ironically, it was Landis himself who convinced the Roosevelt administration that the president had the authority to remove Humphrey at will, since Landis was so familiar with the *Myers* precedent. When Roosevelt eventually lost the case because he had followed Landis's advice, Landis was nonetheless quite pleased: the defeat for the president was meaningless in comparison with the great independence for administrators that the *Humphrey's* decision helped to secure.[49] This incident also helps to show that Landis was much more concerned with the freedom of administrators from politics than was Roosevelt. It was, after all, partly as a result of Roosevelt's belief that administrators should be tied more closely to his political agenda that he appointed the Brownlow Commission, the conclusions of which Landis ridiculed in *The Administrative Process*.[50]

When Landis reflected on the status of administration in his 1960 *Report on Regulatory Agencies,* he continued to urge an even greater independence for administrators from political influence. To the extent that administrative agencies had failed to live up to the vision with which they were created, Landis made clear that the problem was not insufficient political control, but rather an insufficient separation of administration from politics. This is why Landis criticized *ex parte* contacts in administrative decision making[51]—where administrators seek or receive input from other parties in the political institutions—and why he warned that politics was playing too great a role in the appointment of administrators. As he elaborated:

> Advances have been nullified by the appointment of members of these agencies on political grounds, and by not advancing to posts of significance within the agencies men experienced by long service in their business. Largely on political grounds, outsiders lacking necessary qualification for their important tasks have been appointed.

[49] For an account of these episodes, see Ritchie, *James M. Landis: Dean of the Regulators*, 24–25, 49.

[50] See ibid., 85–86.

[51] James M. Landis, *Report on Regulatory Agencies to the President-Elect*, Committee on the Judiciary of the U.S. Senate, 86th Congress, 2d Session, December 1960, section I.D.

> There has also been too much of the morale-shattering practice of permitting executive interference in the disposition of [cases] and controversies delegated to the agencies for decision.[52]

Landis readily acknowledged that keeping administrative decision making free from the influence of politics, and providing administrators with the latitude to exercise legislative, executive, and judicial powers, weakened the protection for individual rights contained within the traditional doctrine of the rule of law. The rule-of-law principle, after all, requires that administrators act only in accord with a preestablished rule. Absent such a principle, individuals and companies have no idea what they have to do in order to avoid the enforcement power of the state, thus putting them at the mercy of administrators who, literally, make up the rules as they go along. Landis complained, however, that the modern need for efficiency and discretion in administration simply made it impossible for administrators to be bound by such an inflexible system.[53]

Furthermore, administrators would be hampered if their decisions were subject to review by an independent court. This bedrock protection for rights, Landis explained, interfered with the notion that administrators were the most expert in their field and thus were the most qualified to adjudicate disputes where individuals or companies were accused of wrongdoing.[54] He even lamented that the problem with allowing individuals or companies to have their cases heard in traditional courts is that such courts must be bound by the "limitations" of the law and judicial procedure put into place to protect rights. Traditional courts must rely only on evidence presented at trial, for example. When administrators adjudicate, by contrast, they do not have to be bound by the evidence presented, but can instead employ their own expertise and understanding of what is truly in the public interest. "For [the administrative] process to be successful in a particular field," Landis argued, "it is imperative that controversies be decided as 'rightly' as possible, independently of the formal record the parties themselves produce."[55] At the very least, Landis considered it essential that agency fact-finding not be second-guessed by an independent judiciary; otherwise, "the very efficiency of the system becomes threatened."[56] These sentiments make perfect sense when one recalls that, for Landis, the ends of government had evolved. Getting a decision "right" in terms of the "well-being" of the general public interest

[52] Ibid., section II.
[53] Landis, *The Administrative Process*, 49–50. For an excellent illustration of how progressive principles of administration undermine the rule of law, see *SEC v. Chenery*, 332 U.S. 194 (1947) and its related cases.
[54] Landis, *The Administrative Process*, 123–24.
[55] Ibid., 38–39. For additional examples of Landis's criticism of the rule of law, see ibid., 30, 35, 133–35.
[56] Ibid., 133.

was, to Landis, a far more important purpose of government than following specific rules and procedures designed to ensure the maximum protection for individual rights.

## D. Why trust administrators?

It is not quite correct to say that Landis disregarded the importance of individual rights. It is the case, rather, that Landis so strongly trusted the objectivity and expertise of administrators that he could not conceive it likely that they would reach unjust decisions, so long as they were given sufficient freedom to do their jobs. It is this trust—or what one commentator has called his "exuberant optimism"[57]—that is really at the core of Landis's entire outlook on reforming government. As we will see in subsequent sections of this essay, Landis was a true Progressive at heart; his trust in the enlightenment and disinterestedness of administrators stands as an instructive contrast to the permanent self-interestedness that the framers of the U.S. Constitution saw in human nature.[58] Just as this sobriety about the potential for tyranny led the framers to circumscribe carefully the authority of the national government, Landis's passionate optimism fueled his call for maximum discretion for administrators. This is not to suggest that the framers denied discretionary power to the national government; no reader of *Federalist No. 23*, or many other papers of *The Federalist* for that matter, could draw such a conclusion. Rather, the framers understood that such discretion had to be channeled through the forms of the Constitution in order to be safe for liberty. Thus, as Alexander Hamilton explained in *Federalist No. 23* and elsewhere, the vigorous discretion that the national government must have is made safe by the "most vigilant and careful attention of the people."[59] For the people to exercise this kind of vigilance, the officers who exercise discretion must do so in a system of clear, electoral accountability. It is precisely this kind of accountability to the realm of politics from which Landis, by contrast, wanted to free administrators.

For Landis, there is something special about civil servants that somehow raises them above the ordinary self-interestedness of human nature. As we will see, for Landis's forebears in the Progressive era, such confidence in civil servants came from a faith that the progressive power of history had elevated public servants to a level of objectivity. They would,

---

[57] Jaffe, "James Landis and the Administrative Process," 319. Jaffe was one of the main critics of Landis's optimism, and he argues in this article that the special circumstances of the New Deal blinded Landis to administration's general susceptibility to corruption. For a listing of other accounts criticizing Landis's excessive optimism, see Ritchie, *James M. Landis: Dean of the Regulators*, 213 n. 6.

[58] See, for example, *Federalist No. 6*, where Publius addresses the Antifederalist and Enlightenment notion that human nature had improved and become less dangerous. He characterizes those holding such notions as "far gone in utopian speculations." *Federalist No. 6*: 28.

[59] *Federalist No. 23*: 150.

accordingly, be able to disregard their own private or particular inclinations in order to dedicate themselves to the objective good. Landis himself spoke glowingly of the selflessness of administrators, describing them as "men whose sole urge for public service is the opportunity that it affords for the satisfaction of achievement." [60] Because of this disinterestedness, restraints on their discretion were unnecessary. Landis took this notion even further, suggesting that the selflessness and objectivity of administrators created a kind of moral imperative that the country allow them to rule:

> Government today no longer dares to rely for its administration upon the casual office-seeker. Into its service it now seeks to bring men of professional attainment in various fields and to make that service such that they will envisage governance as a career. *The desires of these men to share in the mediation of human claims cannot be denied; their contributions dare not casually be tossed aside.* The grandeur that is law loses nothing from such a prospect. Instead, under its banner as a commanding discipline are enlisted armies of men dedicated to the idea of justice.[61]

For Landis, this dedication and the expertise of administrators together cure any potential problem that might come from removing the traditional separation-of-powers protections for individual rights. In the case of granting adjudicatory power to administrators, for example, Landis explained that this is a good thing both for individuals and for the common good, because the expertise of administrators makes them more competent than traditional courts and thus more likely to reach a just result. Therefore, he argued, "it is only delay that results from the insistence upon independent judicial examination of the administrative's [*sic*] conclusion." [62]

## E. Reconsiderations?

Landis's faith in the competence and objectivity of administrators had not receded when he wrote his 1960 evaluation of the system he helped to create. It is true that Landis was disappointed with the record of what agencies had done with their discretion, and he had also had his own unsatisfactory experience with national administration. He even

---

[60] Landis, *The Administrative Process*, 28.

[61] Ibid., 154; emphasis added.

[62] Ibid., 142–43; see also 125. In *Withrow v. Larkin*, where the Supreme Court upheld combining prosecutorial and adjudicative functions in the same set of agency hands, Justice Byron White employed a Landis-like trust of administrators, writing of a "presumption of honesty and integrity in those serving as adjudicators." *Withrow v. Larkin*, 421 U.S. 35 (1975), at 47.

made what must have been a painful concession, admitting that "a deterioration in the quality of our administrative personnel has taken place, both at the top level and throughout the staff."[63] But Landis did not draw from his disappointment over the actual experience of administration the conclusion that agencies might not have been so deserving of the trust he had placed in them or of the latitude they were given as a consequence of the New Deal. "Their continued existence is obviously essential for effective government," Landis wrote. "The complexities of our modern society are increasing rather than decreasing. . . . [These complexities] all call for greater surveillance by government."[64] Landis's 1960 evaluation is thus animated by a call for agencies to do even more, and for them to exercise even greater discretion in making national policy. If anything, in Landis's view, agencies had not abused their discretion but had, instead, been too deliberative and cautious.[65]

The question for Landis in 1960, therefore, was how administration could be helped along to fulfill the great role that he still envisioned for it. First, Landis urged more money and more manpower. It was a frequent observation of Landis's report that agency inaction seemed to come, at least partly, from too great a workload. With greater budgets and staff, agencies would be able to regulate even more zealously.[66] Second, Landis saw a need to attract higher quality personnel into administrative positions. The problem was not that administrators had abused their trust, but rather that they had not been trusted enough. The way to attract better administrators, Landis argued, was to put even more power in administrative positions, thus demonstrating to the most talented individuals that national administration was a place where they could make a real difference. Thus, Landis advocated further insulating administration from politics, and contended that political interference had harmed the morale of agencies and had even kept good men away from administration entirely. The other way to attract higher quality administrators was to offer higher compensation and longer tenure. Longer tenure would, especially, give administrators "freedom from worry" about political influence.[67] Landis also worried about excessive procedural impediments to agency action. Perhaps more than anything else, regulatory activity had been slowed because agencies were being overly cautious in their procedures. Again, the problem was not too much discretion for agencies, but too little. As Landis observed, "The tendency here is again further to judicialize [sic] the administrative process and, in the opinion of many

---

[63] Landis, *Report on Regulatory Agencies*, I.C.
[64] Ibid., Introduction.
[65] Ibid., I.A, I.C, Summary.
[66] Ibid., I.F, II.A.9.
[67] Ibid., II.B.

observers, to over-judicialize it to a point where stagnation is likely to set in."[68]

If Landis's faith in the competence and objectivity of administrators was at odds with the founders' sobriety over the self-interestedness of human nature, experience with the poor quality of administration did not lead him to change his mind. When Landis fretted in 1960 that administrators were making decisions out of concern for advancing their careers, or that administrators might be attracted by more money or increased job security, he did not draw the conclusion that these observations might just be evidence that the founders were correct about the self-interestedness of human nature. He wanted, instead, to see administrators take on an even greater role in national governance.

At first glance, Landis's faith in the objectivity of administrators, expressed in 1938 and affirmed in 1960, may seem at odds with a subsequent development in 1970s administrative law often referred to as "capture theory." This development refers to a growing sentiment, especially among environmental interest groups, that administrators too frequently became "captured" by the industries and businesses they were supposed to regulate. These interest groups began to turn, in the 1970s, to increasingly receptive federal courts, seeking intervention either against agency inaction or against agency action deemed to be insufficiently vigorous.[69] In one sense, such action by interest groups and courts suggests a lack of confidence in the ability of administrators to do their jobs—not a sentiment one would easily associate with Landis. It is also the case, however, that Landis's views in 1960 prefigured the sentiments of activists in the 1970s. That is, Landis wanted agencies to do more, to be more active and zealous in regulating. And Landis, too, worried about the "capture" of regulators:

> Industry orientation of agency members is a common criticism, frequently expressed in terms that the regulatees have become the regulators. . . . The real problem relates to those who are originally oriented towards the public interest but who gradually and honestly begin to view that interest more in terms of the private interest.[70]

Landis and the 1970s activists thus shared a vision about the proper role of administration; both believed that administrators needed to be out

---

[68] Ibid., I. See also I.A.

[69] Gary Lawson has an excellent account of this phenomenon, to which my understanding of it is indebted. See Gary Lawson, *Federal Administrative Law*, 2d ed. (St. Paul, MN: West Group, 2001), 245–55. For examples of the kinds of cases that reflect court action in response to "capture theory," see especially *Citizens to Preserve Overton Park v. Volpe*, 401 U.S. 402 (1971); and *Motor Vehicles Manufacturers Association of the U.S. v. State Farm Mutual Automobile Ins.*, 463 U.S. 29 (1983).

[70] Landis, *Report on Regulatory Agencies*, II.C.

front in acting on behalf of the public good. Both shared, in other words, in the original, New Deal vision for the role of agencies in national governance. Landis did not call, of course, for increasing judicial intervention in order to make administrators fulfill his vision for them; he thought that more money, power, and freedom of action would solve the problem. But the basic understanding of the broad role and mission of administration remained relatively consistent throughout the post–New Deal period. No one, in other words, sought to revive the nondelegation doctrine as a means of correcting any problems that were perceived with agencies or those who staffed them.

### IV. Woodrow Wilson and the Origins of the Politics-Administration Dichotomy

The key principle at work in the twentieth-century developments in administrative law and policymaking described in Section II, and in James Landis's vision for the modern regulatory state described in Section III, is the destruction of separation-of-powers constitutionalism and its replacement by the separation of politics and administration. While Landis and the New Dealers were responsible for taking this principle and transforming it into reality, it did not originate with them. The idea of separating politics and administration—of grounding a significant portion of government not on the basis of popular consent but on expertise—was introduced into the United States by Progressive reformers who had, themselves, learned the principle from German historicism and state theory. In this regard, no one was more important to the origins of the administrative state in America than Woodrow Wilson and Frank Goodnow.[71]

The idea of shielding administration, at least to some degree, from political influence had been around in the United States for some time—at least since the reaction against the nineteenth-century spoils system, in which many jobs in the federal bureaucracy were doled out on the basis of one's affiliation with the party currently in power as opposed to one's actual merit or skill. While the establishment of the Civil Service Commission, through the Pendleton Act of 1883, marked a significant victory for opponents of the spoils system, it took the Progressives, starting with Wilson and Goodnow, to take this rather narrow inclination against the influence of politics in administration and make it part of a thoughtful,

---

[71] This discussion connecting Wilson and Goodnow to the development of the administrative state builds on my earlier work on Wilson. The account here of Wilson's vision for administrative discretion thus represents a brief summary of the more detailed argument in my introduction to *Woodrow Wilson: The Essential Political Writings* (Lanham, MD: Lexington Books, 2005), 22–25, and in my *Woodrow Wilson and the Roots of Modern Liberalism,* 117–28, 221–52. For a very different account of Wilson, see Eldon J. Eisenach, who contends that Wilson was not even a Progressive. His election in 1912 instead marked the end of the Progressive movement, Eisenach argues. Eldon J. Eisenach, *The Lost Promise of Progressivism* (Lawrence: University Press of Kansas, 1994), esp. 3, 124–25.

comprehensive critique of American constitutionalism and part of a broader argument for political reform. Moreover, while the opponents of the spoils system certainly wanted to shield administration from political cronyism, they did not offer a vision of a vastly expanded role for administration; the Progressives, by contrast, made such an expansive role a vital cog in their reform argument. Wilson introduced the concept of separating politics and administration—of treating administrative governance as an object of study entirely separate from politics—in a series of essays in the latter part of the 1880s. Goodnow, while he never directly acknowledged Wilson's role as far as I am aware, expanded upon this Wilsonian concept in the 1890s, and eventually published a book in 1900 titled *Politics and Administration*. Goodnow is often given more credit today for his role in the origins of administrative law, both because his seminal writings on the topic were more voluminous than Wilson's and because administrative law was the field in which Goodnow worked and published for decades. Wilson's administrative writings, by contrast, were but one element of his academic work, and his presidency naturally occupies most of the attention he receives from scholars. Nonetheless, there is very little in Goodnow's understanding of politics and administration, and in his critique of separation-of-powers constitutionalism, that does not build on the principles of Wilson's work from the 1880s, when Wilson was in the early stages of a prolific academic career that would see him in posts at Bryn Mawr College, Wesleyan University, and Princeton (of which he became president) prior to his entry into political life in 1910.

As Landis's writings make clear, the fundamental assumption behind the vast discretion that new liberals wanted to give to administration was a trust in or optimism about the selflessness, competence, and objectivity of administrators, and thus a belief that the separation-of-powers checks on government were no longer necessary or just. If the framers had instituted the separation of powers out of fear of majority faction—fear that the permanent self-interestedness of human nature could make government empowered by democratic majorities a threat to the natural rights of citizens—then the advocates of administrative discretion concluded that such fears, even if well founded in the early days of the republic, no longer applied in the modern era. Thus, administration could be freed from the shackles placed upon it by the separation of powers, in order to take on the new tasks that new liberals had in mind for the national state. This key assumption behind the separation of politics and administration is exemplified in Wilson's political thought.[72]

---

[72] For a different point of view—one that suggests important continuities between Wilson's administrative vision and that of the American founders—see Herbert J. Storing, "American Statesmanship: Old and New," in *Toward a More Perfect Union: Writings of Herbert J. Storing*, ed. Joseph M. Bessette (Washington, DC: AEI Press, 1995), 412–14; Paul P. Van Riper, "The American Administrative State: Wilson and the Founders—An Unorthodox View," *Public Administration Review* 43 (November/December 1983): 479–80; and Rohr, "The

Wilson subscribed thoroughly to the doctrine of historical progress that he had learned from reading German state theorists like G. W. F. Hegel and Johann Bluntschli, and from his own teachers such as Richard T. Ely, who had received their education at German universities. Wilson believed, accordingly, that history had solved the problem of faction, that human nature was no longer a danger in democratic government. He wrote frequently of a "steady and unmistakable growth of nationality of sentiment," of a growing unity and objectivity in the American mind, and thus concluded that the power of the national government could be unfettered because one faction or part of the country was no longer a threat to abuse the rights of another.[73]

With the threat of faction having receded due to historical progress, Wilson argued that a new understanding of the ends and scope of government was in order. This new understanding required, just as it would for Landis, an evolutionary understanding of the Constitution—one where the ends and scope of government are not determined by looking to constitutional forms, but instead to the new demands placed upon government by contemporary historical circumstances. Thus, in his New Freedom campaign for president in 1912, Wilson urged that the rigid, mechanical, "Newtonian" constitutionalism of the old liberalism be replaced by a "Darwinian" perspective, adjusting the Constitution as an organic entity to fit the ever-changing environment. Wilson blamed separation-of-powers theory for what he believed to be the inflexibility of national government and its inability to handle the tasks required of it by the modern era:

> The trouble with the theory is that government is not a machine, but a living thing. It falls, not under the theory of the universe, but under the theory of organic life. It is accountable to Darwin, not to Newton. It is modified by its environment, necessitated by its tasks, shaped to its functions by the sheer pressure of life. No living thing can have its organs offset against each other, as checks, and live.[74]

Wilson saw the separation of powers as a hindrance because, as Landis would later explain, the modern era values efficiency over anything else. As Wilson claimed in 1885, efficiency had become the preeminent principle in government because history had brought us to an age where the administrative functions of government were most important: "The period

---

Constitutional World of Woodrow Wilson," 43–44. For a more detailed response to these arguments, particularly as they relate to Wilson, see my *Woodrow Wilson and the Roots of Modern Liberalism*, 237–38.

[73] Woodrow Wilson, *Congressional Government*, 15th ed. (1885; Boston: Houghton Mifflin, 1900), 42.

[74] Woodrow Wilson, *The New Freedom* (New York: Doubleday, Page and Company, 1913), 47.

of constitution-making is passed now. We have reached a new territory in which we need new guides, the vast territory of *administration*." [75]

Wilson's work on empowering administration with significant discretion to regulate national progress seems to have taken off immediately following his graduate education at Johns Hopkins University. It was at Hopkins that Wilson imbibed deeply in the administrative writings of German authors who belonged to the Hegelian tradition, especially Bluntschli, and that he learned from teachers like Ely, who had studied under Bluntschli at Heidelberg. Wilson's first sustained work on administration came right at this time, in an unpublished essay written in November 1885, titled "The Art of Governing." This work led to the writing, the following year, of Wilson's seminal essay "The Study of Administration," where the case for separating politics and administration is made explicitly for the first time in the United States. [76] Wilson subsequently elaborated on this case in notes he prepared for an annual lectureship at Johns Hopkins from 1888 to 1897. Even prior to entering graduate school, however, Wilson's views on administration had been taking shape, as evidenced by his 1882 essay "Government by Debate." It was in this essay that Wilson first suggested freeing administration from political influence because large parts of national administration were, he contended, apolitical and based on expertise. Administrative departments, Wilson wrote then, "should be organized in strict accordance with recognized business principles. The greater part of their affairs is altogether outside of politics." [77]

---

[75] Woodrow Wilson, "The Art of Governing," November 15, 1885, in *The Papers of Woodrow Wilson* (hereafter cited as *PWW*), 69 vols., ed. Arthur S. Link (Princeton, NJ: Princeton University Press, 1966–1993), 5:52; emphasis in original.

[76] Some scholars suggest that Wilson did not really urge a strict separation between politics and administration. See Kent A. Kirwan, "The Crisis of Identity in the Study of Public Administration: Woodrow Wilson," *Polity* 9 (Spring 1977): 332; Larry Walker, "Woodrow Wilson, Progressive Reform, and Public Administration," *Political Science Quarterly* 104, no. 3 (1989): 511; John M. Mulder, *Woodrow Wilson: The Years of Preparation* (Princeton, NJ: Princeton University Press, 1978), 118; Phillip J. Cooper, "The Wilsonian Dichotomy in Administrative Law," in Rabin and Bowman, eds., *Politics and Administration*, 79–94; and Kendrick A. Clements, "Woodrow Wilson and Administrative Reform," *Presidential Studies Quarterly* 28, no. 2 (Spring 1998): 320–36. Clements even suggests that Wilson's previous assertion of a strict separation between politics and administration "was not really what he meant to say" (322).

[77] Woodrow Wilson, "Government by Debate," December 1882, in *PWW*, 2:224. Wilson's precise role as a founder of the modern discipline of "public administration" has been the topic of some debate. For examples of those who see Wilson as the founder of public administration, see Arthur S. Link, "Woodrow Wilson and the Study of Administration," in Link, *The Higher Realism of Woodrow Wilson and Other Essays* (Nashville, TN: Vanderbilt University Press, 1971), 44; and Leonard D. White, *Introduction to the Study of Administration* (New York: Macmillan, 1929), 5–9. For examples of those who contest Wilson's status as the founder of public administration, see Lynton K. Caldwell, "Public Administration and the Universities: A Half-Century of Development," *Public Administration Review* 25, no. 1 (1965): 53–58; Daniel W. Martin, "The Fading Legacy of Woodrow Wilson," *Public Administration Review* 48 (March/April 1988): 632–35; and Van Riper, "The American Administrative State," 479.

Wilson's thesis in his works on administration was that it was far better and more efficient for a professional class of experts, instead of a multiplicity of politicians with narrow, competing interests, to handle the complex business of the modern state. To the objection that entrusting administrators with such discretion might not comport with the Constitution's distribution of power, Wilson responded that administrative principles and constitutional principles were distinct, and thus constitutional limitations could not easily be applied to the exercise of administrative authority. The constitutional principle of checks and balances, for example, interfered with efficiency and should not be applied to the exercise of administrative power: "Give us administrative elasticity and discretion," he urged, "free us from the idea that checks and balances are to be carried down through all stages of organization."[78] Relying heavily on European models of administrative power, Wilson laid out a vision for administrative discretion that could easily be used as an encapsulation for what Landis would later write in *The Administrative Process*. Wilson wrote, in 1891:

> The functions of government are in a very real sense independent of legislation, and even constitutions, because [they are] as old as government and inherent in its very nature. The bulk and complex minuteness of our positive law, which covers almost every case that can arise in Administration, obscures for us the fact that *Administration cannot wait upon legislation, but must be given leave, or take it, to proceed without specific warrant in giving effect to the characteristic life of the State.*[79]

Wilson well understood that this wide latitude for administrative action undermined the separation of powers, which he attacked and contrasted with what he called the "actual division of powers," where there are many "legislative and judicial acts of the administration."[80]

As would later be the case with Landis, Wilson's argument for freeing administrators from close political control was grounded in a confidence in the expertise and objectivity of the administrative class. For years, Wilson had been urging special education for future administrators at elite universities. He argued that "an intelligent nation cannot be led or ruled save by thoroughly trained and completely-educated men. Only comprehensive information and entire mastery of principles and details can qualify for command." Wilson had faith in the power of expertise, of "special knowledge, and its importance to those who would lead."[81] He

---

[78] Woodrow Wilson, "Notes for Lectures at the Johns Hopkins," January 26, 1891, in *PWW*, 7:122.

[79] Ibid., 7:121; emphasis added.

[80] Ibid., 7:134–38.

[81] Woodrow Wilson, "What Can Be Done for Constitutional Liberty," March 21, 1881, in *PWW*, 2:34–36.

later referred to "the patriotism" and "the disinterested ambition" of the new administrative class.[82] Wilson is thus a critical figure for the new liberal vision of administration, because he is largely responsible for applying Hegelian optimism about the objectivity of administrators to the American system. Wilson assumed, just as Hegel had in the *Philosophy of Right*, that a secure position in the bureaucracy, with tenure and good pay, would relieve the civil servant of his natural self-interestedness, thereby freeing him of his particularity and allowing him to focus solely on the objective good of society.[83] This is exactly the assumption relied upon by Landis, both in 1938 and later in 1960, when Landis called explicitly for improving the pay and tenure of bureaucrats in order to improve their public-spiritedness.

Wilson's model for this conception of administrators, he freely acknowledged, was almost entirely foreign to American constitutionalism. Yet it was his own notion of the distinction between politics and administration, Wilson argued, that cleared the way for importing what was essentially a Prussian model of administration into the United States. Precisely because administration was to be insulated from politics, an administrative system that had come from a monarchy could be brought to America without harming America's republican political institutions. As Wilson memorably put it in "The Study of Administration":

> It is the distinction, already drawn, between administration and politics which makes the comparative method so safe in the field of administration. When we study the administrative systems of France and Germany, knowing that we are not in search of *political* principles, we need not care a peppercorn for the constitutional or political reasons which Frenchmen or Germans give for their practices when explaining them to us. If I see a murderous fellow sharpening a knife cleverly, I can borrow his way of sharpening the knife without borrowing his probable intention to commit murder with it; and so, if I see a monarchist dyed in the wool managing a public bureau well, I can learn his business methods without changing one of my republican spots.[84]

Or, as Wilson asked elsewhere in the same essay, "Why should we not use such parts of foreign contrivances as we want, if they be in any way serviceable? We are in no danger of using them in a foreign way. We

---

[82] Wilson, "Notes for Lectures," in *PWW*, 7:122.

[83] See G. W. F. Hegel, *Philosophy of Right*, trans. T. M. Knox (Oxford: Oxford University Press, 1967), 191–92. For criticisms of this assumption of administrators' disinterestedness, see Herbert J. Storing, "Political Parties and the Bureaucracy," in Storing, *Toward a More Perfect Union*, 312; and Robert D. Miewald, "The Origins of Wilson's Thought: The German Tradition and the Organic State," in Rabin and Bowman, eds., *Politics and Administration*, 18–19, 27.

[84] Woodrow Wilson, "The Study of Administration," November 1886, in *PWW*, 5:378.

borrowed rice, but we do not eat it with chopsticks."[85] Wilson knew, then, that his vision for administration was a novelty in America. In fact, when he later taught administration in the 1890s, he said that there was only one author other than himself who understood administration as a separate discipline: Frank Goodnow.[86]

## V. FRANK GOODNOW AND THE DEVELOPMENT OF THE POLITICS-ADMINISTRATION DICHOTOMY

When Wilson identified Goodnow as the only other American of whom he was aware to treat administration as an object of study separate from politics, he was referring to Goodnow's *Comparative Administrative Law*, published in 1893. That book certainly put Goodnow on the map, although his real contributions to the modern understanding of administration's place in the political order came primarily with the publication of *Politics and Administration* in 1900. Two other works—*Social Reform and the Constitution* (1911) and *The American Conception of Liberty and Government* (1916)—later helped to clarify Goodnow's Progressive agenda, especially for the courts, and to fill out his views on the fundamental purposes of civil government. Goodnow produced almost all of this work while he was a professor at Columbia University, where he had been brought by his mentor, John Burgess, to teach political science and law, and where he became the first to teach administrative law in the United States. Prior to teaching at Columbia, Goodnow had spent a year studying in France and Germany; he would go on to finish his career at Johns Hopkins University, where he served as president until his retirement in 1929.[87] Although a student of Burgess, Goodnow did not adopt Burgess's political conservatism. Instead, Goodnow looked for ways that American national government could be modified to accommodate Progressive policy aims; this goal could best be accomplished, Goodnow believed, by freeing up administration to manage the broad scope of affairs that Progressives believed needed government intervention.

### A. The evolving ends and scope of government

Like Wilson, Goodnow argued that government needed to adjust its very purpose and organization to accommodate modern necessities;[88]

---

[85] Ibid.

[86] Wilson, "Notes for Lectures," in *PWW*, 7:118–20. Wilson's mention of Goodnow came in an 1894 revision he made to these notes.

[87] Samuel C. Patterson, "Remembering Frank J. Goodnow," *PS* 34, no. 4 (December 2001): 875–81; Charles G. Haines and Marshall E. Dimock, "Introduction," in *Essays on the Law and Practice of Governmental Administration: A Volume in Honor of Frank Johnson Goodnow*, ed. Haines and Dimock (Baltimore, MD: Johns Hopkins Press, 1935), vii–viii.

[88] Frank J. Goodnow, *Social Reform and the Constitution* (New York: Macmillan, 1911), 1.

and, like Wilson, he believed that history had made obsolete the founders' dedication to protecting individual rights and their consequent design
of a carefully limited form of national government. In *Social Reform and
the Constitution*, Goodnow complained about "reverence" for the Constitution, which he regarded as "superstitious" and an obstacle to genuine political and administrative reform.[89] In *Politics and Administration*,
Goodnow made clear that his push for administrative reform was not
simply or even primarily aimed at correcting the corruption of the
spoils system. Rather, administrative reform was, for Goodnow, instrumental to the end of achieving Progressive, big-government liberalism.
Progressives had in mind a wide array of new activities in which they
wanted national-government involvement; such involvement could not
be achieved with the old system of placing administration under political direction:

> Before we can hope that administrative officers can occupy a position
> reasonably permanent in character and reasonably free from political
> influence, we must recognize the existence of an administrative func-
> tion whose discharge must be uninfluenced by political consider-
> ations. This England and Germany, and France though to a much less
> degree, have done. To this fact in large part is due the excellence of
> their administrative systems. Under such conditions the government
> may safely be intrusted with much work which, until the people of
> the United States attain to the same conception, cannot be intrusted
> to their governmental organs.[90]

Understanding administrative reform this way—as a means to securing
the broader aims of Progressive liberalism—is what makes the work of
Goodnow, and Wilson too, so much more significant to the development
of modern American thought and politics than had been the case with the
civil-service reformers.

Goodnow and his fellow Progressives envisioned an almost entirely
new purpose for the national government. Government itself, therefore,
had to be viewed through a historical lens. The principles of the original
Constitution, Goodnow reasoned, may have been appropriate for the
founding era, but now, "under present conditions, they are working harm
rather than good."[91] The error that the founders made was not in constructing government as they did, but rather in thinking that their particular construction and manner of conceiving politics would transcend
their own age, and would be appropriate for future ages as well. They did

---

[89] Ibid., 9–10.
[90] Frank J. Goodnow, *Politics and Administration* (1900; New Brunswick, NJ: Transaction,
2003), 86–87.
[91] Goodnow, *Social Reform and the Constitution*, 2.

not realize the historical contingency of their principles.[92] The modern situation, Goodnow argued, called for less focus on constitutional principle and form, and much greater focus on empowering and perfecting administration. He even repeated, using almost the same words, Wilson's proclamation from 1885 that the nation had to move from constitutional to administrative questions. Wrote Goodnow: "The great problems of modern public law are almost exclusively administrative in character. While the age that has passed was one of constitutional, the present age is one of administrative reform."[93] In order to address the administrative questions that history was pressing upon the nation, Goodnow urged a focus not on the "formal" governing system (that is, the rules and procedures of the Constitution) but on the "real" governing system, which becomes whatever is demanded by the necessities of the time.[94]

The focus of the old liberalism on government's permanent duty to protect individual rights was an impediment to the marked expansion of governmental power that Progressives desired; thus, the ideas that animated the old-liberal conception of government had to be discredited. Goodnow understood the political theory of the founding quite well. He knew that the notion that government's primary duty was to protect rights came from the theory of social compact—a theory which held that men are naturally endowed with rights prior to the formation of government, and thus consent to create government only insofar as it will protect their natural rights. The founders' system of government, Goodnow acknowledged, "was permeated by the theories of social compact and natural right." He condemned these theories as "worse than useless," since they "retard development"[95]—in other words, they prevent the expansion of government by their focus on individual liberty. The separation-of-powers limits on government, Goodnow realized, came from the founding-era concern for individual liberty: "It was the fear of political tyranny through which liberty might be lost which led to the adoption of the theories of checks and balances and of the separation of powers."[96]

Goodnow's critique of the founders' political theory came from the perspective of historical contingency. Their understanding of rights and the role of government, he argued, was based upon pure "speculation" and "had no historical justification."[97] Here Goodnow employed the same

---

[92] Frank J. Goodnow, *The American Conception of Liberty and Government* (Providence, RI: Brown University Colver Lectures, 1916), 20.

[93] Frank J. Goodnow, *Comparative Administrative Law,* student edition (New York: Putnam, 1893), iv. See Wilson's similar statement in "The Art of Governing," in *PWW,* 5:52, quoted above.

[94] Goodnow, *Politics and Administration,* xxxi, 1–3.

[95] Goodnow, *Social Reform and the Constitution,* 1, 3. See also *The American Conception of Liberty and Government,* 13, where Goodnow identified the main problem with the American conception of liberty and government as its foundation in nature.

[96] Goodnow, *The American Conception of Liberty and Government,* 11.

[97] Ibid., 9.

critique as his fellow Hegelian Wilson, who had written in 1889 that the idea of social compact had "no historical foundation."[98] Instead of an understanding of rights grounded in nature, where the individual possesses them prior to the formation of government, Goodnow urged an understanding of rights that are granted by government itself. He remarked favorably upon European trends in understanding rights as contingent upon government: "The rights which [an individual] possesses are, it is believed, conferred upon him, not by his Creator, but rather by the society to which he belongs. What they are is to be determined by the legislative authority in view of the needs of that society. Social expediency, rather than natural right, is thus to determine the sphere of individual freedom of action."[99]

Goodnow found it necessary to critique the theory of natural rights because he knew it was the foundation for the requirement of government based upon consent.[100] The principle of government by the consent of the governed was a problem for Goodnow and those with his vision of administrative power. Goodnow's vision required significant deference to expertise. The empowering of administrators, as he saw it, was justified not because the administrators had the consent of the people, but because they were experts in their fields. This is why Goodnow wanted to improve administration not by making it more accountable to politics and to the consent of the governed, but by making it less accountable. He observed and conceded that the doctrines of "sovereignty of the people and of popular participation in the operations of government" were an integral part of American political culture. He therefore acknowledged that this aspect of the culture would be a difficult hurdle for his vision of administration to overcome. "Our governmental organization developed," he explained, "at a time when expert service could not be obtained, when the expert as we now understand him did not exist."[101]

## B. Discretion for administrators and the separation of politics and administration

Since administrative experts were now available, Goodnow urged that they be employed and empowered with significant discretion to manage the new tasks that Progressives had in mind for the national government. In *Politics and Administration*, Goodnow featured chapters on the "Function of Politics" and the "Function of Administration." Both chapters have exactly the same aim: to show that politics ought to be kept out of admin-

[98] Wilson, *The State*, 13.
[99] Goodnow, *The American Conception of Liberty and Government*, 11.
[100] For a good explanation of the foundation of consent in the Declaration of Independence, see Thomas G. West, "The Political Theory of the Declaration of Independence," in Pestritto and West, eds., *The American Founding and the Social Compact*, 120–30.
[101] Goodnow, *The American Conception of Liberty and Government*, 45; see also ibid., 36.

istration's way. Put differently, the function of politics is to refrain from influencing administration, and the function of administration is to exercise discretion by avoiding the influence of politics. Goodnow's distinction between the roles of politics and administration was a response to what he believed had been the corrupting influence of politics on national administration. While Goodnow, for example, championed the potential of the party system (as a means of circumventing the separation of powers), he did so only under the condition that party politics be kept entirely out of administration.[102] Administrative decision making, Goodnow argued, was politically neutral and required expertise. Where administration had been "subjected too much to the control of politics in the United States," he claimed, the effect had been the "decreasing of administrative efficiency."[103] Thus, political institutions, Goodnow concluded, ought to concern themselves only with ensuring that administrators remained neutral, and such institutions were to be kept out of influencing the *substance* of administrative decisions. He explained: "All that the legislature, or any political body, can do is to see to it, through the exercise of its control, that persons discharging these administrative functions are efficient and impartial. Their general conduct, but not their concrete actions, should be subject to control."[104]

Goodnow was well aware that insulating administration from political control in this way ran up against the traditional, constitutional role for administration, where administrators are subservient to the chief executive. He explained that his conception of administration was novel, since it considered the sphere of administration to lie outside the sphere of constitutional law; indeed, this new conception was exactly what Wilson had given Goodnow credit for in 1894. Emphasizing the distinction between the constitutional and administrative spheres, Goodnow remarked that the student of government "is too apt to confine himself to constitutional questions, perhaps not considering at all the administrative system."[105] It is for this reason of considering administration as an object of study outside of the Constitution that Goodnow's landmark book on administrative law, *Comparative Administrative Law,* relies almost entirely upon an account of foreign administrative systems.[106] He knew, as Wilson did, that such a concept was a novelty in the American political tradition. Modern administrative law, therefore, would take it for granted that the political branches of government had to cede significant discretion to administrative agencies; the new body of law would be dedicated to establishing a framework for governing the *extent* and *organization* of this discretion.[107]

---

[102] Goodnow, *Politics and Administration,* 37.
[103] Ibid., 43.
[104] Ibid., 81.
[105] Ibid., 5–6.
[106] Goodnow, *Comparative Administrative Law,* v.
[107] Ibid., 1:10–11.

Careful readers of Goodnow's work will note that in making his case for freeing administration from political influence, he did not speak of a strict or rigid separation between politics and administration; indeed, Goodnow noted that the boundary between the two is difficult to define and that there would inevitably be overlap.[108] This overlap, however, seems to be in one direction only, in a manner that enlarges the orbit of administration; that is, Goodnow seemed to contemplate instances where administrative organs would exercise political functions, but he apparently did not contemplate instances of political organs engaging in administrative activity. He characterized the function of politics as "expressing" the will of the state, while the function of administration is to "execute" the will of the state. He made it clear, however, that the overlap between politics and administration would come in the form of administrative agencies taking a share in "expressing" as well as "executing" state will:

> No political organization, based on the general theory of a differentiation of governmental functions, has ever been established which assigns the functions of expressing the will of the state exclusively to any one of the organs for which it makes provision. Thus, the organ of government whose main function is the execution of the will of the state is often, and indeed usually, intrusted with the expression of that will in its details. These details, however, when expressed, must conform with the general principles laid down by the organ whose main duty is that of expression. That is, the authority called executive has, in almost all cases, considerable ordinance or legislative power.[109]

The notion that Goodnow might see administration as subordinate to politics—as confined only to executing previously expressed will[110]—is hereby called into question. Moreover, Goodnow's statement essentially laid the foundation for the abandonment of the nondelegation doctrine. He elaborated: "As a result, either of the provisions of the constitution or of the delegation of the power by the legislature, the chief executive or subordinate executive authorities may, through the issue of ordinances, express the will of the state as to details where it is inconvenient for the legislature to act."[111]

Goodnow shed further light on the role administration might play in "expressing" the will of the state when he categorized the kinds of decisions in which administrative agencies are legitimately involved. When administrators make "executive" decisions, he explained, they are sub-

---

[108] See, for example, Goodnow, *Politics and Administration,* 16. For an account of this point, see Patterson, "Remembering Frank J. Goodnow," 878.

[109] Goodnow, *Politics and Administration,* 15.

[110] For an example of Goodnow's making such a claim, see ibid., 24.

[111] Ibid., 17.

ordinate to previously expressed will. But in reasoning that would later be adopted by the Supreme Court in the *Humphrey's* case, Goodnow contended that administrators engage not only in "executive" decisions but also in decisions that are quasi-legislative and quasi-judicial. In doing so, administrators not only execute the will of the state, but also play a role in its expression. When administrators are merely executing state will, Goodnow explained, it is appropriate for them to be subject to the supervision of politics. When they are expressing state will in their quasi-legislative or quasi-judicial role, however, administrators require freedom from political influence. As Goodnow wrote, the "executive function must therefore of necessity be subordinated to the function of politics. No such close connection, however, exists between the function of politics and the other branches of the administration of government. No control of a political character can bring it about that administrative officers will discharge better their *quasi*-judicial duties, for example. . . ." [112] In other words, when administrators are merely functioning as executives by following previously expressed will, political accountability can be brought to bear; but it is at the point when they exercise even more power, acting as legislators or judges by aiding the expression of state will, that they must be the most free from political accountability.

## C. Why trust administrators?

The key to trusting administrators with the kind of discretion that Goodnow envisioned was his profound faith in the expertise and objectivity of the administrative class—just as it had been for Wilson and would be for Landis. Administrators could be freed from political control because they were "neutral": their salary and tenure would take care of any self-interested inclinations that might corrupt their decision making, liberating them to focus solely on truth and the good of the public as a whole. As Goodnow explained, "such a force should be free from the influence of politics because of the fact that their mission is the exercise of foresight and discretion, the pursuit of truth, the gathering of information, the maintenance of a strictly impartial attitude toward the individuals with whom they have dealings, and the provision of the most efficient possible administrative organization." [113] A natural objection here would be that freeing administrators from political control is a recipe for corruption: that it is precisely through the electoral connection of public officials that we "make their interest coincide with their duty," as Hamilton puts it in *The Federalist*.[114] For Goodnow, though, it was just this connection to electoral politics that would make administrators corrupt,

---

[112] Ibid., 79.
[113] Ibid., 85.
[114] *Federalist No. 72*: 488.

while the absence of accountability to the electorate would somehow make them pure. Politics, Goodnow explained, is "polluted" and full of "bias," whereas administration is all about the "truth."[115]

Goodnow's confidence in the objectivity of administrators, like Wilson's, is a sign of his Hegelianism, and it shows that he accepted Hegel's premise that bureaucrats could be freed of their particularity and could will only the objective good of the state.[116] In his introduction to the recent edition of Goodnow's *Politics and Administration*, bureaucracy scholar John A. Rohr concludes that Goodnow's "Hegelian starting point" doomed his attempt at crafting a realistic administrative reform.[117] Goodnow himself worried, in 1900, that the emphasis in American political culture on popular sovereignty and individual rights would pose a formidable obstacle to the enactment of his vision for administration. The people, given their historical background, might resist deferring to a permanent, administrative class:

> When we take into account on the one hand the environment in which men lived in this country prior to the middle of the nineteenth century, and on the other hand the prevailing political philosophy with its emphasis on individual liberty, and popular sovereignty, and its abhorrence of a permanent governing class, we can well understand the development of the idea which was so commonly held that rotation in office was a cardinal doctrine in American government.[118]

Goodnow also worried that this public hostility to "experts" would make it hard to attract talented individuals into the bureaucracy, although he subsequently consoled himself with the possibility that change was on the horizon. In 1916, Goodnow hoped he was seeing a change in attitude, where the people were becoming less attached to their sovereignty so that experts could be allowed to rule:

> Generally speaking, however, the power of the people to elect directly public officers is diminishing. The change is not, however, as has been pointed out, due to any decrease in the belief in the general theory of popular sovereignty. The people through the referendum and initiative are exercising greater power than ever over the determination of questions of policy. They have, however, in the interest of efficient government, been willing to surrender powers of choosing public officers which they at one time regarded with great jealousy.[119]

---

[115] Goodnow, *Politics and Administration*, 82.
[116] See note 81 above.
[117] John A. Rohr, "Introduction," in Goodnow, *Politics and Administration*, xxviii–xxix.
[118] Goodnow, *Politics and Administration*, 46.
[119] Goodnow, *The American Conception of Liberty and Government*, 62.

## D. Goodnow's new categories of state power

Goodnow's vision for administrative governance is grounded in a set of categories he employs to describe the different types of state power. Contrary to the American separation-of-powers framework, which divides power into three categories, Goodnow's framework contains only two. When the state exercises power, Goodnow argued in *Politics and Administration*, it does it either by "expressing" will or by "executing" will that has previously been expressed.[120] This is an elaboration of an expression that Goodnow had employed in his first book, *Comparative Administrative Law,* where he referred to the "expression of the will of the state."[121] The distinction between "expressing" and "executing" translates directly into Goodnow's distinction between "politics" and "administration"—the very distinction at the heart of the administrative state today. As he explained, "There are, then, in all governmental systems two primary or ultimate functions of government, viz. the expression of the will of the state and the execution of that will. There are also in all states separate organs, each of which is mainly busied with the discharge of one of these functions. These functions are, respectively, Politics and Administration."[122] As Wilson had done in his essay "The Study of Administration," Goodnow emphasized the separation between politics and administration in order to pave the way for importing a foreign administrative science into the American system of government. Since administration, under this scheme, is not involved in politics—since it is only involved in "executing" previously expressed will—Goodnow saw no danger in adopting a monarchic system of bureaucracy in a democratic regime. As I have noted, however, Goodnow did not always talk so strictly or rigidly about the separation between politics and administration, and he acknowledged that there are many instances where administration will have a role in "expressing" as well as "executing" state will.

Within that part of the state responsible for "executing" will, Goodnow made a further division into three parts. It is this division of the executive branch of government that is central to his argument for the independence of administration and that represents the most distinctive part of his overall argument for reform. The three elements of the executive are: (1) the judiciary; (2) the administrative agencies; and (3) what would

---

[120] Goodnow, *Politics and Administration,* 9. Goodnow thus relies on a division of power which, at least at the surface, comports more with Locke's division (between legislative and executive) than with Montesquieu's (between legislative, executive, and judicial). Rohr cites this connection to Locke for the purpose of arguing that Goodnow is not completely "out of touch with American political thought" (Rohr, *To Run a Constitution,* 88). But this is only a superficial connection to Locke, as the purpose of Locke's separation is to protect individual rights from the arbitrary exercise of state power, whereas the purpose of Goodnow's is to provide the most efficient mechanism for the delivery of state power.

[121] Goodnow, *Comparative Administrative Law,* 2:106.

[122] Goodnow, *Politics and Administration,* 22.

traditionally be called the constitutional executive—the president, state governors, etc.[123] What most immediately stands out here, of course, is the inclusion of the judiciary within the executive. Goodnow explained that the founders had erred in following Montesquieu's portrayal of the judiciary as its own independent branch of government. Judges, Goodnow reasoned, were essentially involved in the *execution* of previously expressed will or law, just like the other elements of the executive.[124] In addition to the inclusion of the judiciary within the executive, it is also worth noting the distinction that Goodnow made between the president and the administrative agencies. Whereas the Constitution would have to consider agencies simply as an extension of the presidency (the president being vested with all of "the executive power"), Goodnow clearly separated agencies from the political office of president.

Goodnow's conception of the executive is also unique in that it considers both courts and agencies to be part of administration. The executive, he explained, involves both the "administration of justice" (by the courts) and the "administration of government" (by agencies). And within the "administration of government," agencies can perform different functions; some of these are purely executive, but others take on more of a judicial or even legislative character.[125] What matters most is that neither kind of administration—neither that done by the courts nor that done by agencies—is confined to the mere execution of previously expressed will. These traditionally administrative elements commonly cross over into the realm of politics, helping to express as well as execute the will of the state. This is true of courts in particular, since they interpret both the law and the Constitution itself.[126]

Goodnow emphasized the independence from political influence that American courts had traditionally enjoyed. But whereas the original idea behind this independence had been the securing of individual rights,[127] for Goodnow it served as a vehicle for granting vast discretion to administration. The key is Goodnow's placing of the courts and agencies alongside one another in the realm of administration. Since the courts traditionally enjoyed independence from politics, and since agencies are partners with the courts in the realm of administration, it follows that agencies (like courts) ought to enjoy independence from political control. Administration—whether it be "administration of justice" in the courts, or "administration of government" in the bureaucracy—is politically neutral and ought not be influenced by the vicissitudes of elections, even though, as Goodnow himself made clear, administration must necessarily

---

[123] Ibid., 17.
[124] Ibid., 11–13.
[125] Ibid., 72–73.
[126] Ibid., 36.
[127] See *Federalist No. 78*: 522–24, where Hamilton explains that the federal courts required independence from politics because of the necessity to safeguard individual liberty.

involve itself in not only executing but giving expression to the will of the state.[128] As Rohr puts it, "by assimilating administrators to judges whom he includes within the concept of executive and excluding constitutional executives from administration, Goodnow neatly carves a niche for the administrator to exercise legitimately a certain degree of independence." [129] Put another way, Goodnow tapped into a traditional feature of American constitutionalism—the relative independence of the judiciary—to argue for something quite untraditional—the independence of administration from political control.

Goodnow's employment of independent courts to secure a similar independence for administrative agencies is useful in placing in its proper perspective the "capture" phenomenon of modern administrative law. As I have noted, much of modern administrative law consists of fights between agencies and judges, who are spurred on by interest groups to intervene in agency decision making out of a belief that agencies are too lenient on regulated industries. From one point of view, such a phenomenon demonstrates that agencies no longer have the discretion that they once enjoyed. Understood from Goodnow's perspective, however, such wrangling between courts and agencies would be largely inconsequential, or merely at the level of an intrafamily squabble, since both courts and agencies were considered by Goodnow to be part of administration. What mattered for Goodnow was not whether courts or agencies had the upper hand, but rather that both of them, as part of administration, were independent of politics. This is also the important point for those of us who are interested in the fate of traditional constitutionalism in today's administrative state: it ought to matter less exactly which unelected entity is most influential in policymaking (agencies or courts), and it ought to matter more that such power has been delegated in the first place by the elected branches of government.

## VI. CONCLUSION

Today's administrative state is built on the death of the nondelegation doctrine. It is on the basis of abandoning nondelegation that administration can be separated from politics—that administrators can act, in other words, with discretion as they employ their expertise free from political influence. Constitutional and administrative law today really do not concern themselves with whether or not administrative agencies can have such discretion delegated to them, or whether or not they may exercise legislative and judicial powers in addition to their executive powers. Instead, the law assumes these things to be entirely legitimate, and concerns itself with the questions of how, and to what extent, such discretion

---

[128] Goodnow, *Politics and Administration,* 39–42, 45–46, 78.
[129] Rohr, "Introduction," xxvii.

can be exercised. Thus, the entire enterprise of the modern administrative state owes its existence to the abandonment of separation of powers as an operative constitutional principle, and its replacement by a system separating politics and administration. While a separation of politics and administration was relied upon by the likes of Landis to build up the administrative state, it originated in the work of Wilson and Goodnow.

There is some debate as to whether Wilson or Goodnow was more important in developing the fundamental concepts of modern administration. On the one hand, the argument for Goodnow is strengthened by the fact that his contributions to the field were far more numerous; administrative law was, after all, the very discipline to which he dedicated his academic career. Wilson's writings, by contrast, are not nearly as exclusively focused on administration, and thus there is no question that Goodnow was able to spend considerably more energy developing the implications of the basic politics-administration dichotomy.[130] On the other hand, there is the fact that Wilson's writings on administration, and, specifically, his explication of the separation of politics and administration, came first. Wilson's most important writings on administration came in the mid-1880s, while Goodnow's first major work appeared in 1893, and it was not until 1900 that Goodnow really laid out his theory of separating politics and administration with any thoroughness. While Goodnow certainly spent more time developing the details of an administrative system, there is little in his basic approach to the question that Wilson had not previously explicated in one way or another. The historicist perspective on politics and on the U.S. Constitution, along with the specific critique of the separation-of-powers framework, had all been laid out by Wilson in the 1880s.

It may therefore be best to conclude that Goodnow built on Wilson's basic principles, and that he made a very significant contribution by his unique argument on the role of the courts. In particular, Goodnow's use of judicial independence to make the case for administrative independence was unprecedented in Progressive thought. It is this element of Goodnow's thought that has given us the two pillars of today's liberal state: unelected judges who make law through constitutional interpretation, and unelected bureaucrats to whom significant policymaking power is delegated on the basis of their expertise.

*Political Science, Hillsdale College*

---

[130] For scholarly accounts crediting Goodnow more than Wilson, see Patterson, "Remembering Frank J. Goodnow," 877; and Haines and Dimock, "Introduction," x–xi. Rohr also gives more credit to Goodnow, claiming that Wilson's thought was more "eclectic" while Goodnow was more of a pure Hegelian. Rohr, "Introduction," xxii. But I would suggest, on the contrary, that Wilson was about as pure a Hegelian as one could find in the United States. See my *Woodrow Wilson and the Roots of Modern Liberalism*, esp. 14–19, 34, 36–37, 41–44, 55, 68–70, 75, 82, 91, 100, 102, 213–16, 225, 228–30, 233, 240, and 263.

# PROGRESSIVISM AS A NATIONAL NARRATIVE IN BIBLICAL-HEGELIAN TIME

By Eldon J. Eisenach

## I. Introduction

It is important to get Progressivism right. The authors of its leading ideas founded the modern American university and created its disciplines and the journals that codified their thoughts. They completed the transformation of sectarian American Protestantism, begun before the Civil War, into an embracive, liberal, and evangelical civil religion. They created the ligaments of the national administrative and regulatory state, and founded and supplied a mass national journalism independent of political party and church. They witnessed and helped legitimate the creation of a national financial and industrial corporate economy that soon became the engine driving the international economy, transforming America into the dominant world power. In the process, they sought to transform an older American liberalism anchored in natural rights and constitutional jurisprudence into a new socialized liberalism anchored in visions of evolutionary progress and the socialization of the self. If Americans cannot understand Progressivism on these terms, they have little hope of understanding themselves and the place of contemporary America in the world.

This essay represents some generalizations about Progressivism exemplified by three figures: Lyman Abbott, Albion Small, and Simon Patten.[1] Each helped shape Progressive political and social thought in national universities, through national journalism and national professional and reform organizations, and by creating powerful reform networks that permeated American society and mobilized its talents and energies to transform the nation. These figures institutionalized a new liberalism that came to dominate major sectors of American political culture and eventually its national politics.

Lyman Abbott (1835–1922) was chiefly known as the editor of *Outlook* (1881–1922), a weekly that began as *Christian Union*. The son of a New England Congregational minister, Abbott studied at New York University, and began his career as a lawyer. Under the influence of the renowned preacher Henry Ward Beecher, however, Abbott left law practice to study theology, first serving churches in the Midwest during the Civil War and

---

[1] See Eldon J. Eisenach, ed., *The Social and Political Thought of American Progressivism* (Cambridge, MA, and Indianapolis, IN: Hackett Publishing, 2006), for a collection of thirty-eight Progressive writings by twenty-five authors.

then directing the Freedmen's Union Commission that provided aid to white war refugees and black freedmen. Under Abbott's editorship, *Outlook* achieved a circulation of 100,000, becoming the preeminent nonsectarian Protestant publication of its day. Following his presidency, Theodore Roosevelt became an associate editor. Booker T. Washington,[2] Jacob Riis,[3] and Edward Everett Hale,[4] along with Roosevelt, published their autobiographies in *Outlook* before releasing them as books. Albion Small and Richard T. Ely[5] were also contributors. Abbott's major book, *The Evolution of Christianity*, popularized the melding of social progress and liberal Christianity. It was continually published from 1892 through 1926 in seven editions. In addition to a popular biography of Henry Ward Beecher, whose pulpit Abbott himself occupied from 1888 to 1899, Abbott authored *The Rights of Man*, a series of lectures that advanced a theory of government integrating the writings of G. W. F. Hegel and prominent British and American political and social theorists. Abbott's thesis was that "self-government is not an assumption on which we are to start in framing a government; it is the goal which we are to reach by means of government." Democracy is not a form of government, but a way of being, "pervaded by the spirit, not merely of good will toward man, and of large hope for man, but also of faith in man."[6] He is credited with having coined and popularized the term "industrial democracy."

Albion Small (1854–1926) was professor of sociology at the University of Chicago at its founding in 1892 until his death. He was a founding member of the American Sociological Society, serving as its president (1912–1914), and the founder and editor of *The American Journal of Sociology* (1895–1926), a leading venue for Progressive scholarship and reform causes. Albion Small's father was a Congregational minister in Maine; his mother, Thankful Lincoln Small, was a descendant of Samuel Lincoln, Abraham Lincoln's earliest American ancestor. After earning degrees from Colby College and Newton Theological Institute, Albion Small studied in

[2] Washington (1856–1915), born into slavery, became president of the Tuskegee Institute in Alabama, an industrial and agricultural training center for freed slaves. He accepted the necessity for legal and social segregation in the South, maintaining that the best path was economic and educational advancement as a prerequisite for claiming civic and political equality. He was a strong supporter of Theodore Roosevelt.

[3] Riis (1849–1914) was a Danish-born American journalist. His book *How the Other Half Lives* (1890), illustrated with his own photographs, documented life in the slums of New York City. The book brought him to the attention of Theodore Roosevelt, who was then serving as the city's police commissioner.

[4] Hale (1822–1909) was a clergyman and popular writer, most notably of *The Man without a Country* (1863). Married into the Beecher family of prominent abolitionists, he later became a prominent advocate of modernist theology and the "social gospel" movement.

[5] Ely (1854–1943), a German-educated professor of political economy at the University of Wisconsin, was a founder and early president of the American Economic Association and of the American Association for Labor Legislation, and author of many books on the relationship between the new industrial economy and political and social reform.

[6] Lyman Abbott, *The Rights of Man* (Boston and New York: Houghton Mifflin, 1901), 100 and 165.

Germany and then returned to receive his Ph.D. from Johns Hopkins University, whose social science faculty also trained in Germany. Albion Small was more influential as founding editor of *The American Journal of Sociology* than as a major sociological thinker. For more than thirty years, Small used his journal as a sort of clearing house for progressive ideas, welcoming Jane Addams,[7] Florence Kelley,[8] and Charlotte Perkins Gilman[9] to its pages, none of whom was a trained sociologist. The integration of women into sociology and reform was also taking place professionally. The sociology department at the University of Chicago welcomed the first female doctoral students in America in 1894 and, by the early 1900s, was producing one-third of all female social science Ph.D.s in America.[10] Small wrote extensively on "social economy"—the relationship of the new industrial economy to moral, social, and political life—and on the role of religion in social reform.

Simon Patten (1852–1922) was born in Illinois, the descendant of eighteenth-century Scotch Irish settlers in New York. Educated at Northwestern University and at the University of Halle, where he received his Ph.D., Patten was one of the many German-trained founders and early presidents of the American Economic Association. Along with Albion Small and six of Patten's doctoral students, he was also one of the founders of the American Sociological Society, serving as its president as well. Patten followed Edmund J. James, another son of Illinois and a Halle Ph.D. (and, later, president of the University of Illinois), to the University of Pennsylvania, where they were professors in the Wharton School, the newly founded professional business school that combined the study of economics, public finance, and business management. Together, Patten and James founded and led the American Academy of Social and Political Science and edited its publication, the *Annals*. This journal became a high-level meeting place not only for German-trained academics in America, but also for leaders in business, finance, and government. Patton's analysis of wages, profits, and rents provided the basis for Charles Beard's

---

[7] Addams (1860–1935) was the founder of Hull House in Chicago, a famous neighborhood settlement house and social laboratory serving the needs of new immigrants. Its volunteer residents, mostly college-educated young women, led many reform movements for factory legislation, municipal reform, the abolition of child labor, and scientific social work. With Florence Kelley, Addams drafted the social and industrial justice planks of the 1912 Progressive Party platform.

[8] Kelley (1859–1932), an early resident volunteer at Hull House in Chicago, was a founder and longtime president of the National Consumers League and associate editor of *Charities*, a journal advocating scientific social work. She was active in organizing women's trade unions, in factory safety legislation, and in the abolition of sweatshops and child labor.

[9] Gilman (1860–1935), a descendant of the Beecher family, supported herself and her children as an editor, lecturer, and writer. Her most notable writings are *Women and Economics* (1898) and a play, *Yellow Wallpaper* (1899).

[10] In 1894, the University of Chicago had twenty-five women and eighty-five men enrolled in graduate study in the departments of political economy, political science, and sociology. Ellen Fitzpatrick, *Endless Crusade: Women Social Scientists and Progressive Reform* (New York: Oxford University Press, 1990), 13, 29–30.

analysis of the sources of political conflicts in America, starting with the Antifederalists and Federalists over the adoption of the Constitution, and continuing through party conflicts to the present day. Patten's basic argument that underlay Beard's political party analysis was simple: the major battle is not between workingmen and capitalists, but between the productivity and profits of the industrial economy and the somewhat parasitic benefits from rents, that is, unearned income from rising land values and local market monopolies that typified small-producer capitalism. The lesson is the one preached by William McKinley against William Jennings Bryan in the presidential election of 1896: the interests of workingmen lie in a thriving industrial capitalism producing economic surplus and not in a class alliance with marginal farmers, main street shop owners, and Southern *rentier* interests against capitalists. Herbert Croly, whose book *The Promise of American Life* (1909) became the definitive statement of national Progressivism, used this same argument in his discussion of the emergence of a permanent class of industrial wage earners. Patten's many graduate students (called "Patten Men") included Walter Weyl of *The New Republic*, Edward Devine, general secretary of the New York Charity Organization Society, and two individuals who later made major contributions to the New Deal: Rexford Tugwell and Frances Perkins. Patten is credited with inventing and popularizing the term "social work."

Three features animate the thought of Abbott, Small, Patten, and other major Progressive figures. The first is the primacy of a narrative. This narrative was historicist in its outline of America's national history and destiny. This historicism, in turn, was grounded in Protestant Evangelical theology and Hegelian philosophy, seeing the structural changes in American social and economic life as signs of an emerging morality and spirit that would lead in the reconstruction of American society. It was this shared narrative, I suggest, that fused together Progressivism and Protestantism, providing the moral, intellectual, and institutional basis for political mobilization. A second feature of Progressive thought flows directly from the primacy of narrative, namely, its hostility to "principled" or abstract-philosophical forms of political and social thought because these were thought to be major barriers to democratic reform. This hostility took many forms, but its chief targets were classical economic theory and prevailing forms of constitutional jurisprudence, both of which treated rights as pre-existing, fixed, and free-standing entities that stand outside of social, economic, and political life. The third feature of Progressive thought is its confidence that historical modes of social and political inquiry would produce "laws" of progress that should guide practice and provide a set of values that would integrate self and society on a democratic foundation.

The analysis that follows addresses five topics central to Progressivism that contain these animating features. Section II addresses the Progressives' intense national patriotism. The Progressives believed that the American nation, if it prepared itself, was destined to become a world-historical actor, shaping the history of the modern world. Section III examines the new industrial economy and its centrality in the new social sciences. Progressives believed that organized social knowledge would make manifest the relationship between material and spiritual progress. Section IV considers the Progressive call for new ethical and civic values required of this new economic and social order. These values were thought to be immanent in the new industrial economy and in the path that social knowledge was taking. Section V explores the religious dimension of this same evolutionary argument, expressed by the term "the social gospel." Finally, Section VI examines the Progressive attack on principles, with particular attention paid to the role of constitutional jurisprudence and law in American political institutions and practices. I conclude with some reflections on the achievements and ironies of Progressive political thought both in terms of the path of academic political theory after the Progressive era and in terms of the rise of conservative political thought in the last quarter of the twentieth century.

## II. America as a Democratic Nation

Progressive intellectuals were children of staunch Republican Party parents who saw Lincoln as the defining figure in American life. Herbert Croly identified Lincoln as the one American political leader who had the intelligence and courage to see that the issue of slavery in the territories was not resolvable inside the bounds of the Constitution and laws as currently understood. Because Lincoln forged a new understanding of the Constitution, slavery was destroyed and America was refounded on a more national and democratic basis. The challenge in confronting the new industrial economy was a direct parallel to that of slavery.[11] In her textbook on social ideals in English letters, Vida Dutton Scudder, a professor of literature at Wellesley, made the Civil War "the third great episode in the national struggle for freedom" that now called Americans to a fourth task, that of realizing "a spiritual democracy for the victims and outcasts of the Old World" now on American shores.[12] To Lyman Abbott, who as a young man had heard Lincoln's Cooper Union Address in 1860,[13] Lincoln had given us the principles we needed to address the labor problem in America.[14]

---

[11] Herbert Croly, *The Promise of American Life* (New York: Macmillan, 1909), chapter 4.

[12] Vida Dutton Scudder, *Social Ideals in English Letters* (New York: Houghton Mifflin, 1898), 205 and 210. The first two episodes were the colonization of New England by the Puritans and the American Revolution.

[13] It was this address against the extension of slavery that galvanized Lincoln's campaign for the Republican Party nomination for president later that year.

[14] "What is the choice of the American people? Do they prefer Communism or Industrial Democracy? The life and teaching of Abraham Lincoln make perfectly clear his answer to that question. . . ." Lyman Abbott, *Silhouettes of My Contemporaries* (Garden City, NY: Doubleday, Page and Company, 1922), 309.

Lincoln and the Civil War symbolized for the Progressives a new commitment—they would say "covenant"—of the American people to create a democratic nation. The period following the Civil War was largely a betrayal of that commitment, as American political life retreated back into a politics of electoral corruption, party patronage, and the dominance of powerful economic interests.[15] Rededication to building a national democracy would require painful adjustments in ways of thinking about American citizenship, about economic life, and even about religion and the family.

In his article "The Bonds of Nationality," Albion Small nicely summarized what was required to create a real nation. National bonds primarily consisted of four elements: (1) a common language, (2) race solidarity, (3) a coherent family type, and (4) a convincing religion.[16] The achievement and strengthening of all four bonds required substantial political, economic, and social reforms. The goal of the new science of sociology was to depict, organize, and make meaningful the democratic social forces that served these bonds of nationality.[17] "The American democracy can trust its interest to the national interest," said Herbert Croly, "because national cohesion is dependent, not only upon certain forms of historical association, but upon fidelity to a democratic principle." The rise of national industrial, financial, legal, political, and labor leaders who operated outside of democratic controls was "driving new wedges into American national cohesion." At the turn of the twentieth century, Croly wrote, "the American people are not prepared for a higher form of democracy, because they are not prepared for a more coherent and intense national life." The nationalization of the American people, so brilliantly evidenced by the North in the Civil War, should not mean, however, "merely to centralize their government." Indeed, now, "among those branches of the American national organization which are greatly in need of nationalizing is the central government" itself.[18]

Academics like Small and Patten, and journalists like Abbott, placed extraordinary faith in the capacity of national institutions like the univer-

---

[15] This era has been termed a regime of courts and parties. See Stephen Skowronek, *Building a New American State: The Expansion of National Administrative Capacities, 1877–1920* (New York: Cambridge University Press, 1982); and Morton Keller, *Affairs of State: Public Life in Late Nineteenth Century America* (Cambridge, MA: Harvard University Press, 1977).

[16] By "race," Small was referring to cultural and moral agreement, or consensus, not biological or genetic identity. By "religion," Small did not mean membership in a common church organization or subscription to a particular theological creed, but rather a nationally shared sense of transcendent purposes and projects. For a similar formulation, see Lyman Abbott, *America in the Making* (New Haven, CT: Yale University Press, 1911), chapter 5. For similar understandings by contemporary scholars, see Harold Bloom, *The American Religion: The Emergence of a Post-Christian Nation* (New York: Simon and Schuster, 1992); and Sidney Mead, *The Nation with the Soul of a Church* (New York: Harper and Row, 1975).

[17] Albion Small, "The Bonds of Nationality," *The American Journal of Sociology* 20 (1915): 629–83.

[18] Croly, *Promise of American Life*, 267, 269, 271, and 273.

sities, public education, churches, professional associations, national magazines, and national reform organizations to become effective schools for national democratic citizenship. From this base, they thought, it might even be possible to transform political parties into nationally oriented institutions instead of temporary and expedient coalitions of local and special interests to capture the national government and reap the spoils of victory. To break through the institutional and legal barriers to reform first required emancipation from "traditional illusions," chief among them, according to Croly, the "tendency to regard the existing Constitution with superstitious awe, and to shrink with horror from modifying it even in the smallest detail." If this emancipation were not achieved, Croly wrote, "the American ideal [would] have to be fitted to the rigid and narrow lines of a few legal formulas; and the ruler of the American spirit, like the ruler of the Jewish spirit of old, [would] become the lawyer." To affirm a new covenant between nationality and democracy—what Croly termed a fusion between Hamilton and Jefferson—would be "in truth equivalent to a new Declaration of Independence" because it would affirm the right of the American people "to organize their political, economic, and social life in the service of a comprehensive, a lofty, and far-reaching democratic purpose."[19]

## III. The New Political Economy

Nowhere were democratic values more lacking than in the organization of the industrial economy. As talented as they were, both business and labor "bosses" wielded undemocratic power to serve narrow and self-interested ends. The existence of a permanent and rapidly expanding class of wage-laborers was the central theme in all branches of the social sciences in the new research universities. Whether the issues were public education, city government, assimilation of new immigrants, public health, or the broader issues of political democracy and social justice, the new industrial economy was central in their analysis. Two formative books giving shape to this perspective were *Studies in the Evolution of Industrial Society* and *Outlines of Economics,* both by Richard T. Ely. Interestingly, these books were first published as part of a "home reading series" of the Chautauqua Movement, a Methodist-inspired summer camp, and later a national lecture series, dedicated to melding together nondoctrinal Christianity, family life, ethical values, and responsible citizenship. *Outlines of Economics* became the standard text in college economics courses, published continuously, in many revisions, between 1893 and 1939. A central thesis of both books is this:

> The multiplying relations of men with one another give us a new economic world. These relations require regulation, in order to pre-

[19] Ibid., 278–79.

serve freedom. The regulation by the power of the state of these industrial and other social relations existing among men is an essential condition of freedom.[20]

Behind that simple thesis lies a much more complex understanding of what constitutes social knowledge and how that knowledge is to be obtained. Ely and Simon Patten largely drafted the statement of principles adopted at the formation of the American Economic Association in 1895. They might well have been speaking of the Progressive ideals of the social sciences generally:

1. We regard the state as an agency whose positive assistance is one of the indispensable conditions of human progress.
2. We believe that political economy as a science is still in an early stage of its development. While we appreciate the work of former economists, we look, not so much to speculation as to the historical and statistical study of actual conditions of economic life for the satisfactory accomplishment of that development.
3. We hold that the conflict of labor and capital has brought into prominence a vast number of social problems, whose solution requires the united efforts, each in its own sphere, of the church, of the state, and of science.
4. In the study of the industrial and commercial policy of governments we take no partisan attitude. We believe in a progressive development of economic conditions, which must be met by a corresponding development of legislative policy.

Albion Small seconded the primacy of the new industrial economy to the study of sociology:

A large part of the confusion in the present stage of transition is due to our acquiescence in conceptions of capital as an exclusively economic phenomenon, and in corollaries from those conceptions which act as automatic adjusters of conduct to those unmoral conceptions. Conflicts centering around capital press for convincing analysis of capital as a social phenomenon. . . .

The clue to a primary analysis of capital from the social standpoint may be found in the question: To what extent is the effectiveness of capital in the economic process due to unaided acts of the owner; and to what extent is its effectiveness conferred by acts of others than the owner?

---

[20] Richard T. Ely, *Studies in the Evolution of Industrial Society* (Chautauqua, NY: Chautauqua Press, 1903), 98–99; and Ely, *Outlines of Economics* (Chautauqua, NY: Chautauqua Press, 1893).

When the answer to this question is partially made out, it shows that there are three distinct types of capital, considered as a social phenomenon, viz., first, capital which is used solely by the owner; second, capital which is used by the owner in some sort of dependence upon the acts of others; third, capital which is employed, as such, wholly by others than the owner, and under conditions which he does not and could not maintain by his individual power.[21]

The most original and far-ranging of the new German-trained political and social economists was Simon Patten. He took as given the superiority of large-scale, integrated economic organizations, and was little troubled by either European cartels or American trusts. What did concern Patten were the social and political implications of these new entities, most especially the implications flowing from their ability to produce ever-cheaper and more abundant goods and services. "In modern nations," he maintained, "the productive power is more than sufficient to produce the minimum of existence. There is a social surplus above the costs of production in which every worker has a right to share."[22] While these economic rights were different from earlier conceptions of political and civil rights, they shared the same ends:

> The rights upon which political freedom depends have already been worked out. They were obtained by picturing a primitive society where men were so isolated that their relations were simple and plain. The problem of economic freedom is to find a modern equivalent for the rights that in earlier times went with land. The workman of to-day should have all that the landowner of the past enjoyed. Freedom consists not merely of political rights, but is dependent upon the possession of economic rights, freely recognized and universally granted to each man by his fellow citizens. These economic rights measure freedom in proportion as there is a mutual agreement concerning their desirability, and as complete adjustment makes their realization possible. Only those rights that American conditions permit and the impulses of unimpeded activity may attain can be properly considered ideal. . . .[23]

The kinds of rights Patten had in mind were all tied, directly or indirectly, to protecting the production of abundance and to the wise use of the social surplus. These rights fall into four categories in Patten's view. The first set of rights are "Public or Market Rights," including rights to an

---

[21] Albion Small, "The Social Gradations of Capital," *The American Journal of Sociology* 19, no. 6 (1914): 722, 725, and 726.
[22] Simon Patten, *The Theory of Prosperity* (New York: Macmillan, 1902), 224.
[23] Ibid., 215.

open market, to publicity (transparency), to security, and to association. Among "Social Rights" are rights to a home, to personal development, to wholesome moral standards, to homogeneity of population, and to decisions by public opinion. Among "Rights to Leisure" are provisions for recreation, clean air and water, and a pleasing visual environment. Among "Exceptional Rights" Patten calls for family provision in the event of unemployment or industrial accidents and for rights to an income both for single women and for women whose husbands have been injured or killed in the line of work.[24]

Behind these programmatic proposals lay Patten's larger theory of human progress, best summarized in his book on the changing requirements of charity and social work, *The New Basis of Civilization:*

> There can be no permanent progress until poverty has been eliminated, for then only will the normally evolving man, dominant through numbers and keen mental powers, force adjustments, generation by generation, which will raise the general level of intellect and character. And when poverty is gone, the last formidable obstacle to the upward movement of the race will have disappeared.[25]

For Patten, ideals are not outside of material life and history, but are immanent in the phenomenal world. This lesson is particularly difficult for philanthropists and charity-workers to learn. "The means of progress are material; its ends are ideal."[26]

## IV. The New Democratic Ethic

Behind Patten's theory of material progress and the means of its achievement is an evolutionary ethical theory that informed theological speculation as well. The transition that marks the coming age is from a pain and scarcity economy to a pleasure and abundance economy. According to Patten, a Hobbesian world of law backed by fear of punishment required a Judeo-Christian God as ruler and punisher. These beliefs and doctrines are now barriers to God's continuing revelation. The new Christ "comes not as the ruler of men, but as their servant." In a society of plenty, the greatest dangers are not external persecution and exploitation, but internal temptation: we need "a model for imitation, one who remains pure even though subject to the passions and temptations of men." In the coming era, "intelligence and self-control will be the great virtues" spread

---

[24] Ibid., 216–29. See also Florence Kelley, *Some Ethical Gains Through Legislation* (New York: Macmillan, 1905); and Seth Low and Richard T. Ely, "A Programme for Labor Reform," *Century Magazine* 39, no. 6 (1890): 938–51. Abbott, *The Rights of Man,* has two chapters summarizing these same rights of labor.

[25] Simon Patten, *The New Basis of Civilization* (New York: Macmillan, 1907), 197.

[26] Ibid., 213.

through imitation and inspiration. This process is already evident in America, the most economically advanced nation on earth.[27]

Many other Progressives voiced this call for a new democratic ethic. In one of his earliest essays, John Dewey sought to identify the specifically ethical dimensions of democracy. Any ethical conception, on his view, must reject from the start an abstract and mathematical conception of democracy, reducing men "into merely numerical individuals, into ballot-projecting units."[28] Ethical democracy rests on the fact that

> [s]ociety and the individual are really organic to each other. . . . [The individual] is not merely [society's] image or mirror. He is the localized manifestation of its life. And if, as actually happens, society be not yet possessed of one will, but partially is one and partially has a number of fragmentary and warring wills, it yet follows that *so far* as society has a common purpose and spirit, *so far* each individual is not representative of a certain proportionate share of the sum total of will but is its vital embodiment. And this is the theory, often crudely expressed, but none the less true in substance, that every citizen is a sovereign, the American theory, a doctrine which in grandeur has but one equal in history, and that its fellow, namely, that every man is a priest of God.[29]

In a socialized and ethical democracy, social progress and personal development are interdependent because both require "a unified and articulate will."[30] Without this will, every association for the achievement of common ends would remain temporary and artificial. In his coauthored and widely used textbook *Ethics*, Dewey stated it this way:

> A common end which is not made such by common, free voluntary coöperation in process of achievement is common in name only. It has no support and guarantee in the activities which it is supposed to benefit, because it is not the fruit of those activities. Hence, it does not stay put. It has to be continually buttressed by appeal to external, not voluntary, considerations; bribes of pleasure, threats of harm, use of force. It has to be undone and done over.[31]

The effective embodiment of a common moral will requires a coherent and consensual "public opinion." The many Progressive social scientists

---

[27] Simon Patten, *A Theory of Social Forces* (Philadelphia, PA: American Academy of Political and Social Science, 1896), 85, 90, and 107.

[28] John Dewey, "The Ethics of Democracy," *Philosophical Papers*, Second Series, No. 1 (University of Michigan, 1888): 8.

[29] Ibid., 14.

[30] Ibid., 16 and 22.

[31] John Dewey and James Tufts, *Ethics* (New York: Henry Holt, 1908), 304.

who wrote on public opinion shared this view of its crucial role in democratic theory. In the words of Charles Horton Cooley, one of Dewey's early colleagues at the University of Michigan, "public opinion is no mere aggregate of separate individual judgments, but an organization, a coöperative product of communication and reciprocal influence. It may be as different from the sum of what the individuals could have thought out in separation as a ship built by a hundred men is from a hundred boats each built by one man."[32] To Franklin Giddings, a sociologist and later colleague of Dewey's at Columbia, "society is democratic only when all people without distinction of rank or class participate in the making of public opinion and of moral authority."[33]

The increased role of public opinion not only marks the progress of democratic government, it signals a higher moral consciousness. Cooley's social psychology textbook put it this way:

> The present epoch . . . brings with it a larger and, potentially at least, a higher and freer consciousness. . . . The general or public phase of larger consciousness is what we call Democracy. I mean by this primarily the organized sway of public opinion. It works out also in a tendency to humanize the collective life, to make institutions express the higher impulses of human nature, instead of brutal or mechanical conditions.[34]

Jane Addams was the most eloquent spokesperson for a new democratic ethic. Famous for the establishment of Hull House in Chicago, whose female residents were soon to lead a host of Progressive reform organizations and causes, Addams was also a prolific and influential writer. In an early essay, "The Subjective Necessity of Social Settlements," her starting point is educated young people who "are seeking an outlet for that sentiment of universal brotherhood which the best spirit of our times is forcing from an emotion into a motive." Educated young people especially feel a great gap between their impulses and their actions:

> They feel a fatal want of harmony between their theory and their lives, a lack of co-ordination between thought and action. . . . These young men and women, longing to socialize their democracy, are animated by certain hopes. . . . These hopes may be loosely formu-

---

[32] Charles Horton Cooley, *Social Organization: A Study of the Larger Mind* (New York: Charles Scribner's Sons, 1909), 121.

[33] Franklin Giddings, *Elements of Sociology* (New York: Macmillan, 1898), 315. See also Edward A. Ross, *Social Control: A Survey of the Foundations of Order* (New York: Macmillan, 1901), 93–105.

[34] Cooley, *Social Organization*, 116 and 118. Cooley's 1909 social psychology textbook was the founding book in this new field, and was in continuous publication through 1929.

lated thus: that if in a democratic country nothing can be permanently achieved save through the masses of the people, it will be impossible to establish a higher political life than the people themselves crave; that it is difficult to see how the notion of a higher civic life can be fostered save through common intercourse; that the blessings which we associate with a life of refinement and cultivation can be made universal and must be made universal if they are to be permanent; that the good we secure for ourselves is precarious and uncertain, is floating in mid-air, until it is secured for all of us and incorporated into our common life. . . .[35]

Addams arranges the impulses behind these hopes and ideals in an ascending hierarchy:

The first contains the desire to make the entire social organism democratic, to extend democracy beyond its political expression; the second is the impulse to share the race life, and to bring as much as possible of social energy and the accumulation of civilization to those portions of the race which have little; the third springs from a certain *renaissance* of Christianity, a movement toward its early humanitarian aspects. . . .[36]

## V. The New Social Gospel

Progressives not only acknowledged the importance of moral and religious vanguards, they made identification with this vanguard a large part of their appeal. This, I think, is most evident in those who explicitly combined Protestant evangelicalism and Progressive social reform.[37]

"Evangelizing" America by establishing new churches and colleges in the west had long been a project of New England and, later, Midwestern Protestants. Additionally, pre–Civil War "evangelical united fronts" created many ecumenical national reform movements, most notably, the temperance and antislavery movements. New England "theocrats" like Horace Bushnell and Henry Ward Beecher had outlined projects of "Christianizing America," projects that included many moral and ethical components. Post–Civil War "social Christianity," which came to be called

---

[35] Jane Addams, "The Subjective Necessity of Social Settlements," in Henry Carter Adams, ed., *Philanthropy and Social Progress* (New York: Thomas Y. Crowell, 1893), 2.

[36] Ibid., 7.

[37] Dewey incorporated these same millennialist hopes into his ethics textbook when he stated that the increase in rights has been accompanied by an increase in personal responsibility as social norms become internalized and widespread in democratic societies and where "the external control of force has been replaced by the moral control of duty." Dewey and Tufts, *Ethics*, 153.

"the social gospel," was unique, however, first in its alliance with the new social sciences, and then in its equanimity at the prospect of having much of the church's social mission taken over by governmental or other secular institutions.

These two features were not begrudged concessions to something called "modernity" or "secularization," but were welcomed and, indeed, more or less implicit in liberal-evangelical theology and in its evolutionary theory of history. Lyman Abbott wrote three books on the evolution of Christianity. The first traces the history of Christianity as a spiritual force, the second, as a social development, and the third as an evolving ethical system.[38] When the three books are set alongside two other books of Abbott's, on the history and evolution of human freedom and on the making of America,[39] the result is a comprehensive narrative underpinning for the Progressive reform project.[40]

Abbott's evolutionary historicism—the theory that higher and more democratic ideals were immanent in the development of new forms of social, economic, and religious life—fed into and reinforced the "myths America lives by."[41] All of Abbott's books substantiated what was called a "New Theology" in American Protestantism that sought to integrate the fruits of higher learning and historical scholarship into Christianity. Many of these fruits grew in German universities; in that sense, Abbott was restating at second-hand the scholarly conclusions of American churchmen and professors who studied in Germany beginning in the 1830s and extending well into the early twentieth century.[42]

[38] Lyman Abbott, *The Evolution of Christianity* (Boston: Houghton Mifflin Company, 1892); Abbott, *Christianity and Social Problems* (Boston: Houghton Mifflin Company, 1896); and Abbott, *The Theology of an Evolutionist* (Boston: Houghton Mifflin Company, 1897).

[39] Abbott, *The Rights of Man*, and Abbott, *America in the Making.* The latter was part of the Yale Lectures on the Responsibilities of Citizenship series; previous lecturers included James Bryce, Charles Evans Hughes, Arthur Twining Hadley, Elihu Root, and William H. Taft.

[40] His contemporary John Bascom (1827–1911), president of the University of Wisconsin, wrote four books that almost exactly parallel those by Abbott: Bascom, *A New Theology* (New York: G. P. Putnam, 1891); Bascom, *An Historical Interpretation of Philosophy* (New York: G. P. Putnam, 1893); Bascom, *Evolution and Religion; or Faith as Part of a Complete Cosmic System* (New York: G. P. Putnam, 1897); and Bascom, *Growth of Nationality in the United States: A Social Study* (New York: G. P. Putnam, 1899).

[41] Richard T. Hughes, *Myths America Lives By* (Urbana: University of Illinois Press, 2004). Some of the myths discussed, in roughly chronological order, are America as a chosen nation, as nature's nation, as a Christian nation, as a millennialist nation, and as an innocent nation. Abbott's *America in the Making* is a restatement of many varieties of these myths discussed by Hughes, beginning with the Puritan migration and ending with our new international responsibilities.

[42] There were also those who received their German scholarship through Samuel Taylor Coleridge, in the manner of Horace Bushnell, one of Abbott's early heroes. On the influence of German scholarship in this period, see Jurgen Herbst, *The German Historical School in American Scholarship* (Cambridge, MA: Harvard University Press, 1965); and Louise L. Stevenson, *Scholarly Means to Evangelical Ends: The New Haven Scholars and the Transformation of Higher Learning in America, 1830–1890* (Baltimore, MD: Johns Hopkins University Press, 1986).

Because it had its origin in the colleges and seminaries of New England Protestantism,[43] the "New Theology" was also called "The New Puritanism."[44] Abbott's formulation was a common one:

> New Theology is neither new nor a theology . . . [but] new only in contrast with the Puritan theology out of which it has sprung, and from which it is a reaction. It is not truly a theology, since its chief inspiration is a deep desire to get away from the questions of the purely speculative intellect, the answers to which constitute theology, to the practical questions of the Hebrew seers, the answers to which constitute religion. . . . The church, then, is coming more and more to conceive of God, not as some one outside of his creation ruling *over* it, but as some one inside his creation ruling *within* it.[45]

In this perspective, experience of the spirit takes place in time and history; for each age of man, authentic religion "is always new" and must find new forms of articulate expression. Christianity is evolutionary because God "manifests himself [to man] in growth."[46] History "is but the record of the process of this evolution of the divinity out of humanity. It is a continuous progressive change, from lower to higher, and from simpler to more complex. It is according to certain definite laws of the moral and spiritual life."[47] Progressive revelation turns religious life toward ethics and the life of the church from inward maintenance to outward action. Because God is disclosed ever more fully only through man in his larger moral and social life, God "is training children to be free like himself, and by their own free choice to become partakers of his nature." Evidence of this disclosure is in man's increasing capacity for "righteousness."[48]

Most striking in Abbott's religious historicism is his contrast of pagan Rome and holy Israel. While this contrast is central to his analysis of the history of the Church after Constantine and up to the Reformation, its larger meaning is theological and political.[49] History is the unfolding of the age-old struggle between Roman "imperialism" and Hebraic "democ-

---

[43] For the crucial role of Yale College and its German-trained faculty, see Stevenson, *Scholarly Means to Evangelical Ends.* Yale College went on to produce the founding presidents of Johns Hopkins, Cornell, and the University of Chicago.

[44] Lyman Abbott, Amory H. Bradford, et al., *The New Puritanism* (New York: Fords, Howard, and Hulbert, 1898).

[45] Abbott, *Evolution of Christianity,* 109–10.

[46] Ibid., iii and v.

[47] Ibid., 254.

[48] Ibid., 237 and 247. This analysis is also found later in the writings of Walter Rauschenbusch, the social gospel theologian most known today by historians of America political thought. See, for example, Rauschenbusch, *Christianity and the Social Crisis* (New York: Macmillan, 1914), 201–10.

[49] Abbott, *Evolution of Christianity,* 154: "The history of the church down to the period of the Reformation is the history of the way in which Christian principles and the Christian spirit pervaded and transformed pagan institutions, and in which Christian institutions

racy." Fulfillment in history, both spiritual and material, is the victory of democracy. The Reformation, especially as it developed in England and the American colonies, was where the battle between "ecclesiastical imperialism" and liberty was most aggressively joined.[50]

Interwoven in Abbott's political-ecclesiastical history is a history of ideas, a *Geistesgeschichte*. Luther, Calvin, and Cromwell are joined by Copernicus and Bacon, who are soon joined by Rousseau, Voltaire, and Hegel. Abbott's lectures, published as *The Rights of Man*, are accompanied by a list of books that inform each chapter. Hegel is the first listed, joined by John Stuart Mill and his major followers, John Morley and Frederic Harrison, the liberal statesmen William Gladstone, and social reformers Sidney and Beatrice Webb. The American churchman Josiah Strong is listed alongside prominent Progressive intellectuals Franklin Giddings, Richard T. Ely, and H. D. Lloyd, who are, in turn, joined by political leaders Theodore Roosevelt and Booker T. Washington.

The "New Theology" is a social and not a theological gospel because religion is seen to migrate from out of the constraints of creed and church in order to permeate the larger society with its higher ethic and advancing social knowledge. America, as the highest embodiment of democracy, is also the highest embodiment of Christianity, for the two are one.[51] In the words of an astute historian of the impulses of liberal Protestantism:

> A key paradox of [American] liberal Protestantism—one that must be a cornerstone of any history of liberal Protestantism—is that its goal has always been, in part, to sanctify the secular, to bring forth out of the natural and human worlds the divine potential contained within them. Secularization can be seen, in some of its forms, as a sign of success for liberal Protestantism, not a marker of defeat.[52]

---

were moulded and pervaded by pagan principles . . . an empire partially christianized, and a church partially paganized."

[50] When Abbott wrote in support of America's entry into the First World War, he repeated this argument: what was at stake for mankind was the victory either of "Rome" or of "Israel." Germany and its Kaiser represented a soulless, external, and authoritarian Rome. America, represented by Lincoln and Wilson, stood for the union of reason, matter, and spirit—what Abbott termed Hegel and Christianity. "He who believes that history is anything more than merely a series of accidental happenings, who believes that there is any continuity and coherence in history, who believes in any ordered social evolution, should find it difficult to believe that this march of the century toward liberty will be halted." Lyman Abbott, *The Twentieth Century Crusade* (New York: Macmillan, 1918), 99.

[51] The last chapter in Abbott's *The Rights of Man* is subtitled "To what extent and in what sense democracy and political Christianity are synonymous." The Hegelian element becomes clear when paired with the subtitle of the previous chapter: "The grounds for believing that democracy in some form is the ultimate and permanent form of government." John Dewey posited this same conflation in an early essay, "Christianity and Democracy," in *John Dewey, The Early Works*, vol. 4 (Carbondale: Southern Illinois University Press, 1971), 3–10.

[52] Richard W. Fox, "Experience and Explanation in American Religious History," in Harry S. Stout and P. G. Hart, eds., *New Directions in American Religious History* (New York: Oxford University Press, 1997), 400. Susan Curtis, *A Consuming Faith: The Social Gospel and Modern American Culture* (Baltimore, MD: Johns Hopkins University Press, 1991), 131, adds that "a

The millennial and utopian strains in Progressive political thought came largely from an alliance of social gospel writers with the emerging science of sociology. Indeed, sociology was seen as the special voice of God's progressive revelation.[53] A meeting of Wisconsin Congregationalists in 1895 proclaimed "the right of sociology to demand that theology be ethicized" and that "the best book for social guidance is the New Testament; the best commentaries are the works of scientific sociology."[54] This alliance declared war on "individualism" and its intellectual allies. Echoing the critique of individualism by political economists, but with a more moralistic edge, Samuel Zane Batten declared in *The Christian State* that "just so far as democracy means the enthronement of self-interest and the apotheosis of individual desire . . . so far it becomes an iniquitous and dangerous thing." George Herron, in *The Christian Society*, declared that "the law of self-interest is the eternal falsehood that mothers all social and private woes; for sin is pure individualism." Simon Patten, who often wrote for social gospel publications, lists as one of the ten principles of social Christianity "the doctrine of social responsibility in contrast to individual rights."[55]

The calls for a new political economy, a new social ethic, and a revitalized social Christianity combined to constitute a deep indictment of

---

revitalized politics promised new life to religion as social gospelers conceived it. A political system responsible for social service and public morality extended the influence of churches into the secular arena and restored the relevance of religion to everyday life. Most important, progressive politics demanded social gospel Protestantism."

[53] Albion Small, in "Bonds of Nationality," wrote: "The crucial problem at the present stage of religious development is not whether this, that, or the other doctrinal formula or system is correct; but the incalculably more radical problem is whether religion is a hand-out from an external authority or a deposit of the evolving output of men's objective experience and subjective interpretations and valuations. . . ." He concluded that it fell to sociology "to represent among scholars the conviction that the world's knowledge, in the degree in which it approaches objectivity, must be capable of demonstrating its objectivity in part by its composability into an organization of knowledge, each portion of which shall corroborate and vitalize every other portion. Nothing less than this is conceivably adequate intellectual support for a religion that should convince all men" (675–76).

[54] Quoted in David Paul Thelen, *The New Citizenship: The Origins of Progressivism in Wisconsin, 1885–1890* (Columbia: University of Missouri Press, 1972), 108–9. George Herron, one of the more influential social gospel ministers, added: "Sociology cannot be dissociated from theology. Sociology and theology will ultimately be one science. Society depends upon theology. Men will be what they think God is. We need a Christian theology that we may have a Christian society." George Herron, *The Christian Society* (Chicago: Fleming H. Revell, 1894), 32.

[55] Samuel Zane Batten, *The Christian State: The State, Democracy, and Christianity* (Philadelphia, PA: Union Press, 1909), 215; Herron, *The Christian Society*, 110; Patten, quoted in Ronald White and Charles Hopkins, eds., *The Social Gospel: Religion and Reform in Changing America* (Philadelphia, PA: Temple University Press, 1976), 133. Batten and Herron were among the most popular social gospel writers and lecturers in America. The centrality of national consensus to achieving "the brotherhood of man" also impelled an attack on existing party-electoral politics. Batten declared that the system of parties and electoral spoils "stands between the people and the government and makes a fully democratic government impossible. . . . A good partisan cannot be a good citizen" (*The Christian State*, 239–40).

America's commitment in the "Gilded Age" to constitutionalism and a rights-based discourse. Whether the issue was states' rights, the claims of private property, the sanctity of contract, or, more generally, the power of courts to intervene in industrial disputes and overturn legislative will, Progressives now had an armory of weapons to challenge these prevailing legal values. More broadly, their project was to transform and to reconstitute the older liberalism on a new ethical and social basis.

## VI. THE PROGRESSIVES' PROBLEM WITH PRINCIPLES

With the exception of Oliver Wendell Holmes (1841–1935), whom Theodore Roosevelt appointed to the Supreme Court in 1902, Progressives displayed a thinly disguised contempt for the American legal mind and its institutional expressions in the upper bar and the courts.[56] Herbert Croly, in his call for reform in *The Promise of American Life*, simply dismisses the legal profession as unqualified to make any positive contribution to this effort.[57] In *Progressive Democracy*, Croly extends this criticism to the Constitution itself when viewed as standing above and outside of democratic political life:

> Public opinion can no longer be hypnotized and scared into accepting the traditional constitutionalism, as the final word in politics. . . .
> The Law in the shape of the Federal Constitution really came to be a monarchy of the Word. . . . Thus the aspirations and the conviction of the early democrats that popular political authority should be righteously expressed hardened into a system, which consecrated one particular machinery of possibly righteous expression. . . .
> The Constitution was really king. Once the kingdom of the Word had been ordained, it was almost as seditious to question the Word as it was to plot against the kingdom. A monarch exists to be obeyed. In the United States, as in other monarchies, unquestioning obedience was erected into the highest of political virtues.[58]

Croly admits that, like European monarchy, American constitutionalism initially served educative political purposes:

> The monarchy of the Constitution satisfied the current needs and the contemporary conscience of the American nation. Its government

---

[56] Richard T. Ely dedicated *Studies in the Evolution of Industrial Society* (1903) to Oliver Wendell Holmes, with the inscription, "In appreciation of the enlightened philosophy so conspicuous in his opinions, which is laying a firm foundation for a superstructure of industrial liberty."

[57] Croly, *Promise of American Life*, 135–37. Croly argued that, in alliance with corporate business, lawyers manipulated popular Constitution worship for their own selfish ends.

[58] Herbert Croly, *Progressive Democracy* (New York: Macmillan, 1914), 25, 44–45, and 131.

was at once authoritative, national and educational. It instructed the American people during their collective childhood. It trained them during their collective youth. With its assistance the American people have become a nation. They have been habituated to mutual association and joint action.[59]

This age has now passed. Democracy and the monarchy of the Constitution are now in conflict, and monarchy must give way:

The ideal of individual justice is being supplemented by the ideal of social justice. . . . Now the tendency is to conceive the social welfare, not as an end which cannot be left to the happy harmonizing of individual interests, but as an end which must be consciously willed by society and efficiently realized. Society, that is, has become a moral ideal, not independent of the individual but supplementary to him, an ideal which must be pursued less by regulating individual excesses than by the active conscious encouragement of socializing tendencies and purposes.[60]

Behind this critique of the Constitution and law lay a social science that posited the growing power of "public opinion" and internal moral controls as the evolutionary mark of democracy. As the sociologist Edward Ross explained:

Public opinion has the advantage of a *wide gamut* of influences. By thus supplementing the coarse and rough sanctions of the law, soci-

[59] Ibid., 145–46.
[60] Ibid., 148–49. Charles Beard's textbook *American Government and Politics*, which dominated collegiate instruction in American politics from its inception in 1910 through the 1930s, made this same historical argument:

No longer do statesmen spend weary days over finely spun theories about strict and liberal interpretations of the Constitution, about the sovereignty and reserved rights of states. . . . It is true that there are still debates on such themes as federal encroachments on local liberties, and that admonitory volumes on "federal" usurpation come from the press. It is true also that conservative judges, dismayed at the radical policies reflected in new statutes, federal and state, sometimes set them aside in the name of strict interpretation. But one has only to compare the social and economic legislation of the last decade with that of the closing years of the nineteenth century, for instance, to understand how deep is the change in the minds of those who have occasion to examine and interpret the Constitution bequeathed to them by the Fathers. Imagine Jefferson . . . reading Roosevelt's autobiography affirming the doctrine that the President of the United States can do anything for the welfare of the people which is not forbidden by the Constitution! Imagine Chief Justice Taney . . . called upon to uphold a state law fixing the hours of all factory labor. . . . Imagine James Monroe . . . called upon to sign bills appropriating federal money for roads, education, public health . . . and other social purposes! . . . Why multiply examples?

Charles Beard, *American Government and Politics* (New York: Macmillan, 1928), 100–101.

ety avoids putting itself into such undisguised opposition to a man's
wishes, and is not so likely to raise the spirit of rebellion. Its blame
does not exclude moral suasion, and its ban does not renounce all
appeal to the feelings.

Public opinion is *less mechanical* in operation than law. The public
can weigh provocation better, and can take into account condoning
or aggravating circumstances of time, place, motive, or office. The
blade of the law playing up and down in its groove with iron precision is hardly so good a regulative instrument as the flexible lash of
public censure. . . .[61]

Charles Horton Cooley saw a relationship between the supremacy of
legalism and stunted social and individual character development:

Underlying all formalism, indeed, is the fact that it is psychically
cheap; it substitutes the outer for the inner as more tangible, more
capable of being held before the mind without fresh expense of thought
and feeling, more easily extended, therefore, and impressed upon the
multitude. . . . The effect of formalism upon personality is to starve
its higher life and leave it the prey of apathy, self-complacency, sen-
suality and the lower nature in general. A formalized religion and a
formalized freedom are, notoriously, the congenial dwelling-place of
depravity and oppression.[62]

In a 1924 essay, "Logical Method and the Law," Dewey drew out the
implications of this argument. At the forefront of his analysis were the
writings of Justice Holmes; in the background lay an evolutionary theory
of history and human development. Logical systemization in legal decisions, on Dewey's analysis, is a necessary part of any instrumental reasoning and, "while it may be an end in itself for a particular student,
[logical systemization] is clearly in last resort subservient to the economical and effective reaching of decisions in particular cases." Legal logic,
then, "is ultimately an empirical and concrete discipline" but, by a process of natural selection "of the methods which afford the better type of
conclusion," those selected become clarified by logical analysis and hard-
ened into scientific formulas.[63]

Despite this underlying experiential practice, courts must justify their
decisions through exposition. The logic of exposition is, however, quite
different from the experimental logic of search and discovery:

---

[61] Ross, *Social Control*, 93–94; emphasis in original. Ross adds that public opinion is a
progressive force not only with the growth of popular intelligence and character, but when
members of the public defer to "the ascendency of the wise" (102).

[62] Cooley, *Social Organization*, 343 and 347.

[63] John Dewey, "Logical Method and the Law," *Cornell Law Quarterly* 10 (1924): 19.

It is at this point that the chief stimulus and temptation to mechanical logic and abstract use of formal concepts come in. Just because the personal element cannot be wholly excluded, while at the same time the decision must assume as nearly as possible an impersonal, objective, rational form, the temptation is to surrender the vital logic which has actually yielded the conclusion and to substitute for it forms of speech which are rigorous in appearance and which give an illusion of certitude.[64]

Dewey concludes his argument on a historicist note. Most contemporary principles of law, especially those regarding property and contract, were shaped in and through the experience of the eighteenth century, when "the great social need was emancipation of industry and trade from a multitude of restrictions which held over from the feudal estate of Europe." Now, however, one sees "in the present reaction against the individualistic formulae of an older liberalism" an "intermittent tendency in the direction of legislation, and to a less extent [sic] of judicial decision, towards what is vaguely known as 'social justice,' toward formulae of a collectivistic character." Those who continue "the sanctification of ready-made antecedent universal principles as methods of thinking" are "the chief obstacle to the kind of thinking which is the indispensable prerequisite of steady, secure and intelligent social reforms in general and social advance by means of law in particular."[65]

The "kind of thinking" that Dewey had in mind already lay at hand in the new social sciences. In the 1890s, the political economist Henry Carter Adams wrote a definitive article in which he charged that contemporary legal thinking was so far removed from the realities of contemporary economic relationships that resort to force by both capital and labor became inevitable.[66] In the first volume of *The American Journal of Sociology*, published in 1895, Albion Small launched a critique of prevailing ideas of property and contract in the face of the rise of large business corporations.[67] Roscoe Pound, who began his twenty-year tenure as dean of Harvard Law School in 1916,[68] wrote three very influential articles in the previous decade that made his reputation and became programmatic

[64] Ibid., 24.

[65] Ibid., 27.

[66] Henry Carter Adams, "Economics and Jurisprudence"; another article by Adams, "The Relation of the State to Industrial Action," was equally influential. Both essays are in Joseph Dorfman, ed., *Two Essays: The Relation of the State to Industrial Action and Economics and Jurisprudence* (New York: Columbia University Press, 1954). The latter essay was Adam's presidential address to the American Economic Association.

[67] Albion Small, "The State and Semi-Public Corporations," *The American Journal of Sociology* 1 (1895): 398–410.

[68] Pound was succeeded by James M. Landis, drafter of legislation establishing the Securities and Exchange Commission and author of a book justifying the use of regulatory agencies rather than courts to regulate most economic relationships. James M. Landis, *The Administrative Process* (New Haven, CT: Yale University Press, 1938).

statements for legal reformers.[69] He concluded one of them with a call to integrate the new social sciences into jurisprudence:

> Let us look to economics and sociology and philosophy, and cease to assume that jurisprudence is self-sufficient. It is the work of lawyers to make the law in action conform to the law in the books, not by futile thunderings against popular lawlessness, nor eloquent exhortations to obedience of the written law, but by making the law in the books such that the law in action can conform to it, and providing a speedy, cheap and efficient legal mode of applying it. On no other terms can the two be reconciled.[70]

The energy and tenacity of the Progressive attack on prevailing juridical and constitutional thinking eventually had its intended effects. By the 1920s—well after the electoral energies of Progressivism had been spent—the key assumptions and values of Progressivism were institutionalized in the curricula of elite law schools, in the federal regulatory bureaucracy, and eventually in the judiciary. By the time of the great realigning election of 1932, the New Deal not only found a well-developed administrative branch to serve its ends, but it found a court system that increasingly deferred to the will of legislative majorities and expert administrators.

## VII. Conclusion: Achievements and Ironies

In the national election campaign of 1844, the Whig Party declared:

> We wish, fully and entirely, TO NATIONALIZE THE INSTITUTIONS OF OUR LAND, AND TO IDENTIFY OURSELVES WITH OUR COUNTRY; to become a single great people, separate and distinct in national character, political interest, social and civil affinity from any and other [sic] nations, kindred and people on earth. . . . We have all the elements of becoming a greater people, a mightier nation, and more endurable government than has ever held a place in the annals of time. The civilized countries of the old world will yet do homage to the wisdom and learning, and science and arts of our people; and the combined powers of all Europe shall bow before the majesty of our power.[71]

Thanks to the antislavery movement, the victory of the Union armies in the Civil War, and the hegemonic electoral victory of the Republican Party

---

[69] Roscoe Pound, "Law in Books and Law in Action," *American Law Review* 44 (1910); Pound, "Liberty of Contract," *Yale Law Journal* 18 (1909); and Pound, "Mechanical Jurisprudence," *Columbia Law Review* 8 (1908).

[70] Pound, "Law in Books and Law in Action," 36.

[71] *American Republican*, November 7, 1844.

in 1896, the intellectual, moral, and political leadership of the Progressives at the turn of the twentieth century led to a substantial fulfillment of this early Whig national vision. Adding to the Whig call to nationalize existing institutions, however, the Progressives created many new and more embracive ones. While many of these institutions were "top down" in organization and leadership, an equal number were "bottom up" federations, joining local and regional organizations to national ones.

This nationalization—including the nationalization of governmental institutions—had a curious two-edged effect. First, it "politicized" private and local activities to the extent that they voiced ends that were explicitly tied to larger national purposes. In the earlier world of the Whigs, this transformation was largely within Protestant churches and the ecumenical reform organizations they created. The Progressives went much further in creating a nonsectarian, nationally oriented and richly complex "civil society" with these same politicized features. And second, like the Whigs, the Progressives "moralized" many political organizations and activities by infusing them with quasi-religious purposes.

The election of 1912 represented the highpoint of Progressive ideas in popular political culture. All three parties, but especially the Progressive Party, a newly formed breakaway from the Republicans, touted various aspects of a Progressive agenda. While all three presidential candidates won a substantial share of the vote, the Democratic candidate, Woodrow Wilson, prevailed with more than 6.6 million votes. Theodore Roosevelt, the Progressive candidate, however, received 4.13 million votes, more than half a million more votes than the Republican Party regular, William Howard Taft. The Progressive Party nominating convention, held in Chicago in August 1912, was a curious affair. In the style of Protestant sects, every delegate was given five minutes for political testimony. Theodore Roosevelt's address was titled "Confession of Faith." Periodically, the delegates would break out singing "Battle Hymn of the Republic." Following the keynote address by former Senator Albert Beveridge, the audience sang "Onward Christian Soldiers" as they paraded through the hall—led by the head of the New York delegation, Oscar S. Straus, a prominent Jewish political leader. The party's platform documented the success of more than three decades of Progressive political and social thought—especially the platform's planks on social and industrial justice, drafted largely by Florence Kelley and Jane Addams. Addams seconded Roosevelt's nomination.[72]

This highpoint was no accident: the major institutions of Progressive ideas, along with the new industrial economy, were thriving. Mass jour-

[72] There were two notable exceptions to this triumph, both involving blacks in the South. The first was the failure to condemn in the party platform violence against blacks, their increasing loss of civil and political rights, and their increasing social segregation. The second involved the refusal to accept and seat a racially mixed delegation from a southern state. See Robert Crunden, *Ministers of Reform: The Progressives' Achievement in American Civilization, 1889–1920* (Urbana: University of Illinois Press, 1984), chapter 7.

nalism, the new universities, citizen-oriented book series, women's clubs, and the infrastructure of reform organizations, churches, social workers, teachers, and professional and academic associations, each with their magazines and journals, were at the peak of their energies and morale. The combined effect was to infuse all three contesting political parties with the language of reform.[73]

In addition to shaping and institutionalizing a national language of democratic reform, a second major Progressive achievement was to link the systematic pursuit of social knowledge to political reform and thereby to tie higher education and the learned professions to the cause of national democracy. Given the undeveloped administrative capacity of the national government, this tie did not yield European "statism," but it did set up durable patterns of cooperation between the universities, the national government, large business corporations, and, later, national charitable foundations, labor unions, and the military.[74] One important result was the development of "welfare capitalism"—what Simon Patten termed "voluntary socialism"—as large corporations took on many functions that in Europe were provided by governments.[75] Another important side-effect of these ties was to turn many academic social scientists into well-known "public intellectuals" (or, better, "public moralists") writing for popular magazines, speaking to large nonacademic gatherings, and cultivating strong personal ties with nonacademic reform leaders from many walks of life.[76] As reform leaders became national institutional elites, so did many academics.

Lastly, the combined effects of Progressive ideas, organizations, and energies helped to complete a new national self-consciousness and national identity. In a recent book on regime periods in American history, Michael Lind, a prominent liberal journalist and public intellectual, distinguishes between "government framers" and "people founders" in terms of their roles in shaping new political regimes.[77] Surely, the Progressives can be said to have completed much of Abraham Lincoln's task of re-founding America, not so much in terms of formal governmental institutions, but in how we see these institutions in relation to shared national purposes. No matter how deeply "rights talk" came later to penetrate American

---

[73] Three books, all published in this period, reflect this optimism: Benjamin Parke De Witt, *The Progressive Movement* (New York: Macmillan, 1915); Walter Lippmann, *Drift and Mastery: An Attempt to Diagnose the Current Unrest* (New York: Mitchell Kennerley, 1914); and Walter Weyl, *The New Democracy* (New York: Macmillan, 1912).

[74] See Olivier Zunz, *Why the American Century?* (Chicago: University of Chicago Press, 1998). When the national media is added, these networks later came to be called "The Liberal Establishment."

[75] Stuart D. Brandes, *American Welfare Capitalism, 1880–1940* (Chicago: University of Chicago Press, 1976).

[76] Crunden, *Ministers of Reform*.

[77] Michael Lind, *The Next American Nation: The New Nationalism and the Fourth American Revolution* (New York: Free Press, 1995).

reformist political discourse, an enduring legacy of the Progressives was to ask that all rights claims be tied to durable national ends.

Recent books by political theorists and public intellectuals on the left have reasserted the relevance of the Progressive tradition for our own times.[78] These commentators see the era beginning in the 1980s—its economic restructurings and dislocations, its growing inequalities of wealth and income, and its explosive growth of immigration—as a new "Gilded Age" calling for an intellectual and political response modeled on that of the Progressive generation one hundred years earlier. Insofar as Progressivism is seen as the progenitor of New Deal liberalism—itself a contentious view—there is a certain irony in this contemporary hope by the American left of a rebirth of Progressivism. With the exception of recent electoral losses, liberalism continues to enjoy a hegemonic position in America's universities and law schools, in public education, in most professional associations, in the national media, and in the upper reaches of the mainline Protestant churches and much of the Catholic Church. When to these redoubts we add much of corporate America, almost all of the major charitable foundations, and much of the federal judiciary and bureaucracy, calls by liberals for a rebirth of Progressivism seem excessive.

There is, however, a deeper reason for this call, and it involves narrative. The rise of "value-neutral" readings of liberal democracy beginning in the mid-twentieth century,[79] and the turn to Rawlsian and Kantian versions of democratic liberalism—especially in constitutional understandings—have entailed the abandonment of national narrative by American liberalism. Contemporary liberalism not only lacks a compelling national narrative, it seems actively hostile in principle to the very idea of a national narrative— let alone a *sacred* one—that honors "ascriptive" or "ethnocentric" values. There have been some notable exceptions.

---

[78] Alan Dawley, *Struggles for Justice: Social Responsibility and the Liberal State* (Cambridge, MA: Harvard University Press, 1991); Dawley, *Changing the World: American Progressives in War and Revolution* (Princeton, NJ: Princeton University Press, 2003); Michael McGerr, *A Fierce Discontent: The Rise and Fall of the Progressive Movement in America, 1870–1920* (New York: Free Press, 2003); Jonathan Hansen, *Lost Promise of Patriotism: Debating American Identity, 1890–1920* (Chicago: University of Chicago Press, 2003); Richard Rorty, *Achieving Our Country: Leftist Thought in Twentieth-Century America* (Cambridge, MA: Harvard University Press, 1998); E. J. Dionne, *They Only Look Dead: Why Progressives Will Dominate the Next Political Era* (New York: Simon and Schuster, 1996); Lind, *Next American Nation*; Michael Tomasky, *Left for Dead: The Life, Death, and Possible Resurrection of Progressive Politics in America* (New York: Free Press, 1996). Jeffrey C. Isaac, *The Poverty of Progressivism: The Future of American Democracy in a Time of Decline* (Lanham, MD: Rowman and Littlefield, 2003) critiques much of this literature. For the most complete overview of contemporary writings on the Progressive period, see Robert D. Johnston, "Re-Democratizing the Progressive Era: The Politics of Progressive Era Political Historiography," *Journal of the Gilded Age and Progressive Era* 1, no. 1 (2002): 68–91.

[79] Two of the most notable are David Truman, *The Governmental Process* (New York: Knopf, 1951), and Robert Dahl, *Preface to Democratic Theory* (Chicago: University of Chicago Press, 1956). For an analysis of the rise of a value-neutral conception of the liberal democratic state in America, see David Ciepley, *Liberalism in the Shadow of Totalitarianism* (Cambridge, MA: Harvard University Press, 2007).

The opening line of Richard Rorty's 1997 Massey Lectures at Harvard reads: "National pride is to countries what self-respect is to individuals: a necessary condition of self-improvement." Lamenting "a widespread sense that national pride is no longer appropriate" among left intellectuals, Rorty draws a sharp contrast between contemporary and early twentieth-century leftist thought as that between "spectators" and "agents." The agency of these earlier reformers (he cites Herbert Croly) was anchored in the earlier national patriotism of Abraham Lincoln and Walt Whitman.[80] Lacking a patriotic and sacred national story, today's left "has no projects to propose to America, no vision of a country to be achieved by building a consensus on the need for specific reforms." A "thoroughgoing secularism" leaves reformers without either a national narrative or a reform-oriented civil religion of the kind prefigured in John Dewey. Rorty concludes that, while America clearly has a cultural left, it does not have a political one; therefore, "the Left is unable to engage in national politics." To reengage the cultural left in politics requires that it can no longer "take the point of view of a detached cosmopolitan spectator."[81]

A more complex attempt to create a liberal national narrative is made by the political theorist Rogers Smith, in his book *Stories of Peoplehood*.[82] This study is important for three reasons. The first is because it so consciously explores the various forms that national narratives take and the range of purposes they serve. Second, while the study clearly distinguishes stories of peoplehood from universalistic liberal-democratic principles, it recognizes their necessary interdependence. Third, this study comes on the heels of Smith's earlier book *Civic Ideals*, a story of America's seemingly endless betrayal of our universalistic civic ideals.[83] And because it was a wholly principled anti-narrative, *Civic Ideals* resonated perfectly with the academic and intellectual left that Rorty charged with being "unable to engage in national politics." Proof of this inability is that *Civic Ideals* quickly became adorned with national academic awards.[84]

*Civic Ideals* was a mea culpa, cataloging the constitutional and legal ways by which African Americans, Native Americans, and women were denied full membership in the political community. Smith posits that

---

[80] Rorty, *Achieving Our Country*, 3 and 10.

[81] Ibid., 19, 91, and 106.

[82] Rogers Smith, *Stories of Peoplehood: The Politics and Morals of Political Membership* (New York: Cambridge University Press, 2003).

[83] Rogers Smith, *Civic Ideals: Conflicting Visions of Citizenship in U.S. History* (New Haven, CT: Yale University Press, 1997).

[84] Two organized sections of the American Political Science Association (Politics and History and Foundations of Political Theory) gave the book the association's annual award. The Social Science History Association made it a co-winner of its annual book award, as did the Organization of American Historians in the category of American intellectual history. Outside of academic organizations, the Association of American Publishers gave the book its highest award in Government and Political Science. Given the number and breadth of the accolades bestowed on the book, to his credit its author was seemingly less satisfied with its conclusions than most of his readers.

these exclusions flow logically from the practice of defining the political community in "ascriptive" terms, that is, terms not based on the universal principle of equal individual consent. The persistent worry in *Civic Ideals* is why Americans seem so willing and able to heed the siren calls of ascriptive national identity in the face of their foundational liberal and civic republican principles. Smith's answer is simple but troubling. In a political democracy, "aspirants to power require a population to lead that imagines itself to be a 'people'," driving "political leaders to offer civic ideologies, or myths of civic identity" in order to achieve power.[85] Smith's somewhat tepid proposal is that holders of universal liberal principles— the authentic ground of American identity—must condescend to form a "party" with an ideology and myth of civic identity in order to compete against illiberal narratives.[86]

In *Stories of Peoplehood*, Smith revisits the issues raised in *Civic Ideals*, but with a decided shift in emphasis. All political regimes, even liberal-democratic ones, are now said to *require* "ethically constitutive stories":

> The problem is not only that, politically, we probably cannot hope to shape communities that can long endure unless people see them as expressing more than their procedural agreements and senses of abstract justice. . . . On these accounts, so long as one preaches democracy, particular memberships then can be expected to emerge rather organically out of fundamentally extra-political factors. But since those "extra-political" forms of intersection and mutual effect need to be articulated in politics as bases of collaboration . . . the pressures and dangers that impel reliance on ethically constitutive accounts of whole particular political societies cannot be escaped. . . . Citizens are at a minimum morally entitled to understand the commitments of those to whom they are entrusting their political destinies.[87]

Even though "the politics of people-making . . . involves continual . . . often invidious, and always exclusionary processes centered on stories and force . . . these processes also do much to make us who we are and to

---

[85] Smith, *Civic Ideals*, 6.

[86] This would be a party with a built-in arrogance as well: we brave/fearless few risk hard and principled choices in a society of intellectually and morally lazy citizens all too willing to support illiberal values and policies. See Smith, *Civic Ideals*, 502.

[87] Smith, *Stories of Peoplehood*, 152. There are two other forms of constitutive stories: economic ones that celebrate the material flourishing of a people (ibid., 60–62, 79–80, and 82–83), and political power stories, celebrating the power of citizens in the government, the popular achievement of independence or revolution, etc. (ibid., 62–64 and 93–95). These two kinds of stories, however, are much less binding and long-lived than ethically constitutive stories, which "are more likely to be religious or quasi-religious, kinship-like, and gendered than economic or political power stories" (ibid., 69). Smith does not see that these other stories can be combined into one larger national narrative, a sacred narrative that I argue the Progressives succeeded in creating.

make it possible for us to flourish on this earth." The philosophical requirements of political life seem now to include a national narrative at its very
center. "I therefore doubt," Smith concludes, "that any kind of politics of
peoplehood . . . is likely to get far in transforming the world for the better
if it simply takes the form of an assault on or dismissal of American
national identity." These assertions are in direct response to those who
would constrain democratic discourse to that which meets philosophically fixed standards of "public reason." These constrainers "appear to
deny, either hypocritically or foolishly, that their own views also express
controversial ethically constitutive accounts of human beings that are far
from self-evident truths."[88]

Whatever implications the arguments by Rorty and Smith have for
the philosophical foundations of contemporary liberal-democratic political theory, there is no question that their calls for national narrative
are in response to the rise of a coherently conservative Republican
Party over the past three decades. This rise suggests an irony in contemporary American political thought, namely, that the *rise* of contemporary conservatism bears some close resemblances to the rise of
Progressivism. Like Progressivism, contemporary conservatism began
as an intellectual "counter-culture" against a prevailing set of frozen
possibilities and static visions. It was now liberalism that seemed frozen, first in its static models of "interest group pluralism," and then in
its legalistic formulas of identity group pluralism.[89] Neither formulation embodied a coherent notion of the public good or a shared ideal
of national purpose. Given the demise of Cold War patriotism during
the Vietnam War period, the only remaining symbol of national unity
for liberalism was an abstract and philosophically grounded rights discourse through which to read the Constitution. Unfortunately, this discourse has been used primarily to buttress the traditional favorites in
the old system of interest groups or to sponsor new favorites in the
emerging system of racial and identity group politics.

What this conclusion suggests is that contemporary conservatism in
America might owe the Progressives more than it acknowledges, both
in shaping public policy consistently oriented to national purposes and in
enlisting the political, moral, and spiritual energies of those who wish to
participate as public-regarding citizens of their country. The Progressives
drew their core values from Lincoln's conception of the American people
as a nation with shared substantive purposes. How and through what
means these purposes were to be achieved was not preordained and fixed

---

[88] Ibid., 56, 177, and 183. Here Smith comes closer to the pragmatic position in Stanley
Fish, *The Trouble with Principle* (Cambridge, MA: Harvard University Press, 1999), chapters
9–11.

[89] Theodore Lowi, *The End of Liberalism* (New York: W. W. Norton, 1969) is the definitive
critique of interest group pluralism; Lind's *The Next American Nation* is an effective critique
of multiculturalism as a national purpose.

PROGRESSIVISM AS A NATIONAL NARRATIVE

for all time because the nation was a living and evolving organism. In the fight against slavery, for example, Lincoln depended less on prevailing constitutional truths and more on the moral energies and historical visions of his compatriots.[90] So, too, the best forms of contemporary conservative thought—let's call them the newest forms of liberalism—must maintain their national orientation, both in their commitment to a substantive public good and in their understanding of the place and distribution of rights.

*Political Science, University of Tulsa*

[90] Lincoln responded to the charge that his decree emancipating slaves in areas under Union military occupation violated the Constitution by asking, "Was it possible to lose the nation, and yet preserve the Constitution?" Letter to A. G. Hodges, April 4, 1864, quoted in Ronald C. White, Jr., *Lincoln's Great Speech: The Second Inaugural* (New York: Simon and Schuster, 2002), appendix II, 207.

# ON JUSTIFYING THE MORAL RIGHTS
# OF THE MODERNS: A CASE OF OLD WINE
# IN NEW BOTTLES*

By Gerald F. Gaus

## I. Something Old, Something New

We are familiar with one divide between "old" and "new" liberalism—
that between classical liberalism and social justice liberalism.[1] Although
this divide between the old and the new is multifaceted, the crux is a
debate about the place of the market, private property, and democracy in
a liberal polity.[2] According to common wisdom, classical liberals insist on
rights of the person against others and against a limited government,
freedom of association, freedom of conscience, and a free market within
a framework of laws against fraud and violence, laws enforcing contracts,
and strong rights of private property, including robust rights of investment, exchange, and inheritance. Limited democracy is endorsed as a
way to control government, but not as a source of fundamental norms.
Social justice liberals, while endorsing traditional civil rights—for example, the freedoms of speech, press, and religion, rights against search and
seizure, the right to a fair trial, privacy rights, equal protection of the
laws, and, generally, liberties of the person—argue that justice fundamentally concerns the distribution of resources or that one's basic claims of
justice are to resources that one needs or deserves. Thus, such liberals lay
great stress on policies to alter the distribution of property, or to enforce
social rights to assistance. Moreover, such liberals emphasize the role of

* Earlier versions of this essay were presented at the University of North Carolina, Chapel
Hill, Philosophy Department workshop on the morality of capitalism, and at the conference
on rights theory at the Murphy Institute, Tulane University. I am grateful for the comments
of the participants; my special thanks to David Schmidtz, Julian Lamont, and Andrea
Houchard for their useful written comments and suggestions.
[1] "Social justice liberalism" is more appropriate than either "welfare state liberalism" or
"egalitarian liberalism." "Welfare state liberalism" is a misnomer since obvious members of
this group—such as John Rawls—believe that the welfare state is inadequate. "Egalitarian
liberalism" is inappropriate since "new liberals" such as L. T. Hobhouse were not egalitarians. All "new liberals," however, have been concerned with the idea of social justice.
Hobhouse's *Elements of Social Justice* (London: Allen and Unwin, 1922) was one of the first
books on the subject. On the division between the old and the new liberalism, see Michael
Freeden, *The New Liberalism: An Ideology of Social Reform* (Oxford: Clarendon Press, 1978),
and Freeden, *Liberalism Divided: A Study in British Political Thought, 1914-1939* (Oxford:
Oxford University Press, 1986).
[2] See my essay "Liberalism at the End of the Century," *Journal of Political Ideologies* 5
(2000): 179-99.

democratic institutions in a liberal polity. Indeed, in recent years, social justice liberals such as John Rawls and his followers have declared themselves to be "deliberative democrats," who value political participation rights equally with civil liberties.[3] While of course inadequate, this familiar stylized contrast between classical liberalism and social justice liberalism captures a good deal of the truth.[4]

Michael Freeden, a contemporary political theorist, has drawn our attention to another interesting contrast between old and new conceptions of liberalism.[5] Freeden plausibly argues that liberal thinking—especially in the United States—has become increasingly the domain of abstract and technical philosophy since, say, the publication of Rawls's *A Theory of Justice* in 1971. Freeden unfavorably compares this new philosophical liberalism to older conceptions of liberalism that were widely accessible and firmly grounded in actual political practice. An upshot of the shift to the terrain of abstract philosophy is, I think, that many theories explicate the requirements of liberalism in an increasingly idealized, indeed often utopian, way. Liberalism is said to require implementation of a fully egalitarian society, or a society with the highest possible minimum income for all, or perhaps some version of market socialism. Although most of the interesting work in this new, highly philosophic approach to liberalism has been by advocates of social justice liberalism,[6] the approach has also been employed by classical liberals and libertarians, offering highly philosophical and abstract arguments based on intuitions about Lockean property rights, unlimited rights of self-ownership, and hypothetical histories.[7] This new variety of liberal theory can be contrasted to the older and more accessible accounts of liberalism presented by public intellectuals such as Herbert Spencer, Liberal Party intellectuals such as L. T. Hobhouse (in his famous little book *Liberalism*, published in 1911), or even philosophers

---

[3] See John Rawls, *Political Liberalism,* paperback ed. (New York: Columbia University Press, 1996), 413. This is often put in terms of the contrast between the "liberty of the ancients and of the moderns": I consider this contrast further in Section VII.D. Originally, Rawls insisted that civil rights were more important than political participation rights, but he came to revise his views. On Rawls's changing views, see note 105 below. Rawls declares himself to be a "deliberative democrat" in Rawls, "The Idea of Public Reason Revisited," *University of Chicago Law Review* 64 (Summer 1997): 764–807, at 772; reprinted in John Rawls, *The Law of Peoples* (Cambridge, MA: Harvard University Press, 1999), and in Samuel Freeman, ed., *John Rawls: Collected Papers* (Cambridge, MA: Harvard University Press, 1999), chap. 26.

[4] I have considered the differences between the old and the new liberalism in a more nuanced way in my essay "Public and Private Interests in Liberal Political Economy, Old and New," in S. I. Benn and G. F. Gaus, eds., *Public and Private in Social Life* (New York: St. Martin's Press, 1983), 183–222.

[5] See Michael Freeden, *Ideologies and Political Theory: A Conceptual Approach* (Oxford: Clarendon Press, 1996), chap. 6.

[6] See, for example, Ronald Dworkin, *Sovereign Virtue* (Cambridge, MA: Harvard University Press, 2000); and Philippe Van Parijs, *Real Freedom for All* (Oxford: Oxford University Press, 1995).

[7] I have in mind, of course, Robert Nozick, *Anarchy, State, and Utopia* (New York: Basic Books, 1974).

such as John Stuart Mill (in *On Liberty*, 1859). All of these were British, but even earlier Americans such as John Dewey in his *Liberalism and Social Action* (1935) presented fairly simple and concise statements of liberal principles that were accessible to most educated members of the public.[8] In the hands of these political theorists, liberalism still looked to be a practical political program rather than a technical and highly idealized philosophic construction.

I believe that there is something right and enlightening about Freeden's version of the "old" and "new" divide, although of course it must be highly qualified. Liberalism has traditionally been a radical doctrine; criticizing the current order and presenting idealized proposals is part and parcel of the liberal tradition. Liberals are often radicals. And, of course, liberal theories were sometimes abstract and technical long before Rawls and the rise of academic liberalism in the United States. The nineteenth-century British philosopher T. H. Green, whose liberalism inspired Hobhouse and others, based his political theory on a version of absolute idealism drawn from G. W. F. Hegel, as abstruse a philosophical doctrine as one is apt to encounter.[9] Still, Freeden has an important insight. If one reads Hobhouse's *Liberalism*, or Dewey's *Liberalism and Social Action* (or, I should add, Isaiah Berlin's "Two Concepts of Liberty"),[10] one encounters a very different genre of liberal theorizing from that found in current philosophy journals and books. While there have always been both genres, I think it is fair to say that today liberalism's center of gravity is in the academy and, especially, in philosophy departments.

The movement from the older, more practical and accessible approach, to the newer, more academic and philosophical approach to liberal theorizing has been a mixed good. In my view, a clear deficit is the plethora of opposed moral blueprints for social institutions, each insisting that departures from its ideal scheme render existing institutions unjust and illegitimate. We now have before us libertarian theories based on self-ownership and rights to initial acquisition (telling us that nearly any redistribution of market outcomes is illegitimate);[11] left-libertarian theo-

---

[8] See Herbert Spencer, "From Freedom to Bondage," in Spencer, *The Man Versus the State, with Six Essays on Government, Society, and Freedom* (Indianapolis: Liberty Fund, 1982), 487–518; L. T. Hobhouse, *Liberalism* (London: Oxford University Press, 1911); J. S. Mill, *On Liberty* (1859), in John Gray, ed., *On Liberty and Other Essays* (New York: Oxford University Press, 1991); and John Dewey, *Liberalism and Social Action* (1935; New York: G. P. Putnam's Sons, 1980).

[9] I should note that, in the hands of British philosophers such as Green, this theory was certainly more intelligible than in its original German version.

[10] Isaiah Berlin, "Two Concepts of Liberty" (1958), in Berlin, *Four Essays on Liberty* (Oxford: Oxford University Press, 1969).

[11] See, for example, Nozick, *Anarchy, State, and Utopia*; and Eric Mack, "Self-Ownership and the Right of Property," *The Monist* 73 (October 1990): 519–43. For an overview, see Eric Mack and Gerald F. Gaus, "Classical Liberalism and Libertarianism," in Gerald F. Gaus and Chandran Kukathas, eds., *Handbook of Political Theory* (London: Sage, 2004): 115–30.

ries also supportive of a conception of self-ownership but often upholding intuitions about the common ownership of the earth (telling us that
extensive redistribution of market outcomes is mandatory for justice);[12]
desert-based theories of various types (some insisting on the necessity of
strong private ownership rights, and others upholding strongly redistributive policies);[13] neo-Kantian theories (some supporting welfare-state rights
to well-being, others leaning toward libertarianism);[14] theories upholding
an equal distribution of resources (or welfare, or basic capabilities) which
challenge strong ownership rights while embracing some version of the
market;[15] and neo-Hobbesian accounts (some defending robust private
property rights, others upholding a right to welfare).[16] As a rule, these
theories worry very little about connecting up with actual social practices
except insofar as the author supposes that his moral intuitions are widespread. It is a caricature—but not an entirely unfair one—to depict all this
as the activity of philosophers, ensconced in their ivory towers, instruct-
ing everyone as to the system of morality and politics that is clearly
demanded by rational reflection, yet talking in a babble of conflicting
voices. Yet the movement to rigorous philosophical analysis has had great
payoffs. A contemporary reader cannot help but be struck by the vague-
ness and, one can only say, sloppiness of the analyses of Hobhouse's
*Liberalism*, Dewey's *Liberalism and Social Action*, or the works of Spencer.
Even John Locke's *Second Treatise of Government* does not fare well by the
standards of current argument. Our understandings of liberty, justice,
equality, and the nature of public reasoning in a diverse society have
improved immensely.

As I said, it is tempting to lay both the praise and the blame—if blame
is appropriate—for the development of this more philosophical brand of
liberal theorizing at Rawls's feet. Rawls's thinking, though, is always
more complex than it first appears, and almost always more subtle than
those whom he inspired. Rawls, we must remember, developed his philosophical liberalism into a political one where the overriding concern was
meshing philosophical analysis with social facts. According to Rawls:

> [E]ven if by some convincing philosophical argument—at least con-
> vincing to us and a few like-minded others—we could trace the right

---

[12] See Hillel Steiner and Peter Vallentyne, eds., *Left-Libertarianism and Its Critics* (Basingstoke: Palgrave, 2000).

[13] For the former, see my *Social Philosophy* (Armonk, NY: M. E. Sharpe, 1999), chap. 9; for the latter, see Julian Lamont, "Incentive Income, Deserved Income, and Economic Rents," *Journal of Political Philosophy* 5 (1997): 26–46.

[14] For the former, see Alan Gewirth, *Reason and Morality* (Chicago: University of Chicago Press, 1981); for the latter, see Marcus Verhaegh, "Kant and Property Rights," *Journal of Libertarian Studies* 18 (Summer 2004): 11–32.

[15] See esp. Dworkin, *Sovereign Virtue*, but there are a host of others who take this view.

[16] For the former, see David Gauthier, *Morals by Agreement* (Oxford: Clarendon, 1986); for the latter, see Gregory Kavka, *Hobbesian Moral and Political Theory* (Princeton, NJ: Princeton University Press, 1986).

to private or social property back to first principles or to basic rights, there is a good reason for working out a conception of justice which does not do this. For ... the aim of justice as fairness as a political conception is to resolve the impasse in the democratic tradition as to the way in which social institutions are to be arranged if they are to conform to the freedom and equality of citizens as moral persons. Philosophical argument alone is most unlikely to convince either side that the other is correct on a question like that of private or social property in the means of production. It is more fruitful to look for bases of agreement implicit in the public culture of a democratic society and therefore in its underlying conceptions of the person and of social cooperation.[17]

Rawls presents us with a paradox. His work was a major impetus to developing abstract theories of distributive justice, and he himself insists that his own rather abstract philosophical theory demonstrates that both laissez-faire and welfare-state capitalism are unjustifiable.[18] However, he insists that "convincing philosophical argument" grounding a justification of capitalism on basic rights is not the right way to go about developing a conception of justice. If we accept this latter idea, much recent liberal political philosophy—whether endorsing classical or social justice liberalism—rests on a mistake: even if its abstract arguments are sound, they cannot achieve their ends.

In this essay, I sketch a philosophical conception of liberal morality that stays true to Rawls's complex insight: although abstract philosophical argument alone cannot resolve our moral differences, careful philosophical reasoning is necessary to see our way to a resolution. Thus, I shall argue, we can develop a "new" (qua philosophical) liberalism that takes existing social facts and mores seriously while, at the same time, retaining the critical edge characteristic of the liberal tradition. However, *pace* Rawls, I shall argue that once we develop such an account, we are led toward a vindication of "old" (qua classical) liberal morality. Hence the old (vintage) wine in the new, more Rawlsian bottles.

Section II begins by sketching the basis for the claim that liberal principles must be "publicly justified"—justified to everyone. Section III argues that our deep disagreements about the proper standards of evaluation pose a challenge to all attempts at public justification. Sections IV through VI analyze methods for publicly justifying a morality under these conditions of disagreement on evaluative standards. Section VII then argues that the morality that is justified under these conditions is not the social justice/deliberative democratic liberalism of

[17] Rawls, *Political Liberalism*, 338–39.
[18] John Rawls, *Justice as Fairness: A Restatement*, ed. Erin Kelly (Cambridge, MA: Belknap Press of Harvard University Press, 2001), 136ff.

Rawls, but closer to what Benjamin Constant called the "liberty of the moderns."[19]

## II. Public Justification Among Free and Equal Moral Persons

### A. Free and equal moral persons

I take as my starting point the supposition that we conceive of ourselves and others as (1) moral persons who are (2) free and equal. Although these features are assumed in this essay, we should not suppose that these assumptions cannot themselves be defended. Rawls rightly argues that this general conception of moral persons is implicit in our public culture.[20] In much the same vein, I have argued that our commitment to the public justification of our moral demands on each other follows from our conception of ourselves and others as such persons.[21] Let me briefly explain each of these fundamental ideas: (i) moral personality, (ii) free moral persons, and (iii) equal moral persons.

(i) A *moral person* is one who makes, and can act upon, moral demands. Moral persons thus conceive of themselves as advancing moral claims on others and being subject to such claims. Alternatively, we can say that moral persons understand themselves as owed, and owing, certain restraints and acts.[22] Not all humans—not even all functioning adult humans—are moral persons: psychopaths do not appear to understand themselves as pressing moral claims on others that demand respect, nor do they see others as moral persons.[23] As well as advancing moral claims, moral persons have the capability to act on justified moral claims made on them. In this sense, moral persons are not solely devoted to their own ends; they have a capacity to put aside their personal ends and goals to act on justified moral claims. Moral persons, then, are not simply instrumentally rational agents;[24] they possess a capacity for moral autonomy. Insofar as moral autonomy presupposes the ability to distinguish one's

[19] See Benjamin Constant, "The Liberty of the Ancients Compared with That of the Moderns," in Constant, *Political Writings,* ed. Biancamaria Fontana (Cambridge: Cambridge University Press, 1988), 308–28.

[20] See John Rawls, "Kantian Constructivism in Moral Theory," in Freeman, ed., *John Rawls: Collected Papers,* 303–58, esp. 305ff. This is not to say that Rawls and I advance precisely the same conception of free and equal moral persons, as will become clear in what follows.

[21] See my *Value and Justification* (Cambridge: Cambridge University Press, 1990), 278ff.

[22] See J. R. Lucas, *On Justice* (Oxford: Clarendon Press, 1980), 7. For a development of this conception of morality, see Thomas Scanlon, *What We Owe Each Other* (Cambridge, MA: Belknap Press of Harvard University Press, 1998), esp. 177ff. On this view, interpersonal claims are the crux of morality, though, of course, such claims need not be explicitly advanced: a moral person "makes claims on herself" in the sense that she accepts as reasons for actions the rights of others, and she acts on these reasons without prompting.

[23] I argue this in *Value and Justification,* 281ff.

[24] See Rawls, *Political Liberalism,* 51.

own ends from the moral claims of others, the idea of a moral person presupposes some cognitive skills.[25]

(ii) In the *Second Treatise*, Locke held that "[t]he natural liberty of man is to be free from any superior power on earth, and not to be under the will or legislative authority of man, but to have only the law of Nature for his rule."[26] To conceive of oneself as *morally free* is to understand oneself as free from any natural moral authority that would accord others status to dictate one's moral obligations. *This is not at all to say that one sees oneself as unbound by any external morality.* Locke thought we have the law of nature as our rule. Although we are by no means committed to a natural-law conception of morality, the crucial point, again one in the spirit of Locke, is that free moral persons call on their own reason when determining the dictates of moral law. A free person employs her own standards of evaluation when presented with claims about her moral liberties and obligations. A free person, we can say, has an interest in living in ways that accord with her own standards of value and goodness. At a minimum, to conceive of oneself as a morally free person is to see oneself as bound only by moral requirements that can be validated from one's own point of view; it is not necessarily to view morality as one's creation or the result of one's will or choice.[27]

(iii) To say that moral persons are equal is to claim, first, that qua moral persons they possess the minimum requisite moral personality so that they are equal participants in the moral enterprise and, second, that each is *equally* morally free insofar as no one is subjected to the moral authority of others. The equality of moral persons is their equality qua free moral persons: it is not a substantive principle of moral equality but a presupposition of the practice of moral justification insofar as it defines the status of the participants in moral justification. While this is a modest conception of moral equality, it rules out some conceptions of moral justification. Rawls not only conceives of moral persons as advancing claims against each other, but stresses that they view themselves as "self-authenticating sources of valid claims."[28] It would seem, and apparently Rawls agrees, that those who understand themselves as authenticating their own claims would not see themselves as bound to justify their claims against others to those others—they would not suppose that only

[25] I argue for this claim in "The Place of Autonomy in Liberalism," in John Christman and Joel Rogers, eds., *Autonomy and the Challenges to Liberalism* (Cambridge: Cambridge University Press, 2005), 272–306.

[26] John Locke, *Second Treatise of Government*, in Locke, *Two Treatises of Government*, ed. Peter Laslett (Cambridge: Cambridge University Press, 1960), sec. 21.

[27] It also provides the basis for understanding morality as self-legislated. I develop this idea further in "The Place of Autonomy in Liberalism."

[28] Rawls, *Justice as Fairness*, 23. The importance of the idea of self-authentication is easily overlooked in Rawls's thinking. It first appeared in his 1951 paper "Outline of a Decision Procedure for Ethics," which conceived of ethics as adjudicating the claims of individuals, which he clearly saw as self-authenticating. See section 5 of that paper, in Freeman, ed., *John Rawls: Collected Papers*, chap. 1.

claims justified to others are valid.[29] To advance a self-authenticating claim against others, however, is not to respect their moral freedom, for others are bound only by moral claims that they can validate through their own reason. The supposition of equal moral freedom thus requires that one's moral claims be validated by those to whom they are addressed.

Many have advanced stronger conceptions of moral equality. Some have claimed, for example, that the very practice of morality presupposes an "equal right of each to be treated only with justification."[30] In a similar vein, S. I. Benn and R. S. Peters, in their classic political theory text, defended the principle that "[t]he onus of justification rests on whoever would make distinctions. . . . Presume equality until there is a reason to presume otherwise."[31] Benn and Peter's principle does not simply require us to justify our moral claims to others: it requires us to justify all our actions that disadvantage some others. Leaving aside whether some such presumptive egalitarian principle could be morally justified,[32] this conception of moral equality is not presupposed by the very idea of a justified morality among free and equal moral persons. If I accept this principle, I claim that others act wrongly if they disadvantage me without good justification. But unless this nondiscriminatory principle itself can be validated by others, I disrespect their moral freedom, as I am making a moral claim on them to nondiscriminatory action that is not validated by their own reason.

Validation from the rational and reflective perspective of another, however, is not the same as her actual consent. To treat another as a free and equal moral person is to accept that moral claims must be validated from her perspective when she rationally reflects upon them. Now, although, as Mill noted, there is a strong presumption that each knows her own perspective best, this is not necessarily so.[33] Just as others can make sound judgments about a person's beliefs and principles, and can be correct even when the person disagrees, so can others be correct, and the moral agent wrong, about what is validated from her perspective. Knowledge of oneself is generally superior to others' knowledge of one, but it is not indefeasible. People may withhold assent

[29] Hence, because of this, parties to Rawls's original position are not required to advance justifications for their claims. Rawls argues this in "Kantian Constructivism," 334.

[30] Hadley Arkes, *First Things: An Inquiry into the First Principles of Morals and Justice* (Princeton, NJ: Princeton University Press, 1986), 70; italics omitted. Compare Ted Honderich: "To have a liberty in the relevant sense, whatever else it comes to be, is to act in a way that has recommendation or justification. You have to have a right." On this view, one may only act if one has a justified claim on others to allow one to act. Ted Honderich, *After the Terror* (Edinburgh: Edinburgh University Press, 2002), 45.

[31] S. I. Benn and R. S. Peters, *Social Principles and the Democratic State* (London: George Allen and Unwin, 1959), 110.

[32] I argue that it cannot in *Justificatory Liberalism* (New York: Oxford University Press, 1996), 162ff.

[33] Mill, *On Liberty*, 84–85 (chap. IV, para. 4). Mill also was aware that this assumption does not always hold true. See his *Principles of Political Economy*, in J. M. Robson, ed., *The Collected Works of John Stuart Mill* (Toronto: University of Toronto Press, 1963), vols. II and III, 947 (bk. V, chap. xi, sec. 9).

for a variety of reasons, including strategic objectives, pigheadedness, confusion, manifestly false beliefs, neurosis, and so on. Nevertheless, respect for the equal moral freedom of another requires that the presumption in favor of self-knowledge only be overridden given strong reasons supporting the conclusion that she has misunderstood what is validated from her own point of view. Suppose that Alf and Betty reasonably disagree about whether some moral principle *P* is validated from Betty's rational perspective. Say that Alf has good reasons to conclude that Betty has misunderstood what is validated from her point of view: *P*, he says, really is validated from her point of view. Betty, we suppose, has reason to insist it isn't. For Alf to insist that his merely reasonable view of Betty's commitments overrides her own reasonable understanding of her moral perspective constitutes a violation of her moral freedom, since Alf is claiming authority to override Betty's own reasonable understanding of her moral commitments with his merely reasonable view.[34] Of course, just where to draw the line between a person's reasonable and unreasonable understandings of her commitments is difficult (I have spent more than a few pages trying to do so).[35] The core idea though, is not obscure. As Jeffrey Reiman argues in his account of justice, when one person's judgment prevails over another's, there is always the suspicion of "subjugation," which Reiman defines as "any case in which the judgment of one person prevails over the contrary judgment of another simply because it can and thus without adequate justification." To "dispel" this suspicion, we must be able to show that our judgment is valid "beyond reasonable doubt."[36]

## B. The principle of public justification

Given the requirements for treating others as free and equal moral persons, the task of publicly justifying a moral principle *P* requires that *P* be validated from the perspective of each (sufficiently) reasonable free and equal moral person. To publicly justify a moral principle is to justify it to all reasonable free and equal moral persons within some public, who confront each other as strangers.[37] I shall assume that the relevant public here is something like a society; we could also define the public in terms of all persons (a universalistic cosmopolitan morality) or a smaller community. As our main concern is with morality insofar as it relates to political justice, focusing on the notion of a society's morality is appro-

---

[34] I deal with this complex question more formally in *Justificatory Liberalism*, parts I and II.

[35] See ibid. and *Value and Justification*, 399–404.

[36] Jeffrey Reiman, *Justice and Modern Moral Philosophy* (New Haven, CT: Yale University Press, 1990), 1–2.

[37] On the concept of the public, see S. I. Benn and G. F. Gaus, "The Liberal Conception of the Public and Private," in Benn and Gaus, eds., *Public and Private in Social Life*, 31–66.

priate. (Moreover, as we shall see, there is some reason to think that societies, broadly conceived, may possess justified moral codes in a way that mankind does not. Should it be the case, however, that cosmopolitan morality is similar to the morality I defend in the later sections of this essay, the restriction may not be significant.)

I have employed the unfamiliar idea of "validating" a principle. Validating is, I think, especially appropriate in this context. To validate a moral principle $P$ is to exercise one's authority to inspect $P$ and confirm that it meets the relevant requirements (as when a visa is validated). Validation is not voluntaristic in the way that consent is, or "acceptance" or "rejection" might be taken to be. Validation first involves substantive requirements: to be valid, $P$ must meet the test of respecting others' rational natures—there must be a conclusive reason justifying $P$. (What else could respecting others' rational natures require, other than providing them with reasons?) But validation is not simply a matter of *in fact* meeting the requirements—of there being a reason for $P$. It requires that this fact be confirmed by one who has the authority to do so. Surely, to respect the free moral and rational natures of others is to provide them with conclusive considerations for $P$ that can be seen as such by them insofar as they are reasonable; given that we are free and equal, each of us alone has the moral authority to confirm principles binding him- or herself. If Alf appeals to $P$, and Betty, a free and equal rational moral person, cannot see how she has adequate reason to accept $P$, then Alf is not respecting her as a free and equal rational moral person if he nonetheless insists that she does have good reason to accept $P$ and thus is morally required to abide by $P$. Alf's understanding of the demands of reason cannot trump Betty's reasonable understanding if he is to respect her as a free and equal rational moral person. To be more precise, let us work with the following understanding of public justification:

$P$ is a bona fide moral principle only if each reasonable free and equal moral person would, upon presentation of $P$, validate it.

According to this understanding of public justification, to possess a bona fide moral claim does not require that everyone has already validated it, and this is the case for two reasons. (i) A bona fide moral claim only requires the validation of reasonable, not actual, moral persons. (ii) Public justification conceives of moral claims as carrying the guarantee that they can be justified to reasonable others, even if these justifications have not yet actually been presented. This, I think, points the way to a plausible version of what Rawls calls "the proviso."[38] Principles that meet the test of public justification are publicly justified principles.

[38] John Rawls, "The Idea of Public Reason Revisited," *University of Chicago Law Review* 64 (Summer 1997): 764–807, pp. 783–84.

### III. The Problem of Evaluative Diversity

An obvious point of departure in publicly justifying moral principles would be to identify some "conception of the good"—involving a systematic relation of the various goods—that is shared by each free and equal moral person in the relevant public.[39] However, it seems most unlikely that free and equal moral persons share any such "comprehensive" understandings of the good or of value.[40] Contemporary liberal theory has stressed the reasonable pluralism that obtains about such comprehensive understandings of value or of the good. Pluralism about the good poses obvious problems for public justification, such as when my comprehensive understanding of value leads me to endorse $P$ on the grounds that $P$ promotes $V_1$, and you deny that $V_1$ is a value; $V_2$, you say, is correct, and it does not validate $P$. This may not entirely preclude public justification, as we might still converge on $P'$ because it promotes both $V_1$ and $V_2$.[41] Still, the difficulties in appealing to such comprehensive systems of value in the justification of moral claims is formidable in a society characterized by deep-seated reasonable differences about what makes life worth living. In any event, I shall put aside this well-discussed problem of clear value disagreement, and consider the problems raised by the case in which we all concur on the normative considerations that justify moral claims. This is not to say that I deny that sometimes our evaluative standards simply clash; however, I wish to stress that *even if we share evaluative standards, the problem of evaluative diversity remains.*

Suppose we disaggregate conceptions of the good, or systems of value, into their component goods, values, and other normative principles. Even though we do not share full-blown systems of values, we do share many specific values, such as the good of bodily integrity, the good of personal resources, and the good of health; we also share moral "intuitions," such as the wrongness of inflicting gratuitous pain on others. Abstracting from the notions of goods, values, moral "intuitions," and so on, let us provisionally say that $\Sigma$ is an *evaluative standard* for moral person Alf if and only if holding $\Sigma$ is relevant to the validation of a candidate moral principle given Alf's rational point of view.[42] Evaluative standards, then, are to be distinguished from publicly justified moral principles. Now assume that everyone in the relevant public holds $\Sigma_1$ and the relevant beliefs about the world such that $P_1$ is validated in the perspective of everyone.

---

[39] Henceforth, the clause "in the relevant public" will be assumed.

[40] I focus on this problem in *Contemporary Theories of Liberalism: Public Reason as a Post-Enlightenment Project* (London: Sage, 2003). See also my *Social Philosophy*, chap. 3.

[41] On convergence as a mode of justification, see Fred D'Agostino, *Free Public Reason: Making It Up As We Go* (New York: Oxford University Press, 1996), 30–31.

[42] I leave aside here whether $\Sigma$ is itself a belief about the world, as ethical naturalists would have it. It is important to stress that nothing in my account precludes moral realism as a metaethical or metaphysical thesis; the epistemic constraint on moral reasons is the crucial principle on which the analysis rests.

Thus, $P_1$ is publicly justified. Assume further that the same holds for $\Sigma_2$ and $P_2$: everyone shares $\Sigma_2$ as a normative standard, and everyone shares the relevant beliefs that validate $P_2$. It would seem that the project of public justification is well under way. However, as Fred D'Agostino, a philosopher of social sciences, recently has shown, so long as individuals order $\Sigma_1$ and $\Sigma_2$ differently, the real problems for public justification remain unresolved.[43] If Alf's ranking is $\Sigma_1 > \Sigma_2$ (read as "$\Sigma_1$ is ranked above $\Sigma_2$"), while Betty maintains that $\Sigma_2 > \Sigma_1$, then if the degree of justification of the moral claims is monotonic with the ranking of normative standards,[44] Alf will hold $P_1 > P_2$, while Betty will maintain $P_2 > P_1$. Thus, in an $N$-person society in which everyone holds all the same normative standards and relevant beliefs, we can still get $N$ rankings of moral principles.

Many believe that a morality requires priority rules.[45] If so, this problem of plurality of rankings is indeed an obstacle to the public justification of a morality. To some extent, perhaps, the necessity of priority rules has been exaggerated. As the great moral theorist W. D. Ross argued, our moral knowledge is about moral principles; the correct way to order the principles in cases where more than one is applicable is, for Ross, a matter of practical judgment about which people will often disagree.[46] Perhaps in many matters of private life it would be enough to agree on moral principles, accepting that priority judgments will vary from person to person. Even this, though, is a cause for some concern, as our account indicates not simply that we disagree about the proper weighting of the principles in specific cases, but that there simply is no publicly justified weighting.

Because so many issues of public morality require not only the justification of a set of moral claims, but some priority rules, we require some way to publicly commensurate individual evaluative standards to arrive at a public ordering of moral claims. The problem, then, is this: A public ranking of moral principle $P_1$ over $P_2$ is obviously justified only if the evaluative standards (and sound beliefs) of each rational and reflective moral person give her good reason to rank $P_1$ over $P_2$.[47] Given reasonable

---

[43] See Fred D'Agostino, *Incommensurability and Commensuration: The Common Denominator* (Aldershot, Hampshire: Ashgate, 2003). I draw upon D'Agostino's insightful analysis throughout Sections III–V and in Section VII. I consider these issues in a different way in "Liberal Neutrality: A Radical and Compelling Principle," in Steven Wall and George Klosko, eds., *Perfectionism and Neutrality: Essays in Liberal Theory* (Lanham, MD: Rowman and Littlefield, 2003), 136–165, 156ff.

[44] This is to say that the normative standard passes on a degree of justification commensurate with its ranking within a perspective.

[45] See Kurt Baier, "The Point of View of Morality," *Australasian Journal of Philosophy* 32 (1954): 104–35.

[46] W. D. Ross, *The Right and the Good* (Oxford: Clarendon Press, 1930), 27ff.

[47] This is too simple. A consistent system of trade-off rates between $P_1$ and $P_2$ need not, and most plausibly will not, be a simple priority according to which the satisfaction of $P_1$, in any circumstance, is ranked above the satisfaction of $P_2$. I focus on this idea in "Why All Welfare States (Including Laissez-Faire Ones) Are Unreasonable," *Social Philosophy and Policy*

evaluative diversity, this, I conjecture, will seldom occur (which is not to say it will never occur; see Sections V and VI below). Indeed, empirical research indicates that the main source of value conflicts among Americans lies in their rankings. According to Milton Rokeach, a psychologist, Americans agree in affirming a set of thirty-six values; what they differ on is "the way they organize them to form value hierarchies or priorities."[48] Our disputes are not generally about what is good, but what is better. And given that all action has opportunity costs—doing one thing means forgoing others—disputes about what is more important result in endemic disagreement about what to do.

The problem of disagreement about public morality arising out of an *agreement* in evaluative standards is even more daunting than I have depicted it. I assumed above that each claim is to be validated by a single evaluative standard (along with relevant beliefs). More realistically, we must allow that, in each individual's perspective, a number of evaluative standards contribute to the validation of a moral principle. Thus, even if we all agree on the same set of evaluative standards and relevant beliefs, and all agree what standards are relevant to the validation of a specific moral claim, we may not all validate *any* specific moral claim. To see this, suppose that both $\Sigma_1$ and $\Sigma_2$ are relevant to the justification of $P$-type principles. If Alf's ranking is $\Sigma_1 > \Sigma_2$, while Betty's is $\Sigma_2 > \Sigma_1$, then Alf may validate $P'$ while Betty validates $P''$. Thus, the initial problem in justifying priority rules becomes a problem of justifying any principle or claim when it is validated by multiple evaluative standards.

## IV. Two Flawed Responses to Evaluative Diversity

Given the assumption of evaluative diversity, how might we endeavor to publicly justify some ranking of principles? Following Rawls, we might suppose a deliberative setting of rational and reflective moral persons evaluating proposed moral principles according their evaluative criteria; what such people would all accept shows what is publicly justified.[49] To fix ideas, suppose that three reasonable moral persons are deliberating about how to rank three moral principles (assume for now that the evaluative perspective of each person provides some reason to accept all three

---

15, no. 2 (1998): 1–33. However, the more complicated analysis would only reinforce the point of the text: different sets of rational evaluative criteria will endorse different trade-off rates.

[48] See Milton Rokeach, *The Nature of Human Values* (New York: The Free Press, 1973), 110; Milton Rokeach, "From Individual to Institutional Values," in Rokeach, *Understanding Values* (London: Collier Macmillan, 1979), 208.

[49] "Understood in this way the question of justification is settled by working out a problem of deliberation: we have to ascertain which principles it would be rational to adopt given the contractual situation." John Rawls, *A Theory of Justice*, revised ed. (Cambridge, MA: Belknap Press of Harvard University Press, 1999), 16.

TABLE 1. *Condorcet paradox rankings*

| Alf | Betty | Charlie |
|:---:|:---:|:---:|
| $P_1$ | $P_2$ | $P_3$ |
| $P_2$ | $P_3$ | $P_1$ |
| $P_3$ | $P_1$ | $P_2$ |

principles). Their rankings are summarized in table 1. Can any social ranking be justified to all three individuals?

## A. *Aggregation*

Let us first consider the familiar process of collective (aggregative) commensuration: Suppose that in our deliberative setting we seek to develop some aggregation procedure that takes, as inputs, each reasonable free and equal moral person's ranking of proposed moral principles (based on his or her own evaluative standards) and generates, as outputs, a publicly justified ordering of moral principles. Now, *ex hypothesi*, the procedure we develop must also pass the test of public justification; moreover, the problem of evaluative diversity resulting in different rankings of principles must not reproduce itself as a rational diversity in rankings of aggregation procedures. Given that all see themselves as *equal* moral persons, we might think that some aggregation procedure reflecting "one person, one vote" might be employed in our deliberative setting to decide on the publicly justified ordering of principles. The hitch, of course, is that the aggregation procedure itself must be justified, and our disputes about the rankings of principles will reproduce themselves as disputes about the rankings of procedures.[50] No candidate aggregation procedure would be ranked best by each. As we know from Arrow's theorem and related work on collective choice rules, reasonable objections can be brought against every procedure for ranking three or more options, or indeed every procedure for choosing from a set of three or more options. As Kenneth Arrow showed, given a social choice over three or more options (with two or more people choosing), there is no aggregation method that (1) is guaranteed to produce a complete and transitive social ordering and (2) meets a set of reasonable conditions.[51] Although some proponents of

---

[50] As Robert Nozick reminds us: "When sincere and good persons differ, we are prone to think they must accept some procedure to decide their differences, some procedure they both agree to be reliable and fair. Here we see the possibility that this disagreement may extend all the way up the ladder of procedures." *Anarchy, State, and Utopia*, 98.

[51] The conditions are these: (1) *Universal domain:* There is a social ordering for every possible set of individual preference profiles. (2) *Monotonicity:* An individual's changing her

collective decision-making seek to dismiss the relevance of Arrow's theorem,[52] it clearly undermines any claim that there is an uncontroversial
way to commensurate all diverse rankings by developing an aggregation
method that rationally and fairly transforms individual rankings into a
publicly justified social ranking. There are a number of such methods, but
all are flawed, and there is no reason to suppose that rational and reflective people will converge on one. Moreover, equally reasonable, flawed
procedures can produce different results, so the choice of aggregation
procedure really does matter.[53] Table 1 depicts Condorcet's famous set of
paradox orderings, in which pairwise majority choice between the options
(options are considered in pairs, with majority vote deciding which of the
pair is the social preference) results in an intransitive social ordering
($P_1 > P_2 > P_3 > P_1$). Thus, rational individual rankings yield an irrational
social ranking: Arrow's theorem can be understood as a generalization of
this result to all plausible aggregation procedures. More generally, the
chaotic characteristics of aggregation procedures such as voting show
that their outcomes can be highly unstable. As Donald G. Saari, a mathematician, observes: "*Beware!* Beware of aggregation procedures because,
in an unexpected manner, they allow unanticipated behavior."[54]

This is not to say that we are never warranted in relying on democratic
procedures to resolve disputes. Given the background justification of
moral and political principles, it may well be that at some point we have
disagreements that we all have reason to believe must be resolved, and no
procedure for resolving them is better than democracy. However, no aggregation procedure is intrinsically fair, stable, and reliable; whatever the
merits of aggregation procedures, they are highly objectionable as ways
to produce a justified, rational social choice of basic moral principles out
of diverse individual orderings.

---

evaluation from {*y* is better than *x*} to {*x* is better than *y*} cannot itself make *x* socially less
preferred than *y*. (3) *Nonimposition:* The social ordering is always a function of individual
orderings. (4) *Pareto optimality:* If everyone prefers *x* over *y*, the social ordering ranks *x* over
*y*. (5) *Independence of irrelevant alternatives:* The social preference between *x* and *y* must
depend only on individuals' preferences between *x* and *y*, and cannot be affected by the
presence or absence of some third alternative, *z*. (6) *Nondictatorship:* There is no person
whose individual ordering over every pair of options is decisive for the social ordering. See
William Riker, *Liberalism Against Populism* (Prospect Heights, IL: Waveland Press, 1988). I
evaluate Riker's criticisms of democracy in my essay "Does Democracy Reveal the Will of
the People? Four Takes on Rousseau," *Australasian Journal of Philosophy* 75 (June 1997):
141–62. For an analysis more nuanced than Riker's, see Dennis Mueller, *Public Choice III*
(Cambridge: Cambridge University Press, 2003). For Arrow's own version, see Kenneth
Arrow, *Social Choice and Individual Values*, 2d ed. (New Haven, CT: Yale University Press,
1963).
   [52] John Dryzek, for example, rejects most of Riker's analysis; see Dryzek, "Democratic
Theory," in Gaus and Kukathas, eds., *The Handbook of Political Theory*, 143–54.
   [53] This point is emphasized by Riker, *Liberalism Against Populism*, chap. 2. On the importance of this for democratic choice, see Gaus, "Does Democracy Reveal the Will of the
People?"
   [54] Donald G. Saari, *Chaotic Elections! A Mathematician Looks at Voting* (Providence, RI:
American Mathematical Society, 2000), 152; emphasis in original.

## B. Elimination (or idealization)

Arrow's theorem relies on the assumption that the aggregation procedure must successfully operate for all possible individual rankings: the procedure must work for every permutation of the options. One way to respond to Arrow's theorem is, to use D'Agostino's term, "elimination": we disallow some rankings so that the paradoxical social choice implied by table 1 does not occur.[55] Elimination of troublesome evaluative standards might be achieved by *idealizing* our deliberative moral persons so that they have "correct" evaluative systems, which thus limit the possible orderings of proposed moral principles. Thus, we might suppose that all rational and reflective moral persons have the sort of evaluative systems devoted to the cultivation of individuality endorsed by John Stuart Mill,[56] or that they all have the same rational insight into natural law or natural rights endorsed by Locke. Those who do not have such evaluations are then eliminated from the deliberative problem. But this is just to weaken our assumption of rational evaluative diversity; such proposals seek to constrain evaluative diversity within some acceptable range and, thereby, produce significant rational consensus. However, this move is question-begging: it assumes that, prior to public justification between rational moral persons, some substantive public evaluative conclusions have been reached about suitable individual standards of evaluation. That, though, looks as if it must mean that some persons assert that, while a certain restriction of evaluative standards could not be validated by all rational reflective moral persons, nonetheless it is warranted and those dissenting can be excluded from public justification. This is to lack respect for the moral freedom and equality of others.

## V. JUSTIFYING PUBLIC MORALITY: ARGUMENTS FROM ABSTRACTION

### A. Abstract and full justification

Is there some way to achieve public justification in the face of evaluative diversity? D'Agostino tells us that one of the great attractions of Rawls's original position is that it provides a device of "social commensuration":

> Rawls's problem is, indeed, one of ranking options in a social setting. The members of some society have to decide, in a way that will be collectively binding, how they are to organize their relations with one another, at least in certain fundamental ways. In particular they have to decide how to rank proposals about the so-called "basic

---

[55] D'Agostino, *Incommensurability and Commensuration*, 91–95.
[56] For an explicit argument of this sort, see Jonathan Riley, *Liberal Utilitarianism: Social Choice and J. S. Mill's Philosophy* (Cambridge: Cambridge University Press, 1983).

structure of society." If each individual appeared in his own identity as a participant in discourse or negotiations about how to organize the "basic structure of society" in a collectively acceptable way, it is unlikely, in the extreme, that any agreement on substantive matters would be possible and, hence, the various options (each a specification of "the basic structure") would remain incommensurable with respect to one another. From a collective point of view we would not know how to order them in a satisfactory way.[57]

The device of the original position aims to provide a public justification of a ranking of some moral claims (such as liberty versus equality) by abstracting from our actual, full evaluative positions, and so providing a shared core perspective that yields a determinate deliberative-justificatory outcome.[58] One function of the veil of ignorance is to locate this shared basis for evaluation. "One excludes the knowledge of those contingencies which set men apart. . . ."[59] Individuals are abstracted to the common status of agents devoted to their own evaluative criteria (values, comprehensive conceptions of the good, and so on), and because "everyone is equally rational and similarly situated, each is convinced by the same arguments."[60] Indeed, abstraction allows us to avoid the problem of interpersonal justification since the problem is reduced to the choice of one person.[61] The success of an argument from abstraction depends on three key claims.

(1) Most obviously, it must be the case that there is a shared perspective that identifies a common basis of evaluation. The aim is to show that once we abstract to a certain shared perspective (and thus, for example, we exclude our desires to dominate or rule others), we do share some evaluative standards. Arguments for abstraction need not deploy a device such as the original position: Alan Gewirth, S. I. Benn, and others have maintained that the perspective of an abstract agent devoted to acting on his or her own evaluative criteria validates basic liberty claims, though they have not utilized a hypothetical choice situation.[62]

(2) This shared perspective must identify especially important shared evaluative standards; it will be of little avail to identify a shared perspective that does not capture really important evaluative standards. We must, as Rawls says, "give very great and normally overriding weight" to the norms prescribed by the shared standpoint.[63]

---

[57] D'Agostino, *Incommensurability and Commensuration*, 100.
[58] Ibid., 100–101.
[59] Rawls, *A Theory of Justice*, 17.
[60] Ibid., 120.
[61] Ibid., 120–21.
[62] Alan Gewirth, *Reason and Morality* (Chicago: University of Chicago Press, 1980), chap. 2; S. I. Benn, *A Theory of Freedom* (Cambridge: Cambridge University Press, 1988), chaps. 6–7. See also my *Value and Justification*, sec. 24.2.
[63] Rawls, *Political Liberalism*, 241.

(3) Related to this point, it must be the case that the deliberative conclusions are not overturned as the process of abstraction is undone and individuals are again understood to be guided by their full set of evaluative standards. It is, I think, seldom appreciated just how important this point is to Rawls's later work. Rawls argues that the political conception can be justified as freestanding: it is based on an *abstract* conception of persons as reasonable and rational, free and equal—a conception that is said to be implicit in our democratic society, and thus, shared by all.[64] Justice as fairness thus expresses "shared reason."[65] Rawls maintains that justice as fairness is a justified political conception because it articulates the requirements of the concepts of the person and society that all reasonable citizens in our democratic societies share. What Rawls calls "freestandingness" is a case of argument from abstraction. However, Rawls does not believe that this exhausts justification. Indeed, he says that this is simply a *pro tanto* (so far as it goes) justification.[66] In what he refers to as "full" justification, citizens draw on their full range of evaluative standards and find further reasons for endorsing the political conception. At this stage, Rawls tells us, the *pro tanto* abstract justification "may be overridden by citizen's comprehensive doctrines once all values are tallied up."[67] What was simply "freestanding" must, if it is to be fully justified, serve as a "module" that fits into each free and equal rational moral person's set of evaluative criteria.[68]

It is, I believe, a serious mistake to think that Rawls's basic notion of justification changed from *A Theory of Justice* to *Political Liberalism*, replacing the focus on shared reasoning in the original position with justification qua "overlapping consensus"—that all reasonable evaluative systems overlap on the basic liberal principles. Rather, the core idea throughout his work is the argument from abstraction in the original position, but Rawls increasingly worried that as the abstraction is undone and people come to know their comprehensive conceptions of value, their devotion to the principles might be "overridden." Full knowledge of evaluative standards may change what is validated from their perspectives. Hence Rawls's claim that under "full" justification the normative importance of the *pro tanto* argument from abstraction is preserved (i.e., condition 3 is met). Let us, then, call this third requirement *the stability of abstract justi-*

---

[64] Ibid., 10.
[65] Ibid., 9.
[66] Ibid., 386.
[67] Ibid.
[68] Most commentators on Rawls mistakenly identify these two ideas. Rawls employs the idea of a "module" when explaining "overlapping consensus" (ibid., 12–13; 144–45), whereas "freestandingness" applies to the appeal to shared conceptions of the person, and lack of metaphysical and other commitments, of the abstract argument for the two principles (ibid., 10, 40, 133, 144). The crucial passage that confuses many readers is on pp. 144–45 of *Political Liberalism*, where Rawls argues that because the political conception is freestanding it can serve as a module; many readers suppose that Rawls is simply equating the two ideas.

*fication under full justification.* This last requirement is immensely important: unless the conclusion of the argument from abstraction can be affirmed in light of a rational and reflective, free and equal moral person's full set of evaluative criteria, the abstract justification will be defeated by these other elements of her evaluative set. When Rawls tells us his main concern in developing political liberalism was to provide an account of the stability of a society based on his principles,[69] we should not think of this as mainly a sociological concern: the fundamental concern is the stability of the abstract justification in the light of the diversity of reasonable and conflicting "comprehensive conceptions of the good."

## B. Rawls's two principles of justice

As is well known, Rawls maintains that two strictly ordered principles are justified via the argument from abstraction:

> First: each person is to have an equal right to the most extensive scheme of equal basic liberties compatible with a similar scheme of liberties for others.
>     Second: social and economic inequalities are to be arranged so that they are both (a) reasonably expected to be to everyone's advantage and (b) attached to positions and offices open to all.[70]

Rawls provides a compelling case that his argument from abstraction for the first principle and its priority over other social values satisfies our three conditions. (1) We do share the perspective of rational agents devoted to our ends. (2) What we are committed to when occupying this perspective is of great importance, since it is always relevant to action based on our evaluative standards. (3) The *pro tanto* case for an extensive and strong scheme of liberty seems stable under full justification. The compelling arguments in Rawls's *Political Liberalism* for overlapping consensus concern basic liberties. Much less compelling is the argument for the second principle. It was notoriously controversial whether the argument from the original position actually endorses the second principle. (Let us focus simply on principle 2(a), the so-called "difference principle.") Rawls's attempts to show that abstract agents would select basic institutions that must distribute universally required goods so as to maximize the share to the least-advantaged group has confronted an array of objections that this would simply not be a rational strategy for such agents. Objectors insist that the abstracted parties would do better to maximize the average payoffs, or, alternatively, to avoid distributions that are disastrous to some,

---

[69] Ibid., xix.
[70] Ibid., 53. Compare the original edition of Rawls, *A Theory of Justice* (Cambridge, MA: Belknap Press of Harvard University Press, 1971), 60.

but once those distributions are omitted choose the distribution that maximizes average payoff, and so on.[71] However, let us leave these well-hoed fields behind. Even if the difference principle is justified by the argument from abstraction, it manifestly is not stable under full justification. Once free and equal reasonable individuals become aware of their evaluative standards (comprehensive conceptions of the good), many find the difference principle highly objectionable. Many people, for example, are strongly committed to notions of desert which clash with the difference principle.[72] We need not, though, focus simply on Rawls's highly controversial difference principle. Consider the much more modest claim of Alan Gewirth that abstract agents would demand rights to welfare as well as freedom.[73] Suppose we grant that abstract agents would accept an unconditional right to welfare: because they value their agency, they would value those things that are necessary for continued agency. However, as our model deliberators become aware of the full range of their evaluative criteria (including notions of desert, responsibility, and prudence) some will rationally reject the results of the abstract justification, showing again that it is not stable under full justification. Consider two such objectors, Prudence and Sylvan.

Prudence is reasonably averse to risk, and spends a good deal of time planning for trouble and how to avoid it. Central to her evaluative criteria is that one is responsible for avoiding the pitfalls of life. Now she has good reason to value a cautious life in which she looks out for her own welfare rather than a life in which we look out for each other. For others may lead riskier lives, and thus put themselves in positions in which they are more likely to be imperiled. Prudence will see welfare-grounded claims to assistance as violating her "comprehensive conception of the good": those whom she considers irresponsible and who reject the value of prudence, or reject taking responsibility for their own lives, will have claims *on her* that are antithetical to her values. People get into very hot water because they seek excitement, or are careless, or are too cheap or lazy to take precautions, or simply would rather spend their time and money having a good time. Prudence's objection is sound. Although, say, healthcare provision often has been enacted on the ground that everyone's basic welfare interests should be protected, experience has shown that the careless or reckless make inordinate demands on health-care systems. Because welfare provision is funded by all, Prudence and others like her end up paying a good deal for the recklessness of smokers and motorcyclists who

---

[71] For evidence that ordinary reasoners tend toward this last option, and thus have non-Rawlsian strategies in original position–like situations, see Norman Frohlich and Joe A. Oppenheimer, *Choosing Justice: An Experimental Approach to Ethical Theory* (Berkeley: University of California Press, 1992).

[72] For a review of the literature on people's beliefs about justice that brings out the importance of desert, see David Miller, "Distributive Justice: What People Think," *Ethics* 102 (April 1992): 555–93. See also my *Social Philosophy*, chap. 6.

[73] Gewirth, *Reason and Morality*, chap. 2.

ride without helmets; thus, Prudence and her like-minded fellows are forced to encourage what they see as vices.

The second objection comes from Sylvan, a nature lover. Sylvan's values are not centered on his own life or well-being, but on the wonders of nature. Although he does what he can to help and protect nature, Sylvan is under no delusion that his survival is necessary for the survival of nature. Because he so loves nature, however, he seeks to devote his life to worshipping it and understanding it; he has a religious awe when in the presence of nature. Now Sylvan may well resist incurring significant costs or transferring resources via taxation to help others; he does not cherish humans—he thinks they are not all that important in the scheme of things. Now, to *respect* and to *cherish* are not the same: Sylvan can respect others as moral persons without cherishing their flourishing. To Sylvan, devoting his resources to being near nature is tremendously more important than saving humans. Of course, Sylvan realizes that some day he may need help, and he is reasonable enough to admit that if he needs help, it would be nice to get it. But his environment-oriented philosophy indicates that it will be no great loss to the universe whether he dies in five, ten, twenty, or forty years. So Sylvan would resist the idea that significant costs should be put on him to assist others.

## C. The moral right to private property

Political philosophers such as Rawls and Gewirth thus contend that, if we consider simply the abstract perspective of ourselves as agents, we appreciate not only the importance we place on agency freedom, but the importance we place on the maintenance of agency, and thus we all endorse strong claims against others to help us maintain our agency. Even if the latter "agency welfare rights" are justified from the abstract perspective, I have argued, they are not stable under full justification: once Prudence and Sylvan are aware of their complete set of evaluate standards, they will reject these claims on them.[74] However, Rawls and Gewirth are certainly right that the perspective of abstract agency does not simply endorse liberty rights. As Immanuel Kant argued, property rights are required for agency.[75] Think about a world without any moral rights to property. From a moral point of view, in such a world an agent can only *possess:* he can physically control objects and resources but never *own* them. And he must allow that there is nothing wrong with others' pos-

---

[74] See Loren Lomasky's argument concerning the "strains of commitment" that are induced by making us responsible for each other, and why this casts doubt on Rawls's claim that the difference principle would be selected in the original position. Lomasky, "Libertarianism at Twin Harvard," *Social Philosophy and Policy* 22, no. 1 (2005): 178–99.

[75] This, of course, supposes that property rights are not freedom rights. I argue for this view in my essay "Property, Rights, and Freedom," *Social Philosophy and Policy* 11, no. 2 (1994): 209–40.

sessing what he would like to have, for there are, we are supposing, no moral rights to property (and that includes no collective moral rights vested in the community). If one rejects the very idea of a moral right to private property by refusing to assert ownership, argued Kant, one must allow that it would be no moral injury to one should others arbitrarily take what one possesses and in so doing undermine one's activity and will. "In other words, it would reduce these objects to naught from a practical point of view and make them into res nullius, although . . . the will [is] involved in the use of these things. . . ."[76] Recall that given the argument from abstract agency, we have, qua agents, a central concern with acting on our evaluative standards. By reducing the objects of his will and plans to "res nullius," one who rejects the very idea of private property rights undermines his own claim qua agent to act on his evaluative criteria: it is never a moral injury to him to "rob" his activities of those parts of the world with which they are intertwined. In sum, without true property rights defining a sphere of moral authority (see Section VII.A below), an agent has no moral claims on others to allow him to employ his evaluative standards over most of social life. Thus, Kant reminds us that claims to property are part of free agency itself: when one claims property over a thing, one claims "that any interference with my using it as I please would constitute an injury to me."[77] This Kantian idea is reflected in the common law. When a thing that is simply possessed becomes integral to one's activity, the common law often supposes that claims are thereby generated. In common law, for example, possession is understood as an implicit act of communication of a claim that gives rise to rights, and often to title. Although possession qua control is understood as *physical* fact, it can give rise to *claims*. Even acts of possession such as killing and carrying away an unowned fox have been held to give title.[78]

Given that a free moral person has an interest in acting in accord with his own evaluative standards (see Section II above), it does not seem that he can reject moral rights to property, even under full justification. This, of course, by no means justifies anything like capitalistic property rights. It merely demonstrates the importance of private property as a moral category for agency. The contours of those rights must be filled in, but

---

[76] Immanuel Kant, *The Metaphysical Elements of Justice*, trans. John Ladd (Indianapolis, IN: Bobbs-Merrill, 1965), 53 (Private Law, sec. 2). *Res nullius* is a thing belonging to no one.

[77] Ibid., 55 (Private Law, sec. 5).

[78] Thus the famous case of *Pierson v. Post* (Supreme Court of New York, 1805; 3 Cai. R. 175, 2 Am. Dec. 264). Post, the plaintiff, was pursuing a fox with his hounds while Pierson came in during the chase, shot the fox, and carried it off. Post sued (invoking something like the labor theory of value) on the grounds that he was pursuing the fox, and so had a claim to it. The court found in favor of Pierson, as he possessed the fox. See Jesse Dukeminier and James E. Krier, eds., *Property*, 5th ed. (New York: Aspen, 2002), 19–24. For a discussion, see Carol Rose, "Possession as the Origin of Property," *University of Chicago Law Review* 52 (Winter 1985): 72–96.

however they are filled in, the property rights must be robust enough to secure the interest in agency and in doing "as I please." Moreover, it must be remembered that whatever principle of property is justified by considerations of abstract agency must be stable under full justification. To accept that there is an intrinsic tie between free agency and property rights, and thus that a system of property rights is morally necessary, also implies certain other conditions: just as only systems of basic liberties that widely distribute liberty can be justified among abstract agents, so too with property. Systems distinguishing "mine and thine" by making everything mine and nothing thine are manifestly unable to be endorsed under full justification. Adequate defenses of private property have always sought to show that, at a minimum, the benefits of property rights are universal: everyone is much better off under a system of private property than without one.[79] However, universal benefit from property may not be sufficient; an unimpaired opportunity to acquire property, or even something closer to a system that is conducive to universal property-holding, may be required.[80]

## VI. JUSTIFYING PUBLIC MORALITY: THE TESTING CONCEPTION

### A. Optimal eligible interpretations

The argument from abstraction identifies, at a minimum, the importance of agency freedom and property rules; let us focus for now on agency freedom, the fundamental liberal concern. As I said, the abstract argument gives us abstract requirements; a wide range of interpretations present themselves about just what freedoms are morally required by agents such as ourselves. To see our way to more specific justifications, let us introduce the concept of a set $\{p_1 \ldots p_n\}$ of *optimal eligible interpretations*

---

[79] The universal benefit of private property has been a fundamental liberal theme. Consider the following canonical liberal passages. First, Adam Smith: "[T]he accommodation of an European prince does not always so much exceed that of an industrious and frugal peasant, as the accommodation of the latter exceeds that of many an African King, the absolute master of the lives and liberties of the thousand naked savages." Adam Smith, *An Inquiry into the Nature and Causes of the Wealth of Nations*, ed. R. H. Campbell and A. S. Skinner (Indianapolis, IN: Liberty Press, 1981), vol. I, pp. 23–24. Now Locke: "There cannot be a clearer demonstration of any thing, than several Nations of the Americans are of this, who are rich in Land, and poor in all the Comforts of Life; whom Nature having furnished as liberally as any other people, with the materials of Plenty, i.e. a fruitful Soil, apt to produce in abundance, what might serve for food, rayment, and delight; yet for want of improving it by labour, have not one hundredth part of the Conveniences we enjoy: And a King of a large fruitful Territory there feeds, lodges, and is clad worse than a day Labourer in England." Locke, *Second Treatise of Government*, 314–15 (sec. 41). In both cases, the claim is that private property is a Pareto improvement over a non-property regime.

[80] For a sensitive discussion, see Jeremy Waldron, *The Right to Private Property* (Oxford: Clarendon Press, 1988), esp. chap. 11. Arguments for a Lockean "proviso" are also relevant here: i.e., the idea that a condition of a justified property right is that it does not interfere with others' opportunities to acquire property.

of an abstract justified principle $P$. Our justificatory problem comes to this: We need to first identify what such a set might be, and then justify identifying one member of it as our public morality. Let us say that each *interpretation p* is put forward as a fully specified scheme of agency freedoms, including any priority rules. An interpretation $p$ is *eligible* if and only if under full justification the interpretation of $P$ qua $p$ would be ranked by every reasonable moral person as better than no $P$ interpretation at all. And let us restrict ourselves to only *optimal* eligible interpretations: if $p_1$ and $p_2$ are both eligible interpretations of $P$, and if under full justification everyone's evaluative standards rank $p_1 > p_2$, then $p_2$ is excluded from the set of optimal interpretations.

I shall suppose, for the moment, that the set of optimal eligible interpretations contains more than one member (but see below). If the set is null, then the abstract argument was not stable under full justification insofar as, for every possible interpretation, at least one reasonable moral person ranks it as worse than a morality without the principle. If the set has one member, then the justificatory task is completed. But the assumption that the set can be reduced to one—in other words, that abstract philosophical argument actually justifies a unique and determinate answer to what our morality requires—strikes me as implausible, and is indicative of disregard for current practices that Freeden (to say nothing of Hume, Hayek, and so many others) warns against. I assume, then, that we have a *nested disagreement:* a rational disagreement about the best choice nested within a rationally agreed upon set.[81] We disagree about the best specification of moral claims, but this disagreement is nested in a rational agreement that moral regulation of this matter is publicly validated.

## B. The testing conception

We seem to have landed back where we started: we have divergent rankings with no best option, though now we do rationally concur that some member of the set must be selected. Of course, we can continue on with abstract philosophical argument: we might, for instance, develop some sort of bargaining theory that would show that some member of the set is the rationally-to-be-selected option.[82] But any proposal for a rationally best solution from the set of optimal eligible interpretations will itself be evaluated differently by various evaluative standards, leading us to a second-level disagreement about the rankings of different bargaining theories. A fresh start is needed. Abstract philosophical construction has done a lot of work; we have arrived at abstract principles and an under-

---

[81] I have given a slightly different account of nested disagreement in *Justificatory Liberalism*, 156ff. For an enlightening discussion, see Micah Schwartzman, "The Completeness of Public Reason," *Politics, Philosophy, and Economics* 3 (June 2004): 191–220.

[82] I sought to do this in *Value and Justification*, chap. 9.

standing of what range of interpretations is rationally admissible. But what is the next step in understanding a morality for free and equal rational agents?

An alternative conception of moral validation has been employed by philosophers such as Kurt Baier. Basic to Baier's analysis is that moralities are social facts. Anthropologists can identify a group's morality, and distinguish it from laws, taboos, and etiquette.[83] To be sure, members of a group may have sharp disagreements about some of the rules and interpretations of them, but an anthropologist could describe them in a fairly accurate way. On this conception, to validate a morality is to test the moral rules of one's group from the moral point of view: we ask whether each person's evaluative standards validate this rule. However, "validation" here does not imply "the best social moral code," "the best of all possible rules from one's perspective," or "the rules that would be arrived at in a perfectly fair bargaining situation." Because, ultimately, moralities are not philosophical creations—they are not at all the same thing as what philosophers call "moral theories"—philosophers cannot construct them by writing books, even quite long ones. They are social facts that confront us. The task of philosophical ethics is to sort out which of these social facts should be acknowledged as imposing obligations and which should be rejected as inconsistent with treating all as free and equal moral persons.[84]

Our abstract construction has provided us with the requisite critical perspective; the task of moral reflection is to apply this perspective to our actual morality. Restricting ourselves now to agency freedom, our actual morality must be within the set of optimal eligible interpretations if all are to have good reason to accept our social morality. If our current interpretation of agency freedom is within the optimal eligible set, then we are confronted with actual moral freedom rights that satisfy the requirements of abstract moral reflection, and would not be rejected by any reasonable moral person under full awareness of her evaluative standards. This does not mean, however, that each person sees this as the best specification, or even one of the best, or even better-than-average. The existing practice may not be close to most people's ideal, but if it is part of the optimal eligible set, it qualifies as publicly justified. Moral obligation is not a tight function of moral perfection. Of course, people can provide arguments to move the current morality in their ideal directions. As Baier observes, "improvements in the society's morality can occur only by changes in the members' morality and these are best brought about by the members' own efforts at convincing one another by their discussions with others (and, of course, by their own critical reflections)."[85]

---

[83] See Baier, "The Point of View of Morality."
[84] See Kurt Baier, *The Rational and the Moral Order* (Chicago: Open Court, 1995), 212.
[85] Ibid., 217.

In contrast, the current interpretation may fail to be justified in two ways: (1) It could be that our current interpretation of liberty rights is part of the set of eligible interpretations, but not in the set of *optimal* eligible moralities. In that case, there is some alternative moral practice that everyone's evaluative criteria ranks as better than the current way of interpreting our agency rights. In that case, our current moral rights to agency freedom, though they represent an eligible option, are irrational because they are suboptimal: we all have reason to adopt the optimal alternative scheme. This raises complex issues. How far, for example, is the current interpretation of $P$ from the relevant optimal interpretation? Certainly there is a case for moral reform here, but whether one has reason to follow the current understanding of our moral liberty rights depends on the details of the case. A reasonable proposal is that in personal interactions one should appeal to the optimal code, as one has the opportunity for showing that it is justified among free and equal moral persons. In relations with strangers, however, it may be morally presumptuous for one to ignore the accepted code.

(2) Secondly, it might be the case that our current moral practice is not within the set of eligible interpretations: it is not justified under some free and equal moral persons' full evaluative standards. In that case, the current interpretation is illegitimate: it does not specify moral rights to freedom. Of course, we might still have pragmatic reasons to pay attention to these positive rights, but they would not be justified elements of our public morality. However, we should not jump to the conclusion that the entire current moral practice involving agency freedom would be undermined. Even if the entire practice cannot be fully justified, some parts of it may survive the scrutiny of full justification and thus morally ground parts of our current agency freedoms. Insofar as we can partition our moral practices,[86] we can distinguish those parts that withstand critical reflection from those that do not. However, should large parts of our current practice fail to be within the set of eligible interpretations of abstractly justified principles, we would be faced with a sort of moral chaos: our current moral practice would then fail to treat each individual in a way required by his status as a free and equal moral person. We would then be faced with a deep moral problem: we are committed to some interpretation of a moral principle, but we cannot identify any publicly justified specific interpretation, so we are unable to arrive at a workable morality even though some moral principles are validated. It is tempting to suppose that democratic decision-making can offer a solution: the law might be understood as a way for us to coordinate on new practices within the eligible set.[87] However, we need to be careful: there

---

[86] This partitioning raises formal problems about the possible interconnectedness of justifications that I do not pursue here.

[87] See Jeremy Waldron, *Law and Disagreement* (Oxford: Oxford University Press, 1999), 104ff.

is no good reason to suppose that majoritarian procedures will focus on practices that would be validated by all, rather than just the majority. If politics and legislation are to help us escape such moral anarchy, we would have to employ carefully constructed extramajoritarian methods to ensure that the outputs were reasonably likely to pass the test of public justification.[88]

## C. Morality as recognized claims

Some object to the testing conception of moral validation because it supposes a "bias" toward current moral practice. Why select the current morality from the set of eligible codes? What could justify this bias toward the actual?

A bias toward the actual is endorsed by a certain *publicity condition on morality*. This requires that a morality be a social fact. To be rationally justified is not sufficient to establish a bona fide moral rule: it must be accepted, taught, and relied upon. Baier sought to capture this publicity condition by requiring as a condition for being a moral rule that a rule "be taught to all children," so that all would know what the rule is.[89] Rawls upheld a publicity condition as a formal constraint on the concept of right: our conception of what is right presupposes that justified moral principles are known to be such by everyone.[90] Some interpret the publicity condition in a weaker way, as simply mandating that the moral rules and principles *could* be made public, and thus their efficacy does not necessarily depend on being restricted to a few. The stronger condition endorsed here (and, I think, by Baier) is that moral principles *must* be public in the sense that they provide the basis of our settled expectations about each other's duties and claims. Moral duty is not *simply* a matter of reason, it is necessarily a practical guarantee and source of mutual recognition of each other as possessing a certain status as free and equal moral persons—in the words of T. H. Green, "a society of men who recognise each other as *isoi kai homoioi* [equals]."[91] If we accept the publicity condition, a necessary condition for $R$ to be a moral right entailing obligations is that it is publicly recognized as part of morality. Only rules that are part of our current code can fulfill that condition.

---

[88] See my *Justificatory Liberalism*, 237ff. See also my essay "The Legal Coordination Game," *American Philosophical Association's Newsletter on Philosophy and Law* 1 (Spring 2002): 122–28.

[89] Baier, "The Point of View of Morality."

[90] Rawls, *A Theory of Justice*, 115. Rawls relates this condition to Kant's justification of publicity in a note, 115n.

[91] T. H. Green, *Lectures on the Principles of Political Obligation*, in Paul Harris and John Morrow, eds., *Lectures on the Principles of Political Obligation and Other Writings* (Cambridge: Cambridge University Press, 1986), sec. 116.

## VII. The Rights of the Moderns

### A. Rights as devices of devolution

Our fundamental moral concern, then, must be whether our current morality is at least within the set of eligible interpretations. Do we have any reason to think it is?

D'Agostino's analysis is again helpful, providing grounds for concluding that our liberal morality does reasonably well at the crucial task of coping with evaluative diversity. Because liberal morality is a morality of rights, its main solution to the problem of divergent evaluative standards, and divergent interpretations of shared principles, is to devolve to individuals the moral authority to decide what evaluative standards to apply in specific situations. A system of rights is an efficient response to the problem of public justification given evaluative diversity. "Civil society, with its individual rights and rights of association, [and] the market, with its foundation of property rights and rights of contract," are, D'Agostino argues, devices of "commensuration" that devolve moral authority: they define spheres of authority that specify whose evaluative standards will be regulative in a social interaction.[92] "In effect, we say that in a society with $n$ individual members, there are $n$ separate spheres in which an answer . . . may be sought, each of which is, in theory, inviolable and particular to the individual who occupies it."[93]

Of course, because there are indefinitely many systems of rights, the devolution solution presupposes that successful arguments from abstraction have identified the eligible systems, and the testing conception confirms that our system is in the set. Granted that, however, we can see how devolution via a system of rights greatly lessens what we might call the burdens of justification. Deep evaluative diversity, we have seen, poses serious obstacles to the public justification of a common morality. The rights solution is to mitigate our evaluative disagreements by granting to each a limited sphere in which an individual's evaluative standards have public standing. This function of rights is almost always overlooked.[94] Liberals are apt to see rights as ways in which individuals are protected against others: they define morally protected zones surrounding each. While rights are certainly that, however, they are typically far more: a moral right gives a person moral authority to decide the social outcome on the basis of his own evaluative standards. If I exercise my moral right against you, my evaluative standards are given social moral standing: they become, on this issue, the voice of public morality.

---

[92] D'Agostino, *Incommensurability and Commensuration*, 105.
[93] Ibid.
[94] For a notable exception, see Eric Mack, "In Defense of the Jurisdiction Theory of Rights," *Journal of Ethics* 4 (January–March 2000): 71–98.

## B. *The impossibility of a Paretian liberal?*

At this point, the argument of Amartya Sen's essay "The Impossibility of a Paretian Liberal" is relevant, and seems to pose an objection to the devolution proposal.[95] Sen conceives of a person having a right $R$ as having authority to decide the social preference over at least one pair of alternatives $(x,y)$ such that if a person chooses $x > y$, that is the social preference; and if the person chooses $y > x$, then that is the social preference. This conception of a right has been disputed, but it perfectly captures the conception of rights as devolved ways to cope with evaluative diversity: instead of a collective choice over the pair $(x,y)$, the social choice is devolved to a single agent.[96] However, Sen shows that attributing such rights to two persons, and assuming all possible orderings of social states are permissible, the social outcome selected by the rights can conflict with the widely endorsed Pareto principle (that if for everyone $x > y$, then the social preference must be $x > y$). More formally, Sen shows how combining rights, the Pareto principle, and no restriction of preference orderings, can result in intransitive social preference. Sen nicely summarizes his argument:

> There is a book (e.g. *Lady Chatterley's Lover*) which may be read by Mr. A ("the prude") or Mr. B ("the lascivious") or by neither. Given other things, these three alternatives define social states, *a, b* and *o* respectively. Consider now the following possibility. The prude A most prefers *o* (no one reading it), then *a* ("I'll take the hurt on myself"), and lastly *b* ("Imagine that lascivious lapping it up"). The lascivious [Mr. B] prefers most *a* ("it will give that lilywhite baby a nice shock), then *b* ("it will be fun"), and last *o* ("what a waste of a good book"). On grounds of individual freedom, since B wants to read the book rather than no one reading it, *b* is socially preferred to *o*; note that in *either* case A does not read the book here. Similarly, since A does not want to read it, *o* is socially better than *a*. But *a* is Pareto superior to *b*, yielding a preference cycle.[97]

Thus, we get $b > o$ (by Mr. B's right); $o > a$ (by Mr. A's right), and $a > b$ (by the Pareto principle, since in both Mr. A's and Mr. B's ordering, $a > b$); therefore, we get $b > o > a > b$ —a cycle.

Some see this as a case against individual rights: such rights can conflict with the Pareto principle, which many see as so intuitively obvious as to

---

[95] Amartya Sen, "The Impossibility of a Paretian Liberal," *The Journal of Political Economy* 78 (January–February 1970): 152–57. For an extended, and accessible, discussion, see Amartya Sen, "Liberty, Unanimity, and Rights," *Economica*, New Series 43 (August 1976): 217–45.

[96] Nozick, for one, criticized this conception in *Anarchy, State, and Utopia*, 165–66. Cf. Sen, "Liberty, Unanimity, and Rights," 229–31.

[97] Sen, "Liberty, Unanimity, and Rights," 218.

be beyond dispute. After all, if *everyone* in society prefers *a* to *b*, then certainly that ought to be the social ordering; but if we combine this principle with individual rights to decide the social preference over some options, we can get a social preference—or a public morality—that is intransitive, and thus irrational. However, Sen saw this not as a case against liberal rights, but as showing "the unacceptability of the Pareto principle as a universal rule."[98] We have especially good reason to discount the Pareto principle *here*.[99] According to our argument from abstraction, morality is to ascribe central importance to agency freedom. Sen's case is an example where people's agency freedom conflicts with what they prefer others to do; preferences about what another does in her sphere of rights thus should be ignored by public morality.

## C. Rights and social recognition

Appreciation of the importance of rights as devices of devolution leads to another consideration (in addition to the publicity condition; see Section VI.C above) supporting the testing conception's "bias" toward actual morality. If a system of rights is to perform the function of devolving moral authority to individuals in society, it is crucial that these rights be socially recognized. In his *Lectures on the Principles of Political Obligation,* Green considers the distinction between de facto and de jure sovereignty.[100] Green resists the idea that de jure sovereignty is simply "rightful authority" that has no practical force, as when appeal is made simply to a "general will, or the mere name of a fallen dynasty exercising no control over men in their dealings with each other."[101] Instead, Green argues, the distinction "has natural meaning in the mouths of those who, in resisting some coercive power that claims their obedience, can point to another determinate authority to which they not only consider obedience due, but to which obedience in some measure is actually rendered. . . ."[102] Green's point—and he seems entirely right—is that a political authority that has no practical effect is no political authority at all, as it cannot perform its main task of sorting out disagreements and harmonizing rights. To be any

---

[98] Ibid., 235.

[99] If the Pareto principle is unacceptable as a general constraint, then we must question Arrow's theorem (see Section IV.A), which also relies on it (see note 51 above). Does this mean that justification via aggregation is a live option again? I think not, both for the reason I explore in the text, and because the formal problems identified by Arrow's theorem are just the tip of the iceberg with aggregation procedures, which display a plethora of worrisome features such as path dependence.

[100] Green, *Lectures on the Principles of Political Obligation,* sec. 105. For defenses of "the rights recognition thesis," see Rex Martin, *A System of Rights* (Oxford: Clarendon Press, 1993); Derrick Darby, "Two Conceptions of Rights Possession," *Social Theory and Practice* 7 (July 2001): 387–417; and Gerald F. Gaus, "Green's Rights Recognition Thesis and Moral Internalism," *British Journal of Politics and International Relations* 7 (2005): 5–17.

[101] Green, *Lectures on the Principles of Political Obligation,* sec. 105.

[102] Ibid.

sort of authority at all, there must be some general recognition of it; only then can it perform its designated tasks. If it is not generally recognized as an authority, we might argue that it ought to be an authority, but we cannot claim that it now is. The job of authority is to regulate and coordinate interaction; if so, an authority that is not recognized simply is unable to perform the office of an authority, just as one who is not socially recognized as a leader is unable to fulfill the position of "group leader." We can say that a person who is not recognized—either explicitly or implicitly—as a leader ought to be the leader, but not that he is the leader.

The application of Green's analysis of sovereignty—understood in terms of the point of authority argument—to rights qua dispersed moral authority is manifest. To the extent that the function of moral rights is to localize moral authority, they cannot fulfill this function at all if they are not generally recognized. If there are no recognized moral rights, we are in a state akin to civil war, with each side seeking to construct its own preferred authority. As Green observes, however, in situations like this, there really is no sovereignty at all.[103] Rights as dispersed moral authority thus require social recognition. Without general recognition, no authority exists.

## D. The rights of the moderns

Benjamin Constant's famous lecture "The Liberty of the Ancients Compared with That of the Moderns" is interesting to us insofar as he set out to compare two interpretations of the freedom principle: the one that we "moderns" have developed and a more ancient one, which still has a pull on us. The liberty of the moderns, Constant tells us, consists in people's freedom from arbitrary arrest and punishment, their freedom of association and religion, their right to exercise influence on government, their right of expression, *and* their right "to choose a profession and practice it, to dispose of property, and even to abuse it; to come and go without permission, and without having to account for their motives or undertakings." Constant contrasts this to the liberty of the ancients, which consisted of "exercising collectively, but directly, several parts of the complete sovereignty."[104] As I said at the outset in Section I, Rawls's final position was that these two types of liberties are of equal status.[105] His

---

[103] Ibid.

[104] See Constant, "The Liberty of the Ancients Compared with That of the Moderns," 310–11.

[105] Rawls appears to change his position from a priority of the liberty of the moderns over the ancients (in his senses) to one of equal status. Compare Rawls, *Justice as Fairness*, 143, and *Political Liberalism*, 106ff. Although *Justice as Fairness* was published after *Political Liberalism*, it expresses Rawls's views from the 1980s. Constant himself held that "[i]ndividual liberty . . . is the true modern liberty. Political liberty is its guarantee, consequently political liberty is indispensable." Constant concludes his essay, however, by insisting that the two sorts of liberty must be combined in free institutions. As Stephen Holmes points out, Constant wrote parts of his famous essay in the first years of the nineteenth century, with left-wing critics

influential interpretation of this distinction, which he attributed to Constant, is troubling in two ways.

First, as Rawls sees it, the liberties of the moderns are, centrally, "freedom of thought and liberty of conscience, and the civil liberties generally."[106] Elsewhere, Rawls adds "certain basic rights of the person and property, and the rule of law."[107] He consistently identifies political liberties with the liberties of the ancients,[108] though Constant was explicit that the liberty of the moderns includes "everyone's right to exercise some influence on the administration of the government, either by electing all or particular officials, or through representations, petitions, demands to which the authorities are more or less compelled to pay heed."[109] For Constant, the liberty of the ancients concerned not simply political rights, but a

> collective exercise of sovereignty; in deliberating, in the public square, over war and peace; in forming alliances with foreign governments; in voting laws, in pronouncing judgments, in examining the accounts, the acts, the stewardship of the magistrates; in calling them to appear in front of the assembled people, in accusing, condemning or absolving them.[110]

Constant did not have in mind, then, simply the distinction between, on the one hand, freedom of conscience and expression, freedom of association, and basic rights of the person, and, on the other hand, political rights. Once we see that political representation is part of the liberty of the moderns, it is uncertain whether the liberty of the ancients holds any attraction whatsoever. The "collective exercise of sovereignty" resulting in a "social jurisdiction" over the commensuration of evaluative standards cannot loom large in modern life, for the familiar reasons I have canvassed. Given (as Arrow and others have shown) the impossibility of devising a way of aggregating preferences into an overall social preference ordering (or, indeed, into a simple social choice) that does not violate reasonable conditions, collective commensuration wilts under the burdens of justification (see Section IV.A above).

Second, Rawls's gloss on the distinction just barely admits the right to private property as one of the "liberties" of the moderns. As I have said,

---

in his sights; much of this part of the essay is critical of the liberty of the ancients. By 1819, when he delivered his lecture, these left-wing critics had passed from the scene, and Constant, worried about overprivatization, added comments sympathetic to the liberty of the ancients. See Stephen Holmes, *Benjamin Constant and the Making of Modern Liberalism* (New Haven, CT: Yale University Press, 1984), chap. 2.

[106] Rawls, *Political Liberalism*, 299.

[107] Ibid., 5.

[108] See Rawls, *A Theory of Justice*, 176–77, 195; Rawls, *Justice as Fairness*, 143; and Rawls, *Political Liberalism*, 396ff.

[109] Constant, "The Liberty of the Ancients Compared with That of the Moderns," 311.

[110] Ibid.

in some places Rawls includes among the liberties of the moderns "basic" rights of property, while at other times no mention at all is made of property.[111] In any event, it is clear that Rawls does not think that a just scheme of agency freedom must include any property rights in productive resources.[112] Constant gave a far more important place to property rights in his account: modern "freedom" (broadly understood here to include a range of liberties, claims, powers, and liabilities) is based on devolution of moral jurisdiction to individuals over wide areas of social life, crucially including a system of robust property rights. To be able "to choose a profession and practice it, to dispose of property, and even to abuse it; to come and go without permission, and without having to account for their motives or undertakings" is fundamental to the morality of people living in complex, evaluatively diverse modern societies. One can act within a sphere without having to account to others because one has moral authority within it. Constant's chief aim was to contrast the modern system of private jurisdictions over parts of social life to the unlimited "social jurisdiction" of the ancients.

Private property is perhaps the chief means by which the authority to employ controversial evaluative standards is devolved to individuals and associations. We thus arrive at a second fundamental argument for private property rights (in addition to the argument from agency; see Section V.C). In the absence of robust private property rights, the rights of freedom of expression and of conscience, freedom of association, and freedom of occupation ineffectively respond to the burdens of justification, as so many of our evaluative standards relate to the disposition of resources. Owners employ controversial standards with which others disagree, yet others recognize a bundle of moral duties and liabilities that give public moral standing to an owner's standard-based activity. Rights in several property, by devolving moral jurisdiction, thus allow for moral claims in the face of evaluative disagreement and in the absence of collective commensuration.[113] As Jeremy Waldron notes in his insightful book on the right to private property: "Ownership . . . expresses the abstract idea of an object being correlated with the name of some individual, *in relation to a rule which says that society will uphold that individual's decision as final when there is any dispute about how the object should be used.*"[114] Ownership, then, implies authority over decisions about the use of objects and parts of the world.[115] A robust system of private ownership is endorsed

---

[111] Property is included in Rawls, *Political Liberalism*, 5, and *Justice as Fairness*, 2; it is omitted in Rawls, *A Theory of Justice*, 195; *Justice as Fairness*, 144; and *Political Liberalism*, 299.

[112] See Rawls, *Justice as Fairness*, 177.

[113] On these points, see Mack, "In Defense of the Jurisdiction Theory of Rights"; and Randy Barnett, *The Structure of Liberty: Justice and the Rule of Law* (New York: Oxford University Press, 1998), 138ff.

[114] Waldron, *The Right to Private Property*, 47; emphasis added.

[115] The idea of ownership as a status against the whole world in relation to a thing remains important in property law. See, e.g., *Armory v. Delamirie* (Kings Bench, 1722, 1

by the very (Rawlsian) idea of public justification under conditions of far-reaching evaluative diversity. As the political theorist John Gray once observed:

> The importance of several property for civil society is that it acts as an enabling device whereby rival and possibly incommensurable conceptions of the good may be implemented and realized without any recourse to any collective decision-procedure. . . . One may even say of civil society that it is a device for securing peace by reducing to a minimum the decisions on which recourse to collective choice — the political or public choice that is binding on all — is unavoidable.[116]

A regime of individual moral rights, including a regime of private or "several" property, is thus a form of public justification or, perhaps better understood, a way to settle the problem of public justification in such a way that in the future it is no longer a collective problem. This point is seldom appreciated. It is, of course, widely accepted that, as the prominent libertarian philosopher Eric Mack puts it, the "organizing idea" of the "private property system . . . [is] the idea of sanctioning expansion of personal spheres of authority so as to secure individuals' inviolability in their respective life projects."[117] (Or, in the words of the left-leaning Charles Reich, "[p]roperty draws a circle around the activities of each private individual or organization. Within that circle, the individual has a greater degree of freedom than without.")[118] This is the abstract argument from agency (Section V), and it should by no means be belittled. What is less appreciated, though, is how this devolution of moral authority allows us to cope with evaluative diversity without ongoing collective commensuration.[119]

## E. The fatal attraction of the liberty of the ancients

What Constant called the liberty of the moderns is, I believe, one of the great modern discoveries: it provides a framework for a common morality that reconciles deep differences in our evaluative standards by devolving moral authority to individuals, giving each a sphere in which her evaluative standards have authority. Yet, puzzlingly, contemporary political theory is enamored with the liberty of the ancients — collective commensuration to reach joint judgments about evaluative standards. The current fascination in contemporary political theory is "deliberative

---

Strange 505), in Dukeminier and Krier, eds., *Property*, 108–9. On the importance of property qua jurisdiction over resources, see Barnett, *The Structure of Liberty*, 64ff.

[116] John Gray, *Post-Enlightenment Liberalism* (London: Routledge, 1993), 314.

[117] Mack, "Self-Ownership and the Right of Property," 536.

[118] Charles Reich, "The New Property," *Yale Law Journal* 73 (1964): 771.

[119] See Barnett, *The Structure of Liberty*, 138ff.

democracy"—a diverse family of views favoring enlarging the scope of democratic decision-making based on widespread public deliberation aiming at consensus.[120] "[T]he aim of the regulative idea is agreement of conviction on the basis of public reasons uttered and assessed in public discourse. . . ."[121] Even Rawls came to embrace some version of this doctrine.[122] Apparently, we are still held captive by the highly idealized picture in our mind's eye of the Athenian polis: Why can't we again be like that? (Was it ever like that?)

This attempt to emulate in practice a romantic image of the past can only lead to oppression. Deliberative democracy supposes that our differences in evaluative standards are, as it were, only on the surface. Once we reason together and talk things through, deliberative democrats hold that our value orderings will be transformed:[123] the range of disagreement will radically narrow so that the problems of social commensuration will become fairly insignificant, if not vanish altogether. Surely, though, this is a fantastic claim: in the end, deliberative democrats acknowledge, we must cut off discussion and take a vote, but then the majority is subjugating others to its judgment in the name of public reason—reason which is not shared by the dissenting minority. Moreover, we know that there is nothing uniquely correct about the outputs of any actual voting procedures. Once we accept that our disagreements are widespread and deep—that the range of possible value orderings is almost unlimited—democratic procedures simply are not up to the task of collective commensuration (again, we come back to Arrow-like problems; see Section IV.A).

## VIII. CONCLUSION: OUR MORALITY OF RIGHTS

I have argued that our commitment to treating others as free and equal moral persons implies a commitment to the public justification of our moral claims. Given reasonable evaluative diversity, the public justification of a morality must, somehow, take these reasonably diverse standards and arrive at a common, justified morality. The burdens of justification are weighty. A regime of rights solves the commensuration problem by devolving moral authority. Thus, I have upheld the liberty of the moderns—understood as a system of individual rights—over the lib-

---

[120] The core work here has been done by Jürgen Habermas. See his "Popular Sovereignty as Procedure," trans. William Rehg, in James Bohman and William Rehg, eds., *Deliberative Democracy: Essays on Reason and Politics* (Cambridge, MA: MIT Press, 1997), 44. See generally the essays in that volume. See also Dryzek, "Democratic Theory."

[121] Gerald J. Postema, "Public Practical Reason: Political Practice," in Ian Shapiro and Judith Wagner DeCew, eds., *Nomos XXXVII: Theory and Practice* (New York: New York University Press, 1995): 345–85, at 356.

[122] See note 105 above.

[123] See Jon Elster, "The Market and the Forum," in Bohman and Rehg, eds., *Deliberative Democracy*, 10–11.

erty of the ancients, which stressed collective decision-making as the primary mode of public commensuration.

But how can we justify a regime of rights? Before we can devolve authority, we must justify a specific rights regime. Philosophical reflection and justification, I have argued, can give us abstract answers regarding which moralities are acceptable to free and equal moral persons, but they cannot create a morality, moral rights, or moral obligations. A morality is a social fact (though not only a social fact) that cannot be conjured up by even the most potent philosophical brews: it involves real norms, which structure actual social interaction. Once we abandon the thoroughly constructivist project, we see that the main aim of normative ethics is to reflect on the moral rights that are recognized in our society, and to determine which of them free and equal moral persons ought to embrace.

*Philosophy, University of Arizona*

# LIBERALISM, ECONOMIC FREEDOM, AND THE LIMITS OF MARKETS*

By Debra Satz

## I. Introduction

Liberalism is often understood as an antipaternalistic and antiauthoritarian fighting creed whose hero is the autonomous decision-maker. Liberals have typically argued that people are entitled to make their own choices, even if those choices are in error. Nevertheless, liberalism has had a complex relationship with the question of market freedom. On the one hand, some liberals see the market as a key forum for carrying out people's uncoerced choices; market relationships are the antithesis of relationships based on authority and compulsion. On the other hand, some liberals defend collective intervention in market choices, particularly in cases in which these choices would lead to serious harms to others, or are based on false information or extremely asymmetric bargaining power.

The term "liberalism" thus encompasses a range of divergent views about market freedom that nevertheless share a core commitment to the value of individual choice. According to a widely shared (but, I will argue, erroneous) view, "classical" liberals are those who insist that unregulated or minimally regulated markets are inseparably entwined with individual freedom. The central thought here is that the dispersion of power that results from an unregulated or minimally regulated market economy is necessary to protect individuals from state control. Freedom, on this view, requires that individuals be free to buy and sell any or all of their goods on a market, without a central authority directing the production and distribution of those goods.

A prominent story about liberalism alleges that classical liberalism was displaced in the late nineteenth and early twentieth centuries by a "revisionist" version.[1] This revisionist liberalism severs the close link between liberty and markets: unregulated or minimally regulated markets are viewed as only contingently related to individual freedom. The central thought here is that a commitment to individual liberty can sometimes require substantial intervention in markets: left to themselves, markets

* I would like to thank the other contributors to this volume, and its editors, for their helpful comments on an earlier draft of this essay.
[1] Cf. Milton Friedman, *Capitalism and Freedom* (Chicago: University of Chicago Press, 1962), 6.

can produce extremely bad outcomes and can lead to large inequalities that undermine liberty.

In this essay, I want to complicate this picture of the relationship between classical and revisionist liberalism by pointing out a revisionist strand in the writings of liberalism's earliest defenders. These "classical" liberals recognized that market liberty was not always compatible with individual liberty. In particular, they argued that labor markets required intervention and regulation if workers were not to be wholly subjugated to the power of their employers. Functioning capitalist labor markets (along with functioning credit markets) were not "natural" outgrowths of exchange, but achievements hard won in the battle against feudalism. Further, and crucially, the existence of such markets required closing off other market choices.

In their writings, the classical liberals offer insights into the limits of the market that are missing from the approach of revisionist liberalism. In presenting the classical theorists' argument about the need for interventions in labor and credit markets, I will appeal to the liberal thinker who is often thought to be particularly hostile to intervention in the market: Adam Smith. My argument will stress Smith's understanding of the distinctions between *kinds* of markets and the need for interventions in labor and credit markets if the increase in substantive freedom that capitalism brings about is to be preserved.

## II. GROUND CLEARING

Markets are institutions in which exchanges take place between consenting parties. The phrase "between consenting parties" is crucial: market exchanges are voluntary.[2] Armed robbery is not an example of market exchange. In market exchange, the parties consent to the exchange. Both buyer and seller have the freedom to refuse an offer and to attempt to strike a better deal with someone else. There is no market where there is no possibility of exit.

Furthermore, a single act of exchange does not constitute a market. For exchanges to turn into markets, there have to be a certain number of them and they have to happen with predictability. Even regular exchange is not sufficient for a market: markets depend on institutions to enforce their terms, "especially if an exchange involves a promise of payment only in the future."[3] In the memorable phrase of legal scholars Lewis Kornhauser and Robert Mnookin, economic transacting in the market occurs "under

---

[2] As Milton Friedman puts it, "The possibility of coordination through voluntary cooperation rests on the elementary—yet frequently denied—proposition that both parties to an economic transaction benefit from it, *provided the transaction is bilaterally voluntary and informed.*" Ibid., 13. It is noteworthy how little time economists have spent on analyzing the concept of a "voluntary" act.

[3] See Ravi Kanbur, "On Obnoxious Markets," in Stephen Cullenberg and Prasanta Pattanaik, eds., *Globalization, Culture, and the Limits of the Market* (New Delhi: Oxford University Press, 2004), 42.

the shadow of the law."[4] The ordinary market participant counts on the state for her security when walking to and from the grocery store; even the extra-ordinary entrepreneur would not engage in high-risk initiatives without a variety of state guarantees. Thus, all markets depend not only on background property rules but also on coercive mechanisms to enforce exchanges.

## III. The Liberal Case for Respecting Voluntary Transactions

Why do so many liberal thinkers emphasize the importance of the freedom to exchange through a market? There are two contemporary arguments in favor of not interfering with people's voluntary transactions on a market: both have roots in Adam Smith's *The Wealth of Nations*. The first argument stresses the connection between market freedom and individual liberty.[5] The second stresses the connection between market freedom and efficient economic production. In recent economic theory, the argument from efficiency has eclipsed the argument from liberty, although, as is well known, liberty was central to Smith's own defense of markets.

With respect to the link between markets and freedom, proponents of this link cite a range of important effects that markets have on an individual's ability to develop and exercise the capacities of a free agent:

1. Markets present agents with the opportunity to choose between a large array of alternatives.
2. Markets provide incentives for agents to anticipate the results of their choices and thus foster instrumental rationality.
3. Markets decentralize decision making, giving to an agent alone the power to buy and sell goods and services without requiring her to ask anyone else's permission.
4. Markets place limits on the viability of coercive social relationships by providing (relatively) unimpeded avenues for exit.
5. Markets decentralize information.
6. Markets help undermine racial, ethnic, and religious discrimination.
7. Markets allow people to practice and try out various alternatives.
8. Markets enable liberal individuals to cooperate without having to agree on a large range of questions of value.

Liberal theories that assign substantial weight to individual freedom thus tend to allot a central role for market allocation, pointing to the market realm as a place where the capacity for individual choice is devel-

---

[4] Robert Mnookin and Lewis Kornhauser, "Bargaining in the Shadow of the Law: The Case of Divorce," *Yale Law Journal* 88 (1979): 950.

[5] In this essay, I use the terms "freedom" and "liberty" interchangeably.

oped. Markets also help minimize the extent to which individuals can be subjected to externally imposed forms of coercion or socially ordained status. Within the bounds of justice, then, liberals tend to believe in, and indeed extol, the principle of freedom of contract.

With respect to the second argument, it is widely recognized that markets are efficient forms of social organization and usually more efficient than nonmarket alternatives. In particular, markets appear to be an efficient means for getting people what they want. Economic theorists see markets as mechanisms that enable the optimal satisfaction of people's preferences.

Efficiency is most often interpreted (by present-day economists) in terms of the concept of Pareto optimality. A social state is Pareto optimal when it is the case that no one can be made better off (in terms of his or her utility) without making someone else worse off. An extremely elegant result, the so-called "fundamental theorem of welfare economics," shows that under ideal conditions all perfectly competitive market equilibria are Pareto optimal. The idea of Pareto optimality has obvious ethical appeal, for it seems clear that it is better to make people better off, and that if one of two prospects is better for someone than the other, and at least as good for everyone else, then it is better.[6]

Thus, liberals celebrate markets because markets are conducive to both individual freedom and economic efficiency, where efficiency is understood in terms of making people better off, that is, yielding greater satisfaction of preferences.[7]

## IV. ENTER REAL MARKETS

The simple story about liberalism and its changing relationship to market freedom runs as follows. Classical liberals such as Adam Smith developed the basis of a theory of ideal markets with the implication that intervention in the economy was (in general) inimical to both freedom and efficient economic development. Revisionist liberals recognized that real markets fail to live up to the textbook fiction of ideal markets in three important ways: transacting agents often lack relevant information; they engage in exchanges with third-party effects; and many markets in which agents participate are distorted by monopolies. According to the simple story, the discontinuity between classical liberalism and revisionist liberalism is primarily a disagreement over the extent to which real markets converge with ideal markets.

---

[6] It is, of course, possible to challenge this claim. See Anne Phillips, *Which Equalities Matter?* (Cambridge: Polity Press, 1999).

[7] There is a complex link between the efficiency and liberty defenses of ideal markets; although they overlap in certain respects, they are also in tension with each other. Amartya Sen has explored the tensions between Pareto optimality and freedom. See Amartya Sen, "The Impossibility of a Paretian Liberal," *Journal of Political Economy* 78 (1970): 152–57.

This story is incorrect. Classical liberals had a greater sensitivity to the limits of ideal markets, and to the problems with real markets, than this narrative suggests. Not only did they recognize the need for intervention in markets characterized by externalities, poor information, and monopoly, but also, as I will show, they saw the need to restrict certain exchanges if even ideal markets were to promote liberty. Below, I will argue that classical liberals like Adam Smith recognized that without some limits on particular markets, the new capitalist freedoms would degenerate into feudalism.[8] In particular, Smith and other classical liberals recognized something that contemporary liberals often overlook: the choices that an agent faces are not exogenously given. Allowing certain types of markets to operate can foreclose other choices that an agent might herself prefer to have and, in the extreme, can render her with no meaningful alternative choice. This important insight will be elaborated below in Section VII.

Some earlier arguments by classical liberals for the restriction of markets do resonate with the revisionist liberal case for regulating markets. To begin with, then, I want to consider the grounds that revisionist liberals appeal to in order to justify interference in the workings of markets. There are chiefly three such grounds: (1) incomplete information, (2) external effects, and (3) monopoly or extremely asymmetric bargaining power.

## A. Incomplete information

Even the most committed proponents of unregulated markets recognize that certain information preconditions must be met for any given exchange if it is to be truly beneficial to the exchanging agents. As Milton Friedman puts it, both parties to an economic transaction benefit from it "provided the transaction is bilaterally voluntary and informed."[9] In the presence of reliable information, an exchange that previously looked attractive may turn out to be mere fool's gold. In fact, an exchange entered into with deficient information may leave me worse off after exchanging than I would have been had I never entered the transaction in the first place (e.g., buying a used car that turns out to be a lemon).[10]

Information is relevant to a person's preferences, and incomplete information may lead a person to enter into transactions that are inconsistent with her preferences. This means that in the presence of faulty informa-

---

[8] John Locke had earlier argued that no one has the right to sell himself into slavery: there are limits to the degree of permissible personal subjection to others. See John Locke, *Second Treatise of Government*, in Peter Laslett, ed., *Two Treatises of Government: A Critical Edition* (Cambridge: Cambridge University Press, 1988).

[9] Friedman, *Capitalism and Freedom*, 13.

[10] Cf. George Akerlof, "The Market for 'Lemons': Uncertainty and the Market Mechanism," *Quarterly Journal of Economics* 84 (1970): 488–500.

tion, we cannot assume that free exchanges will be Pareto optimal. Just how faulty information has to be to justify interventions or to overturn previously agreed on exchanges is, of course, a difficult question of social policy.

Faulty information is relevant to a person's preferences and thus to Pareto optimality. Yet even if free exchanges based on misinformation are inefficient, perhaps they should be respected. Shouldn't agents be free to engage in inefficient exchanges? After all, information is not only a precondition of choice but also an object of choice. Even if greater knowledge is desirable to an agent, it is often costly to acquire. A rational agent decides how much information it is worth her while to acquire: in many cases, deficient information stems from her own agency.

This response, while it raises an important consideration, overstates its case. It neglects the role that information itself plays in the idea of free choice. An agent needs a certain amount of information in order to imagine and distinguish among alternatives, and to assess them. In this sense, some information is a precondition of choosing. Where information is grossly defective, where an agent is mistakenly ignorant of any possible alternatives to her action, her "agency" is weakened.

In cases in which time and uncertainty break the link between perceived and actual consequences, it becomes questionable whether (and to what extent) the agent actually consented to (i.e., chose) those consequences. Consider the case of an individual selling a body part, such as a kidney. It is doubtful that this person can really know the consequences of selling her kidney, especially as those consequences extend far into the future. Insofar as this is true, then, we can question the extent to which the individual can be said to truly consent to a contract to sell her kidney, since she might not have entered into the contract had she had more information. Of course, we have to tread carefully here, because choice by competent adults under some amount of imperfect or limited information is still, in an important sense, choice. Nevertheless, it is reasonable to assume that the more defective the information, the weaker the person's "agency" in the transaction will be, and the less clear it is that the person is choosing to make that actual transaction. The greater the information omissions or distortions, the more uncomfortable many liberals will be about enforcing a contract. Liberal discomfort with an exchange is likely to be even higher when the outcomes of decisions made with poor information are very bad for at least one of the parties, and the results are irreversible.[11] Such considerations have led at least some liberals to object to kidney markets and to enforcing commercial surrogacy agreements.

---

[11] See Debra Satz, "Noxious Markets: Why Some Things Should Not Be For Sale," in Cullenberg and Pattanaik, eds., *Globalization, Culture, and the Limits of the Market*, 11–38.

## B. External effects

One important reason to interfere in real-world markets is that sometimes the consequences of people's free transactions "spill over" and impose significant costs on (unwilling) third parties. These costs are usually referred to as "externalities," and they form the core of the theory of market failure.[12] So, for example, the effects of pollution cannot be restricted only to the parties whose market exchanges produce it. Likewise, sales of weapons on the international market have effects on people who are far removed from the parties to the transaction. These spillover consequences can render certain exchanges inefficient.

Spillovers need not be taken as support for market restriction; indeed, economists often view spillovers as evidence that the market has not been sufficiently enlarged. Externalities exist because there is a mutually advantageous exchange that is unexploited. The theory of market failure is not so much a theory of what is wrong with certain markets, but of what goes wrong if and when additional markets are not available. For example, if the costs of pollution could be bought and sold on the market, then the externality would be internalized by the contracting parties. In principle, there are no limits to the market. In reality, however, many markets are missing or incomplete, and economists will often look to intervention to curtail or redress a market's external effects.

Third-party effects, like imperfect information, are ubiquitous. If all the cases where third parties bear costs could count to prohibit an exchange, freedom of contract would largely be at an end. Thus, liberals have focused on developing a theory of those third-party effects that should be considered harms. In a rough-and-ready way, the presence of these harms is taken to require societal intervention. This is only a rough-and-ready case because it is important to consider that regulatory institutions are liable to interest-group capture and bureaucratic sclerosis. A little inefficiency might be preferable to a lot of red tape.[13]

While many liberals are likely to view harmful externalities as a reasonable justification for market regulation, those who are libertarians generally do not. Libertarians do not deny that market outcomes sometimes produce bad consequences for others. Instead, they claim that these effects, as the unintended consequences of voluntary actions, are not morally objectionable unless they interfere with rights or are based on force or fraud. Since libertarians tend to eschew welfare rights, the question is whether markets have external effects on people's liberty or prop-

---

[12] Other bases of market failure include the existence of natural monopolies, non-zero transaction costs, and economies of scale.

[13] A classic defense of private property rights is that such rights allow people to internalize externalities: without private property rights, the commons would deteriorate. See Harold Demsetz, "Toward a Theory of Property Rights," *American Economic Review: Proceedings and Papers* 57 (1967): 347–59.

erty rights. If such violations occur as by-products of free exchanges, then libertarians might well see a case for market restriction, or at least for compensation for those whose rights are violated.[14]

## C. Asymmetry of bargaining power

Monopoly in the market wreaks havoc with the fundamental theorems of welfare economics, severing the link between unregulated markets and Pareto optimality. Whereas mainstream economic analysis tends to rely on a framework in which agents do not have market power—since no one agent is taken to be able to determine the market price, and entry and exit from the market is unimpeded—in real-world markets there may be pockets of market power working even when there is no issue of monopoly in the classic sense.

Many real-world markets allow one agent to exercise considerable power over another, as when a moneylender in a small village charges usurious rates of interest or when big corporations have, with respect to their employees, an asymmetric power to exit from an economy.[15] Consider the example of asset sales of livestock and land at "fire sale prices," which regularly happen in drought-stricken areas in poor countries. Even when there is no element of monopoly in the operation of these markets, they set in motion processes of dispossession of assets by the poorest and accumulation by the richest. Such markets involve people forced by their own necessity to sell at a price that is well below what people who are less poor would hold out for. In such cases, it might be argued that markets are actually compatible with de facto monopoly pricing.

In fact, even perfect competition, where every agent is paid according to the marginal product of the factor she owns, may not be enough to correct for highly asymmetric bargaining power. This is because an agent's bargaining power is affected not only by her assets at the moment, but by her assets overall, including her wealth and property. The point here is simply to note that background property rights and wealth partly determine each party's relative ability to hold out for more acceptable terms. Property rights thus distribute market power as well as goods; and certain distributions may yield such asymmetric bargaining power between the agents as to approach monopoly power.

In sum, revisionist liberals endorse three reasons to intervene in markets, all of which can arise when real-world markets diverge from ideal markets. Imperfect information, external effects, and monopoly pricing all generate inefficiencies; moreover, imperfect information and monopoly can objectionably weaken the agency of transacting individuals, while

---

[14] Robert Nozick, *Anarchy, State, and Utopia* (New York: Basic Books, 1974).
[15] This paragraph is drawn from my essay "Noxious Markets."

externalities distribute costs on individuals who are not treated as transacting agents at all.

## V. Revisionism in Classical Liberalism

Adam Smith, of course, knew nothing about the "fundamental theorem" of welfare economics, which he greatly antedated. Smith's defense
of unregulated markets did not rest on their purported allocative efficiency, but rather on the tendency of markets to promote the accumulation of capital and the growth of income, and principally on their connection
to freedom. However, Smith does recognize that there are contexts in
which markets require governmental restriction: contexts in which there
are market failures.

The most important case Smith sees for governmental intervention on
grounds of externalities is education. Because parents have little time for
the education of their children, and because the children of poor families
must be put to work at an early age, many children have no chance to
acquire the skills for any but the most mindless occupations. This "corruption and degeneracy of the great body of people" [16] is inevitable without some attention from the government. Smith argues that basic education
(for example, literacy) provides a communal benefit that transcends the
gains of the person being educated. Conversely, failure to educate children can produce public ills: less labor mobility, greater poverty, and less
economic growth. Smith harshly criticizes the irrationality of failing to
provide public expenditures for education: "For a very small expense the
publick can facilitate, can encourage, and can even impose upon the
whole body of the people, the necessity of acquiring those most essential
parts of education." [17]

In addition to its role in education, Smith saw roles for the government
in certifying the quantity and quality of traded commodities, in the mint-
ing of coins, in the administration of justice, [18] and in the provision of
public works and national defense. [19] In each of these cases, allowing
unfettered markets has public costs, even though such markets may benefit the individuals involved in the private transactions. For example,
even though individual families might benefit from pulling their children
out of school and immediately putting them to work, their private action
has costs for the society as a whole.

In his writings against usury, Smith also demonstrated an awareness of
the informational problems inherent in certain types of markets. Few
commentators have called attention to Smith's advocacy of legal restric-

---

[16] Adam Smith, *An Inquiry into the Nature and Causes of the Wealth of Nations* (1776), ed. R.
H. Campbell and A. S. Skinner (Oxford: Oxford University Press, 1976), 781.
[17] Ibid., 785.
[18] Ibid., 814.
[19] Ibid., 815.

tions on usury. While Smith objected to the legal banning of charging interest on loans, he granted his qualified approval to the existing usury laws in Great Britain that limited the rate of interest to 5 percent:

> In countries where interest is permitted, the law, in order to prevent the extortion of usury, generally fixes the highest rate which can be taken without incurring a penalty. . . .
>
> The legal rate, it is to be observed, though it ought to be somewhat above, ought not to be much above the lowest market rate. If the legal rate of interest in Great Britain, for example, was fixed so high as eight or ten percent, the greater part of the money which was to be lent, would be lent to prodigals and projectors, who alone would be willing to give this high interest. Sober people, who will give for the use of money no more than a part of what they are likely to make by the use of it, would not venture into the competition. A greater part of the capital of the country would thus be kept out of the hands which were most likely to make a profitable and advantageous use of it, and thrown into those which were most likely to waste and destroy it.[20]

The economist Amartya Sen correctly reads this passage as expressing Smith's recognition that in some contexts the pursuit of private gain (by prodigals and projectors) can lead to social loss.[21] There is, however, another aspect of this passage that Sen does not note: Smith's understanding that credit markets are characterized by asymmetric information. The actions of the prodigal borrower—pursuing misguided or myopic ventures—make a default on repayment likely. If credit markets are characterized by asymmetric information and moral hazard, then rationing by government may be a needed feature of such markets.

Finally, Smith seems to recognize the problems that can arise when agents in a market have extremely asymmetric power. In his writings on the regulation of wages, he notes: "When the regulation . . . is in favor of workmen, it is always just and equitable; but it is sometimes otherwise when it is in favor of the masters."[22] Smith recognized that merchants tend to use their market power to pursue their own interests by wielding political influence. In Book IV of The Wealth of Nations, Smith attempts to unmask the ways that merchants use their inordinate economic power to influence politics, particularly by influencing restrictions on imports. Likewise, he objects that the apprentice system is enacted in the interests of the powerful and subjects workers to the power of their masters; and he supports a tax on carriages such that "the indolence and vanity of the rich

[20] Ibid., 356–57.
[21] Amartya Sen, Development as Freedom (New York: Alfred Knopf, 1999), 124–25.
[22] Smith, Wealth of Nations, 157–58.

is made to contribute in a very easy manner to the relief of the poor,"[23] thus placing the poor in a better bargaining position on the market.

Smith recognizes both the advantages of markets and the ways that particular markets require regulation if economic growth is to be preserved and individual freedom secured. In at least some strands of his writings, then, he shows an awareness associated with the revisionist liberals: real markets deviate from ideal markets in important ways. Some real markets are built on asymmetric information, give rise to externalities, or manifest profoundly unequal bargaining power.

## VI. The Issue of the Limits of the Market Recast

Consider a voluntary transaction in which all the features of a perfect market are present. That is, there is perfect knowledge on the part of all of the transacting agents; there are no externalities; and there is no monopoly power. Do liberals have any reasons for forbidding this transaction?

Some people believe that under these conditions it would be illegitimate to interfere with private choices on the market. Under such conditions, markets would function, as the philosopher David Gauthier once put it, as moral "free zones."[24] Although many contemporary liberals have recognized that real-world markets are often rife with asymmetric information, monopoly, and third-party harm, they have said little about the need to place limits on market freedom under ideal conditions. Indeed, the two dominant schools of liberal economics—Paretian welfarism[25] and libertarian public choice[26]—defend an ideal market without limits. The primary normative properties of the general equilibrium system—including the fundamental theorem of welfare economics mentioned above—*depend on* there being a market in everything, including futures and uncertainty. The distinctive contributions of the public choice school are derived from *assuming* that commodity-like relationships determine outcomes in arenas not customarily thought of as economic, including voting.

In *Anarchy, State, and Utopia*, Robert Nozick draws out the implications of the view that ideal markets should not be regulated, and claims that respect for liberal freedom in ideal conditions entails that individuals even have the right to sell themselves into slavery.[27] Here, Nozick recognizes a point made earlier by John Stuart Mill: while slavery is usually rooted in an initial act of coercion, it is not necessary for slavery to originate in violence and force. People driven by poverty or preference

---

[23] Ibid., 725.

[24] David Gauthier, *Morals by Agreement* (Oxford: Oxford University Press, 1986), 95.

[25] See Kenneth Arrow and Frank Hahn, *General Competitive Analysis* (San Francisco: Holden-Day, 1971).

[26] Some key public choice economists are James M. Buchanan, Gordon Tullock, and Anthony Downs.

[27] Nozick, *Anarchy, State, and Utopia*, 331.

might have reasons to opt to become slaves: this was, in fact, the case in some parts of medieval Europe. Both bonded labor and serfdom have, at times, been voluntarily chosen.[28] However, unlike Nozick, Mill attempts to articulate a principle that, while asserting the priority of individual freedom, would nevertheless disallow contractual, voluntary slavery. In *On Liberty*, Mill argues that allowing the voluntary alienation of one's freedom through a slave contract is incompatible with a recognition of the priority of that freedom. He writes:

> In this and most other civilized countries, for example, an engagement by which a person should sell himself, or allow himself to be sold, as a slave would be null and void, neither enforced by law nor by opinion. The ground for thus limiting his power of voluntarily disposing of his own lot in life is apparent, and is very clearly seen in this extreme case. The reason for not interfering, unless for the sake of others, with a person's voluntary acts is consideration for his liberty. . . . But by selling himself as a slave, he abdicates his liberty; he foregoes any future use of it beyond that single act. He therefore defeats, in his own case, the very purpose which is the justification of allowing him to dispose of himself. He is no longer free, but is thenceforth in a position which has no longer the presumption in its favor that would be afforded by his voluntarily remaining in it. The principle of freedom cannot require that he should be free not to be free.[29]

Note that Mill does not base his argument against voluntary slavery contracts on potential harm to others, or the presence of faulty information, or asymmetric bargaining power. Mill's argument against voluntary self-enslavement contracts appeals to liberty.

What should we make of Mill's argument? Although it is rhetorically suggestive, I do not find it (at least as stated) a powerful argument. Why is respecting voluntary slavery contracts inconsistent? Mill views liberty largely in terms of noninterference, and if I sell my*self* into slavery no one is interfering with me. Indeed, Mill's claim about slavery is especially puzzling since, in *On Liberty*, he argues that a person should be free to kill himself by jumping off a bridge. Why is freedom compatible with killing myself but not with selling myself? Mill's text gives us no answer.

As we reflect on Mill's and Nozick's views on voluntary slavery, we are left with a more general question: Does a commitment to freedom require that one respect all market choices, including bonded labor contracts and

---

[28] Cf. Orlando Patterson, *Slavery and Social Death* (Cambridge, MA: Harvard University Press, 1982).

[29] John Stuart Mill, *On Liberty* (1859), ed. Elizabeth Rappaport (Indianapolis, IN: Hackett Publishing, 1978), 101.

credit contracts at usurious interest rates, if made under ideal conditions? I believe that the classical economists can help provide us with an answer.

## VII. ADAM SMITH AND THE LIMITS
## OF IDEAL MARKETS

There are two aspects of Smith's thought that I want to draw on in answering this question about the limits of ideal markets. The first is Smith's understanding that without intervention in certain types of market choices the advance in freedom that capitalism represents over feudalism will not be preserved. The second is Smith's understanding that markets differ in kind and that some markets can shape their participants in troubling ways.

### A. Smith as an anti-feudal thinker

If we read Smith as a classical liberal according to the canonical story, then he believed that market regulation is to be rejected because it strengthens the hand of governmental power and compromises individual freedom. That is, the main danger to the new system of natural liberty is the overexpansion of governmental power. Smith's "invisible hand" of the market shows us a way to organize society that can replace the visible fist of government. On this interpretation, Smith can be seen as a close forerunner of Friedrich Hayek; the invisible hand brings about a kind of spontaneous order—order without coercion and, indeed, without any social planning.[30]

Yet the invisible hand was not central to Smith's economic and moral thought. The economic historian Emma Rothschild has shown, in her well-documented book *Economic Sentiments,* that Smith only used the term "invisible hand" three times, one of which was clearly meant to be ironic.[31] The term only appears once in *The Wealth of Nations,* in the context of an argument that legislators should leave merchants alone to pursue their private interests since so doing is actually most conducive to the public good. Interestingly, however, in the same chapter Smith also says that merchants and manufacturers are "always demanding a monopoly against their countrymen" and that they "are the people who derive the greatest advantage from it [monopoly]."[32] In this context, Smith is worried that government action would simply strengthen the merchants' hand, by legally granting them rights to monopoly.

At the same time, if the merchants were actually able to secure a monopoly over productive assets or with respect to essential goods on their own,

---

[30] See John Gray, *Liberalism* (Minneapolis: University of Minnesota Press, 1986), 42.

[31] Emma Rothschild, *Economic Sentiments: Adam Smith, Condorcet, and the Enlightenment* (Cambridge, MA: Harvard University Press, 2001), 117.

[32] Smith, *Wealth of Nations,* 467.

then leaving them alone would not likely serve the public good. For example, Smith supported government intervention to oblige employers to pay their workmen in money, not in kind, when prices were falling, and he supported wage regulation when it was in favor of the workmen but not when it was in favor of the owners.

Rather than seeing Smith as opposed to government intervention per se, it might be helpful to recall that Smith's arguments against intervention in markets are focused on a specific social order: feudalism. Many of the regulations that Smith vociferously condemned were vestiges of a precapitalist order: the vested interests of the merchants seeking to protect their inflated profits, the powerful guilds that restricted the free entry of individuals into professions and trades. Smith celebrated the freedom to buy and sell not only as an impetus to economic growth and wealth, but also as a form of emancipation from a particular form of political oppression. Markets undermined social relationships built on servility:

> Commerce and manufactures gradually introduced order and good government, and with them, the liberty and security of individuals, among the inhabitants of the country, who had before lived almost in a continual state of war with their neighbors and of servile dependency upon their superiors. This, although it has been the least observed, is by far the most important of their effects.[33]

Smith contrasted the freedom of the new industrial order based on market exchange with the organization of feudal society. Under feudalism, peasants and laborers were dependent on the feudal landowners for their subsistence and for protection from violence by others. This extreme dependency supported relations of servility between the lord and his subjects: the peasant's bowing and scraping before his "superior." Peasants had a duty to obey any of the lord's commands, no matter how arbitrary, humiliating, or costly such commands were. An important point about this servile relationship between serf and lord is that it was voluntary: the serf was tied to his master by apparently voluntary acts of loyalty. Given his economic, political, and cultural circumstances, subservience to the lord was the peasant's best option.

Markets liberated individuals from this abject dependence on one powerful person by allowing producers to sustain themselves through exchanges with thousands of anonymous and indifferent customers:

> Each tradesman or artificer derives his subsistence from the employment, not of one, but of a hundred or a thousand different customers.

---

[33] Ibid., 412.

Though in some measure obliged to them all, therefore, he is not absolutely dependent on any one of them.[34]

Freedom of commerce, according to *The Wealth of Nations*, brings about individual emancipation from personal, political, and, indeed, physical oppression. According to Smith, this end of abject servility to masters, along with good government, was "by far the most important" of all the effects of markets. Market freedom undermined the relations of personal subjection and servility that characterized feudalism. In particular, the extension of the market made possible a society of horizontal relationships—a society in which relationships between people were based on free interaction, equality, and reciprocity.

However, Smith also recognized that the ability of laborers to escape from their servility to one master was dependent on a number of conditions, including how competitive the labor market actually was. He was extremely aware of the tendency of the merchants to attempt to bring the state in as an ally in controlling their workers—a tendency that he argued must be resisted. But to resist this tendency required limits on markets: not only must state officials be able to operate independently of the interests of the merchants, but there must be restrictions on the ability of merchants to enter into (contractual) collusion with each other to drive down the price of labor; and there must be measures taken to prevent workers from becoming overly dependent on a single employer.

Rather than propounding a doctrine of spontaneous order, Smith continually stressed that markets can function as vehicles of freedom and efficiency only under very definite institutional arrangements. Markets require a "separate independent state" to promote the well-being and freedom of the poor, a state cut loose from the power of merchants, guilds, religious groups, and prejudicial social norms. Smith wrote that the system of law would never be completely secure against such interests and would need to be counteracted by a universal system of education, and by regulation of labor markets to protect the freedom of the workers.

The danger to workers was not merely that employers might collude to hold down wages; even if employers did not collude, workers were harder to organize than employers, since workers existed in greater numbers. Furthermore, workers had fewer resources to engage in protracted struggles with their employers. For this reason, Smith was far more sympathetic to intervention on behalf of workers in labor markets than to government intervention in other markets. Unfortunately, as Smith recognized, most government intervention tended to be on the side of the employers. Even legally protected guilds, which look like combinations of workers, actually serve only the interests of employers by obstructing

---

[34] Ibid., 420.

the free circulation of labor. Smith writes of such combinations that "a thousand spinners and weavers" may be dependent on "half a dozen wool combers," who by refusing to take on apprentices can "reduce the whole manufacture into a sort of slavery to themselves."[35]

Ironically, the main schools of contemporary liberal economic thought that support the expansion of the market domain—libertarian public choice and Paretian welfare economics—are unable to represent the capitalist transformation of the labor market, from a relation of dependency between servant and lord to one of equality between producers and consumers, as an improvement. For that transformation depended on limiting the power one person could exercise over another, and this, in turn, depended on setting limits on the scope of markets and limits on freedom of contract.

Consider a contemporary example. Millions of people today work in conditions that can only be characterized as bonded labor, debt peonage (where a debtor is held in servitude by a creditor), and serfdom. But these conditions are often entered into voluntarily in order to escape acute poverty or starvation. According to contemporary welfare economics, if the laborers are rational individuals maximizing their utility, then they must be better off. According to public choice theorists, if the laborers are competent adults, then to restrict their choices is to treat them paternalistically as wards of the state. Neither theory can explain what is wrong with such contracts, except insofar as they generate externalities, reflect imperfect information, or arise in situations of monopoly.

Yet to appreciate the problems with these forms of labor, we have to move beyond these dimensions of markets. A central problem with bonded labor contracts and other contracts that put people into relationships of extreme dependency with others emerges when we consider that the set of choices a person faces is not given. The range of choices an individual has is not exogenously determined, but largely endogenously (internally) determined by the existing property rules, distribution of power, and social norms. Smith saw that relationships of servile dependency produced choices that undermined the freedom and good government that capitalism brings.

Child labor provides an interesting illustration of the phenomenon by which permitting a particular "choice" (to be utterly dependent on an employer) can lead to far fewer available choices for the agent. Poor parents in developing societies often send their children to work because they can see no other way of supporting their families. For each individual family, child labor looks to be the family's best option for survival: child labor can generate the income that keeps family members from starving to death. At the same time, however, the availability of child labor may serve to drive down the wages of adult laborers, thus making child labor necessary for every family's survival. The availabil-

[35] Ibid., 143.

ity of child labor can thus trap families and societies in a low-wage, low-productivity equilibrium in which children are raised to be ignorant and uneducated, with few options open to them. Not only would children be better off in such circumstances if they went to school, but so too would their families. The institution of child labor restrains the set of alternatives available to poor families, so that they have no better choice than to send their children to work.[36] Child labor also, and perhaps most centrally, restrains the choices of poor children, since it corrupts their development, causing them to have less ability to choose than they would have had if they had been educated. Interestingly, permitting child labor is in the interests of some employers, since it provides them with a cheaper source of labor than adults. Such employers may seek to manipulate the choice environment.

The economist Garance Genicot provides an example of the ways that landlords can strategically restrain the choices available to laborers such that these laborers voluntarily accept bonded labor. In her model, peasants choose between bonded labor and casual labor, and landlords and local credit institutions compete with each other on the credit market. If bonded labor is allowed, the enforcement capabilities of the landlords and the local credit institutions will be different. Since bonded laborers agree to work for the landlord over the period of the loan, the landlord can subtract the amount due directly from the laborers' wages. By contrast, local credit institutions have to rely on implicit agreements in which the threat of losing future credit opportunities prevents borrowers from defaulting on loans. Genicot shows that the (mere) possibility of entering into bondage, even if not taken, harms poor peasants' access to credit by improving their options in the case of default. A poor peasant who defaults on a loan to a local credit institution now has another option to obtain credit. She can now sell herself into bondage to secure a loan. Thus, bonded labor has the potential to render the implicit promise to repay a loan unenforceable and therefore prevents asset-less peasants from gaining access to formal credit. Moreover, landlords can set the terms of bonded labor such that peasants are denied credit from local institutions.[37]

Voluntary bondage, child labor, and debt peonage replicate the feudal relations between individuals that Smith denounces. Those in bondage are entirely dependent on one individual for their survival, and they have few if any alternative options. Enforcing genuinely free labor markets requires restrictions on bonded labor, laws that guarantee the right to exit from employment, education that makes this right not merely a right in name only, and restrictions on monopoly and monopsony, with perhaps an additional role for the state as a source of credit to poor families.

[36] See Debra Satz, "Child Labor: A Normative Approach," *World Bank Economic Review* 17, no. 2 (2003): 297–309.

[37] Garance Genicot, "Bonded Labor and Serfdom: A Paradox of Voluntary Choice," *Journal of Development Economics* 67, no. 1 (February 2002): 101–27.

Because of the endogenous nature of the choices an agent faces, we need to focus not only on the moment of individual choice, but also on the way that institutions can enhance or restrict her range of choices. If it is true that without limits on labor or credit markets, such markets would degenerate into relations characterized by subordination and extreme servility, then it is not concerns of paternalism or efficiency that prompt restrictions on markets but an argument about the need for collective self-protection. Without some restrictions on markets and property rights, a person's real opportunities could shrink to zero and she could become extremely dependent on a small set of individuals who would wield great power over her. The most important of the market's effects—its erosion of servile dependency and its promotion of the liberty and security of individuals—would be dramatically undercut. Bonded labor, whether contractual or not, is objectionable because it constitutes a relation of personal subjection, in which one party enjoys arbitrary power over another. It also changes the options that are open to an agent, whether she wants to engage in bonded labor or not.

The examples of child labor and bonded labor illustrate the blurriness of the distinction between the imposition of an institutional form of servitude and the limitations placed on individual choice by the lack of alternatives. Powerful agents often act to restrict the set of choices open to less powerful agents, who then voluntarily accept the choice that is in the best interest of the powerful.

Adam Smith recognized that free contract employment was a momentous instance of progress, liberating individuals from the tyranny of servitude. While he advocated the use of markets in many circumstances, he did not hesitate to investigate those economic circumstances where particular restrictions could enhance liberty. Thus, although he was hostile to labor market regulations that benefited employers, he was tolerant of such regulations when they were in favor of workers: "When the regulation . . . is in favor if the workmen, it is always just and equitable, but it is sometimes otherwise when it is in favor of the masters."[38] Smith's recognition that there are good reasons to reject institutions (including underlying systems of property rights) that reduce an agent's options so that servile dependency is her best alternative opens the door to limitations on freedom of contract. The reasons for imposing these limitations overlap with, but also go well beyond, the revisionist liberal's reasons for regulating markets (externalities, incomplete information, and monopoly). For it is not only consistent with Smith's analysis that bonded labor, child labor, and usury be prohibited, but also that incorporated (company) towns be banned, as well as markets in political influence. The point is that without restraints on

---

[38] Smith, *Wealth of Nations*, 157–58.

freedom of contract, we do not get capitalism. We get a system of voluntary feudalism.[39]

## B. Market heterogeneity

Adam Smith saw the market as a heterogeneous set of institutions. Smith and his followers offered distinct theories of the functioning not only of markets for goods, but also of markets for land, credit, and labor. Land, credit, and labor were considered to be peculiar in a variety of ways: land had fixed natural limits; credit was forwarded on the basis of a future promise to pay with uncertain enforcement; and labor was a commodity embodied in human beings.

It is because Smith saw labor as a special kind of commodity that he viewed labor markets in a way that differed from the way he viewed other kinds of markets (for example, a market in corn). Unlike a corn market, a labor market directly shaped the capacities of human beings:

> The employment of the great body of the people comes to be confined to a few operations; frequently to one or two. But the understandings ... of men are necessarily formed by their ordinary employments. The man whose whole life is spent performing a few simple operations of which the effects too are perhaps always the same ... has no occasion to exert his understanding or to exercise his invention in finding out expedients for removing difficulties which never occur. He naturally loses, therefore, the habit of such exertion and generally becomes as stupid and ignorant as it is possible for a human creature to become. ... [He is incapable] of forming any just judgment concerning many even of the ordinary duties of private life. Of the great and extensive interests of his country, he is altogether incapable of judging. ... .[40]

Smith recognized that a worker's preferences and capabilities were shaped by the structure of the labor market. For this reason, Smith objected to the one-sided training of the apprenticeship guilds, to the power of incorporated towns, and to the degradation of workers into mere things at work. He was aware that markets have not only economic but also social and political effects: in particular, markets push forward the development of the division of labor, which in turn produces not only economic growth but also a one-sided worker incapable of taking part in

---

[39] See also Elizabeth Anderson, "Adventures in Contract Feudalism," http://left2right. typepad.com (February 10, 2005).
[40] Smith, *Wealth of Nations*, 781–82.

social decision-making. The growth of the division of labor deprives workers of their "intellectual, social and martial virtues."[41]

In his discussions of the pin-making factory, Smith detailed how workers spent their waking hours focusing on one small facet of pin production. How could such workers—if shaped only by these tasks—rise to the level of citizens participating in choosing their circumstances and goals? Smith's striking admission of the limited nature of industrial workers in a capitalist economy was later developed by Hegel and Marx in their ideas of the alienation of labor. Like these later social critics, Smith recognized that the functioning of labor markets inevitably raises questions relevant to the structure of public life, in a way that the functioning of a market in apples does not.

For Smith, labor markets are not only economic institutions that allocate labor across industries and distribute income; they are also political and cultural institutions. Labor markets shape our culture, foster or thwart various human capacities, and support or undermine structures of power. For Smith, the market would fail even if it were efficient and "voluntary" if it also supported an undemocratic structure of power, or fostered political opportunism, or placed workers in relations of servile dependence with manufacturers. In contrast to the excessively abstract, formal representations of freedom, efficiency, and markets in contemporary economic theory, Smith understood that the virtues of capitalism lay in the concrete social relations, motivations, and norms through which market exchange takes place. In modern parlance, we might say that Smith recognized that labor markets were endogenous insofar as they shaped the values, preferences, and choice-sets of workers.[42]

## VIII. Conclusion

Revisionist liberals have more in common with the classical liberals than is often supposed. But the classical liberals, as exemplified by Adam Smith, offer key insights on the relationship between markets and freedom that are missing from contemporary liberal approaches. I have sought to recover two important Smithian insights.

First, the distinction between externally imposed restrictions on choice and internally limited choice-sets is not sharp. Institutions, including markets, shape the range of choices that are open to an agent and thus her degree of effective freedom. If certain markets—child labor markets, bonded labor markets, credit markets—can restrict the choices open to an agent, independently of whether or not she chooses to participate in them, then

---

[41] Ibid., 782.
[42] See also Samuel Bowles and Herbert Gintis, "The Revenge of Homo Economicus: Contested Exchange and the Revival of Political Economy," *Journal of Economic Perspectives* 7, no. 1 (1993): 83–102.

this makes these markets problematic. Moreover, this restriction in the range of choice is not simply a problem of "externalities": the choice-sets of even those who choose to participate in such markets (e.g., voluntary bonded laborers) may be forever altered.

Second, liberals should address markets as cultural and political institutions as much as economic ones. Certain markets shape individuals: consider labor markets, or child-care markets. These markets are constitutive. How such markets are organized has a significant bearing on the development of our capacities, preferences, and choice-sets. Thus, labor markets can be organized in very different ways, ways that not only change the prevailing wages of workers but also give employers more or less control over their employees. The implication of this is not that such constitutive markets should be abolished, but rather that we should structure such markets to preserve relations based on reciprocity and not on coercion. In thinking about the interconnections between markets and freedom, we need to pay attention to the relationships that different markets support as well as to the distributions that they achieve.

*Philosophy, Stanford University*

# POPULIST PERFECTIONISM:
## THE OTHER AMERICAN LIBERALISM

By Thomas A. Spragens, Jr.

## I. Introduction: Three Debates about American Liberalism

Scholarly studies of American political thought over the past several decades have devoted a great deal of attention to three important debates. The first concerns the ideological origins of the American Revolution. The second concerns the merits of the competing interpretations of liberal rights championed by libertarian theorists such as Robert Nozick on the one side and egalitarian theorists such as John Rawls on the other. The third debate has been between rights-based liberals and their communitarian critics.

The first of these debates was initiated principally by the colonial historian Bernard Bailyn with his pathbreaking and iconoclastic book *The Ideological Origins of the American Revolution* (1967). Before the publication of that work, the conventional scholarly wisdom—paradigmatically expressed in Louis Hartz's *The Liberal Tradition in America* (1955)—was that the American political tradition was grounded in a Lockean liberalism so deeply taken for granted and so widely subscribed to as to be largely invisible.[1] Bailyn, soon seconded by intellectual historians such as Gordon Wood and J. G. A. Pocock,[2] contended that this belief was mistaken: instead of being grounded in Lockean liberalism, the ideological inspiration and justification for America's rebellion against the mother country was instead derived more from the civic republican tradition, particularly in its appropriation by the "country party" in Great Britain. In turn, other scholars have disputed some of the evidentiary base Bailyn relied upon and have also taken issue with the understanding of Lockeanism upon which Bailyn and Pocock depended in constructing their interpretations.[3]

The second debate was kicked off by Rawls's notable feat of reconstructive hermeneutics in his *A Theory of Justice* (1971).[4] Rawls argued there that the moral foundations of democratic society were best accounted

---

[1] Louis Hartz, *The Liberal Tradition in America* (New York: Harcourt, Brace, and World, 1955); Bernard Bailyn, *The Ideological Origins of the American Revolution* (Cambridge, MA: Harvard University Press, 1967).

[2] See Gordon Wood, *The Creation of the American Republic* (Chapel Hill: University of North Carolina Press, 1969), and J. G. A. Pocock, *The Machiavellian Moment* (Princeton, NJ: Princeton University Press, 1975).

[3] An excellent treatment of these issues is provided by Steven Dworetz in *The Unvarnished Doctrine: Locke, Liberalism, and the American Revolution* (Durham, NC, and London: Duke University Press, 1990).

[4] John Rawls, *A Theory of Justice* (Cambridge, MA: Harvard University Press, 1971).

for within the tradition and the animating moral intuitions of liberalism's contractarian individualism, but that the normative implications of this tradition properly understood pointed in the direction of an economically redistributive welfare state rather than toward a night-watchman minimal state devoted to the protection of individual liberties and property. Robert Nozick responded by criticizing some of the most problematic and controversial claims and assumptions upon which Rawls's conclusions were based, seeking to recapture deontological liberalism for the sort of political economy championed by people like F. A. Hayek and Ludwig von Mises.[5] The ensuing commentaries and arguments regarding the proper way to understand the content of liberal rights and distributive justice have become a substantial cottage industry.

Finally, the so-called liberalism-communitarianism debate had multiple and overlapping sources—in Charles Taylor's neo-Hegelian critique of liberal individualism, in Michael Sandel's criticism of the philosophical anthropology he found embedded in Rawls's theory and other rights-based liberal theories, and in Amitai Etzioni's criticisms of what he saw as the destructive consequences of the fixation upon individual rights in both the contemporary left and the contemporary right.[6] The communitarians argued that our public philosophy and our policies both needed to pay more attention to the common good, to personal and communal responsibility, to the civic virtues required of democratic citizens, and to the health of the institutions of civil society. Liberal individualists, both left and right, replied that aspirations on behalf of operative conceptions of virtue and a putative common good were inappropriate in principle and likely to be oppressive in practice in today's pluralistic societies.

Each of these debates has been an important one, and the arguments they inspired have contributed a great deal to our understanding of American political thought and the assumptions, implications, and ambiguities of liberal political theory in the broad sense of that term. It is also worth noting that each of these debates has been driven in part by tacit ideological concerns. The disputants were engaged in what often were presented as historical and hermeneutic enterprises. Nonetheless, how we understand our past, our traditions, and the moral and philosophical presuppositions behind them tends to have performative implications. The self-understanding of a society produces—perhaps for psychological reasons more than logical ones—a kind of "value slope" (to borrow a term from Charles Taylor) that favors some contemporary political orientations over others. Accounts of "the American political tradition" or "the liberal tradition" function partly as rhetorical redescriptions with

---

[5] See Robert Nozick, *Anarchy, State, and Utopia* (New York: Basic Books, 1974).

[6] See Charles Taylor, *Sources of the Self: The Making of the Modern Identity* (Cambridge, MA: Harvard University Press, 1989); Michael Sandel, *Liberalism and the Limits of Justice* (Cambridge: Cambridge University Press, 1982); and Amitai Etzioni, *The New Golden Rule: Community and Morality in a Democratic Society* (New York: Basic Books, 1997).

normative force. As evidence here, consider not only the contentious political debates that erupt over the teaching of American history in the public schools but also the perennial partisan disputation over who is and who is not standing in the "mainstream" of American politics. In a political society enjoying a high level of legitimacy among the citizenry, capturing the mantle of orthodoxy tends to confer political benefits.

Thus, the attempt to downplay the Lockean provenance of the ideology of the American Revolution and to emphasize the strands of civic republicanism in the mix was motivated partly by a worry that the prior conventional wisdom about America's founding ideology seemed to accord pride of place to individualistic and inegalitarian norms, leaving out the concerns for the public weal and for civic equality that were more important in the republican tradition. Although Rawls's ostensive adversary in *A Theory of Justice* was utilitarianism, part of his motivation was almost certainly a desire to appropriate contractarian and rights theories for welfare state liberalism and to keep these moral touchstones from serving as the exclusive preserve of laissez-faire and libertarian political philosophies. And although Amitai Etzioni largely conceded that hermeneutic battle over the meaning of liberalism to rights-based individualisms of left and right, preferring to style himself as an ideological innovator, others who shared his worries about the decline of civil society were motivated to insist upon a concern within the liberal tradition itself for community and liberal civic virtue.[7]

Nevertheless, to the extent that the parties to these scholarly controversies were engaged in a de facto debate about "the genius of American politics," to borrow a phrase of historian Daniel Boorstin's, I would want to insist that none of the political-philosophical orientations staked out within these debates provides a persuasive account of what that genius might be. Without taking sides on the merits of any of these orientations, I would simply call attention to their collective limitations and lacunae. However significant it may be as an exercise in historical hermeneutics, the controversy over the ideology of the American Revolution seems a bit of a sidebar to any serious debate about the goals and aspirations of a democratic society. Justifications of any political rebellion, and that was what was going on in the pamphlets, sermons, and treatises at issue here, constitute a discourse of legitimacy and not an account of social goals. This is a discourse focused upon the questions of political obligation and legitimate authority; and claims about the purposes of political society are pertinent only insofar as they bear upon those consuming issues. The Rawls-Nozick debate takes place on the basis of a common presumption that the moral foundations of democracy are deontological in nature (that

---

[7] See, for example, Philip Selznick, "Foundations of Communitarian Liberalism," in *The Essential Communitarian Reader*, ed. Amitai Etzioni (Lanham, MD: Rowman and Littlefield Press, 1998); Richard Dagger, *Civic Virtues* (New York and Oxford: Oxford University Press, 1997).

is, grounded in beliefs about rights and justice rather than beliefs about the human good) and that the only question at issue concerns the content and persuasiveness of the relevant rights claims. Moreover, the debate between communitarian critics of liberalism and their detractors turned to a very considerable degree around competing diagnoses of some fairly specific contemporary social trends and problems. Even when these several debates and competing arguments are taken collectively, therefore, a lot that is pertinent to any attempt to characterize the liberal tradition(s) of America in a larger way and from a more comprehensive perspective gets left out of the picture.

The three scholarly disputes I have mentioned, whatever the motivations and larger implications involved, take place on historical terrain prior to 1787 or after 1960. That marginalizes a rather large chunk of American political thought and experience when it comes to the evidentiary basis for characterizations of the animating purposes of America's version of democratic liberalism. Perhaps this relative ignoring of such a large swath of American history results from the judgment that there really is not much in the way of serious, profound, and distinctive political theorizing to be found here. And it is certainly true that, from the standpoint of political philosophy, we could fast forward from *The Federalist Papers* to *A Theory of Justice* without missing much that could offer the kind of intellectual credentials expected of epic political theories. Some of what is found here, moreover, largely replicates rights-based and republican ideas.

## II. HEGEL AND MILL:
### AN ALTERNATIVE PHILOSOPHICAL INSPIRATION

If we look more closely at the more "progressive" or "democratic" modes of thought during this period, however, we find another important philosophical orientation at work—one that cannot be shoehorned into the standard republican or rights-based categories. If we look at apologists for Jacksonian democracy like George Bancroft (whose historical meta-narratives performed core functions of public philosophy), at Abraham Lincoln, at Walt Whitman, at John Dewey and Jane Addams, there seems to be a political sensibility on display which is not a derivative of either rights-based theories or civic republicanism. That is not to say that these interpreters of democratic purposes do not believe in government based on consent, or in the kind of rights guaranteed by the first ten amendments to the Constitution, or in public-spirited equal citizenship, or in the rule of law. They accept all these core liberal tenets which John Locke, Immanuel Kant, and the republican tradition championed, but their principal concerns lie elsewhere and their goals are more ambitious and extensive. Taking rights and civic equality for granted, they want to address the deeper and larger purposes and hopes of democratic society. They see these purposes as historically novel to some extent, and they see the hopes as a work in progress.

For want of a better name, I want to call this genre of democratic public philosophy "populist perfectionism." Each of the terms immediately invites misunderstanding and therefore needs some specification. By "populist" I do not mean to refer to a straightforward class-based politics in which the economic interests of the many are promoted over the vested interests of the wealthy and powerful—although a concern for the general economic well-being of the commoners is certainly part of the equation. Moreover, I do not mean to refer to the championing of a straightforward plebiscitary form of democratic decision-making—although a concern for the political participation and competence of the citizenry at large is also part of the picture. The central meaning of the word "populist" in my characterization is pretty much what G. W. F. Hegel depicted as the axial moral claim or discovery of "the Germanic peoples": that is, the insistence that it is not just the one or the few but the many—indeed, all people— who are able and destined to be free. For most of human history, the common folk were not able or entitled fully to pursue lives of their own, to build their lives around purposes of their own determination, so much as they were externally dominated functionaries in the service of the purposes of their masters and governors. The true motto of populism in this sense was captured in the words of Thomas Rainborough, a colonel in Oliver Cromwell's New Model Army, when he said during the Putney Debates of 1647: "For really I think that the poorest he that is in England hath a life to live as the greatest he." The ultimate goal of "populism" in this signification is to achieve what political scientist Benjamin Barber has called, in a deliberately paradoxical phrase, "an aristocracy of everyone."[8]

The second term in my formula, "perfectionism," has served in contemporary debates and analyses within democratic theory to designate political philosophies that incorporate some teleological conception of human fulfillment. In a broad and general sense, the American expositors of the meaning and purpose of democratic society whom I am concerned with here can be said to fall into this category. This is not to say that they have some single, narrow, and fully comprehensive model of the good human being whose creation it is democracy's purpose to accomplish. It means that these theorists believed that the larger purposes of a novel form of social order only in its infancy—a democratic one—were not confined to or exhausted by mere mechanisms of political authority and governance and were not concerned only with protecting the security and effective functioning of the basic civil order. Instead, the ultimate aspirations of democratic society as these theorists conceived them extended to matters of the mind, heart, and spirit. The ultimate glory and justification

---

[8] Benjamin Barber, *An Aristocracy of Everyone* (New York: Oxford University Press, 1992).

of a democratic society would be its success in fashioning social institutions incarnating a "way of life" conducive to the flourishing of the human capacities of all of its members.

Insofar as this orientation received inspiration from canonical works in political philosophy instead of being an indigenous American amalgam, the most relevant figures are not Locke, Kant, or Algernon Sidney so much as Hegel and John Stuart Mill. The nineteenth-century representatives of what I am calling "populist perfectionism" broadly shared the conviction that brought Alexis de Tocqueville to American shores in 1831. Like Tocqueville, they believed that the seemingly inexorable historical trend toward more democratic forms of governance had the status of what he called "a Providential fact." As Tocqueville wrote, "It has all the chief characteristics of such a fact: It is universal, it is durable, it constantly eludes all human interference, and all events as well as all men contribute to its progress." Also, like Tocqueville, they believed that "the magnitude of what already has been done prevents us from foreseeing what is yet to be accomplished."[9] These convictions made nineteenth-century American democrats like Bancroft and Whitman amenable to Hegel's historical metaphysics. The inexorable progress of democratization represented the unfolding of freedom and spirit through time. A major part of the task of political philosophy, therefore, was to do what Tocqueville said was difficult: to "foresee what is yet to be accomplished in this process." That meant that a political philosophy which began with a proper understanding of the determinative dynamics of historicity would be, to borrow the terminology of the third-generation neo-Hegelian Friedrich Engels, an exercise in visionary "science" more than a "utopian" attempt to conjure up happier social circumstances by an act of freewheeling imagination. What would make this exercise "scientific," however, was not the crystal-ball gazing of pure positivist prediction but the unpacking of the full implications of the logic of democratization: what would human life and society look like when everyone was politically equal and genuinely free?

Because "freedom" in this democratic neo-Hegelian sensibility was understood not merely as a "negative" liberation from all impediments to desire but also as the "positive" fulfillment of the potentialities of the human spirit, the abstract answer to this latter question was understood to be essentially coterminous with what Jürgen Habermas has designated as the fundamental moral and political aspirations of the revolutionary liberal Enlightenment: autonomy and self-realization. This "revolutionary consciousness," Habermas writes, "gave birth to a new mentality" which incorporated "the understanding of political practice in terms of self-determination and self-realization. . . . Autonomy and

---

[9] Alexis de Tocqueville, introduction to *Democracy in America* (1835), trans. Henry Reeve and Frances Bowen (New York: Mentor Books, 1956), 29.

self-realization are the key concepts for a practice with an immanent purpose, namely, the production and reproduction of a life worthy of human beings."[10]

These core ideals of autonomy/self-determination and fulfillment/self-realization received expression and some degree of elaboration in the epigram and the justly famous third chapter ("Of Individuality") of John Stuart Mill's *On Liberty* (1859). To be truly human, Mill wrote there, people cannot live lives of mere "ape-like imitation," abjectly conforming to preexistent models prescribed for them. Instead, "it is the privilege and proper condition of a human being, arrived at the maturity of his faculties, to use and interpret experience in his own way."[11] Devising and pursuing one's own "plan of life" not only constitutes that autonomy which is the hallmark of a genuinely human existence but also constitutes an essential component of the other core goal of self-realization. The "grand, leading principle" to which *On Liberty* was devoted and which was expressed in its epigram taken from Wilhelm von Humboldt "is the absolute and essential importance of human development in its richest diversity." And it is in the conscious choosing and planning of one's life that a person "employs all his faculties."[12] Moreover, because human beings are "not indistinguishably alike" but instead possess many different talents and capabilities, when they do each and all freely and fully develop these talents and capabilities in all their multifarious glory, "human life becomes rich, diversified, and animating," and "human beings become a noble and beautiful object of contemplation."[13]

## III. LIBERAL PERFECTIONISM: WALT WHITMAN AND JOHN DEWEY

Walt Whitman's "Democratic Vistas" (1871) provides us with one of the best and most important exemplifications of a perfectionist account, inspired in part by Hegel and Mill, of the purposes and justification of American democracy. Whitman was not much of a philosopher. He was a poet and a journalist, not a systematic normative theorist who constructed the kind of logical arguments that make their way into the philosophical canon. Nevertheless, he thought a lot about the meaning and significance of America's experiment with self-governance, and his hopes and understandings pretty clearly fell into the pattern of what I have called "populist perfectionism."

[10] Jürgen Habermas, "Popular Sovereignty as Procedure," a lecture given in December 1988, trans. William Rehg, in James Bohman and William Rehg, eds., *Deliberative Democracy: Essays on Reason and Politics* (Cambridge, MA, and London: MIT Press, 1997), 39, 41.
[11] John Stuart Mill, *On Liberty* (1859; Indianapolis: Bobbs-Merrill, 1956), 70.
[12] Ibid., 71.
[13] Ibid., 82, 73.

America should be understood, Whitman tells us, as a "grand experiment of development."[14] It represents the leading edge in a vast cosmic process of spiritual unfolding animated by "divine purpose." Citing Hegel, Whitman admonishes us that "we have peremptorily to dismiss every pretensive production, however fine its esthetic or intellectual points, which violates or ignores, or even does not celebrate, the central divine idea of All, suffusing universe, of eternal trains of purpose, in the development, by however slow degrees, of the physical, moral, and spiritual kosmos. I say he has studied, meditated to no profit, whatever may be his mere erudition, who has not absorbed this simple consciousness and faith. It is not entirely new—but is for Democracy to elaborate it."[15]

American democracy, in the context of this cosmic drama, should be seen as only in the earliest stages of its own development. It is "at present in its embryo condition." Its "fruition" and "the only large and satisfactory justification of it . . . resides altogether in the future."[16] This ultimate "fruition" of democracy will consist in its attainment of purposes that are not simply material and institutional but moral and spiritual in nature. "The world evidently supposes . . . that the States are merely to achieve the equal franchise, and elective government—to inaugurate the respectability of labor, and become a nation of practical operatives, law-abiding, orderly and well off. Yes, those are indeed parts of the task of America; but they not only do not exhaust the progressive conception, but rather arise, teeming with it, as the mediums of deeper, higher progress. . . . For so long as the spirit is not changed, any change of appearance is of no avail."[17]

What, then, are these deeper and higher purposes of democracy? As jumping-off places from which to answer that question, Whitman refers us to two famous texts. The first of these is Lincoln's peroration in his Gettysburg Address. "Few probably are the minds, even in these republican States," Whitman writes, "that fully comprehend the aptness of that phrase, 'THE GOVERNMENT OF THE PEOPLE, BY THE PEOPLE, FOR THE PEOPLE,' which we inherit from the lips of Abraham Lincoln; a formula whose verbal shape is homely wit, but whose scope includes both the totality and all minutiae of the lesson." The second text is "John Stuart Mill's profound essay on Liberty," which is the place to look to understand "the distinctive points contrasting modern European and American political life with the old *Asiatic cultus*," and which explains "the lessons of variety and freedom" with which Mill "begins his speculations."[18]

[14] Walt Whitman, "Democratic Vistas" (1871), in *Walt Whitman: Poetry and Prose,* ed. Justin Kaplan (New York: Literary Classics of the United States, 1996), 972.
[15] Ibid., 1009.
[16] Ibid., 983, 980.
[17] Ibid., 1001–2.
[18] Ibid., 967, 953.

Whitman, as we shall see, weds Lincoln's version of "populism"—the insistence upon democracy as governance of, by, and for the people—with Mill's "perfectionism"—the insistence that the criterion for judging political regimes is their contribution to the mental and moral development of the people.[19] And in doing so, Whitman winds up celebrating the two axial social aspirations that Habermas identified in his account of the "new concept of political practice" found in the "revolutionary consciousness" of the Enlightenment: "self-determination and self-realization."[20] Whitman may not be the clearest and most precise of political theorists, but he does very clearly indicate to his readers at one point in "Democratic Vistas" that he is zeroing in on the most fundamental purposes of democratic governance. He wants to tell them about "the mission of government, henceforth, in civilized lands" and about "the ulterior object of political and all other government." These ultimate purposes are the deeper meaning of the phrases "by the people" and "for the people" respectively.

Democracy's insistence on government "by the people," Whitman writes, is grounded in its moral conviction that "each single individual" is entitled to be "a separate and complete subject for freedom." Therefore, "the mission of government, henceforth, in civilized lands, is not repression alone, and not authority alone, not even of law ... but ... to train communities through all their grades, beginning with individuals and ending there again, to rule themselves."[21] Democracy's insistence on government "for the people" translates into a dedication to the development or actualization of their personal capacities—the very "grand leading principle" of "the absolute and essential importance of human development" in the von Humboldt quotation Mill uses as his epigram to *On Liberty*. This is what Whitman refers to as "the grand experiment of development—whose end, perhaps requiring several generations, may be the forming of a full-grown man or woman."[22] So it is that "the ulterior object of political and all other government" is "not merely to rule, to repress disorder, etc., but to develop, to open up to cultivation, to encourage the possibilities of all beneficent and manly outcroppage, and of that aspiration for independence, and the pride and self-respect latent in all characters."[23]

I do not believe, moreover, that what I am calling the "populist perfectionist" persuasion in democratic public philosophy is an isolated nineteenth-century phenomenon. If we examine John Dewey's explanation and justification of the goals and animating principles of democratic governance, for example, it seems fairly clear that his account is a lot

---

[19] See John Stuart Mill, *Considerations on Representative Government* (1861; Chicago: Regnery, 1962), 35–36.

[20] Habermas, "Popular Sovereignty," 39.

[21] Whitman, "Democratic Vistas," 971.

[22] Ibid., 972.

[23] Ibid., 970–71.

closer to John Stuart Mill than it is to John Locke, John Rawls, or civic republicanism. It would be silly, of course, to style Dewey as simply a later version of Walt Whitman. There are important differences and important innovations here. But there are also enough similarities to warrant the claim that Dewey's democratic pragmatism conforms broadly to the pattern I have been describing.

Like Whitman and Mill, Dewey understands democracy not merely as a set of institutions of governance but as a larger way of life. We must, he writes, "get rid of the habit of thinking of democracy as something institutional and external and to acquire the habit of treating it as a way of personal life."[24] Like Whitman, Dewey sees democratic society as very much a work in progress, with its realization something to hope for in the future rather than a *fait accompli* with the implementation of representative institutions. And, again like Whitman, he cites Hegel with approval for his "attempt to fill in the empty reason of Kant with the contents of history" and for the way he "lifted the idea of progress above that of fixed origins and fixed ends, and presented the social and moral order, as well as the intellectual, as a scene of becoming" and "located reason somewhere within the struggles of life."[25] The common attraction to Hegel in Dewey and Whitman reflects not simply their belief in the historical unfolding of a democratizing entelechy, but their common conviction that the achievement of this process—and of history—is ultimately a self-realization of the human spirit, of *Geist*. Dewey interprets this spiritual achievement mostly by reference to the pragmatically rational communal practices paradigmatically embodied in scientific inquiry, rather than by reference to the artistic creations of the "great literatus," as in Whitman. Nonetheless, both of these accounts depict the essence of the democratic way of life as cultural and spiritual rather than as merely economic and governmental.

Most importantly, when he seeks to articulate the ultimate purposes and defining norms of democratic liberalism, Dewey seems to stand clearly within the tradition of the "revolutionary consciousness" cited by Habermas. In *Liberalism and Social Action* (1935), Dewey argues that the "social control of economic forces" is necessary in the context of advanced industrial societies, but it is a necessity not in order to change the social goals traditionally associated with liberalism but rather to achieve them. These "enduring values," he writes, "are liberty, the development of the inherent capacities of individuals made possible through liberty, and the central role of free intelligence in inquiry, discussion, and expression."[26]

---

[24] John Dewey, "Creative Democracy—The Task Before Us" (1939), in Dewey, *The Political Writings*, ed. Debra Morris and Ian Shapiro (Indianapolis, IN, and Cambridge: Hackett Publishing Company, 1993), 244.

[25] John Dewey, "Intelligence and Morals," in Dewey, *Political Writings*, 72.

[26] John Dewey, *Liberalism and Social Action*, reprinted in Michael Levy, ed., *Political Thought in America* (Chicago: Dorsey Press, 1988), 412.

The first two of these "enduring values" are Habermas's self-rule and self-realization, the same "ulterior" purposes of democracy Whitman cited in his own rendering of what government "by the people" and "for the people" meant. And Dewey's endorsement of the third of these values, which he creatively developed in his model of pragmatic and scientific inquiry, closely resembles the argument of the second chapter of Mill's *On Liberty*, which Whitman cited as inspiration for his "Democratic Vistas."

These accounts of the social hopes and moral preoccupations of Whitman and Dewey are cursory and cryptic. Even so, I hope they provide adequate grounds for the claim that there is another important American liberal tradition in addition to those more commonly accorded pride of place within attempts to characterize the philosophical genius of American politics. This is a perspective on democratic purposes that takes its bearings not so much from Locke's account of legitimate government, or from rights-based philosophies more generally, or from the dominant themes of civic republicanism. Instead, it takes its bearings more from nineteenth-century philosophies of historical progress such as those of Mill and Hegel. And it takes as its ultimate social aspirations not the protection of life, liberty, and estate or the creation of civic communities modeled on Sparta, republican Florence, or Geneva: instead, it sees it as the mission of democratic politics to achieve freedom for everyone—to create a form of social life in which everyone becomes, to cite Whitman once again, "a separate and complete subject for freedom" and a "full-grown man or woman."

## IV. THE CONTEMPORARY RELEVANCE OF WHITMAN AND DEWEY

The question that now presents itself is whether this insistence upon the historical presence within American political thought of an alternative conception of democratic hopes centered around self-rule and self-realization is of merely archaeological significance or whether it can serve constructive contemporary purposes. Should the form of democratic liberalism represented by people like Whitman and Dewey be regarded as a historical curiosity best placed in an academic museum, or can it provide relevant inspiration for us as we contemplate the moral and political challenges of the twenty-first century? One prominent voice in debates about contemporary democratic theory and practice, Richard Rorty, has recently argued that a recovery and reinvigoration of Whitman's and Dewey's form of democratic idealism is precisely what American reform liberalism needs in order to recapture its waning vitality and political relevance. In contrast, Rawlsian rights-based liberals would rather clearly regard any attempt to resurrect teleological or perfectionist conceptions of democratic purposes—including those of Whitman or Dewey—as both unnecessary and inappropriate. I want to conclude my argument, therefore, by engaging these different responses to the question I have posed about the contemporary pertinence of the "populist perfectionist" account of democratic purposes. I want to concur in part with Rorty but also dissent in part from his views. I agree with him that Whitman, Dewey, and "populist perfectionism" represent a form of public philosophy that remains pertinent and useful for all of us who concern ourselves with the future strength and success of democratic regimes. I do not, however, find his postmodernist reading of the content and implications of Whitman's and Dewey's political philosophies fully compelling. Finally, I want to explain why I think that neither I nor Rorty should be deterred from our endorsement of democratic idealism of the Whitman/Dewey sort by the standard objections to perfectionist theories.

In his recent book *Achieving Our Country,* Rorty argues that the American left—or at least the academic American left—has largely become politically irrelevant in the sense of having any meaningful stance or impact upon real-world political issues and battles.[27] This self-disempowerment, he contends, is a result in the first instance of disgust and shame at America's past oppressions, enslavement, and violence against African Americans and Native Americans—and at its more recent role in international politics, which is seen as imperialistic and supportive of authoritarian regimes. This dismay at American transgressions has, Rorty argues, engendered in the left unfortunate theoretical inclinations. It has led American leftists to be too much in thrall to the antiquated economics, the delusionary philosophy of history, and the sectarian puritanism of Marxism. This fixation has been misleading and destructive. In point of fact, "Marxism was not only a catastrophe for all the countries in which Marxists took power, but a disaster for the reformist left in all the countries in which they did not."[28] Even worse, perhaps, members of America's academic left have allowed their dismay with American political transgressions to seduce them into accepting Martin Heidegger's depiction of American democracy as a totalitarian technological moral wasteland and into accepting Michel Foucault's account of liberal polities as disciplinary regimes grounded in discourses of power that legitimate elite dominance.

Rorty holds that viewing America—and, by association, liberal democracy—in this way makes "pride in American citizenship impossible." It makes American patriotism seem "an endorsement of atrocities" and national pride seem "appropriate only for chauvinists." But "national pride is to countries what self-respect is to individuals: a necessary con-

---

[27] Richard Rorty, *Achieving Our Country* (Cambridge, MA, and London: Harvard University Press, 1998).
[28] Ibid., 41.

dition for self-improvement." Thus, the American left has become alienated, politically irrelevant, and impotent. It has succumbed to "the spirit
of detached spectatorship" in the mode of Henry Adams's incapacitating
political cynicism, and to an "inability to think of American citizenship as
an opportunity for action." [29]

Here is where Rorty's embrace of Whitman and Dewey comes in. They
played a central role "in creating the image of America which was ubiquitous on the American left prior to the Vietnam War." Their optimistic narrative of American society as a liberating work in progress gave liberal
reformers the hope and the national pride they needed in order to be constructive participants in political struggles on behalf of greater inclusion,
equality, and social justice. Moreover, Rorty argues, the views of Whitman
and Dewey remain capable of giving us "all the romance, and all the spiritual uplift, we Americans need to go about our public business." And that
is a good thing, too, for "nobody has yet suggested a viable leftist alternative to the civic religion of which Whitman and Dewey were prophets." [30]

I agree with Rorty's insistence that Whitman, Dewey, and the account
of democratic purposes they provide remain pertinent and valuable guides
and resources for reform liberalism today. They are valuable in part for
the reason Rorty emphasizes: that their hopeful narratives encourage
avoidance of the temptation for reform liberals to fall into the politically
self-defeating posture of alienated spectatorship. They are also valuable
because their most central hermeneutic and normative claims are important and correct. American democracy is a work in progress: it may
continue to exhibit patterns of dominance and deep inequalities that systematically thwart the aspiration that all may be free; but it has also
exhibited the ability to overcome many of these barriers over time, to
become less discriminatory, to become more inclusive, to provide more
equal protection of the law, and to enhance the life chances of more of its
disadvantaged members. The normative insistence of Whitman and Dewey
upon what Dewey called the "enduring values" of self-rule and "the
development of the inherent capacities of individuals made possible
through liberty" is also crucial, because it recalls us to the deepest purposes of liberalism and democracy.

That does not mean that Whitman and Dewey should be disinterred
fully intact and unmodified. It would be unreasonable to expect that they
need no revision to be serviceable to us in the altered circumstances of the
twenty-first century. Values may endure, but times do change: we learn
from intervening events, and we encounter new problems and opportunities. Let me give several examples—not a complete list—of needed
emendations. First, the residual influence of a Hegelian philosophy of
history should be set aside, or at least greatly attenuated. The at times dis-

---

[29] Ibid., 7, 3, 11.
[30] Ibid., 11, 97, 101.

maying evidence of the past century undermines any belief in democracy as the inexorable wave of the future. We should also know that this belief in providential guarantees and authorization can be dangerous, leading to self-arrogating claims of "manifest destiny." And we should by now clearly understand that creating a stable, free, self-governing society is a difficult— and fragile—achievement. This recognition may be discouraging, but need not be crippling, to the democratic hopes championed by Whitman and Dewey. Those dedicated to the promise of democracy may have to give up the comforting delusion of guaranteed triumph; but the enduring values and goals Whitman and Dewey champion can be fully grounded in and logically derived from the basic moral premises and legitimacy claims of liberalism and democracy. Civil rights, civil liberties, and popular sovereignty retain their moral purchase for all those who retain Hegel's hope that all shall be free even after we abandon his assurance that the self-actualizing rationality of history will bring this freedom about.[31]

If Rorty is correct to say that for Whitman "we are the greatest poem because we put ourselves in the place of God," and that Whitman would urge us to "redefine God as our future selves," this also is a notion that begs to be jettisoned. Self-deification is more corrupting morally and much more dangerous politically than either orthodox belief in God as "wholly other" (Karl Barth's phrase) or straightforward atheism. Rorty does not explicitly endorse this kind of cosmic narcissism, but he also does not criticize it. Perhaps he thinks this is what life as strong poets in a purely contingent universe means. If this is the case, then Rorty's postmodernist version of touting humanity—perhaps the democratic portion of it—as divine should also be rejected. Again, however, none of this anthropotheism seems essential to the democratic faith of Whitman or Dewey or Rorty about the desirability and possibility of creating a society where all people can run their own lives, participate in communal self-governance, and have the opportunity and resources to pursue happiness.

Lastly, some have depicted Dewey as a positivistic technocrat and as someone who ignored the role of power and self-interest in democratic politics. Reinhold Niebuhr famously levied the latter criticism of Dewey, seeing him as sharing the utopian delusion of Enlightenment figures like Condorcet, who told us that "all errors in politics and morals are based on philosophical errors and these in turn are connected with scientific errors."[32] I will not try to judge here whether these are jus-

---

[31] Rorty argues that Whitman and Dewey were not implicated in the Hegelian/Jacksonian belief that an entelechy of reason in history provided cosmic impetus for democratizing: "they [i.e., Whitman and Dewey] rejected any idea of Divine Providence and any idea of immanent teleology." I am not as certain as Rorty is about this, especially about the immanent teleology part. Either way, however, this widespread belief of nineteenth-century democrats can be set aside.

[32] Marie Jean Antoine Nicolas Caritat de Condorcet, *Sketch for a Historical Picture of the Progress of the Human Mind*, trans. June Barraclough (London: Weidenfeld and Nicolson, 1955), 163.

tified criticisms. Dewey was, to put it kindly, not always the clearest and most consistent of philosophers. As Justice Oliver Wendell Holmes once waspishly observed, Dewey spoke to us as God would speak to us were He somewhat inarticulate but exceedingly anxious to tell us how things were. Thus, while there are textual warrants in Dewey for these criticisms, there are other words of his which seem more politically realistic than utopian and more inclined toward participatory politics than toward governance by experts. The proper conclusion here, I think, is to say that if Dewey was in fact guilty of naiveté about the corruptions of power and interest or guilty of temptations toward technocracy, these failings can properly be rejected without damage to his core conception of the virtues and aspirations of democratic governance.

## V. Assessing Rorty on Whitman and Dewey

Although I endorse Rorty's recommendation that reform liberalism should identify itself with the democratic hopes and aspirations of Whitman and Dewey, I have some reservations about his philosophical construction of the two theorists. Especially given the undeniable polyphony and ambiguity of both men, it is hard not to grant Rorty—or anyone else who tries to interpret them, for that matter—a considerable degree of hermeneutic license. It is nonetheless pretty clear that Rorty chooses to characterize Whitman's and Dewey's beliefs in ways that make them assimilable to his own philosophical outlook. Moreover, I think that in turning Whitman and Dewey into proto-postmodernists, Rorty arguably misconstrues them in several respects. Perhaps it would be most accurate to say that he says things about them that amount to misleading half-truths. Some of these discrepancies, as I see them, have implications for both democratic theory and democratic practice. Thus, while I am willing to grant Rorty the hermeneutic license to rhetorically redescribe these two thinkers he admires in ways he finds comfortable for his own convictions, I want to enter a few reservations that are no doubt driven in part by my own somewhat different philosophical commitments.

There are three points at issue here. The first is Rorty's attempt to ascribe to Whitman and Dewey the postmodern depiction of human selves as entirely contingent. The second is his characterization of Whitman and Dewey as thoroughgoing secularists. The third is his claim that they "substituted social justice for individual freedom as our country's principal goal."[33] Each of these claims includes an important truth about Whitman and Dewey. But each of these assertions also includes—or at least could easily be taken to imply—something about them which is inaccurate and misleading.

[33] Rorty, *Achieving Our Country*, 101.

Rorty tells us that "Dewey's philosophy is a systematic attempt to temporalize everything, to leave nothing fixed. This means abandoning the attempt to find a theoretical frame of reference within which to evaluate proposals for the human future." He attributes to both Whitman and Dewey the idea that "the trouble with Europe . . . was that it tried too hard for knowledge: it tried to find an answer to the question of what human beings should be like." He claims that von Humboldt, whose advocacy of "the absolute and essential importance of human development in its richest diversity" was used by Mill as his epigram for *On Liberty*, suggested "abandoning this hope" for finding such an answer. Moreover, Rorty claims that in "picking up this particular ball from Mill" Whitman bought into this view—that Whitman's "romance of endless diversity" assumed that there was nothing fixed in human nature, no "template on which to model our future."[34]

There is some truth to this characterization. Dewey did indeed speak about modern man as inhabiting "a wide open universe, a universe without bounds in time or space, without final limits of origin or destiny, a universe with the lid off." He also spoke of "the abandonment of a fixed and static moral end." However, Dewey also took seriously, as I have noted, what he called the "enduring values" of liberalism: freedom, individual development, and the techniques and norms of rational inquiry. These were, for him, not merely contingent constructs up for grabs. The abolition of the notion of a single "final goal" of humankind was not, in his mind, to be succeeded by mere whimsy or custom but instead by a "diversity of specific goods." And the abandonment of the idea of "the separate and infallible faculty in morals" (Dewey's characterizations of positions he opposed were sometimes as caricatured as Rorty's rhetorical reconstructions of the views of his own targets) was not to be succeeded by mere will or emotion but by a "progressive science of both things and morals."[35] Similarly, the undeniable "romance of diversity" exhibited by Mill, Whitman, and Dewey entailed their common recognition of valuable differences among human beings and their common anticipation of unimaginable and novel forms of human life in the future. Mill, however, found that view entirely compatible with his insistence that not only were there such things as mental and moral development but that these provided the paramount standard for judging the goodness and legitimacy of various political regimes.

Rorty is also correct, but only partly so, in saying that "the most striking feature of [Whitman and Dewey's] redescription of our country was its thoroughgoing secularism." "Secularism" is an ambiguous and multivalent notion. It is surely correct to call the political ideals of Whitman and Dewey "secularist" both in the sense that they were interested in the

---

[34] Ibid., 20, 23–24.
[35] Dewey, "Intelligence and Morals," 67, 74.

fulfillment of human potentialities in this world rather than in a post-humous Kingdom of God and in the sense that their account of this fulfillment was not governed by religious doctrine. But "secularism" is also taken at times to mean a fixation upon material rather than spiritual goods and to connote ideas incompatible with religious belief. Although Whitman and Dewey (and Mill also, for that matter) were unbelievers in the traditional sense, their enthusiasm for democracy was clearly a function of what they thought it could achieve for the human spirit rather than for material advance. Their account of democratic faith was, as Rorty says, a kind of civic religion. This is a civic religion, moreover, that—though no doubt incompatible with some forms of religious faith—is not necessarily beyond acceptance on the part of believers in transcendental verities. An example of such a believer comes from Rorty's own extended family, in fact: his maternal grandfather, the social gospel theologian Walter Rauschenbusch.

It is also, I believe, only partly true—or only true in a certain sense—that Whitman and Dewey "wanted the struggle for social justice to be the animating principle" of their civic religion.[36] This claim may be correct in the sense that Whitman and Dewey thought the promise of democracy was that all should and could be free—that all the members of a fully developed democratic society should be "full-grown" men and women, as Whitman put it. And for that to happen, the distribution of material resources in the society had to permit it—had to be less unequal than in previous forms of society, where the serfs, plebes, or commoners essentially served more as fodder for the lives of their betters than as "separate and complete subjects for freedom."[37] In that sense, a demand for "social justice" is indeed an important part of their vision of a more democratic future.

That said, two caveats need to be entered, not only to understand the civic religion of Whitman and Dewey properly, but also to make clear the difference between them and contemporary rights-based social justice liberals. The first caveat concerns what Whitman and Dewey considered as the content of social justice; the second concerns what they saw as its status in the pantheon of political goods. Social justice, for them, did not mean the greatest possible degree of social and economic equality. They presumed not only that some differences in social standing and economic achievement would be part of the democratic future but that these differences were "pre-institutionally" justifiable, as contemporary analysts of conceptions of justice would put it. Rorty himself, in his characterization of "the reformist left," probably gets this about right: "By 'justice' they all meant pretty much the same thing—decent wages and working conditions, and the end of racial prejudice."[38] For Whitman and Dewey,

[36] Rorty, *Achieving Our Country*, 18.
[37] Whitman, "Democratic Vistas," 971.
[38] Rorty, *Achieving Our Country*, 59.

social justice did not mean maximum feasible equality of what Rawls calls the "social primary goods" of power and opportunities, income and wealth, and social status. It meant the achievement of civic equality and an end to economic exploitation, political oppression, and social exclusion. Moreover, so far as the status of social justice among political goods was a question for people like Whitman and Dewey—and for those I have called "populist perfectionists" in general—they certainly considered it an essential virtue of social institutions. But they would not have considered it to be the first virtue of social institutions, if that were to mean its attainment was the highest purpose of democracy. That pride of place goes instead to the neo-Aristotelian good of self-realization, along with the self-rule necessary for it. "What does civilization itself rest upon?" Whitman asks rhetorically. "What object has it, with its religions, arts, schools, etc., but rich, luxuriant, and varied personalism? To that, all bends, and it is because toward such result democracy alone . . . breaks up the limitless fallows of humankind, and plants the seed, and gives fair play, that its claims now precede the rest." [39]

## VI. Liberal Deontology or Liberal Perfectionism?

This last point, indeed, provides a point of departure for what I earlier mentioned as a needed supplement to Rorty's brief on behalf of Whitman, Dewey, and those who share their account of the hope and ideals of democracy. That supplement is a few words in explanation of why Rorty could recommend the Whitman-Dewey account of the moral foundations of democratic society to us over the account of those foundations offered by rights-based social democrats. This latter account, after all, remains a very influential one which arguably has as many or more adherents as does the "cultural left" that Rorty takes as his rhetorical adversary. The absence of any riposte in this direction seems a notable and curious one: it is striking to observe that the index of Rorty's *Achieving Our Country* includes eight references to Foucault, six to Heidegger, three to Jacques Lacan, and exactly zero to John Rawls. Moreover, Rawlsian rights-based liberals would certainly be in agreement with Rorty's contention that social justice should be "the country's animating principle" and that it should be "substituted for individual freedom as our country's principal goal." [40] So the obvious question—to which Rorty offers no apparent answer—becomes: Why bother trying to resurrect Whitman and Dewey for our edification and inspiration? Why not just say something like: American political reformers should forget Continental theorists like Heidegger and Foucault and just stick with John Rawls?

[39] Whitman, "Democratic Vistas," 982.
[40] Rorty, *Achieving Our Country*, 18, 101.

This is a large and important question requiring a lot more space than is available here to answer properly. Let me settle for stating in cryptic form what I think Rorty might have and should have said in response to the question he begs. The best one-sentence answer to the question "If social justice is the principal goal of American progressivism, why not just endorse Rawls?," I think, was provided by William Galston when he wrote that "Rawls offers us a dangerously one-sided reconstruction of the liberal tradition, the inadequacies of which are mirrored in the national electoral disasters of contemporary liberalism."[41] I agree with both the theoretical and the practical judgments encapsulated in this assessment; but I will confine my remarks here to the theoretical issues at hand, and of these issues I will focus on what seem to me the most central fissures between Rawlsian liberalism and the Whitman-Dewey version that Rorty and I favor.

Rawls has two basic reasons for rejecting the kind of liberalism found in people like Whitman and Dewey. Each of these reasons is embedded in the central thesis and underlying assumptions of one of his two major books. The first reason is set out in the argument of *A Theory of Justice*.[42] Based upon that argument, Rawls would insist that the conception of social justice in the Whitman-Dewey tradition was unnecessarily vague and inadequately demanding. Instead of settling for the rather general and indeterminate conception of social justice found in this older tradition— more or less the "decent wages and working conditions and the end of racial prejudice" referred to by Rorty—we can, Rawls argued, ascertain a much more precise standard for social justice. By taking the moral intuitions at the foundation of contemporary liberal democratic societies as our axioms and working out their implications for distributive principles, we can produce a "moral geometry" whose conclusions will provide us a determinate conception of social justice. When we perform this rational-choice thought experiment, moreover, we can say with confidence that the demands of social justice are highly egalitarian—that what justice demands is that our constitutional provisions and social policies operate so as to maximize the absolute welfare of the least well-off members of society. Returning to the earlier, more indeterminate, and less demanding account of social justice found in people like Whitman and Dewey, therefore, would constitute, in Rawls's view, a kind of moral backsliding.

Rawls's second basic objection to the Whitman-Dewey tradition is the central difficulty he seeks to surmount in his *Political Liberalism*.[43] The problem Rawls seeks to solve with his account of "political liberalism," he would argue, is one that afflicts and ultimately morally invalidates not only the Whitman-Dewey version of democratic hopes but all other ver-

---

[41] William Galston, *Liberal Purposes* (Cambridge: Cambridge University Press, 1991), 162.
[42] Rawls, *A Theory of Justice* (see note 4 above).
[43] John Rawls, *Political Liberalism* (New York: Columbia University Press, 1993).

sions of "perfectionist" liberalism. The self-delegitimating difficulty Rawls sees as common to all "perfectionist" social theories is this: If the highest goal of a society is to be "self-realization," the society must de facto endorse a particular conception of the human good. We can orient our social enterprise around "mental and moral improvement" (Mill) or "the forming of a full-grown man or woman" (Whitman) only if we have and enforce a single determinate model of human perfection. In a morally and religiously pluralistic society, however, where citizens affirm multiple divergent conceptions of the good life, this must have the consequence of violating the norms of reciprocity at the heart of the equal protection of the laws and must also have the consequence of constraining the freedom of those who do not accept the officially endorsed account of human self-realization. In short, all perfectionist accounts of democratic purposes—and that includes those offered by Whitman and Dewey—are discriminatory and oppressive. To retain our liberal bona fides, therefore, Rawls would insist, we must reject their accounts, limit our common purposes and the moral foundations of our society to the principles of justice upon which we can agree despite the variance in our conceptions of human fulfillment, and simply leave it to each of us freely to pursue happiness as we see fit after we get the distribution of social resources properly taken care of.

These are weighty objections, which have seemed compelling to many. Neither of these objections, however, is in my view finally persuasive. In defense of Whitman, Dewey, and what I have called their "populist perfectionism," Rorty could have responded as follows.

To the complaint that their conception of social justice is too indeterminate and insufficiently stringent by egalitarian standards, there are two proper rejoinders: First, any fully determinate account of absolute fairness in the distribution of social and economic resources is delusionary. Second, the moral assumptions necessary to sustain a rigorously egalitarian conception of social justice, such as the one offered by Rawls,[44] are not only at odds with the considered judgments of many, if not most, of the members of contemporary democratic societies, but also stand in tension with other widely held moral beliefs that are intimately connected with liberal democratic practices and principles. Given the moral tragedies, complexities, and uncertainties endemic to the human condition, that condition admits of no "moral geometry" when it comes to arriving at principles of distributive justice. The various members of all societies, including democratic ones, differ in their natural talents, in the contingent

---

[44] This is the standard found in Rawls's second principle of justice, his "difference principle," whose imperatives are "basic throughout . . . [his] general conception of justice." That general conception is that "all social values—liberty and opportunity, income and wealth, and the bases of self-respect—are to be distributed equally unless an unequal distribution . . . is to everyone's advantage"; and "to everyone's advantage" is to mean "to the greatest benefit of the least advantaged." Rawls, *A Theory of Justice*, 83, 62.

circumstances in which life places them, in their levels of productive effort, in their willingness to delay or sacrifice gratification on behalf of future benefits or common purposes, and in the conceptions of the human good that shape their actions. Moreover, our cognitive limitations do not permit us to know with any great degree of reliability the relative causal contributions of these various differences in creating the inequalities of social and economic goods found in all societies. Nor do reasonable people fully agree about which of these differences in our attributes and behaviors provide moral justification for such inequalities and to what extent they may so function. As a result, claims that there is such a thing as a moral geometry of social justice and that its conclusions can be consensually subscribed to by all reasonable citizens of contemporary democracies are not sustainable. Once these claims are rejected, we no longer have grounds for dismissing the conception of social justice within the Whitman-Dewey tradition because its standards are not fully determinate: all accounts of social justice are contestable by reasonable people, even within the bounds of adherence to liberal and democratic norms. What Rawlsians depict as a failure of the older account of social justice is, therefore, no failure at all, but simply an unavoidable concession to reality and a proper recognition of the moral complexities of fairness within the somewhat tragic circumstances of justice.

Upon examination, moreover, it turns out that the Rawlsian identification of distributive justice with the greatest degree of equality consistent with collective rationality depends upon the assumption that nothing people do can provide them any moral warrant for claiming they have "earned" anything. This denial of all pre-institutional desert, in turn, seems to depend on a "naturalistic" account of behavior incompatible with standard notions of moral responsibility. And the abandonment of that notion serves not only, as Galston observes, to "sever [liberalism's] bonds with the moral convictions of the working class," but also to "flatly reject the conception of the person underlying our beliefs and practices."[45] The stringency of the content of their conception of social justice, which Rawlsian liberals cite as a sign of the superiority of their account to earlier liberal accounts, turns out instead to be a moral step backward in other respects.

Rawls's charge that the kind of perfectionism embodied within the political tradition represented by Whitman and Dewey is oppressive and violates the liberal principle of legitimacy also seems unconvincing. This argument is based on a stylized distinction Rawls seeks to make between "political" and "comprehensive" models of liberalism. "Political" conceptions "remain on the surface" philosophically, resting only on moral

---

[45] Galston, *Liberal Purposes*, 161. These beliefs and practices include the conception of human freedom and dignity widely associated with the idea of human and civil rights and the conception of accountability for one's deeds incorporated in the doctrine of *mens rea*.

assumptions regarding fair terms of social cooperation and eschewing any commitment to particular conceptions of the human good. "Comprehensive" conceptions, in contrast, endorse and depend upon some complete and particular account of the human good. Thus, the argument runs, "political" models of liberalism can deal even-handedly with all the citizens in a pluralistic democratic society, who govern their lives by different and incompatible moral and religious beliefs about the good life. In contrast, "comprehensive" models of liberalism cannot treat all citizens in such a pluralist society with equal respect and will not allow them all the same freedom to pursue happiness as they see fit.

The defect in this argument is that the stylized contrast it rests on may make sense in abstract philosophical space but breaks down when applied to the real world. The fact is that no liberal theory—probably no public philosophy of any sort—can fulfill the neutrality condition of the abstract ideal-typical model of a "political" conception. None can be so teleologically abstemious. All are at least "minimally perfectionist," as Galston puts it; and that certainly includes Rawls's own favored model.[46] And on the other side of the ideal-typical dichotomy, only extremely detailed and dogmatic conceptions of the good society (such as, say, a Taliban-style theocracy) approach dependence upon a genuinely "comprehensive" conception of the form of human life to which the social order is dedicated.

Certainly, in any case, the minimally perfectionist norms of self-realization found in Whitman's and Dewey's democratic idealism do not answer to Rawls's characterization. The implausibility of this way of characterizing, and consequently rejecting as illiberal, the role and degree of commitment to a specific account of the humanly good life in Whitman, Dewey, or Mill seems obvious when one wonders how these theories could be depicted simultaneously as dependent upon a comprehensive conception of the good (by Rawls) and as exhibiting a quasi-postmodernist affirmation of riotously diverse ways of life (by Rorty). The truth of the matter, I believe, falls somewhere between these extremes. The form of democratic idealism represented by Whitman and Dewey is properly seen as perfectionist, but theirs is a partial and "open-ended" perfectionism. They envision all the members of the democratic societies they hope for as displaying all the capacities people require in order to be able to be full subjects of freedom and as exhibiting those civic virtues necessary for democratic self-rule to succeed. After that, the members of society are turned loose—free and able to pursue their own versions of personal fulfillment. Whitman, for example, hopes for "the copious production of perfect characters among the people," but that refers to the democratic civic virtues. Whitman certainly does not envision or celebrate the kind of "narrow theory of life" that Mill attributes to Calvinism or the alleged "Chinese ideal of

---

[46] Ibid., 177.

making all people alike" that Mill specifically denounces in the very text Whitman cites as the inspiration for his "Democratic Vistas."[47] Instead, although all the citizens in the democratic future Whitman envisions will share a "democratic character," the lives they lead will be "rich, luxuriant, and varied."[48] He anticipates and exults in the prospect of the open-ended and unimaginable individual diversity that Mill celebrates as "noble and beautiful."[49] To construe this kind of partially perfectionist democratic idealism as oppressive and inappropriate for a pluralistic society such as ours could seem plausible, I think, only to someone in the grip of a profoundly misleading kind of academic scholasticism.

## VII. CONCLUSION

Somewhat lost in the shuffle amid the recent prominence of rights-based liberalism, republicanism, and communitarianism is another kind of American liberalism. That liberalism, best represented by figures such as Walt Whitman and John Dewey, might be called "populist perfectionism," because its ultimate political aspiration is that all democratic citizens should become enabled to rule themselves and to actualize their talents and capabilities to the fullest possible extent. Philosophically speaking, the inspiration for this orientation comes more from Mill and Hegel than from Locke, Kant, or civic republicanism.

Although this conception of democratic purposes no doubt requires updating and revision to be fully pertinent to the challenges of American society in the twenty-first century, that is a task that contemporary adherents of reform liberalism might well consider undertaking. For populist perfectionism is a democratic idealism that is devoted to social justice without being encumbered by the problematic features of rights-based liberalism or entangled in the alienating fatalism that, as Richard Rorty observes, seems to incapacitate the cultural left.

*Political Science, Duke University*

---

[47] Mill, *On Liberty*, 75–84.
[48] Whitman, "Democratic Vistas," 982–83.
[49] Mill, *On Liberty*, 76.

# PROCEDURAL VERSUS SUBSTANTIVE JUSTICE:
## RAWLS AND NOZICK

By David Lewis Schaefer

## I. Introduction

For over three decades, it has been common to represent John Rawls's *A Theory of Justice* (1971, revised edition 1999) and his Harvard colleague Robert Nozick's *Anarchy, State, and Utopia* (1974) as exemplifying the fundamental alternative paths available for liberal political philosophy in the contemporary world.[1] Both authors hold that justice must take primacy over merely utilitarian considerations. Both authors, broadly imitating the social-contract tradition of early modern liberalism, derive the principles of justice from a hypothetical, prepolitical condition in which human beings are conceived as equal and free (although Nozick, unlike Rawls, refrains from founding justice on a hypothetical contract). Nonetheless, they differ over the implications of that freedom and equality for the content of justice.

For Rawls, the sense of justice that we share dictates that the parties who lay down the principles of justice be conceived as acting under a "veil of ignorance" that prevents anyone from knowing his particular abilities or even his conception of the good, so that he cannot bias the choice of principles to favor himself. One critical implication, according to Rawls, is that the principles of justice must be designed to safeguard each individual against the worst possible outcomes. As a consequence, Rawls argues, the parties would be most likely to agree on a set of principles that dictate (1) the priority of the equal, "basic" liberties for each person, guaranteeing him against the possibility of subjugation under a hierarchical regime, as well as against the elevation of other conceptions of the good over the one he will find he holds (once the veil is lifted); and (2) the regulation of primary goods other than liberty according to the rules of (a) legal equality of opportunity for all and (b) the "difference principle."

[1] John Rawls, *A Theory of Justice*, revised ed. (Cambridge, MA: Belknap Press of Harvard University Press, 1999); Robert Nozick, *Anarchy, State, and Utopia* (New York: Basic Books, 1974). References to these two books—abbreviated as *TJ* and *ASU*, respectively—will be inserted parenthetically in the text.

Parts of Section VI of this essay derive from my article "Libertarianism and Political Philosophy: A Critique of Robert Nozick's *Anarchy, State, and Utopia*," *Interpretation: A Journal of Political Philosophy* 12, nos. 2–3 (May–September 1984): 301–34. Additionally, Section V draws on my forthcoming book *Illiberal Justice: John Rawls vs. the American Political Tradition* (Columbia: University of Missouri Press, 2007). I am grateful to the publishers for permission to reprint this material.

© 2007 Social Philosophy & Policy Foundation. Printed in the USA.

The difference principle, in turn, ordains that inequalities in social and economic goods besides liberty are allowable only to the extent that they improve the lot of the "least advantaged" members of society, compared to what their lives would have been like without such inequalities (*TJ*, 266). Rawls uses the difference principle to mandate not only an extensive welfare state, but also the adoption of tax, antitrust, and other policies designed to guarantee that under a regime of private property, ownership of the means of production is "widely distributed." (Rawls leaves it open whether the difference principle is best effectuated in given circumstances under such a "property owning democracy" or a "liberal socialist" regime [*TJ*, 228, 235].)

By contrast, Nozick conceives the inhabitants of his prepolitical condition (which he calls the "state of nature") as more *like* actual human beings, in that he imagines no veil of ignorance to constrain their decisions. Moreover, unlike Rawls, he uses his account of the prepolitical condition to determine the nature of legitimate government, rather than to articulate comprehensive principles of justice. But his account of the prepolitical situation is no less abstract than Rawls's, since he portrays it as a condition of relatively peaceful coexistence among independent individuals, without attempting to demonstrate that such a condition ever has existed, or could exist, among actual human beings. Instead, he simply rejects Thomas Hobbes's account of the state of nature as a war of every individual against every other in which life is "solitary, poor, nasty, brutish, and short," on the ground that such "awful descriptions" of the prepolitical condition "rarely convince," since "[t]he subjects of psychology and sociology are far too feeble to support generalizing so pessimistically across all societies and persons." Moreover, Nozick maintains, the argument inferring the need for government from such fearsome accounts of the alternative is inconsistent, "since the argument depends upon *not* making *such* pessimistic assumptions about how the *state* operates" (*ASU*, 4; emphasis in original). It would be more useful and persuasive, Nozick believes, "to focus upon a nonstate situation in which people generally satisfy moral constraints and generally act as they ought." Only "if one could show that the state would be superior even to this most favored situation of anarchy, the best that realistically can be hoped for, or would arise [from it] by a process involving no morally impermissible steps" could one morally justify the existence of a state at all (*ASU*, 5).

I shall not trace here the process by which Nozick represents a "minimal" or "night-watchman" state, and *only* such a state, as hypothetically evolving from the prepolitical condition in a manner that conforms fully to moral constraints, in that it does not violate anyone's right to autonomy. Rather, I wish to focus on certain respects in which Rawls and Nozick, despite their seeming disagreement about whether just government must regulate the economy so as to ensure a "fair" distribution of wealth and income, *agree* on certain more fundamental points. Those points of agreement include (1) the attempt to substitute a "procedural" account of justice for a substantive one; and (2) their view of the good and just society as one that is not grounded in any substantive view of the good life, but aims simply to provide human beings with the greatest freedom to live as they choose (so long as they obey the constraints of justice as the two authors respectively conceive it). After summarizing Rawls's procedural approach and Nozick's response to it in Sections II and III, I shall identify what I believe to be the root problems in that approach in Section IV. In Sections V and VI, I address the problems inherent in the moral libertarianism on which Rawls's and Nozick's visions of "utopia," or a perfectly just society, are grounded. Section VII pursues the contrast between their ultimately historicist visions of morality and the principles of natural right enshrined in the American Declaration of Independence. Finally, Section VIII more broadly contrasts the abstract visions of a free and just society devised by Rawls and Nozick with the actual, realistic constitutional-liberal principles on which the American political regime was founded.

## II. Rawls's "Procedural" Justice

Central to Rawls's project, both in *A Theory of Justice* and in his later book *Political Liberalism,* is the aspiration to achieve a "consensus" on the principles of justice, the absence of which he thinks constitutes evidence that existing societies are not "well-ordered" (*TJ,* 4–5). He believes that deriving principles from an original position in which all human beings are fairly represented as "moral persons" can help to supply that consensus (*TJ,* 11). In turn, having a set of agreed-on principles by which to measure the justice of a given political, social, and economic regime should assist us in making actual societies more just.

When it comes to applying his second principle of justice (regarding the distribution of goods other than the basic liberties), however, Rawls acknowledges that we cannot expect actual regimes to embody a *substantive* justice, in the sense that individuals are likely to receive what their own particular merit or moral desert entitles them to. He treats the question of distributive justice "as a matter of pure procedural justice," with the "social system" being designed "so that the outcome is just whatever it happens to be," at least "within a certain range" (*TJ,* 74). The "principle of fair opportunity" insures this result: "against the background of a just basic structure, including a just political constitution and a just arrangement of economic and social institutions," this principle enables one "to discard as irrelevant" (that is, irrelevant to the problem of justice) information about "the varying relative positions of individuals" or about particular transactions (*TJ,* 76).

Going beyond these claims, Rawls justifies his difference principle by denying that any individual deserves his "native endowments," or even "the superior character that enables us to make the effort to cultivate our abilities." Hence, Rawls denies that those blessed with superior endowments, or with the disposition to make the best of their endowments, "deserve" the greater rewards that those endowments might enable them to attain, unless those rewards are somehow "compensated for" to benefit the less advantaged (for instance, by spending "greater resources . . . on the education of the less rather than the more intelligent") (*TJ*, 86–89).

Finally, Rawls challenges the tendency of "common sense" to suppose that "the good things in life . . . should be distributed according to moral desert," so that the notion of justice as "happiness according to virtue" should be regarded as an "ideal" that society ought to aim to approximate. To the contrary, in Rawls's theory, "the principles of justice that regulate the basic structure" of society "do not mention moral desert, and there is no tendency for distributive shares to correspond to it." Since even "the effort a person is willing to make is influenced by his natural abilities and skills," there is no reason to try to reward such effort as a matter of justice. Thus, even under the best circumstances, there is "no tendency for distribution and virtue to coincide." Instead of seeking such a coincidence, we should be satisfied with knowing that "a just scheme gives each person his due" only in the sense that "it allots to each what he is entitled to as *defined* by the scheme itself," and the principles of justice that are selected in the original position "*establish* that doing this is fair" (*TJ*, 273–76; emphasis added).

### III. Nozick's Response

Nozick offers a trenchant critique of Rawls's account of distributive justice in chapter 7 of *Anarchy, State, and Utopia*. As Nozick observes, the very term "distributive justice" is misleading, since it implies that all goods originate in some "central distribution," rather than being acquired by individuals from others "in exchange for something, or as a gift" (*ASU*, 149). Nozick invites us to imagine a set of Robinson Crusoes, each working alone for two years on a separate island. Once these Crusoes eventually came into contact with one another, they would not "owe" some part of their product to the others, merely on account of that contact. Similarly, the sheer fact of social cooperation on which Rawls grounds his second principle of justice does not obviously entail such a debt (*ASU*, 185–86). And in a single society, if the better-endowed in Rawls's sense "manage to accomplish something of great advantage to others, such as new inventions" or the exercise of great productive skills, are they not *already* benefiting their less-advantaged peers? Why punish their industry by demanding that they pay a further "tax" to profit the less advantaged? (*ASU*, 193–95).

Rawls's veil of ignorance, Nozick observes, invites the parties to the original position to treat goods as if they "fell from heaven like manna," rather than having any connectedness to the individuals who produce them (*ASU*, 198–99). And doesn't Rawls's treatment of particular human excellences, including even the disposition to cultivate one's talents, as "the products of factors outside the person's control," and hence morally "arbitrary," embody an "unexalted picture of human beings" that sits uneasily with the conception of "human dignity" that Rawls wishes to advance? (*ASU*, 214). Moreover, doesn't Rawls's treatment of individuals' natural abilities as a "collective asset" embody precisely the fault that he attributes to the utilitarians of failing "to take seriously the distinction between persons"? (*ASU*, 228).

These are powerful objections to Rawls's view of justice. Yet it is not evident that Nozick himself offers a more solid foundation on which to build an account of justice. He seems to represent Rawls's theory as a "patterned," "current time-slice," or "end-result" account, one that aims to actualize a certain vision of what the just "distribution" (level of inequality) ought to look like at any particular moment (*ASU*, 153–64, 198–204). By contrast, Nozick's own "entitlement" theory is a "historical" one, which determines the justness of a distribution simply by examining "how it came about" (*ASU*, 153). "If the world were wholly just," Nozick writes, "justice in holdings" would be determined entirely by whether individuals had justly acquired a given good (through a just acquisition or transfer), and nobody would be entitled to a holding except by that means (*ASU*, 151).

The hypothetical premise I have just quoted, however, undercuts the very foundation of the entitlement theory. There is no reason to suppose that any actual person's present holdings derive from an unbroken series of "just" transactions stemming back to the origins of human history. Within existing polities, of course, the settlement of disputes among private parties over the title to a given piece of property commonly depends on the legal origins of that title, and whether it was transferred to anyone else in a legal manner. But the quest to authenticate a title in a court of law ordinarily ends, in even the most extreme cases, with the historical foundation of the political and legal regime from which the court derives its authority. (Even suits by American Indian tribes to regain title to lands represented as having been wrongly confiscated by other Americans depend on alleged violations of treaties signed with American governmental authorities, not on broader claims that the whole of America "belongs" to the Indians.)

Recognizing this difficulty, Nozick is forced, for the sake of consistency, to take back what he had "given" with his entitlement doctrine through what he calls "the principle of rectification." Having concluded that Rawls's principles by themselves offer no justification for mandatory economic redistribution, Nozick then suggests viewing "patterned principles of justice" such as Rawls's "as rough rules of thumb meant to approximate the general results of applying the principle of rectification of injustice." Since we lack "much historical information" about the ultimate origins of present holdings, Nozick even proposes adopting Rawls's own difference principle, on the (admittedly questionable) hypothesis that "those from the least well-off group" in a society "have the highest probabilities of being the (descendants of) victims of the most serious injustice who are owed compensation by those who benefited from the injustices." This assumes that those beneficiaries (or rather, it would appear, their descendants) are now among "those better off" (*ASU*, 230–31).

Nozick, then, offers no justification on his own terms for barring government from instituting far-reaching programs of economic redistribution, or racial and ethnic quotas in hiring and education. Indeed, his suggestion of targeting the rich as the most likely beneficiaries of past "injustice" not only flies in the face of continuing evidence of a high degree of intergenerational socioeconomic mobility in a constitutional democracy with a (largely) free-enterprise economy like the United States, but contradicts Nozick's own earlier criticism of Rawls for denying people moral title even to those goods they acquire as a result of their own efforts to develop their talents.[2]

## IV. "Procedural" versus Political Justice

Nozick thus proves to be no real friend of economic liberty or of the principle of treating people as individuals (as called for under the natural-rights doctrine of the American Declaration of Independence), rather than as members of more or less arbitrarily defined economic, racial, or ethnic groups. But his failure to offer an effective defense of liberty is rooted, I suggest, in the abstract, "theoretical" approach that he adopts to justice, in common with Rawls—an approach that ignores the actual human or political circumstances in which issues of justice arise, and gives short shrift to what Rawls called our "common-sense" (but, according to Rawls, erroneous) opinions about justice.

---

[2] Since the fact of continuing socioeconomic mobility in the United States not only undermines the ground for Nozick's proposed application of his rectification principle, but also challenges the need for anything like Rawls's difference principle, it will be worthwhile to cite some of the relevant evidence. Statistics commonly cited to show the alleged persistence of fixed economic differences among "classes" in America commonly mislead because they fail to follow the course of *individuals'* economic circumstances over time: even as the incomes of many members of the "lower" class rise over time, their place is often taken by new immigrants who most often start at the bottom. Individual incomes naturally rise, as well, as people age, then decline once they retire. Hence the economist Thomas Sowell notes that studies that tracked individual Americans over a period of years "have found that most do not stay in the same quintile of the income distribution for as long as a decade," and that "only 3 percent of the American population remained in the bottom 20 percent for as long as eight years. More who began in the bottom 20 percent had reached the top 20 percent by the end of that period than remained where they were." Thomas Sowell, *The Quest for Cosmic Justice* (New York: Simon and Schuster, 1999), 38–39. See also Bruce Bartlett, "Class Struggle in America?" *Commentary* 120, no. 1 (July–August 2005): 33–38, at 34; and W. Michael Cox, "It's Not a Wage Gap but an Age Gap," *New York Times*, April 21, 1996, p. 15 (citing the University of Michigan Panel Survey on Income Dynamics).

Despite Nozick's distinction between his ostensibly "historical" account of justice and Rawls's "time-slice" or "end-result" account, Nozick explicitly *agrees* with Rawls that a just distribution of goods is not to be measured by people's moral desert (*ASU*, 217), and more generally that the justice of any given distribution should be assessed solely by the justice of the *procedure* that generated it (*ASU*, 151, 159). The apparent difference in their conclusions is simply a consequence of the different aspects of human existence that they abstract from at the outset. Nozick rightly takes Rawls to task for abstracting from the fact of human individuality and (partial) self-ownership, which entails that no one's natural gifts or efforts may justly be treated as if they were merely a "common asset" whose fruits may be redistributed in accordance with some theorist's fancy. In turn, however, Nozick himself abstracts from the essentially political character of human existence, which entails that no individual can properly be regarded as the sole producer or "owner" of the goods he lawfully acquires, without any concomitant obligations to his fellow citizens. Contrary to Rawls, it is not the vague fact of "social cooperation" that makes us interdependent, but our mutual dependence on a political structure of government and laws, as well as on the readiness of other citizens to risk their own lives, when necessary, to defend the lives and liberties, and the property, of their countrymen.

Nozick dismisses the social-cooperation argument by comparing it to the demand that any inhabitant of a neighborhood that establishes a "system of public entertainment" or a street-sweeping program is obliged to contribute to it, just because he benefits from it (*ASU*, 93–94). But government, unlike entertainment or even clean streets, is not an "optional" benefit for human beings. Contrary to Nozick, Hobbes's argument that stable government is the precondition of all other worthwhile human activity depends not on a "pessimistic" view of humanity—Hobbes explicitly denies such a claim[3]—but rather on the evident facts of human life, specifically the natural conflict of interests and desires among human beings, given their unlimited desires and the limited stock of good things (including honor and political power as well as economic goods) available to satisfy them.

While Hobbes may have underestimated the need to structure government so that it does not itself become oppressive of the rights that it is properly instituted to secure, his successor John Locke fully anticipated Nozick's counsel against that danger. But while Locke is the immediate source for Nozick's account of just acquisition, Locke's treatment of how an individual might become the "owner" of an object or piece of land simply by applying his labor to it is a prepolitical one. While asserting that each human being is naturally the proprietor of

---

[3] See Thomas Hobbes, *Leviathan*, ed. E. M. Curley (Indianapolis, IN: Hackett, 1994), chap. 13, par. 10: "The desires and other passions of man are in themselves no sin."

his own life, liberty, and property, Locke also notes that these rights would be wholly ineffectual—for practical purposes, meaningless—in the absence of a government established to protect them. And agreeing to the establishment of government entails forfeiting our unlimited right to "execute" the laws of nature against trespassers—in return for more secure, albeit limited, rights to the security of our lives, lawfully acquired property, and lawful liberty under government.[4] As Locke observes near the end of the chapter on property in his *Second Treatise*, "in Governments the Laws regulate the right of property, and the possession of land is determined by positive constitutions."[5] Contrary to Nozick's hedging assertion that taxation of people's earnings is "on a par with forced labor" (*ASU*, 169), Locke holds that the critical security against abusive taxation (as well as other forms of oppression) is a government whose authority ultimately derives from the governed, in which legislative and executive authorities are separated, legislators are themselves subject to the laws they enact, and taxes may not be levied without the consent of the people's elected representatives.[6]

Of course, there is no *guarantee*, under the Lockean system or under any other, that people's earnings or wealth will be proportionate to their effort or their moral desert. Certainly, however, the Lockean presumption against arbitrary confiscation of one's property (and against arbitrary imprisonment or arrest), as well as the institutionalization of government by consent, makes it *more likely* than under an absolutist dictatorship or monarchy (or a hereditary caste system) that individuals will enjoy the opportunity to advance themselves in accordance with their own efforts and talents. This fact itself should weaken the disposition toward the envy of other people's attainments that Nozick rightly suggests underlies Rawls's doctrine (*ASU*, 229).

Nonetheless, the mere fact of having to acquire wealth through one's own labor (or that of one's parents or ancestors) will not suffice to legitimize a political or economic regime, unless the system is seen *on the whole* to encourage desirable moral traits besides economic enterprise. How can real human beings be brought to suppress their common-sense judgments of morality and justice in favor of a procedure that merely "defines" what is just as the outcome of a certain procedure?[7] Can any successful

---

[4] John Locke, *Second Treatise*, in Locke, *Two Treatises of Government*, ed. Peter Laslett (New York: New American Library, 1963), chap. 9.

[5] Ibid., chap. 5, sec. 50, lines 14–16.

[6] Ibid., chap. 7, sec. 94 (lines 20–32), and chap. 11, secs. 138, 140–42. For a thorough analysis of the meaning of consent in Locke, stressing its democratic implications, see Peter Josephson, *The Great Art of Government: Locke's Use of Consent* (Lawrence: University Press of Kansas, 2002).

[7] Cf. David Wiggins's response to Rawls's account of "pure procedural justice": "It is not an accident that human beings have always made it a requirement on human justice that one should be able to see as just that which really is just." Wiggins, "Neo-Aristotelian Reflections on Justice," *Mind* 113, no. 451 (July 2004): 506. On the need for the system of free enterprise

political regime be founded on the demand that we avoid assessing the substantive justice of the way of life it engenders, as Rawls and Nozick would have us do?

These questions lead me to address a further commonality between Rawls's and Nozick's doctrines: their representation of an ideally just society as a regime in which government makes no moral demands, and sets no moral restrictions, on its citizens, other than those directly entailed by each author's respective account of justice.

## V. RAWLS'S UTOPIA

It is symptomatic of the narrowness of focus of much of today's academic, liberal political philosophy that Rawls and Nozick are commonly treated as if they represent almost polar opposites, because of their seeming difference on the issue of economic redistribution, or "social justice," when they agree so thoroughly on other aspects of the good and just society. This agreement is evident if one compares Rawls's interpretation of his first principle of justice (mandating the priority of equal liberty over other goods), along with his account of the good society in Part III of *A Theory of Justice*, with the last chapter of Nozick's *Anarchy, State, and Utopia*, titled "A Framework for Utopia."

One of the more curious aspects of Rawls's veil of ignorance is his mandate that the parties who are to arrive at principles of justice must be kept ignorant not only of their particular talents and abilities (so as to prevent them from "fixing" the rules to favor their own interests), but also of their conceptions of the good. Rawls justifies the latter requirement by articulating his "notion of a free person." He describes free individuals as people "who do not think of themselves as inevitably bound to . . . the pursuit of any particular complex of fundamental interests," but rather "give first priority" to preserving their liberty to "revise and alter their final ends." It follows, according to Rawls, that they will want to rank that liberty above other goods in order to guarantee "their highest-order interest as free persons" (*TJ*, 131–32).

This argument is tautological. It amounts to saying that people who prefer freedom to other goods will also prefer to be governed by principles that elevate freedom over other goods. One must question, however, whether this account of the relation between people's freedom and their "final ends" is at all coherent or psychologically intelligible. If people's first priority is to retain the right to revise their final ends whenever they choose, it appears that *no* end is ever meaningfully final. In what sense can we speak of such individuals' expressing "devotion to these ends"

---

to be perceived as resting on a higher moral principle than that of sheer self-interest, see Irving Kristol, "Horatio Alger and Profits," and "When Virtue Loses All Her Loveliness," in Kristol, *Two Cheers for Capitalism* (New York: Basic Books, 1978), 84–89, 257–68.

(*TJ*, 132), as opposed to being devoted to their right to revise them? Doesn't devotion to an end, a cause, or another human being entail committing oneself *not* to desert them? Despite Rawls's pretense of making the deliberations in the original position independent of any particular conception of the good, it would appear that he has actually presupposed a particular, highly questionable view of the good—preeminently, the merely abstract "freedom" to change one's commitments—without submitting this view to critical assessment.

Be this as it may, Rawls infers from the priority of liberty as he understands it a sweeping right to "liberty of conscience" that encompasses far more than that right has traditionally been understood to entail. Since (thanks to the veil of ignorance) the parties in the original position "do not know ... what their religious or moral convictions are, or ... the particular content of their moral or religious obligations as they interpret them," and do not even "know that they think of themselves as having such obligations" at all, "they cannot take chances with their liberty" by adopting a principle that would allow "the dominant religious or moral doctrine to persecute or to suppress others." What is in question, however, is not merely religious "suppression" or "persecution" as these terms are ordinarily understood. Rather, beyond specifying that "the state can favor no particular religion" and may not penalize dissenting religious sects (*TJ*, 186), Rawls holds that in accordance with the principle of neutrality among conflicting moral beliefs, government must also avoid regulating people's conduct on the basis of any particular view of human excellence or dignity. Hence, he explains, government may not prohibit sexual relationships that are thought to be "degrading and shameful," since such judgments reflect "subtle aesthetic preferences" about which individuals may disagree (*TJ*, 291).

Rawls's prescription of strict governmental neutrality on issues of personal morality accords well with political beliefs that are widespread in the contemporary academy, as well as with the thrust of numerous Supreme Court decisions over recent decades (for instance, the Court's 2003 ruling in *Lawrence v. Texas* that state laws against homosexual sodomy are unconstitutional, and earlier decisions severely restricting the capacity of local governments to prohibit the dissemination of pornography). But even the Supreme Court has not (yet) pushed the principle of moral neutrality to its logical limit (e.g., by striking down laws banning polygamy). Moreover, regardless of whether one judges this judicial policy to be sound, it is hard to see how the prescription of governmental neutrality regarding sexual morality can properly be described as a pure dictate of impartial *justice*. (Contrary to the misleading impression engendered by Rawls's veil of ignorance, justice is normally understood to entail the impartial treatment of actual human beings, not an unqualified agnosticism regarding alternative conceptions of the good.) Rather, in holding that government must be firmly neutral among competing religious and moral beliefs on the ground that to do otherwise would improperly make some individuals the interpreters of other people's religious and moral duties (*TJ*, 182–83), isn't Rawls really setting *himself* up as the authoritative interpreter of everyone's religious and moral duties?[8] And what qualifies him to exercise this authority?

Having devised the rules of justice so as ostensibly to accommodate the greatest diversity in people's conceptions of the good or "life plans," Rawls then proceeds in Part III of *A Theory of Justice* to try to show how such diversity is at the same time compatible with or conducive to the greatest possible degree of social unity. Here he explains that his doctrine views human beings as social creatures who share "final ends" and value their "common institutions and activities." Borrowing from the nineteenth-century liberal theorist Wilhelm von Humboldt (a source for John Stuart Mill's notion of individuality in *On Liberty*), Rawls explains that it is only through social union that each person overcomes the limitations of his own capacities and opportunities so as to share in his fellows' "realized natural assets." This community extends over time, so that we profit from our predecessors' achievements and in turn develop our own capacities for the benefit of our descendants (*TJ*, 458–60). When all citizens have "a shared final end and accepted ways of advancing it" that facilitate "public recognition" of everyone's attainments, we can say (as Socrates ironically maintains of the best city in Plato's *Republic* [462c–d]) that "all find satisfaction in the very same thing" (*TJ*, 462).

Such profound thinkers as Edmund Burke have plausibly represented civilization as a partnership among generations.[9] Indeed, the notion of political society as having a shared good that transcends individual interests can be said to characterize preliberal political philosophy as a whole, as well as liberal political thought as articulated by statesmen like Abraham Lincoln. Yet outside the realm of religious prophecy, no serious thinker ever promised such a unity of "satisfaction" among citizens as Rawls attributes to his well-ordered society.[10] (Isn't this unity more nat-

---

[8] Cf. Benjamin Barber, "Justifying Justice: Problems of Psychology, Politics, and Measurement in Rawls," in Norman Daniels, ed., *Reading Rawls* (New York: Basic Books, 1975), 313–14; Victor Gourevitch, "Rawls on Justice," *Review of Metaphysics* 28, no. 3 (March 1975): 494–98; and John Gray's valuable distinction between Rawlsian neutrality and toleration properly understood in Gray, *Enlightenment's Wake: Politics and Culture at the Close of the Modern Age* (London: Routledge, 1995), 19–20.

[9] Edmund Burke, *Reflections on the Revolution in France*, ed. J. G. A. Pocock (Indianapolis, IN: Hackett, 1987), 85.

[10] Perhaps the most sweeping call for civic unity in the tradition of American political thought is John Winthrop's appeal, in his 1630 shipboard sermon on "Christian Charity," that the Puritan settlers "abridge our selves of our superfluities, for the supply of others' necessities" and endeavor to "delight in each other, make others' conditions our own, rejoice together, mourn together, labor and suffer together." But the ground of this ideal of community (an exemplary "city upon a hill") is the Christians' communion with God, a promise of salvation that, of course, has no counterpart in Rawls's utopia. See Winthrop, "Christian Charity: A Model Thereof," in Edmund S. Morgan, ed., *Puritan Political Ideas* (Indianapolis, IN: Bobbs-Merrill, 1965), 92–93. (I have modernized Winthrop's spelling and punctuation.)

urally to be approached in a harmonious marriage, or in the relation of close friends?)

Remarkably, after having based his doctrine on the assumption that the only objective ("primary") goods are those for which we compete with others (wealth and power) or at least seek to enjoy without other people's interference (liberties), Rawls now justifies his doctrine on the basis of an abstract, communized conception of humanity in which the individual's identity collapses into the whole. In place of any natural wholeness that the individual might achieve through understanding—the reason why Plato's Socrates represents philosophy as an essentially erotic activity—or at least through love, friendship, and family, as well as a meaningful public or private vocation—Rawls offers only an artificial "happiness," reducing the individual to a cog in the social machine, extending the division of labor from the factory floor to the whole of life.[11]

What is most distinctive about Rawls's notion of community—unlike Socrates' ostensibly just city in the *Republic*—is its nonjudgmental character. In accordance with the principle of "democracy in the assessment of one another's excellences," Rawls stresses that high scientific, artistic, cultural, or religious achievements "have no special merit from the standpoint of justice." It is better, he suggests, to understand social cooperation on the model of a game, in which each person's "zest and pleasure" presupposes a joint commitment to "fair play."[12] Every individual is fitted neatly within his society, so that his "more private life . . . [is] so to speak a plan within" society's overall plan. And all members of society appreciate "the collective activity of justice" as "the preeminent form of human flourishing" (*TJ*, 462–63). (Rawls proffers no evidence to support the latter judgment.)

The most fundamental difficulty with Rawls's account of the just society as a union of social unions is that it abstracts from the existence of deep-seated *disagreements* about ends, such that it misleadingly assumes that everyone else's development of his potentialities, or the fullest development of all kinds of particular unions, necessarily contributes to *my* happiness or well-being. It is obvious that, say, Hitler's or Saddam Hus-

---

[11] Again, we are reminded of the ironic "best regime" in Plato's *Republic*, which eliminates the family in the name of the greatest civic unity, thereby evincing Plato's view of the dangers of a fanatical pursuit of justice. Cf. Aristotle, *Politics*, II.1-4; and Mary Nichols, *Socrates and the Political Community* (Albany: State University of New York Press, 1987), chap. 3.

[12] Rawls's game metaphor, which played a key role in the original development of his theory, is not apropos here for several reasons. First, even though a game presupposes its members' playing by the rules, their "final end" within the game is typically to win rather than to ensure the maximum of fairness. Second, within a game, some actions (hitting a home run) are clearly ranked above others (striking out). Finally, whereas the rules of a game are by definition artificial, the same cannot be said of the activities of society as a whole. Don't we inevitably think of some undertakings (such as the education of youth, or the governance and defense of one's country) as more serious than other, purely recreational ones?

sein's full development of his potential for tyranny is contrary to the happiness of nearly all other human beings.[13] In a similar vein, it is highly doubtful that from the standpoint of a believing member of one religious faith, the fullest development of alternative religious possibilities is desirable—as distinguished from a unity of human belief that is grounded in the true religion. Moreover, if we take seriously Rawls's mandate of nonjudgmentalism with respect to artistic or scientific excellence, it would follow that the scientist is obliged to applaud the "advance" of astrology and alchemy, and to acknowledge that these "sciences" are no less praiseworthy than mathematical physics. Similarly, "art" works like "Piss Christ" (a statue of Christ immersed in a bottle of the artist's urine that earned a temporary celebrity in the 1990s) must be accorded recognition as the equivalent of a Rembrandt portrait, lest the self-esteem of the "creator" of the former be weakened. How could any political society subsist on the basis of such a merely formal agreement among its citizens' ends?

## VI. Nozick's Utopia

Unlike Rawls, Nozick does not assert the possibility of a society in which all individuals' life plans harmonize neatly with one another. Instead his utopia is a "meta-utopia," a "framework" within which people whose aspirations differ may form their own associations, thereby enabling all "to do their own thing" (ASU, 312). This utopia, however, like Rawls's counterpart, rests on a premise supposedly derived from the observation of human diversity: the fact that "different individuals find their happiness in doing different things" (TJ, 359), or that "people are [so] different . . . in temperament, interests, intellectual ability, aspirations, natural bent, spiritual quests, . . . the kind of life they wish to lead [and] the values they have" that "[t]here is no reason to think that there is *one* community which will serve as ideal for all people and much reason to think that there is not" (ASU, 309–10; emphasis in original). In what he appears to offer as decisive evidence in this regard, Nozick rhetorically asks whether there is "really *one* kind of life which is best" for each of the personages on a long list he supplies, ranging from Moses to Hugh Hefner, and including Socrates, Yogi Berra, Thomas Jefferson, drug guru Baba Ram Dass, the Lubavitcher Rebbe, and the reader's own self and parents (ASU, 310; emphasis in original).

---

[13] More generally, as John Schaar observes, it is impossible for all talents to be "developed equally in any given society," since each society will inevitably admire and reward some potentialities more than others. John Schaar, "Equality of Opportunity, and Beyond," in *Nomos IX: Equality*, ed. J. Roland Pennock and John W. Chapman (New York: Atherton, 1967), 230. Rawls himself stresses the need for particular conceptions of the good to be constrained by justice, thus ruling out tyranny as a way of life. Nonetheless, to the extent that he overcomes the problem of conflict among human ends by excluding from the just society any ways of life that don't fit, his representation of that society as entailing a complementarity of ends reduces itself to tautology.

For both Rawls and Nozick, the sheer fact of human difference suffices to demonstrate that political society has no need or right to try to provide its citizens with authoritative guidance on how to live—as if the only alternative to extreme open-endedness in this regard were a Spartan-like regimentation. (Whereas Rawls was particularly concerned to uphold the right to engage in sexual practices that others might judge degrading, Nozick is eager to advertise his own recreational drug use [*ASU*, 221] as well as rendering homage to Baba Ram Dass.)

But let us note how Nozick's list of diverse personages begs the essential questions: (1) it presupposes that the best way of life for a person must be the one he presently desires or "values" (*ASU*, 309); (2) it implies that no particular model of the good society can allow for an adequate diversity of ways of life to accommodate the natural differences among human beings, unless it is arranged to be entirely "nonjudgmental" about how they live;[14] and (3) it emphasizes the differences of belief and inclination among people who have already been formed by their respective societies, thus ignoring the possibility that Hugh Hefner (to take an extreme example) might have chosen a different way of life from the one he did—and one much less opposed to Moses'—had he been reared in a community that was governed according to the Mosaic law. Given that people's aspirations are inevitably shaped in part by the character of the political society in which they live, shouldn't a healthy regime seek to encourage the young to aspire to emulate individuals like Socrates, Picasso, or Jefferson rather than Hugh Hefner or Baba Ram Dass?

The feature that seemingly distinguishes Nozick's utopia from that of Rawls is Nozick's stress on "experimentation." In the spirit of the pragmatist thinkers John Dewey and Oliver Wendell Holmes, Jr., Nozick treats the construction of the good society as an experiment in which nothing can be known to be good or bad, right or wrong, without first having been "tried out" in practice. (And even if it was tried before and failed, it should still be "retried" to see whether it can be made to work under different conditions [*ASU*, 315–17].)[15] Even "crackpots" and "maniacs"

---

[14] Nozick acknowledges that "no utopian author has everyone in his society leading exactly the same kind of life," but infers from this fact that no single kind of *community* can be best for all men either (*ASU*, 311). Yet the contrary inference would seem to follow just as easily, or more so.

[15] See John Dewey, *The Public and Its Problems* (New York: Henry Holt, 1927). For Holmes's experimentalism, see his dissenting opinions in *Abrams v. United States*, 150 U.S. 616 (1919), and in *Gitlow v. New York*, 268 U.S. 652 (1925), stressing the need for a "free" society to remain open to the possible triumph of "proletarian dictatorship"; and especially his opinion in *Buck v. Bell*, 274 U.S. 200 (1927), sanctioning another sort of experimentation (mandatory sterilization of the retarded) to enable society to "prevent those who are manifestly unfit from continuing their kind."

Holmes also voted to uphold the constitutionality of a state law authorizing a form of indentured servitude, perhaps a step in the direction of a right to sell oneself into slavery (a right supported by Nozick [*ASU*, 331]): see Holmes's dissenting opinion in *Bailey v. Alabama*, 219 U.S. 219 (1911).

should be given the chance to try out their schemes (*ASU*, 316); who are we to say what sanity is?

Nozick himself is prepared to carry the experimental principle to the extreme of guaranteeing an individual's right "to sell himself into slavery" (*ASU*, 331). It is not entirely clear why he does not go further and sanction the retrial of some of the more terrifying social "experiments" of the last century. To be sure, not all the participants or victims of such experimentation participated voluntarily, as Nozick insists they must in a legitimate system (although he qualifies that caveat, as I will note below). Nonetheless, if no political truths can be fixed without having been "proved" through social experimentation, how do we know that freedom itself has such merit as Nozick attributes to it? Once the principle of scientific experimentation is given primacy over belief in an objective morality, consistency seems to dictate that no holds should be barred.

These problems aside, it is not obvious how Nozick's account of the utopia-building process can be reconciled with his previous defense of the minimal state. His identification of the latter with the "framework for utopia" depends critically on a distinction he draws "between a face-to-face community and a nation" (*ASU*, 322). According to this distinction,

> though there is great liberty to choose among communities, many particular communities internally may have many restrictions unjustifiable on libertarian grounds: that is, restrictions which libertarians would condemn if they were enforced by a central state apparatus. For example, paternalistic intervention into people's lives, restrictions on the range of books which may circulate in the community, limitations on the kinds of sexual behavior, and so on. But this is merely another way of pointing out that in a free society people may contract into various restrictions which the government may not legitimately impose on them. Though the framework is libertarian and laissez-faire, *individual communities within it need not be,* and perhaps no community within it will choose to be so. (*ASU*, 320; emphasis in original)

The main ground of this distinction between the legitimate spheres of state and communal authority is that "[i]n a nation, one knows that there are nonconforming individuals, but one need not be directly confronted" by them, whereas "in a face-to-face community one cannot avoid being directly confronted with what one finds to be offensive." Additionally, "[a] face-to-face community can exist on land jointly owned by its members, whereas the land of a nation is not so held." For both these reasons, a community is free to regulate the ways in which its members live, in a manner that Nozick's principles forbid to the nation as a whole (*ASU*, 322). But how far can this distinction hold, and how adequately can it reconcile the competing demands of liberty and community?

I note, to begin with, that Nozick's distinction can apply only to nations large enough to have a number of face-to-face communities within them. It would not apply to a polity that was coextensive with one such community, that is, something like the ancient *polis*. (It would seem to follow that the members of a city-state are free to restrict liberty in an indefinite variety of ways, including interference with what Nozick had previously represented as nigh-absolute individual rights.) And how far can members even of a community that is part of a large nation really avoid being confronted with phenomena that they reasonably find morally offensive— porn theaters situated in a city's downtown, prostitutes soliciting customers, or drug addicts wandering the streets after procuring their latest (legal) "hit," for instance—if the larger government is prohibited from interfering with them? Nor does the criterion of joint ownership of land add anything: since no present property-holders can demonstrate their possession of an unblemished "title" to their land deriving from its first "owners," in the fundamental sense the "property" of *every* political community *is* "jointly held" by its citizenry, if it belongs to anyone at all. All private land titles, in other words, are subordinate to, and derivative from, the collective one.

We must next ask how far Nozick's nation-community distinction actually serves to protect liberty, even within those polities to which it applies. On the surface, it appears to offer very great protection: individuals are free to institute whatever sorts of community they desire, and no one is subjected to restrictions to which he personally has not chosen to submit. However, this seeming liberty operates fully only at the time when communities are originally founded: Nozick denies that an already existent community is obliged to accommodate an individual who wishes to reside there but "opt out" of its practices (*ASU*, 321–22). Ultimately, once communities have been formed throughout the nation or the world, presumably choosing to occupy the most desirable land, the nonconforming individual may have few, or no, real options:

> Even if almost everyone wished to live in a communist community, so that there weren't any viable noncommunist communities, no particular community need also (though it is to be hoped that one would) allow a resident individual to opt out of their sharing arrangement. The recalcitrant individual has no alternative but to conform. Still, the others do not force him to conform, and his rights are not violated. *He has no right* that the others cooperate in making his nonconformity feasible. (*ASU*, 322; emphasis added)

Only when the foregoing passage is put together with several other aspects of Nozick's account of the "framework for utopia" does the passage's full significance emerge. These aspects include (1) Nozick's recognition of each community's right to restrict "the range of books which may circulate" within it (*ASU*, 320); (2) his inability to resolve the conflict between children's right to be informed of "the range of alternatives in the world" and their parents' possible desire to withhold such knowledge from them (*ASU*, 330); (3) his affirmation of people's "right" to sell themselves into slavery (*ASU*, 331); and (4) his hesitation even about how far the individual possesses a right to emigrate from a community, "if [he] can plausibly be viewed as *owing* something to the other members of a community he wishes to leave" (*ASU*, 330; emphasis in original).[16] Strikingly, after considering these remarks together, we find that Nozick— starting from a "libertarian" perspective—has succeeded in offering a recipe for universal tyranny! All that a universal network of tyrannical communities need do to legitimize itself, it would appear, is demonstrate that each community's original founders determined its rules on the basis of a free contract. But after a period of some years (or centuries) had elapsed, during which an appropriate censorship of books was maintained, who would know the truth of the matter? Moreover, from the perspective of an individual who comes on the scene after all communities have been founded, and who therefore "has no alternative but to conform," what possible difference can it make?

No doubt providing a rationale for universal tyranny was the farthest thing from Nozick's mind when he wrote *Anarchy, State, and Utopia*. Nonetheless, the fact that his argument seems to culminate in such a rationale confirms the insufficiency of his understanding of freedom. Even though Nozick's reasoning on behalf of the utopian framework is intended to be independent of his previous argument for the minimal state, with which it nonetheless ultimately "converges" (*ASU*, 333), we must note that the latter argument is not really separable from the former. The reason is that the minimal state, taken by itself, is by Nozick's own account too "pale and feeble" to command people's deepest loyalties or give adequate "luster" to their lives (*ASU*, 297). Life lived in a merely minimal state is banal and meaningless; but life in the total "community" that the minimal state is intended to facilitate may leave no room for freedom. Has Nozick not gone radically astray somewhere?

## VII. EXPERIMENTALISM VERSUS NATURAL RIGHT

In calling for the establishment of a federation of communities that are free to experiment with the institution of various ways of life, without being subject to most of the restrictions that the American government (or any other government) imposes on them, Nozick curiously recapitulates, at a broader level, the position taken by Stephen A. Douglas in defense of

[16] Rawls, similarly, alludes vaguely to the need for "suitable qualifications" to the right of emigration. See John Rawls, *Political Liberalism*, rev. ed. (New York: Columbia University Press, 1996), 222, 277.

the principle of "popular sovereignty" during the slavery controversy that culminated in the American Civil War. According to the view Douglas maintained in his debates with Abraham Lincoln over the extension of slavery, such an extension was not to be judged by parties other than citizens of the state or territory involved, but should be left to local citizens themselves to "try out," as it were, if they chose.[17] Nozick's experimentalism is really a form of historicism: the denial that there is any natural standard accessible to human reason for assessing the justice or goodness of alternative ways of life. Similarly, Rawls observes near the end of *A Theory of Justice* that, in devising principles of justice, "we must rely upon current knowledge," including the "scientific consensus," but must "concede that as established beliefs change . . . the principles of justice which it seems rational to acknowledge may likewise change." While Rawls cites the movement away from "the belief in a fixed natural order sanctioning a hierarchical society" as favoring his two principles (*TJ*, 480), I would note that, by his account, there is no such order sanctioning people's equal, inalienable rights, either. In their abstraction from nature as a standard for justice, both Rawls and Nozick leave our fundamental rights on much shakier ground, or rather on no ground at all.

As the historian Wilfred McClay observes, it is a misuse of language as well as a violation of the principles of the Declaration of Independence to treat constitutional government as if it were an endless "experiment," with even the most fundamental moral principles, as well as the broad institutional means of fulfilling them, forever up for grabs. The purpose of a scientific experiment is to test a hypothesis: the experiment either confirms or disconfirms the hypothesis. When the authors of *Federalist No. 1*, and Lincoln in his Gettysburg Address, represented the United States as a test of free government, they did not mean that Americans must remain committed to an endless process of experimentation, in which the principle of natural rights and the Constitution itself are to be regarded perpetually with only tentative approval, pending further tests.[18]

For Nozick, "utopia" is itself only an endless "process," as distinguished from the "static" visions of the good society advanced by other theorists (*ASU*, 332). In fact, within the framework of the Constitution, American society continues to exhibit a remarkable dynamism, inventiveness, and spirit of enterprise. But how could a mere process, severed from any substantive moral foundation (and hence from appropriate reg-

---

[17] See especially Douglas's remarks in his 1858 debate with Lincoln at Alton, Illinois: "We in Illinois . . . tried slavery, kept it up for twelve years, and finding that it was not profitable, we abolished it for that reason, and became a free State." Robert W. Johannsen, ed., *The Lincoln-Douglas Debates* (New York: Oxford University Press, 1965), 299.

[18] Wilfred McClay, "Is America an Experiment?" in Gary L. Gregg II, ed., *Vital Remnants: America's Founding and the Western Tradition* (Wilmington, DE: ISI Books, 1999), 1–32. For *Federalist No. 1*, see Alexander Hamilton, John Jay, and James Madison, *The Federalist Papers*, ed. Clinton Rossiter (New York: Mentor Books, 1999).

ulations in support of morality) command the attachment—let alone the "eloquen[ce]" (*ASU*, 332)—of anyone other than a philosophy professor, issuing pronouncements from his ivory tower?

Let us note, finally, the misleading character of the claims both Rawls and Nozick make to found their teachings about liberty on the recognition of "diversity." As I have noted, in purporting to derive justice from an impartial treatment of various conceptions of the good, Rawls really imposes his own view of the good on other human beings. And as Nozick suggests, Rawls's difference principle, far from treating actual human beings with equal regard for their rights, actually entails subjugating more talented or industrious individuals to the service of their less-successful peers. In response to individuals who might doubt that Rawls's principles actually serve *their* good, whether through economic collectivism or through moral libertarianism, Rawls's ultimate response is simply, "their nature is their misfortune" (*TJ*, 504). (In other words, tough luck!) As for Nozick, after misleadingly implying that individuals like Moses or Socrates could flourish in one of the subordinate communities his utopia would allow, he responds to "imperialistic utopians" who demand "universal realization" of their own vision of how people should live (as distinguished from Nozick's) by remarking, "Well, you can't satisfy everybody" (*ASU*, 319–20). Some diversity!

## VIII. Conclusion

Let us return, then, from the world of utopian theorizing to an actually existent liberal polity, the United States. Nozick's strictures about the extent of "redistributive" legislation notwithstanding, the example of this country (as well as other constitutional, liberal democracies) demonstrates that it is possible for a nation to survive and flourish while leaving its citizens free to pursue a relatively wide variety of particular ways of life, if not that of Napoleon or Mohammed. (A majority of the individuals on Nozick's list of personages exemplifying diverse vocations and views of the good were residents of the United States, few of whom encountered legal obstacles to their pursuits.)[19] Americans have also traditionally enjoyed a broad freedom to form voluntary communities of various sorts: religious communities, socialist communities, etc. (During the golden age of utopian experimentation in the first half of the nineteenth century, among the better-known of such communities were Robert Owen's socialist village New Harmony in Indiana; its counterpart in New England, Brook Farm, fictionally depicted by Nathaniel Hawthorne in *The Blithedale Romance*; and the various

---

[19] The exceptions to the latter qualification include a tax protester (Henry David Thoreau), a militant anarchist (Emma Goldman), and a purveyor of illegal drugs (Baba Ram Dass, né Richard Alpert).

Shaker religious communities.)[20] Indeed, Alexis de Tocqueville, in *Democracy in America* (written in the 1830s), represents Americans' knowledge and practice of the "art of association" as one of the keys to our political prosperity.[21]

What fundamentally distinguishes the context of such communities from Nozick's "framework," however, is that the national and state governments do not grant particular associations the latitude Nozick would award them to control their members' lives, or to violate what are generally regarded as the moral foundations of civil life in a free republic. Hence, all children must be granted an appropriate education; slavery is illegal, whether "voluntary" or not; polygamy is banned; and no community may prevent one of its members from departing because of what he "owes" to it. Nor can membership in a particular community excuse anyone from obeying the other laws by which citizens in general are bound, including the laws requiring him to pay taxes for the support of the common welfare and defense.

Even though a liberal regime like the American one will never satisfy religious fanatics (along with various other "crackpots"), the broad support it has traditionally given to fundamental precepts of moral decency and even (*pace* the recent Supreme Court) to a generalized, nonsectarian piety enables it to earn the respect of most religious human beings as well as sensible nonbelievers. By outlawing debilitating habits like the use of mind-altering drugs, the American government at the same time fortifies the character required of an independent, self-governing citizenry. And by proscribing such practices as prostitution and polygamy, it reinforces the sense of human dignity on which respect for our equal rights as individuals depends.

Similarly, despite Rawls's unsupported denunciations of the United States and other existing liberal polities for their allegedly grave injustices toward the poor (e.g., *TJ*, 246–47), he never succeeds in demonstrating (nor could anyone) that the economic inequalities that exist in this country violate his difference principle. That is, he never demonstrates that these inequalities are not the inevitable by-products of a system that, by leaving people relatively free to pursue economic gain through lawful means, generates a high level of economic growth that raises the standard of living, as well as the opportunities, available to the poor far beyond what they would otherwise be. Nor does Rawls consider the inherent link between economic and political freedom: because the opportunity to

---

[20] For an intriguing account of the fate of New Harmony and other secular socialist communities modeled on it, and the lessons that anyone with a genuinely empirical outlook might have learned from the experience of these communities, see Joshua Muravchik, *Heaven on Earth: The Rise and Fall of Socialism* (San Francisco: Encounter Books, 2002), chap. 2. The median lifespan of those communities, Muravchik reports, was two years (ibid., 51).

[21] Alexis de Tocqueville, *Democracy in America*, trans. Harvey C. Mansfield and Delba Winthrop (Chicago: University of Chicago Press, 2000), I.ii, chap. 4; II.ii, chap. 5.

acquire wealth independently of government enhances citizens' overall self-sufficiency, it fortifies their capacity to dissent from governmental policies.[22] Meanwhile, following the argument of *Federalist No. 10*, economic liberty diversifies people's interests in a way that reduces the homogeneity of their political opinions and hence mitigates the danger of majoritarian tyranny.

The natural-rights teaching enshrined in the Declaration of Independence on which American institutions rest is neither libertarian (in Nozick's sense) nor socialist. On the one hand, the Lockean property-rights doctrine reflected in that document clearly entails a right to derive profits from the ownership of means of production, rather than being limited to employment by the state.[23] On the other hand, not only does the secure ownership of one's property entail the obligation to pay taxes for the common good, as ordained by the people's elected representatives; the enjoyment of our rights also requires submitting to those regulations minimally necessary to preserve the moral requisites of citizenship and national prosperity. As Michael Zuckert observes:

> Government conducted under the aegis of the Declaration's theory is not committed to indifference on moral matters. . . . Various qualities of character, e.g., a disposition to respect others and their rights, conduce to the institution and maintenance of a reliably rights-protecting society. No liberal society can be merely indifferent to the existence of these qualities in its citizens; no liberal society is required to be "neutral" among all possible character types or life styles.[24]

Zuckert notes, moreover, that a liberal government, dedicated to the aim of securing rights, has both the right and the need to enact legislation providing for a "rights infrastructure" (such as public education) as a means of securing those rights. While "the natural rights theory is quite certain in affirming the ends of political life" (i.e., protecting our natural rights) and government is *ipso facto* prohibited from pursuing policies that

---

[22] On the inherent link historically between the security of private property and individual and political liberty, see Richard Pipes, *Property and Freedom* (New York: Random House, 1999). On Locke's intention in this regard, see Harvey C. Mansfield, "On the Political Character of Property in Locke," in Alkis Kontos, ed., *Powers, Possessions, and Freedom* (Toronto: University of Toronto Press, 1979), 33–38.

[23] For Jefferson's upholding of the natural right to property, despite its omission from the triumvirate of rights mentioned in the opening paragraph of the Declaration, see his Second Inaugural Address, in Adrienne Koch and William Peden, eds., *The Life and Selected Writings of Thomas Jefferson* (New York: Modern Library, 1944), 344; and his letter to Samuel Dupont de Nemours, April 24, 1816, in Gilbert Chinard, ed., *Correspondence of Jefferson and Du Pont de Nemours*, reprint ed. (New York: Arno Press, 1979), 258. On the status of property rights in Jefferson's thought and in the Declaration, see also Michael Zuckert, *Launching Liberalism: On Lockean Political Philosophy* (Lawrence: University Press of Kansas, 2002), 220–23.

[24] Zuckert, *Launching Liberalism*, 227. See also William Galston, *Liberal Purposes* (Cambridge: Cambridge University Press, 1991), esp. chap. 12.

would manifestly violate those rights, such as the establishment of a national church to which all must subscribe, the theory still leaves open "a great range of possibilities" regarding the means of protecting our rights.[25] In a constitutional, republican regime like the American one, it is elected officials and the civil servants subordinate to them who make the particular decisions on what policies best serve the ends enunciated in the Declaration and the Constitution—subject, ultimately, to the will of the electorate.

Policies developed in this manner will never meet the theoretical demands of philosophy professors who seek to devise precise formulas for "just" public policies. Then again, the failure of those widely esteemed thinkers Rawls and Nozick to develop meaningful and salutary standards suggests the imperviousness of human and political phenomena to the demand for theoretical neatness, and the impossibility of subsuming political phenomena under "moral philosophy," as such writers would have us do (ASU, 6).[26]

Above and beyond recognizing the impossibility of transforming political life to conform to the demands of any "theory" of justice, and the folly of trying to do so, one should view with caution the rhetoric that Rawls and Nozick sometimes employ to demonstrate the gap between the American liberal regime (and others) as they exist and these theorists' ostensibly more elevated standards. Examining this rhetoric can serve as a reminder of the dangers of political utopianism grounded in abstract theorizing. Consider the ringing words with which Nozick concludes Anarchy, State, and Utopia, informing us that no state other than his "minimal" one is "morally legitimate" or "tolerable" (ASU, 333). Can he really have believed that the American regime, which Abraham Lincoln termed the "last best hope on earth" for justice and freedom, is morally intolerable? Even more striking are Rawls's repeated disparagements of the United States in his later writings for its many "grave injustices," such as the lack of public campaign financing, the existence of "a widely disparate distribution of income and wealth," and the failure to provide universal, governmentally financed health care.[27] Elsewhere, Rawls even questions whether the contemporary United States is more democratic than "Germany between 1870 and 1945" (i.e., including the Nazi period).[28]

Respect for the people's right of self-government—and gratitude for the benefits that all Americans, but especially college professors, enjoy

---

[25] Zuckert, *Launching Liberalism*, 226.

[26] For a critique of an early attempt to reduce political phenomena to theoretically neat categories, see Aristotle, *Politics*, II.8. On why Aristotle does not propound a "theory" of justice, see Delba Winthrop, "Aristotle and Theories of Justice," *American Political Science Review* 72, no. 4 (December 1978): 1201–16; and Bernard Yack, *The Problems of a Political Animal* (Berkeley: University of California Press, 1993), chap. 5.

[27] John Rawls, "Reply to Habermas," in Rawls, *Political Liberalism*, 398, 407.

[28] John Rawls, *Justice as Fairness: A Restatement* (Cambridge, MA: Harvard University Press, 2002), 101n.

thanks to America's political regime and the sacrifices of their fellow citizens and forebears to support it—would suggest the need for academics to temper their indignation at their fellow citizens for failing to adopt the particular policies that the professors happen to favor. As an antidote to the ingratitude that Rawls and Nozick display toward the American constitutional regime, by disregarding and hence effectively denying the vast moral differences that distinguish it from most regimes that have existed and still exist in the world, I shall close this essay by quoting the judgment of a young American Jewish journalist, Bret Stephens, upon visiting his grandfather's homeland in Moldova. Considering what would have befallen his family had they not emigrated to America following the pogrom of 1903, Stephens remarks, "It was only because of the United States that they were saved."[29] This remark could be multiplied by many millions of similar stories.[30]

*Political Science, Holy Cross College*

---

[29] Bret Stephens, "Coming to America," *Wall Street Journal*, January 2, 2002, A18.
[30] As Joshua Muravchik reports of Robert Dale Owen, the most distinguished of Robert Owen's five children (all of whom led accomplished and successful lives in America once they abandoned the socialist hopes with which their father had imbued them and took advantage of the opportunities available to all in a land of lawful freedom), he "found the 'Land of Promise' not in New Harmony, but in America itself" (Muravchik, *Heaven on Earth*, 59).

# LIBERTARIANISM AND THE STATE*

## By Peter Vallentyne

### I. Introduction

Liberalism comes in two broad forms. Classical liberalism emphasizes the importance of individual liberty, and contemporary (or welfare) liberalism tends to emphasize some kind of material equality. The best-known form of libertarianism—right-libertarianism—is a version of classical liberalism, but there is also a form of libertarianism—left-libertarianism—that combines classical liberalism's concern for individual liberty with contemporary liberalism's robust concern for material equality. In this essay, I shall assess whether libertarianism in general, and left-libertarianism in particular, can judge a state to be just without the universal consent of those it governs.

Although Robert Nozick has argued, in *Anarchy, State, and Utopia*,[1] that libertarianism is compatible with the justice of a minimal state—even if it does not arise from universal consent—few have been persuaded.[2] Libertarianism holds that individuals have very strong rights of noninterference, and all nonpacifist versions of the theory also hold that individuals have strong enforcement rights. Given that these rights are typically understood as protecting choices, it is very difficult to see how a nonconsensual state could be just. Those who have not consented to the state's powers retain their enforcement rights, and the state violates their rights when it uses force against them to stop them from correctly and reliably enforcing their rights.

I shall outline a different way of establishing that a nonconsensual libertarian state can be just. I shall show that a state can, with a few important qualifications, justly enforce the rights of citizens and extract payments from wrongdoers to cover the costs of such enforcement. Moreover, certain versions of left-libertarianism, unlike right-libertarianism, can justify the redistribution of resources to the poor and investment in infrastructure to overcome market failures.

I should emphasize that my goal is rather modest. I shall merely sketch a possible libertarian position that recognizes the justice of significant

* For very helpful comments, I am indebted to Dani Attas, Ellen Frankel Paul, Robert Johnson, Brian Kierland, Mike Otsuka, Eric Roark, and the other contributors to this volume.
[1] Robert Nozick, *Anarchy, State, and Utopia* (New York: Basic Books, 1974).
[2] See, for example, the criticisms raised in Murray Rothbard, *The Ethics of Liberty* (Atlantic Highland, NJ: Humanities Press, 1982), chap. 29.

state activity. Although I believe that this version is indeed plausible, I shall not attempt here to defend its plausibility.

## II. Justice and the State

The term "justice" is used in several different ways. Sometimes it designates the moral permissibility of political structures (such as legal systems). Sometimes it designates moral fairness (as opposed to efficiency or other considerations that are relevant to moral permissibility). Sometimes it designates legitimacy in the sense of it not being morally permissible for others to interfere forcibly. Finally, sometimes it designates what we owe each other in the sense of respecting everyone's rights. This final concept is the concept of justice to which I shall appeal. It can be understood broadly to include duties we owe ourselves (if there are any) or narrowly to exclude such duties. In the present context, this distinction does not matter, since agents of the state will not normally violate their own rights in their official capacity.[3] For simplicity, I will therefore understand justice broadly. The justness of the state is thus a matter of the extent to which it operates without violating anyone's rights.

I shall focus on a threshold conception of justice according to which a state is just if and only if it violates rights as rarely as can be reasonably expected of humans in general. Justice in this sense is compatible with occasional violation of rights. I focus on the threshold concept because states are run by humans and humans are fallible. It is thus inevitable that states will sometimes (e.g., inadvertently) violate someone's rights. Justice in the threshold sense only requires that such activities be sufficiently rare relative to what is reasonably feasible for humans.

It is important to note that the justness of a state does not conceptually guarantee that it has any *political authority* over citizens in the sense that citizens in its territory typically have at least a pro tanto *moral obligation to obey* its dictates. Ideally, a state should have political authority, but it is not conceptually necessary for justice. Just as an individual citizen can behave justly without having any political authority over others, so too can the state (or agents thereof). Consequently, we shall not be concerned here with the important issue of political authority.[4]

---

[3] This is not to say that the issue of whether individuals have rights against themselves is irrelevant to justice—broadly or narrowly construed. If an individual violates his own rights (e.g., by mistreating his body) and others are permitted to enforce those rights even against his will, then it will be just, broadly and narrowly, to do so. Of course, almost all libertarians deny that we have rights against ourselves, and those who accept such rights deny that they may be enforceable against a person's will.

[4] For insightful discussion of political authority in the context of libertarian theory and John Locke's quasi-libertarian theory, see A. John Simmons, "Consent Theory for Libertarians," *Social Philosophy and Policy* 22, no. 1 (2005): 330–56; and A. John Simmons, *On the Edge of Anarchy* (Princeton, NJ: Princeton University Press, 1993).

A state, then, is just, in our sense, if and only if, at least typically, it violates no one's rights. But what is a state? Defining statehood is no easy matter, and there is no uncontroversial comprehensive definition. Something like the following, however, seems at least roughly right for our purposes: A *state* is a rule-of-law-based coercive organization that, for a given territory, effectively rules all individuals in it and claims a monopoly on the use of force. This can be unpacked as follows: An organization is *coercive* just in case it prohibits at least some activities, threatens to use force against individuals who do not comply with its dictates, and generally implements its threats. A coercive organization is *rule-of-law-based* just in case (roughly) it uses force only in a reasonably impartial and reliable manner in response to the violation of dictates that are reasonably knowable in advance (e.g., public, clear, and stable dictates), where violation is reasonably avoidable (e.g., because the dictates are not retroactive and compliance is not unreasonably difficult). An organization *effectively rules* the individuals of a given territory just in case those individuals generally conform to its dictates (in the sense of obeying them in part because the organization issued the dictates). An organization *claims a monopoly on the use of force* just in case it prohibits the use of force (or credible threat thereof) without its permission.[5]

I shall show that, on this view of justice, almost all forms of libertarianism can recognize certain kinds of states as just. Following that, I shall show that a certain form of left-libertarianism can view reasonably robust states as just. First, however, we need to clarify the nature of libertarianism.

## III. Libertarianism

Libertarianism can be advocated as a full theory of moral permissibility or merely as a theory of justice (i.e., a theory of what rights individuals have). The difference concerns impersonal duties (duties owed to no one).[6] Impersonal duties are duties that are not the correlates of any right. Because libertarianism is a purely rights-based theory (i.e., considers only those duties that correspond to someone's rights), it does not specify any impersonal duties. Thus, if there are impersonal duties, libertarianism is mistaken as a full theory of morality. Although I would argue that there are no impersonal duties, I shall not consider that issue here. Instead, I shall simply take libertarianism—as effectively all libertarians do—to be a theory of justice. So understood, libertarianism is only concerned with

---

[5] Note that, to be a state, an organization need neither have, nor claim to have, a de jure (i.e., rightful) monopoly on the use of force. It just has to prohibit the use of force without its permission (i.e., it has to claim a de facto monopoly).

[6] Recall that I understand justice broadly to include duties to oneself. If justice were understood narrowly to exclude duties to oneself, then such duties would be a second difference.

interpersonal duties and is silent on whether there are any impersonal duties.

Libertarianism is sometimes advocated as a derivative set of rules (e.g., on the basis of rule utilitarianism or contractarianism). Here, however, I reserve the term for the natural rights doctrine that agents initially *fully own themselves*. Agents are full self-owners just in case they own themselves in just the same way that they can fully own inanimate objects. Stated slightly differently, full self-owners own themselves in the same way that a full chattel-slave-owner owns a slave. Throughout, we are concerned with moral ownership and not legal ownership.

Full self-ownership consists of full private ownership of one's person (e.g., one's body). Full private ownership of an object consists of a full set of the following ownership rights: (1) *control rights* over the use of the object (liberty-rights to use it and claim-rights against others' using it); (2) *rights to transfer* these rights to others (by sale, rental, gift, or loan); and (3) *immunity to nonconsensual loss of any of these rights* as long as one has not violated anyone else's rights. Full private ownership also includes some bundle of: (4) *rights to compensation* if someone uses the object without one's permission; (5) *enforcement rights* (rights to use force to prevent the violation of these rights or to extract compensation owed for past violation); and (6) *immunities to nonconsensual loss when one has violated the rights of others* (i.e., limits on what rights are lost as the result of a right-violation). Because these last three elements are in tension with each other, the concept of full ownership is indeterminate with respect to what mix of these last three elements is required. At one extreme is the view that full owners have an absolute immunity to the nonconsensual loss of their rights (even if they violate the rights of others). This view entails that full owners do not have any rights of compensation or enforcement (since those rights require that those who violate their rights lose some of their control rights and thus do not have an absolute immunity). At the other extreme is the view that individuals have some kind of absolute rights to compensation and enforcement (e.g., you may kill a person to stop her from touching your car). This view entails that full owners have very minimal immunities to loss when they violate the rights of others.[7]

One possible version of libertarianism, then, is radical pacifist libertarianism, which holds that individuals have absolute immunities to losing any of their self-ownership claim-rights against others' using their person. As a result, radical pacifist libertarians hold that it is never permissible to use force against another individual without her permission.

---

[7] For more on the indeterminacy of full self-ownership with respect to compensation rights, enforcement rights, and immunities to loss, see Peter Vallentyne, Hillel Steiner, and Michael Otsuka, "Why Left-Libertarianism Isn't Incoherent, Indeterminate, or Irrelevant: A Reply to Fried," *Philosophy and Public Affairs* 33 (2005): 201–15.

Because all states use, or threaten to use, force, radical pacifist libertarians deny that any state can be just.[8]

Another possible, but implausible, version of libertarianism holds that individuals have certain rights of enforcement, but no individual, or group of individuals, has any right to enforce *someone else's* rights. I may use force to stop you from assaulting me or to recover compensation from you after you have assaulted me, but this does not justify anyone else's use of force against you for this purpose. To do so would violate your rights, on this view. On this view, individuals do not have the moral power to authorize the use of force by others against their aggressors. Like radical pacifism, this version of libertarianism precludes the justness of a state. All versions of libertarianism hold that it is unjust to use force to stop activities that violate no one's libertarian rights. The view under consideration also holds that it is unjust to use force to stop activities that *do violate* someone else's libertarian rights. This leaves no room for just state activity.

In what follows, I shall set aside these two positions and focus solely on nonpacifist versions of libertarianism that permit third parties to enforce the rights of individuals with the consent of those individuals. I shall attempt to show that such versions of libertarianism can judge certain kinds of states to be just.

All forms of libertarianism endorse full self-ownership. They differ with respect to the moral powers that individuals have to acquire ownership of external things. The best-known versions of libertarianism are right-libertarian theories, which hold that agents have a very strong moral power to acquire full private property rights in external things. Left-libertarians, by contrast, hold that natural resources (e.g., space, land, minerals, air, and water) belong to everyone in some egalitarian manner and thus cannot be appropriated without the consent of, or significant payment to, the members of society.

In what follows, I shall restrict my attention to unilateralist versions of libertarianism, which are those versions that allow agents, under certain conditions, to use and appropriate unowned resources without the collective approval of others. All versions of right-libertarianism are unilateralist—as are almost all versions of left-libertarianism (because they allow appropriation without approval as long as an appropriate payment is made, as I discuss below). The only articulated form of libertarianism that this rules out is joint-ownership left-libertarianism, which holds that natural resources belong to everyone collectively and thus that appropriation—and perhaps (much more radically) even use—

---

[8] Radical pacifists do not deny that individuals have a duty not to violate rights and a duty to pay compensation for past violations. They merely deny that anyone may use force against violators to make them fulfill their duties. Radical pacifists may even allow for a person's property to be confiscated in order to compensate victims—when this can be done without using force against a person.

requires collective consent of some sort (e.g., majority or unanimous consent). This form of libertarianism makes it relatively easy to justify state activity—since all will consent to allowing some kind of state-protected private property rights—but it is not very plausible. Any minimally plausible version of libertarianism will allow some appropriation without the consent of others, and I shall therefore focus solely on unilateralist versions.

## IV. General Libertarian Limits on the State

I shall argue below that (given our background assumptions) libertarianism in general, and a certain version of left-libertarianism in particular, leaves some significant room for just state activity. First, however, let us briefly identify the kinds of state activities that all forms of (unilateralist) libertarianism condemn as unjust—except, of course, where the activities are carried out in accordance with a consensual agreement or in response to the violation of someone's rights (which qualifications I leave implicit in what follows). Because different versions of libertarianism can take different positions on the ownership of external resources (i.e., resources other than the bodies and minds of agents), it is difficult to generalize about the libertarian limits on state restrictions on the use of such resources. All versions of libertarianism, however, endorse full self-ownership, and I shall therefore focus on the limits that this places on just state activity.

First, all libertarians judge it unjust for the state to use force to make individuals promote (by personal service) a merely impersonal good. Merely impersonal goods are features of the world that are morally desirable, but not in virtue of being good for any individual (e.g., perhaps the preservation of cultural artifacts when this benefits no one). Because libertarians, like most people, hold that failing to promote merely impersonal goods violates no one's rights, they hold that the state violates rights of self-ownership if it uses force to make someone promote such goods. All libertarians thus condemn as unjust the state's use of force for this purpose.

Second, effectively all libertarians condemn as unjust the use of force against a person for her own benefit but against her will (i.e., strong paternalism). Here we must distinguish between two ways that rights in general, and those of self-ownership in particular, can be understood. Rights can be understood in choice-protecting terms or in interest-protecting terms. Almost all libertarians endorse self-ownership understood in choice-protecting terms. So understood, only valid consent can waive a right of self-ownership (e.g., make it permissible for you to touch me) or transfer a right from me to you (e.g., as in the case of a binding contract to perform personal services for you). It is possible, however, to endorse self-ownership in interest-protecting terms. So understood, using force against a person without her consent need not violate her self-ownership, if it is not against her interests. Thus, for example, it may not violate a person's self-ownership to forcibly prevent her from smoking, when this use of force is genuinely in her self-interest. Like most libertarians, I believe that the interest-protecting conception of rights licenses far too much paternalism.[9]

Unlike many libertarians, however, I believe that the choice-protecting conception is too restrictive. It is incompatible with young children having any rights, and, without some fancy footwork, it judges that a person's self-ownership is violated when I push her to the ground without her permission to prevent her from being hit by a car. A more promising account, I believe, is a hybrid account according to which rights protect both interests and choices—with the protection of choices being lexically prior. More specifically, I would defend the following conception: A person has a claim-right against others that they not perform action X if and only if it is wrong for others to perform X when (1) she has validly *dissented* from their X-ing (i.e., communicated her opposition to their X-ing), or (2) she has *not validly consented* to their X-ing and their X-ing is *against her interests* (on some appropriate conception of interest). If self-ownership is so understood, then the use of force to benefit a person without her consent sometimes may not violate her rights: namely, when it is not against her interests and she has not dissented (e.g., pushing someone to the ground to prevent her from being hit by a car).[10]

In what follows, I shall assume that the rights of self-ownership protect choices in this hybrid sense. This is a controversial assumption and does some important work below. One immediate implication is that it is unjust to use force against a person for her own benefit *but against her will* (although it may sometimes be permissible to use such force without her consent).[11]

Third, all libertarians condemn as unjust the state's use of force to make a person provide personal services for the benefit of others—assuming, as we are, that the individual has not violated anyone's rights. Most people agree that it is unjust for the state to force people to clean the houses of the needy, but libertarianism's claim is much more radical. It holds that it

---

[9] There are, of course, many different interest-protecting conceptions of rights, and here I assume a particular fairly direct form. For insightful discussion of the debate between choice-protecting and interest-protecting conceptions of rights, see Matthew H. Kramer, N. E. Simmonds, and Hillel Steiner, *A Debate over Rights* (Oxford: Oxford University Press, 1998).

[10] Note that the hybrid account holds that an action does not violate a person's rights when she does not validly dissent and the action is not against her interest. The account does not require that the action be in her interest (she might be unaffected). I would argue against altering the account to require that the action must be in her interest, on the ground that this would sometimes make it impermissible to provide an enormous benefit for others with no adverse effect on the right-holder.

[11] Admittedly, it is most natural to think of property rights as choice-protecting rather than as interest-protecting. Those bothered by an interested-protecting conception of property rights can take them to be quasi-property rights.

is unjust for the state to force individuals to serve in the military, to serve on juries, or even to testify in court cases. Of course, there may be ways to soften this implication. Perhaps it is not unjust for the state to provide incentives (e.g., tax breaks or extra governmental services) to individuals who commit to so serving. Nonetheless, libertarians have fairly radical views on this topic.

Fourth and finally, all libertarians judge it unjust for the state to use force to prevent individuals from exercising their enforcement rights (e.g., using suitable force to prevent someone from violating one of their rights). As I have noted, libertarianism is compatible with different views about what enforcement rights individuals have, but all forms (even radical pacifist libertarianism) agree that, whatever rights these are, it is unjust for the state (or others) to interfere forcibly with their proper exercise. Moreover, this applies even when the enforcement rights are applied against agents of the state. Assuming (as we are) that individuals have at least some enforcement rights, an otherwise innocent agent violates no rights when she properly applies those rights (e.g., uses the minimal force necessary to prevent her rights from being violated) against agents of the state who are (1) attempting to falsely arrest her, or (2) attempting forcibly to prevent her from correctly exercising her enforcement rights against others. It is a violation of her self-ownership, and hence unjust, for the state to intervene forcibly in such cases.

Given our background assumptions, no state is just according to libertarianism if it engages in the foregoing kinds of activities. Can a state nonetheless be deemed just by some versions of libertarianism if it carefully avoids such activities? I shall argue that it can.

Libertarianism holds that individuals have—in virtue of their self-ownership and property rights in external things—various liberty-rights, claim-rights of noninterference, and powers to transfer these rights to others. If everyone consensually transfers some of these rights to each other so as to create a state, and the state fulfills all the obligations generated by these transfers, then the state is just, no matter what it is like. Even a highly communistic state could be just in principle. Thus, universal mutual consent is one uncontroversial, uninteresting, and very unlikely way that a state can be just according to libertarianism.

Even if no one transfers enforcement powers to the state, a state can be just according to (a given version of) libertarianism, if its dictates have the right content and the state is sufficiently reliable in enforcing its dictates. Call a state "a libertarian private-law state" just in case (1) it prohibits (and enforces its prohibitions against) only those activities (a) that violate someone's libertarian rights, (b) for which the victim has a libertarian right to enforce those rights, and (c) for which the state has a libertarian liberty to enforce (e.g., because the victim has consented to enforcement on her behalf); and (2) it respects the libertarian rights of all (including any derivative contractual obligations that it may owe). Although such a state claims a monopoly on the use of force, it is very restrictive in what it prohibits. As a result, if it enforces its prohibitions reliably, such a state will only rarely violate anyone's libertarian rights and will be, according to libertarianism, a (sufficiently) just state.

A libertarian private-law state is much less extensive than any modern state. Indeed, it is much weaker than the "night-watchman" state that some libertarians (e.g., Nozick) are willing to defend. Here we can briefly note some of its key features. One is that it may not involve any *public criminal law*. First, the state prohibits only activities that violate someone's libertarian rights, and it does not enforce anyone's rights against her will. If all those who have had their rights violated by a given action waive their enforcement rights, the state does not pursue the matter. Second, unless one holds—implausibly, in my view—that libertarianism recognizes certain "crimes against society" (e.g., murder, assault, theft), the members of society in general have no enforcement rights with respect to some specific rights violations, except as authorized by specific individual victims. Thus, for example, if the person assaulted waives her enforcement rights, the state does not pursue the matter.[12] (Of course, murder, where the victim no longer exists, requires some special treatment, but I shall not attempt to discuss the matter here.)

Note also that, under a libertarian private-law state, individuals maintain the right to enforce their rights on their own, without any role for the state. That is, a libertarian private-law state does not require that individuals use its enforcement procedures. It merely requires that individuals use enforcement procedures that it has *authorized* (and thus, indeed, claims a monopoly on the use of force). Because it authorizes all libertarian self-enforcement procedures, the libertarian private-law state violates no one's libertarian rights in imposing such a requirement.

A libertarian private-law state can exist and be just without anyone irrevocably consensually transferring any enforcement rights to the state. Its justness thus does not require anyone's consent in this sense. Nonetheless, on a standard choice-protecting conception of rights (to be addressed in the next section), the justice of any particular use of force by a libertarian private-law state against a particular person requires (something like) either (1) her consent or (2) where she has violated someone

---

[12] In *Anarchy, State, and Utopia*, pp. 133–42, Robert Nozick seems to suggest that, for certain kinds of right-violations, others—either individually or collectively—have the right to punish the violator even against the will of the victim. I would argue that a plausible version of libertarianism will limit enforcement to *prevention* of right-violations (including failures to compensate for past violations) and will not include any right to punish as such (to inflict harm on the violator for its own sake). Moreover, even if there is a right to punish, I would argue that it is a right possessed only by the (primary) victim of the right-violation (although she may authorize others to exercise it on her behalf). For more on the rejection of the right to punish, see Randy Barnett, "Victim's Rights: Restitution or Vengeance," *Ethics* 87 (1977): 279–301; Randy Barnett, "The Justice of Restitution," *American Journal of Jurisprudence* 25 (1980): 117–32; and Randy Barnett, *The Structure of Liberty: Justice and the Rule of Law* (Oxford: Clarendon Press, 1998), chaps. 10–11.

else's rights, the consent of that victim (given the latter's enforcement rights). There is thus a weak sense in which the justice of a libertarian private-law state depends on the consent of at least some of those governed. Below, I shall identify a hybrid conception of enforcement rights that will sever this dependency.

We have not yet dealt with the issue of how a libertarian private-law state is financed. We know that it respects libertarian property rights, but, on this issue, the various versions of libertarianism disagree on what kind of taxation, if any, is allowed. I shall now argue that a libertarian private-law state can be financed by forcibly extracting the costs of enforcement from those who violate rights. Following that, I shall argue that, according to a certain form of left-libertarianism, a libertarian private-law state can also involve significant taxation for the purpose of promoting equality of opportunity and financing certain goods and services that the market fails to provide.

## V. Enforcement Rights

As we have seen, libertarianism is compatible with a wide range of views concerning enforcement rights. We have set aside two possible views: (1) radical pacifist libertarianism, which denies that individuals have any enforcement rights, and (2) pure self-enforcement versions of libertarianism, which hold that third parties have no rights to enforce an individual's rights, even with her consent. We shall now examine more carefully the conditions under which third parties in general, and the state in particular, may enforce the rights of individuals.

On a narrow choice-protecting conception of enforcement rights, others are permitted to enforce a person's rights only when she grants them permission. I shall now identify how the hybrid conception of rights (sketched in Section IV) can make it permissible for others to enforce a person's rights under a broader range of conditions. Suppose that you steal my wallet and knock me temporarily unconscious. Alternatively, suppose that you steal my wallet and I haven't realized it yet. Alternatively, suppose that I realize it, but haven't yet decided whom, if anyone, I want to authorize to enforce my rights to recover the wallet. The narrow choice-protecting view of enforcement rights under consideration here says that a third party who witnesses the theft, and who can easily stop the thief, is not permitted to do so because I have not given my permission. This is very implausible. Perhaps there is a broader choice-protecting conception of enforcement rights that avoids this implausible result, but I shall not purse this possibility. Instead, I shall show that a hybrid conception of enforcement rights can judge third-party enforcement to be just in these cases.

On the hybrid conception of rights (with choice-protection lexically prior to interest-protection), others are permitted to enforce my rights when and only when (1) I have validly consented, or (2) I have not validly dissented (i.e., expressed my opposition) and enforcement is not against my interests. For these purposes, let us stipulate that enforcing a right (in a particular context in a particular way) is not against the right-holder's interest if and only if the expected well-being of the right-holder is at least as great with this particular enforcement as it is without it. (Other accounts are, of course, possible, but I will assume this one for the sake of illustration.)[13] Note that the baseline is not nonenforcement generally, but rather nonenforcement by this particular person in this particular situation in this particular manner. Thus, for example, the expected well-being accompanying such nonenforcement takes into account the probabilities that the right will be enforced by others (who may do it more effectively). One is not permitted to enforce someone else's rights without consent when someone else is sufficiently more likely to do a better job.

Assuming that enforcement in the foregoing cases is not against my interests, the hybrid conception holds that others are permitted to enforce my rights in the above kinds of cases. Although I believe that this is a more plausible account than the narrow choice-protecting account, I shall not argue that here. The crucial point is that, if the hybrid conception of rights is accepted, then a third party, and hence the state, may enforce rights under reasonably broad conditions. The right-holder can, of course, renounce the enforcement claim against the right-violator, in which case no one may enforce the right. The right-holder can also dissent from certain others enforcing the right, in which case they are not permitted to enforce the right. In the absence of these two conditions, however, third parties, and the state in particular, may enforce the rights of a right-holder when she consents or when, given the absence of dissent, it is not against her interests.

I shall now discuss a second relevant aspect of enforcement rights. Suppose that you violate my rights and owe me $100 compensation. Suppose further that the only way to get you to pay me this amount is for someone to track you down and force you to pay up. Suppose that the cheapest way of so enforcing my rights costs $50. (For example, perhaps the cheapest way is for me to enforce my rights myself and I would pay up to $50 to avoid doing it myself. Alternatively, perhaps someone else is a more efficient enforcer in this case and she would do so for no less than $50.) I suggest that the right-violator has an enforceable duty to pay for these enforcement costs. Of course, if she immediately and voluntarily pays the $100 compensation, then there are no enforcement costs. If, however, someone has to spend resources on getting her to pay, then the violator is liable for the cheapest (reasonable) way of getting her to pay. Again, this is a controversial issue that requires a defense. Although I

---

[13] I believe that an objective account of the expected consequences is the relevant one, but, of course, several views are possible.

would defend something in the spirit of this position, here I am simply flagging it to explore its implications for the justness of a libertarian private-law state. In what follows, I shall assume that violators have a duty to cover enforcement costs in addition to a duty to compensate their victims.

Right-violators, of course, are not always caught, and when they are caught, it is not always possible to extract full compensation. Here I shall briefly comment on how these issues might be dealt with. I suggest that the payments that may be extracted from apprehended right-violators include payments to cover (when possible) the expected value of the unrecovered payments from them. There are many ways of fleshing out this idea, but here is one. Suppose (1) that a violator imposes a harm worth $100 and enforcement costs of $20, and (2) that there is (a) an 80 percent chance that the violator will be caught and will fully compensate the victim and (b) a 20 percent chance that he will not be caught and will provide no compensation. Given that there is only an 80 percent chance of recovering compensation and enforcement costs, in order for the violator to cover the full expected costs of his right-violation, we must recover $125 ($100/.8) compensation for the victim and $25 ($20/.8) for the enforcer (so that their expected values are $100 and $20 respectively). This ensures that, where possible, the violator covers the full expected costs that she imposes on the victim and the enforcer.[14] Of course, it is sometimes not possible for violators to fully compensate their victims (e.g., because the victim is dead, has suffered an uncompensable harm, or has suffered a finite harm that is greater than it is possible for the violator to compensate). In such cases, I suggest that the recoverable enforcement payment is the efficient cost of maximizing compensation to the victim. Obviously, these and many further related issues need a thorough development.[15] Here I am merely identifying them to explore their implications for the justness of the state.

The core idea is that violators have an enforceable duty to compensate their victims as much as possible and to cover the efficient costs of any enforcement procedures that are needed to ensure that they do compensate their victims as much as possible. If this view is accepted, then we have a financing mechanism for the state. The state may enforce the rights of citizens with their consent or when it is in their interests and they do not dissent. Moreover, the state may forcibly extract efficient enforcement costs from right-violators when the state enforces the rights of citizens. Of

---

[14] Note that, on this proposal, the relevant probabilities of nonpayment are those for the specific violator for the specific violation. Thus, individuals do not foot the bill for other individuals.

[15] Extracting compensation from violators may involve forcing them to labor in their most productive capacity and having compensation and enforcement payments deducted from their paychecks. If the individuals are reasonably reliable, they need not be imprisoned. If they are sufficiently unreliable, they may need to be imprisoned in a labor camp. For more on this view, see Barnett, *The Structure of Liberty*, chap. 14.

course, the enforcement costs that it may extract are limited to something like the cheapest feasible cost. Thus, if the state is inefficient in its enforcement procedures, it will not be able to recover the full costs of enforcement. Unless inefficient states receive voluntary contributions from individuals, they will not be able to sustain their operations without violating the rights of individuals. Efficient states, however, will be able to extract the costs of enforcing rights from right-violators.

A libertarian private-law state, then, can provide enforcement services and forcibly extract financing for those services from the right-violators. I shall now argue that such a state can also (1) redistribute resources to individuals who are disadvantaged through no fault of their own, (2) help provide goods and services that the market does not provide adequately, and (3) forcibly extract financing for those activities.

## VI. REDISTRIBUTION

The modern state often redistributes resources from those who have a lot to those who have little. Can a libertarian private-law state do this? Clearly, it cannot (normally) redistribute resources from all rich people to all poor people, since at least some of the rich may have a libertarian right to those resources. Any redistribution will have to be from those who have resources to which they have no libertarian right to individuals who have a libertarian right to those resources. I shall now examine some different versions of (unilateralist) libertarianism and see what their implications are for just redistribution. The key issue concerns what property rights individuals have.

One version of right-libertarianism is *radical right-libertarianism*, which holds that individuals have the power to appropriate unowned things simply by claiming them (or mixing their labor with them, etc.). Radical right-libertarians deny that any further conditions are relevant. In particular, they deny the necessity of satisfying any Lockean proviso that "enough and as good" be left for others. There is thus no room for the state to redistribute resources to the needy or to finance projects to overcome market failures.[16]

*Lockean libertarianism* agrees that individuals have the moral power to appropriate unowned things by (for example) claiming them, but it insists

---

[16] See, for example, Rothbard, *The Ethics of Liberty*, and Murray Rothbard, *For a New Liberty: The Libertarian Manifesto*, rev. ed. (New York: Libertarian Review Foundation, 1978). One might wonder whether even radical right-libertarianism would permit taxation to overcome market failure and make everyone better off (or at least some better off and none worse off), if it were based on the hybrid conception of rights. The version of the hybrid conception that I would defend does *not* have this implication. First, such taxation violates property rights if the owner dissents, and many or most would dissent. Second, without consent, the particular extraction of taxes must not make the owner worse off, and this condition will typically not be satisfied. Although all people may be better off if all are taxed, all else being equal, taxing an individual makes her worse off.

that this is conditional on satisfying some kind of Lockean proviso.[17]
Different versions of Lockean libertarianism specify different versions of
the Lockean proviso. *Nozickian right-libertarianism* interprets the proviso
as requiring that no one be left worse off with the appropriation than she
would be if the thing appropriated were in common use.[18] Thus, a Nozickian right-libertarian private-law state would redistribute resources by
taking from those who have appropriated things but not satisfied the
proviso and transferring them to those who are made worse off by the
appropriation. *Equal share left-libertarianism*[19] interprets the Lockean proviso as requiring that no one be worse off than she would be if no one
appropriated more than an equal share of the competitive value of natural resources (i.e., the value based on supply and demand). Thus, an
equal share left-libertarian private-law state would redistribute resources
from those who have appropriated unowned resources in violation of this
proviso to those who have been left with less than an equal share. Finally,
*equal opportunity (for well-being) left-libertarianism*[20] interprets the Lockean
proviso as requiring (roughly) that no one be worse off than she would be
if no one appropriated more than is compatible with everyone having an
equally valuable opportunity for well-being. Unlike all the previous versions of libertarianism, this version gives greater entitlements to external
resources to individuals who are disadvantaged in terms of internal
resources (such as beauty, intelligence, and strength). I shall focus on this
version of left-libertarianism.[21]

Equal opportunity left-libertarianism (like other versions of libertarianism) comes in several variations. Here I will focus on the following
version. Agents who do not own any natural resources (i.e., those who
merely use resources, but with no rights of exclusive use) have no duty to
promote equality of opportunity for a good life. If agents appropriate
natural resources (i.e., claim and acquire rights of exclusive use), however, the rights acquired are conditional on the payment of competitive
rent for the rights acquired (i.e., the supply and demand equilibrium price

---

[17] For superb analysis of Locke's own quasi-libertarian views, see A. John Simmons, *The Lockean Theory of Rights* (Princeton, NJ: Princeton University Press, 1992).

[18] See, for example, Nozick, *Anarchy, State, and Utopia,* 175–82. There are many exegetical questions about how Nozick intended his version of the Lockean proviso to be understood, but this is one natural reading.

[19] See, for example, Hillel Steiner, *An Essay on Rights* (Cambridge, MA: Blackwell Pub-lishing, 1994).

[20] See, for example, Michael Otsuka, *Libertarianism without Inequality* (Oxford: Clarendon Press, 2003).

[21] For more on left-libertarianism generally, see Peter Vallentyne and Hillel Steiner, eds., *The Origins of Left Libertarianism: An Anthology of Historical Writings* (New York: Palgrave Publishers Ltd., 2000), and Peter Vallentyne and Hillel Steiner, eds., *Left Libertarianism and Its Critics: The Contemporary Debate* (New York: Palgrave Publishers Ltd., 2000). For a critical assessment of left-libertarianism, see Barbara Fried, "Left-Libertarianism: A Review Essay," *Philosophy and Public Affairs* 32 (2004): 66–92, and Vallentyne, Steiner, and Otsuka, "Why Left-Libertarianism Isn't Incoherent, Indeterminate, or Irrelevant."

for those rights in some suitable hypothetical auction or market).[22] Moreover, if the rights are later transferred to someone else, the duty to pay such rent is also transferred.[23] That is, ownership of natural resources is always conditional upon the payment of this rent. Finally, the rent payment must be used to promote equality of opportunity as much as reasonably possible.[24] If, for example, an individual has rights over land that have a competitive rent value of $100 per year, then she has a duty to promote equality of opportunity as much as is reasonably feasible for her with a budget—covering all implementation costs (including her time and effort)—of $100 per year. This duty is owed to those individuals who are the beneficiaries of the equality-promoting payment. The beneficiaries, that is, have a right to such payments, although the right is highly qualified and conditional: they have a right to a payment only when it turns out that they are the beneficiaries of the most effective way of promoting equality with the sum in question. These beneficiaries' rights, like all libertarian rights (we are assuming), are enforceable. As indicated above, the state is permitted to enforce these rights with the consent of the right-holders, or when it is in the holders' interests and they have not dissented from such enforcement.[25]

An equal opportunity left-libertarian private-law state thus redistributes resources by taking from those who own natural resources but have not fully discharged their equality-promoting duties relative to the competitive rent owed for the rights they hold. Of course, there are significant limitations on the distributive activities of such a state. It does not tax income or wealth other than natural resources. It does not take resources from all rich people nor give them to all poor people, since many rich people have fully discharged their equality-promoting duties and many poor people have had an equal opportunity for well-being and have simply made bad choices or been unlucky in the risks they freely under-

---

[22] Although rights over natural resources can be sold to others, their price, given the accompanying duty to pay competitive rent, will be close to zero. Artifacts (including improvements to natural resources), however, are not subject to any rent payment, and thus their actual market value will not be so reduced.

[23] I would argue that acquisition of property by gift also generates a duty to promote equality of opportunity as much as reasonably possible with the competitive value of that gift. For simplicity, however, I ignore this issue here.

[24] Throughout, when I speak of promoting equality, it should be understood as shorthand for promoting equality in Pareto-optimal ways. Thus, for example, an unequal distribution should be chosen over perfect equality, if everyone is better off under the former distribution. For more on combining equality with Pareto efficiency, see Bertil Tungodden and Peter Vallentyne, "On the Possibility of Paretian Egalitarianism," *Journal of Philosophy* 102 (2005): 126–54.

[25] It is worth noting that, on this version of equal opportunity left-libertarianism, both individuals and the state will have a duty to help enforce the rights of individuals when this is what the relevant equality-maximization duty requires. (This will tend to favor enforcement of the rights of the disadvantaged over enforcement of the rights of the advantaged.) Moreover, where the state is reasonably efficient at promoting equality of opportunity for well-being, individuals will also tend to have a duty to establish and maintain such a state.

took. Moreover, this version of the libertarian private-law state redistributes resources in this way only when the beneficiaries have consented to the state's enforcement of their rights or when they have not dissented and it is not against their interests (i.e., enforcement does not decrease their expected benefits). Finally, the state is permitted to recoup only the costs of efficient enforcement, and thus, if the state is an inefficient enforcer—either in general for certain kinds of right-violations, or in specific cases—it will typically not make sense for the state to get involved.

So far, then, I have shown that the state's enforcement of rights can be just according to nonpacifist libertarian theories that allow third parties to enforce rights. The range of cases in which this is so will be much broader on versions of libertarianism that adopt a hybrid conception of rights (for which consent is not necessary for third-party enforcement) rather than a narrow choice-protecting conception. Moreover, if enforcers are permitted to use coercion to extract the costs of enforcement from violators, then the state, if suitably efficient, can justly finance its enforcement activities. Finally, according to equal opportunity left-libertarianism, individuals have enforceable rights to a certain level of equality-promotion against those who appropriate natural resources, and the state may justly enforce such rights.

Let us turn now to our final topic: the justness of the state's activities to overcome market failures.

## VII. Overcoming Market Failures

Under ideal conditions (e.g., perfect competition), the market is an efficient provider of goods and services. Under other conditions, however, the market is not an efficient provider in the sense that it is not Pareto optimal: some other feasible arrangement would make some individuals better off without making anyone worse off. This is so, for example, when the market provision of a good (e.g., vaccination against contagious diseases) brings with it significant positive externalities, and therefore encourages free-riding (e.g., one can benefit from the vaccination of others without being vaccinated oneself). This is also true when a good to be provided is nonexcludable; an example here is national defense, where it is not practically feasible to provide the good only to those who pay for it. These are cases of market failure.

Of course, the mere fact that the market fails to be efficient does not guarantee that state intervention will be efficient, or even more efficient than the free market. There can be government failure as well. Market failure merely opens up the possibility that government provision might be more efficient. Modern states typically subsidize a variety of activities for which there is some degree of market failure (e.g., national defense, research, and education). I shall now show that a libertarian private-law state can do the same, according to equal opportunity left-libertarianism.

Recall that, according to equal opportunity left-libertarianism, those who appropriate natural resources have a duty to promote equality of opportunity for well-being as much as possible with the payment that they owe for the rights that they claim over such resources. The most natural way of understanding this requirement is that appropriators have a duty to promote *long-term* equality of opportunity, and it is this version that I shall consider here. Thus, if government investment of the sum owed for appropriation better promotes long-term equality of opportunity, then individuals have no right to receive any benefits from that sum in the short run. Individuals have a right to the benefits they would receive if the payments were used efficiently to promote long-term equality of opportunity.[26]

This is particularly relevant because one thing that individuals—and the state—can do is invest justly extracted rental payments in ways that increase the competitive rent of natural resources and thus increase the rental payments owed in the future. The competitive rent of rights over natural resources (e.g., land) is sensitive to the availability and price of various goods and services. For example, each of the following features will make land more valuable (all else being equal): (1) the presence of effective legal and national defense systems; (2) the presence of low-cost and well-functioning transportation, communication, energy, and information systems; and (3) the presence of healthy, knowledgeable, hardworking, and trustworthy individuals. Where markets work well, it is counterproductive (i.e., it is not equality-maximizing) for the state to invest funds to provide such goods and services. Where markets work poorly (e.g., because of indivisibility in the production of goods, nonexcludability of goods in exchange, or positive externalities in use), however, state investment may be an effective way of promoting long-term equality of opportunity. First, the benefits provided by investment in such goods and services may sometimes themselves help promote long-term equality (by providing significant benefits to the relevantly disadvantaged). Second, and more importantly, such investment, when made wisely, will typically increase the total rental payments owed by owners of natural resources by more than the cost of the investment. Such investments will, that is, increase the long-term pool of funds available for promoting equality of opportunity for well-being. Of course, beyond some level, such investments will cost more than the increase in rental payments that they generate. When this is so, the equal opportunity left-libertarian private-law state will not use rental payments for such purposes.

In general, then, for any given budget, there is some, typically positive, optimal level of investment in "market-failure" goods and services with

---

[26] Given that sometimes there is more than one way of maximizing equality of opportunity with the payment owed—with different people being beneficiaries—a more careful statement of the relevant right would be suitably conditional.

respect to maximizing long-term (Pareto efficient) equality of opportunity for well-being. Individuals who appropriate resources thus have a duty to invest their payments at the appropriate level in such goods and services, and the state has the duty to do so if it justly extracts such payments. This tells us nothing, of course, about what the required level of investment is in the real world. It might be small or it might be great. That is an empirical question (given the requirements of equal opportunity left-libertarianism). The important point here is simply that, in principle, a libertarian private-law state may indeed, at least sometimes, invest where the market fails.

## VIII. Conclusion

I have argued that a state can be just according to libertarianism. The first step was to understand justice as a threshold concept that merely requires respecting rights as much as is reasonably feasible. Justice is thus compatible with occasional lapses due to ignorance, reasonable implementation errors, etc. The second step was to focus on states that are sufficiently modest in what they prohibit and sufficiently reliable in how they enforce those prohibitions. More specifically, we focused on states that prohibit only activities that violate libertarian rights, that are reasonably cautious in enforcing those prohibitions (and thus rarely use morally excessive force), and that do not engage in other activities that violate libertarian rights. Such states are libertarian private-law states. Although they claim a monopoly on the use of force in their territories, they prohibit the use of force only when it violates libertarian rights, and they normally (occasional mistakes aside) use force only when it violates no libertarian rights.

Even such states are judged unjust both by radical pacifist libertarianism and by versions of libertarianism that hold that third parties are not permitted to enforce someone's rights. These, however, are not very plausible positions, and, in any case, I restricted my attention to versions of libertarianism that hold that it is permissible for third parties to help enforce rights with the consent of the right-holder.

I then showed how a libertarian private-law state could be reasonably extensive if certain additional—undefended, but plausible in my view—assumptions were made. First, if rights are understood on the proposed hybrid conception, then the state may enforce the rights of citizens even without their consent; it may also enforce their rights when the enforcement is not against their interests and they have not dissented. Second, if right-violators have a duty to bear the costs of any efficient enforcement procedures, then the state has the means to cover the costs of efficient enforcement. Third, if we assume (as I do) equal opportunity (for well-being) libertarianism, then the state may justly use force, where this is efficient, to ensure that those who have rights over natural resources pay the competitive rent of the rights that they claim and that these funds are used to promote equality of opportunity. Finally, if we assume (as I do) that it is *long-term* equality of opportunity for well-being that matters, then the extracted rental payments may be partly invested in goods and services that the market fails to provide efficiently—provided that the costs of such investments are less than the increase in the rental payments that they generate.

Although I believe that each of these assumptions is plausible, I have not attempted to defend them. Thus, the implications are modest: I have merely attempted to show the possibility of some version of libertarianism recognizing the justice of significant state activity. The assessment of whether such a version of libertarianism is plausible must await another occasion.

If my argument is correct, then, almost all minimally plausible forms of libertarianism are compatible with the justice of some kind of state, and some forms of left-libertarianism are compatible with a reasonably robust state. This does not, of course, mean that any existing state is just on libertarian grounds. Indeed, this is clearly not so. Existing states typically tax inappropriately (e.g., income taxes); they are significantly inefficient in how they use resources; they restrict people's freedom against their will for their own benefit (e.g., drug laws and helmet laws); and they require forced labor for the public good (e.g., jury duty, court testimony, and military service). Still, the possibility of a libertarian just state—perhaps a robust one—helps show that libertarianism, and left-libertarianism in particular, is not a utopian dream.

*Philosophy, University of Missouri–Columbia*

# LIBERALISM BEYOND BORDERS

## By Loren E. Lomasky

### I. Introduction

Political philosophy is an anachronism. The institutional structure that provided its bearings—the *polis*—is more than two millennia defunct. Nonetheless, the discipline carries on, turning its attentions to the workings of empires, principalities, and forms in between. Its modern efflorescence coincides with and focuses on the development of the nation-state. With few exceptions, the subject matter of the preceding four centuries' political philosophy is the inner workings of the sovereign modern state. Those within its borders are clients to be served, and state institutions are assessed in terms of how effectively they vindicate individuals' rights, dispense justice, and promote overall well-being. Nowhere is this characterization more apt than in the theory of liberalism. From Thomas Hobbes and John Locke at one end to John Rawls at the other, the state is conceived as the self-contained object of analysis, whether in the mode of omnipotent leviathan or cooperative venture entered into at birth and exited only at death.

It now can be asked of modern liberal political theory whether it too has become an anachronism. Although the nation-state, unlike the *polis*, is still very much with us, no longer is it the unique juncture at which all political avenues meet. Rather, lines of influence and authority are diverse, including interstate, infrastate and nonstate entities. To do political theory as if the only noteworthy claims of justice are those resolvable within borders is to trade on an increasingly unrealistic conception. As communications and economics have gone global, so too must political philosophy. Otherwise, it risks not only anachronism but also obtuseness and irrelevance.

This should not produce an existential crisis among liberals. The deep structure of liberalism is friendly to a global outlook. Classic liberal manifestos are grounded on universal human rights, with the state and its privileged status derivative therefrom. But because everyone has valid claims on everyone, for noninterference if not for more, there is prima facie plausibility to the idea that a fully adequate model of political justice will have to incorporate bonds of obligation that extend beyond national borders.

That this universalist strand lies mostly latent in the tradition is explicable in terms of the context within which liberal philosophy emerged and evolved. First, its development coincided with the history of the burgeoning nation-state as it ascended to political dominance. Because this was the central problem of the seventeenth century (and beyond), it is entirely natural that philosophers would concentrate on the task of exploring its parameters and possibilities. Second, intensity of interaction was once a rapidly decreasing function of distance. In an era when most people lived their entire lives within the county, let alone country, in which they were born, relations across national borders were few and limited. Third, communication was no more rapid than the fastest boat or caravan could travel between population concentrations. Even where there existed a will to extend efficacy abroad, epistemic barriers made it difficult to do so. Fourth, to the extent that a theory of justice in international relations was pursued, it primarily addressed ramifications of traditional just war theory and hospitality to commercial travelers. Any prospect of more extended rule-governed interaction was thoroughly utopian.[1]

It is, perhaps, unnecessary to note that much has changed. The nation-state is mature (some would say verging on senescence),[2] markets for virtually all goods and many services are worldwide, communications across continents proceed at the pace of those conducted across the street, and populations in one country are profoundly affected by legislative enactments and stock-market fluctuations in another. Moreover, individuals are often subject to authority other than that of the sovereign nation-state via international treaties and multinational organizations such as the European Union and the United Nations. It is no longer the case that separate peoples occupy the world in a condition of general detachment from one another. Rather, John Donne's dictum that no man is an island now extends with equal force to communities, regions, nations, continents—and, for that matter, to islands. Along innumerable lines of influence, we affect each other for better and for worse. Because there are substantial gains (or losses) to be incurred through appropriately (or inappropriately) formulated rules of conduct, it seems impossible to deny, or even to ignore, the need to acknowledge principles of justice governing global transactions.

Another change is of special salience to political philosophers. In *A Theory of Justice*, John Rawls developed the theory of justice as fairness for a sovereign nation-state.[3] In that book, he offered only a promissory note concerning the requirements of justice beyond borders. That note was cashed in *The Law of Peoples*.[4] Although the inherent philosophical merits of the latter book are vigorously debated, it is incontrovertible that attention by Rawls to an issue amplifies its visibility many times over. Even prior to the publication of *The Law of Peoples*, philosophical allies of Rawls had endeav-

---

[1] See Immanuel Kant, *Perpetual Peace*, in H. S. Reiss, ed., *Kant: Political Writings* (Cambridge: Cambridge University Press, 1970), 93–130.
[2] See Christopher Morris, *An Essay on the Modern State* (New York: Cambridge University Press, 1998).
[3] John Rawls, *A Theory of Justice* (Cambridge, MA: Harvard University Press, 1971).
[4] John Rawls, *The Law of Peoples* (Cambridge, MA: Harvard University Press, 1999).

ored to extend the theory of justice globally.[5] These treatments typically involved application of Rawls's difference principle (privileging the status of the least well-off members of society) to the entire world population, with massive wealth redistribution as the inescapable consequence. However, when Rawls himself decided to extend the theory of justice, his own take on its ramifications was substantially different. *The Law of Peoples* is only modestly redistributive, with the difference principle explicitly rejected as a basis for international cooperation.[6] Those who believe that the extraordinary disparity in access to primary goods between the world's haves and have-nots constitutes a massive injustice that demands rectification find little to cheer in the book. Therefore, the international-justice debate in the philosophical literature is being waged at least as much by Rawlsian against Rawlsian as by Rawlsian against anti-Rawlsian.

This is an essay in developing cross-border implications of liberalism. Both in motivation and in some of its findings it is in sympathy with *The Law of Peoples*. But as with the critics of Rawls, it proposes a theory of international justice that is continuous with national justice. Like those critics of Rawls, it argues that rich states impose grave and systematic injustices on the poorer peoples of the world. However, these are not attributed to insufficient zeal in applying the difference principle beyond borders. Rather, the flaw is rooted more deeply in a transgression against the grounding theory of liberalism: denial of equal liberty to those with whom one transacts.

Section II discusses the relationship between distance and the stringency of moral ties among persons. The world's peoples are strikingly diverse with regard to possession of the ingredients of well-being, and Section III examines some of the conditions that underlie these differences. Section IV is the most extended of the essay. Five guiding principles of a liberal theory of international justice are set out and defended. Section V offers a brief conclusion.

## II. MORAL TIES AND MORAL CLAIMS

Many people believe that their obligations to co-nationals are weightier and more extensive than those owed to extra-nationals. This is, of course, a disputable proposition, but it is one of a family of claims that closeness, literal or figurative, matters for morality. Near kin and friends are due more consideration than distant relatives and casual acquaintances. The latter, however, take precedence over anonymous members of one's community,

---

[5] See, for example, Charles Beitz, *Political Theory and International Relations* (Princeton, NJ: Princeton University Press, 1979); and Thomas Pogge, *Realizing Rawls* (Ithaca, NY: Cornell University Press, 1990).

[6] The difference principle is, of course, the principle that in a just society, social and economic inequalities are to be arranged so that they work to the greatest benefit of the least advantaged. See Rawls, *A Theory of Justice*, section 13.

who in turn count for more than distant compatriots, who in turn count for more than residents of foreign lands. Such judgments are in tune with our uninstructed moral sentiments. They also are in tune with the basic precept of rationality that the greater the value one places on some item, the more cost one has reason to bear in order to safeguard that item. Some theorists object that concern for personal interests is trumped by moral principles of impartial concern for the well-being of all persons, regardless of their connection to oneself.[7] Not only is that view counterintuitive, but it also forfeits any prospect of constructing an account of morality, including political morality, built on foundations of rational prudence.

Although there are respects in which it is accurate to characterize Rawls as an egalitarian, commitment to a thoroughgoing universal impartialism is not one of them. Rather, a founding assumption of his theory of justice is that persons possess distinct conceptions of the good that afford them individuated reasons to act on behalf of the ends that are distinctively their own. The possibility of reciprocal benefit prompts construction of principles of justice which, if generally adhered to, generate a cooperative surplus. It is in this respect that the theory of justice is said by Rawls to be "a part, perhaps the most significant part, of the theory of rational choice."[8]

How, then, is the Rawlsian difference principle to be understood? First, it does not annul the conception of justice as cooperation for mutual benefit but rather specifies how the cooperative surplus is to be distributed. Second, it applies only under tightly delimited circumstances. In a striking characterization of its range of applicability, Rawls declares, "In justice as fairness men agree to share one another's fate."[9] The implied corollary is that where dealings among people are too occasional or superficial to constitute the basis of any such fate-sharing agreement, the supposition that they could be obligated one to another by anything as strong as the difference principle lacks foundation. Instead, a basic order of live-and-let-live may be all that is rationally sustainable. How strong a spin should be given to the notion of "sharing fate" is open to debate, as is the feasible scope of application. Even to suppose that the citizens of a populous and diverse sovereign state are drawn together in so tight a circle is far-fetched;[10] it is all the more far-fetched to extend the perimeter to encompass all the peoples of the world. This explains, I believe, why

---

[7] See, for example, Peter Singer, "Famine, Affluence, and Morality," *Philosophy and Public Affairs* 1 (1972): 229–43; and Larry Temkin, "Thinking about the Needy: Justice and International Organizations," *Journal of Ethics* 8 (2004): 349–95.

[8] Rawls, *A Theory of Justice*, 16. But see also John Rawls, *Political Liberalism* (New York: Columbia University Press, 1993), 53 n. 7, for a partial retraction of this characterization.

[9] Rawls, *A Theory of Justice*, 102.

[10] I make this objection in "Libertarianism at Twin Harvard," *Social Philosophy and Policy* 22, no. 1 (2005): 178–99. Rawls himself may have been implicitly reconsidering the applicability of this conception when, in the revised edition of *A Theory of Justice* (Cambridge, MA: Harvard University Press, 1999), he omitted without explanation the "share one another's fate" sentence. Possibly, his own later work on international justice had persuaded him to moderate this aspect of the theory, but that is speculation.

when Rawls comes to write *The Law of Peoples,* he eschews grand principles of transnational redistribution in favor of considerably more modest
articles mandating respect for the independence and sovereignty of other
national units. Aid comes into the picture only to enable disfavored peoples to establish a minimally just and decent social order so that they then
might proceed in their own preferred direction.[11] Somewhat surprisingly,
such autonomy is accorded not only to liberal democratic regimes but
also to old-fashioned autocracies (dubbed here "decent hierarchical
peoples").

Rawls, then, is to be located among those theorists who hold that the
weight of moral obligation is a decreasing function of distance. This helps
to explain what some find a puzzling feature of his theory of international
justice: the parties to the global original position are not the world's *people*
but its *peoples.* One can, of course, imagine some sort of compact that a
conclave of six billion souls might produce behind a veil of ignorance, but
why on the other side of the veil they should acknowledge its terms as
binding them in their subsequent dealings admits of no satisfactory answer.
The qualitative and quantitative dimensions of their interactions are so
slight that they can in only the most attenuated sense be described as
cooperators for mutual advantage. Peoples, however, at least those that
carry recognition as sovereign entities, do regularly interact as parties to
treaties, members of international organizations, and transactors in commercial relationships. Therefore, they qualify as potentially reciprocating
beneficiaries and so are subject to principles of justice that they would
endorse as free and independent parties in a suitably characterized original position. Thus the structure of *The Law of Peoples.*

The preceding sketch is not intended to endorse Rawls's conclusions
concerning the terms of international law. As I will argue in Section IV, the
articles he presents are at best incomplete, holding for relations between
states but silent concerning obligations of justice to individual foreign
nationals. My sketch is, however, intended to endorse Rawls's method of
attentiveness both to what may be called the supply side as well as the
demand side of a theory of justice. Not much moral acuity is required to
perceive the massive want and despair that disfigure the global arena.
Questions expressing protest and indignation spontaneously follow: "What
kind of world order is it in which some 2.8 billion people live on an
income of less than two dollars a day, 1.2 billion of whom subsist on less
than one dollar a day?" "When 30,000 children die *each day* from disease
due to inadequate nutrition, doesn't that show that something is very
wrong with the way resources are distributed?" As with other rhetorical
questions, these do not invite extended reflection prior to ascertaining the
indicated answer. Yet the phenomena adduced do not, as such, signify the
existence of an injustice, let alone identify the offending party. Poverty,

[11] Rawls, *The Law of Peoples,* 37.

hunger, and disease naturally call forth instincts to compassion, but who, if anyone, are the parties accountable either for having brought about or for now addressing these circumstances is a further question, the answer to which is not obvious. The planet's poor, let us agree, no more deserve to bear their misery than do the citizens of rich nations of the West deserve to have been born to the affluence that they enjoy. This is lamentably bad fortune for one, good fortune for the other. On what grounds, though, can a claim for recompense be lodged by the former against the latter? If the better-off owe their wealth to unfair dealings with the worse-off, that would, of course, constitute the basis of a strong claim for reparations. However, the fact of inequality, even very great inequality, does not by itself amount to evidence of any prior injustice. Nor, absent a question-begging egalitarian premise, does it show that the wealthy have any duty to acquiesce in a transfer of some share of their resources to the poor. It may be *kind* of them to do so, a matter of laudable *charity* or *generosity*, but that is not equivalent to maintaining that they *must* (as a requirement of justice) do so. To put it slightly differently, that many people stand in urgent need of aid from those who might be able to provide assistance is unassailable. But why and how that need constitutes a valid claim on the actions of others is less clear. What people owe each other is, in the broadest sense, the subject matter of a theory of justice, and it is only within the framework of such a theory that global inequality and distress can accurately be translated into a language of rights and duties.

Parties intimately joined to each other by shared activities and aspirations are bound by a rich web of moral obligations. At the extreme, the bonds are encapsulated in the dictum "Love your neighbor as yourself." The key word in this injunction is, of course, "neighbor." The degree of neighborly closeness invoked to render the requirement comprehensible even as a counsel of perfection is extreme.[12] Although not quite so extreme, the degree of continuing care that would render it reasonable, in Rawls's words, "to share one another's fate" is high. Therefore, the circumstances under which anything approaching these conditions obtains are special and cannot be extrapolated into a general theory of morality, let alone a theory of justice. Instead, the proper starting point for an account of what human beings as such owe each other will presuppose no antecedent ties of affection or association. On what terms, then, is it reasonable for anonymous individuals to interact?

A plausible general morality is necessarily shaped by attention to *reciprocity*. Rational agents will reject any demand to sacrifice some share of their own good so as to confer benefits on moral strangers. Instead, they will put themselves under only those rules and institutional structures from which they deem themselves to be securing benefits that outweigh

---

[12] "Good fences make good neighbors" stands at the opposite extreme.

the costs they are obliged to bear. The paradigmatic example of reciprocal transaction is trade. When Jones parts with $x$ units of apples in order to secure from Smith $y$ units of oranges, each party judges herself to be rendered better off. Jones need not care about what Smith will do with the apples or, indeed, about Smith's welfare at all. All she needs to know for the transaction to be well-judged from her point of view is that she herself has improved her prospects by agreeing to give up the apples for the oranges. Vice versa for Smith. Note that the parties need not concur with regard to the relative value of oranges to apples in order to fix a contract price for their transaction; indeed, it is precisely because their valuations differ that they transact.

Liberal theorists bring the contract model to their accounts of political association. In two respects, the social contract differs from trading wares: (1) the contract that grounds civil society is multiparty rather than pairwise; (2) the transactors proffer to each other not some tangible commodity but rather their noninterference.[13] What renders the social contract recognizably contractual, however, is its exemplification of reciprocity understood as mutual benefit. That which each party forgoes is valued from that individual's perspective less than that which is secured. It is only because Jones values Smith's-noninterference-with-Jones more than she does Jones's-interference-with-Smith that it is rational from her perspective to give deference in exchange for getting deference. The result is generalizable.[14]

Although the social contract presents itself as grounding the sovereign state, reciprocal noninterference enjoys a wider, indeed universal, scope in theories of basic human rights. A right is properly basic if and only if it is a claim owed to everyone and held against everyone. Because the relationship in which rights-holders stand to each other is reciprocal, it is also symmetrical. There are no separate classes of givers and receivers, but rather what each gives to others is also received from them. For that reason, duties correlative to basic rights are all negative, refrainings rather than positive performances. Rights to life, liberty, and property are claims not to be killed, not to be imprisoned, not to be stolen from, rather than entitlements to receive life-, liberty-, or property-preserving bounty. The logic of reciprocity supporting universal human rights is identical to that underlying the social contract. That is why it is plausible to extend classical liberalism's regime of noninterference globally, while Rawlsian lib-

---

[13] A third respect in which they might differ is if the social contract is stipulated to be tacit or hypothetical, perhaps entered into behind a veil of ignorance. No further attention will be paid to these complications.

[14] This is not a theorem of the abstract theory of rationality but rather presupposes a certain view of human nature. Only if people by and large place higher value on being left alone to advance their own projects than they do on meddling with the projects of others will they subscribe to an order of mutual forbearance. Classical social contract theories attempt in different ways to embed mutual and reciprocal willingness to forgo meddling into their accounts.

eralism, especially its difference principle, does not travel comfortably across borders.

Wherever the further reaches of a theory of international justice lead, if the theory does not commence in an order of reciprocal noninterference, it goes nowhere at all. Perhaps just global institutions can evolve structures transcending noninterference in something like the way that the special relationships among citizens of a liberal regime generate claims and obligations that extend beyond respect for basic rights. However, the indicated analytical starting point is simple noninterference.

This is the method employed by Rawls in developing his law of peoples. At the center of this law are requirements of noninterference, with an additional requirement of fidelity to pacts made and a contingent duty of aid to distressed peoples. Whether the account is inadequate in virtue of lacking strongly egalitarian redistributionist principles is vigorously debated. More open to criticism, I believe, is the absence of principles governing the behavior of peoples toward individual foreign nationals. By his espousal of the case of respect for human rights, Rawls is committed to the seriousness of such principles. Thus, for example, a state/people may not take the life of a foreign national. To do so is not merely to wrong the people to which that individual belongs but, also and more fundamentally, to wrong the person. Similarly, foreigners may not be enslaved, may not be stolen from, and so on. All this may seem too obvious to bear repeating, but if developed in parallel to intranational liberal theory, the consequences are far-reaching. Just as it is impermissible for Williams to interfere with Smith and Jones so as to prevent their transacting, so too is it a violation of liberty rights for the United States or France or Nigeria to block transactions between willing parties.[15] That holds true just as much for interactions across borders as within them. The noninterference requirement is modest, no more than a pro forma geographical extension of familiar principles of freedom of association within a state. However, if consistently put into practice it would force radical revision of the control that states exercise over their citizens' relations with foreign nationals. It would, in a word, be to establish a liberalism beyond borders.

## III. Causes of the Wealth (and Woe) of Nations

Some time between the end of the religious wars of the seventeenth century and the present, human circumstances changed profoundly. Whereas wealth was heretofore very much the exception, now it is the

---

[15] Strictly speaking, this claim should bear a *ceteris paribus* qualifier. If the transaction between A and B incorporates infliction of a material harm on C, then principles of self-defense legitimate C's acting so as to block the arrangement. In this respect, international transactions do not differ from domestic ones.

rule. Or to be more precise: in selected locales it is the rule. But we can be more precise still. To oversimplify only slightly, the representative person's prospects for living a tolerably long, prosperous, and decent life are excellent in virtually every location in which there obtains robust protection of private property under the rule of law—that is, wherever liberal structures hold sway. (The only exceptions of which I am aware result from great natural disasters or war.) This result holds both for small island nations and for continental powers; it holds where natural resources are abundant and where they are scarce; it holds in the heart of the developed West and in recently impoverished corners of Asia. Social science is not physics, and the sort of precision exemplified by physical laws is not to be expected in mappings of social phenomena. Yet here if anywhere we have something approaching the status of a general law of societal achievement. The macro-problem of human misery has been solved—in theory but, in far too many venues, not in practice.

Whatever may have been the case some decades back when general prosperity was the special possession only of a small number of populations bordering the Atlantic, and when socialist fancies were the primary domain in which speculations about transformation of the human condition played themselves out, it is no longer credible to proceed on the assumption that poverty around the globe is a phenomenon to be understood in the first instance as the result of stinginess in transfer payments from the rich. If a people can provide for itself a basically liberal order, then its citizens will do well. Otherwise, they are in jeopardy. More effective than the transfer of financial assets from wealthy to poor lands is transfer of the institutional structures within which such assets are generated. One might imagine that accounts of international justice would automatically take this phenomenon as central to their analyses. Egalitarian theories, however, tend to resist or ignore this result. That calls for explanation.

If the dominant reason why poor countries[16] remain poor is because their own institutions are deficient, then the responsibility for the poverty of some is not the wealth of others. Children in America eat well, often too well for their own good, but in Somalia many starve. American plenty does not, however, explain African dearth. The world's wealth is not zero-sum, and thus to consume more is not to visit a harm on those who consume less. Disparities in holdings are, for the most part, explicable by noting how the rich have made themselves rich and the poor have made

---

[16] Selecting an appropriate term to refer to those states in which per-capita income hovers perilously close to the destitution line is difficult. Speaking of them as "developing countries" blissfully ignores the key problem that most are conspicuously failing to develop. "Third World nations" was lamentably vague when the Soviet Union pretended to be a functional regime and is just plain innumerate now. "Burdened society" seems to suggest an external burdener; "failed state" is pessimistic and abruptly final. I shall for the most part, then, unimaginatively speak of poor and wealthy countries.

themselves poor. As Rawls observes, "the problem [of poor countries] is commonly the nature of the public political culture and the religious and philosophical traditions that underlie its institutions. The great social evils in poorer societies are likely to be oppressive government and corrupt elites." [17] This is not to deny that gross inequalities among peoples are evidence of injustice, but it does strongly suggest that the claims of the world's poor are mostly to be addressed against their own governing institutions. However, in a moral environment in which the greatest of all offenses is to "blame the victim," stating this reasonably evident fact strikes some as indecent. Does it mean that the fortunate citizens of the West (and, increasingly, of other parts of the developed world) are at liberty to shrug off the plight of the world's destitute billions by saying, "That's their doing, not ours"? In a word, no. As I will argue, there is quite enough blame to go around, including blame ascribable to wealthy countries for committing injustices against their own citizens which simultaneously visit hardships on those in other countries who are least able to cope. The aim is not to let wealthy nations off the hook but to urge that they be pegged to the right one.

During the 1980s and 1990s, something on the order of 100 million Chinese were lifted above the dollar-a-day income threshold. This represents the single greatest rollback of abject poverty in the history of the world. That Chinese renaissance continues to accelerate, and alongside it a liftoff of comparable magnitude is occurring in India. Compared to these profound changes in the condition of poor peoples, the impact of foreign aid transfers has been minor. What has made the difference in China, as previously in smaller countries of southeast Asia, is security of property holdings coupled with openness to world markets. Conversely, those nations in which access to capital and enterprise formation are jealously controlled by ideological or kleptocratic state bureaucracies remain places in which prospects for leading decent lives have stagnated. Encouragingly, no Periclean exemplars of wise government have been needed to enable escape from general misery. China remains an undemocratic gerontocracy in which respect for human rights is patchy, especially for those entitlements that are deemed to challenge perquisites of the ruling political class. India, although firmly democratic, still has far to go in loosening the bureaucratic hobbles bequeathed by Fabian-inspired colonial overlords and its first generation of indigenous governors. The good news is that no more than a minimal level of political virtue, most especially the virtue of restraint, is needed to catalyze that initial jump into wealth-creation which then, barring backsliding, becomes self-sustaining.

The bad news, of course, is that too many regimes fall conspicuously short of even that minimal level. It seems hideously unfair that populations should suffer grievously from the failures of their domestic institu-

---

[17] Rawls, *The Law of Peoples*, 77.

tions, institutions over which they themselves have virtually no influence. Unfair indeed it is, but this is not an injustice readily addressable by well-meaning external donors. When tens of millions of Chinese citizens were class-struggle casualties of Mao's Great Leap Forward [*sic*] and then the misbegotten Cultural Revolution of the late 1960s, the injustices from which they suffered were almost entirely domestic in origin. And when they began to benefit from initial forays into the arena of global capitalism, melioration was also predominantly domestic. It is, therefore, misleading to characterize the gross wealth disparities that obtain in different sectors of the world as the subject matter of international (in)justice. These are far more the effect of depredations within borders than across them. That is not to say that poverty in other lands holds no moral relevance for the activities of well-off foreign agencies and individuals, but they are secondary respondents rather than primary instigators. In that restricted capacity, they can do some genuine good, but only if they realistically assess their efficacy.

It is much easier to transfer money than salutary social structures. In the extreme, dollar bills can be shoveled from helicopters to waft to waiting hands below. To the best of my knowledge, foreign aid has never been extended in such aerial form,[18] yet it would have one distinct advantage over formal intergovernmental transfers. Helicopter largesse, despite its windborne randomness, would find its way directly to primary beneficiaries, while aid extended via a stricken population's government passes first into just those hands that have shown themselves to be deficient. At best, funds extended may soften the edges of rough-hewn policies; at worst, they will strengthen the position of whichever thief or tyrant has lately taken up residence in the presidential palace. Because the natural interlocutors of a government are other governments, states are likely to have only limited facility in addressing the plight of distressed foreign populations. Even if there were a requirement of justice to alleviate misfortunes that are not of one's own making, direct foreign aid must be quite far down on the list of measures holding out a promise of efficacy.

A much stronger case can be made, in principle, for direct intervention to force maladroit or malevolent rulers to act on behalf of subject populations. That would be to address the proximate cause of distress rather than to apply financial salve in hit-or-miss fashion. The qualifier, however, looms large. Colonialist paternalism has been out of fashion for the last half-century, and the historical record does not make this a cause of regret. Western powers had their innings in Africa, the Middle East, and Asia; by and large, they did a sorry job of tending to the welfare of those over whom they ruled. There would be no reason at all to feel nostalgic for the reigns of viceroys and colonial governors were it not for the fact

---

[18] The 1948–49 Berlin airlift comes close.

that home rule has, in many cases, shown itself to be even more sangui-
nary and corrupt. Nonetheless, it is now a firmly settled convention of
international relations that sovereign states are, apart from exceptional
circumstances, to be left alone to make their own way in the world. And
when those exceptional circumstances have obtained—in Rwanda in 1994,
in Srebrenica in 1995, and now in Darfur—the international community
has shown itself to be less than adroit in stemming genocide, let alone
establishing the underpinnings of benign social structures. That is not to
conclude that foreign intervention is never justified on humanitarian
grounds (see Section IV.E), but it is to suggest that this, too, is an uncertain
device. America, it seems, did rather well for its client in postwar Japan,
rather poorly in Somalia. The jury is still out in Iraq. However, the price
of regime change is measured not only in dollars but also in blood.
Reluctance on the part of democratic electorates to bear these costs for the
sake of benefits that may or may not be bestowed on a distant people is
neither surprising nor discreditable. Thus, the role of direct intervention
to alter dysfunctional political and economic structures abroad will remain
at most a small component of international justice.

## IV. PRECEPTS OF LIBERAL INTERNATIONAL JUSTICE

The preceding section should not be taken as a counsel of despair. The
plight of the world's poor does not put them beyond hope. Almost without exception, they are but one step away from getting on the path to
prosperity and decency. That step is replacement of malignant socio-
political structures with tolerably humane and effective ones. With socialist nostrums now consigned to the dustbin of history and with the example
of dozens of societies that have successfully made the leap from poverty
to adequacy and then along to plenty, it is now well-known what such a
transformation entails. It is also well-known what is not required: foreign
aid packages, overgrown development bureaucracies, a "third way" that
skirts the alleged excesses of both communism and capitalism. These are
useless, worse than useless if they are seen as a substitute for commitment
to robust property rights and free markets. But to say that embracing
market institutions and the rule of law is "all" that is required to lift
societies from abject want to increasing plenty is not a prediction that
such progress will be widespread or rapid. Cooperation for mutual benefit is one way in which people can seek to advance their interests, but
another is predation by the strong on the weak. Where predatory structures are well-established, they can display depressing stability. Those on
top are loath to give up their status to those on whom they fatten, and
those on the bottom may have no aspiration burning more intensely in
their breast than to turn the tables and despoil their despoilers. Predation
is supported by ideologies of racial, national, and religious domination,
and these are alive and well in the first decade of the twenty-first century.

Moreover, many members of the intelligentsia of wealthy nations partake in esoteric rites of simulated self-flagellation in which they confess the culpability of their societies for the distress of the world's poor. (It is simulation because they exclude themselves from the strata of their societies who are blamed.) Even if not widely believed, they afford cover to those who are content to locate culpability closer to Washington, D.C., and London, say, than to Mogadishu and Damascus. Nor is it a sure thing that those who have leaped onto the train to increasing prosperity will not jump off. Over preceding centuries, peoples have shown a remarkable capacity to wed themselves to policies that lay themselves low; there is no reason except hubris to suppose that we have permanently lost the ability to imitate the lemmings as we jubilantly scramble toward the cliffs.

Nonetheless, and with all disclaimers duly noted, the proper attitude is one of optimism. For the first time in human history, it is at least possible for the entire world's population to live well. This is terrific news! Broadsides headlining wealth disparities between the wealthy 20 percent and the remainder should not be allowed to disguise the epochal significance of this alteration of the human condition. There are innumerable reasons why the world's poor suffer from hunger, disease, and the manifold brutalizations consequent on want and despair, but reluctance by the wealthy societies of the West to admit additional new members into their club is not among them.

If this essay is not a foray into pessimism, neither is it a rationalization of the conduct of the world's wealthy and powerful. To say that they are not the primary perpetrators of global distress is not to find them blameless. I have maintained that most so-called violations of international justice are in fact better understood as rooted in domestic failings, and that nearly all the world's peoples would enjoy lives of decency and prosperity if they were beneficiaries of tolerably adequate internal governance. It is only at the margin that external transactors make a difference—but when summed over billions of persons, these marginal effects are considerable.

Liberalism, especially in its classical version, is a theory about required omissions rather than commissions. To respect the rights of others is first and fundamentally to afford them noninterference. Positive provision of welfare goods is, if present at all, secondary. To extend the theory of liberalism across borders is to commend noninterference by both governments and private parties with foreign nationals. To the extent that this has not been forthcoming, there are justifiable complaints to be lodged against the members of the Organization for Economic Cooperation and Development (OECD) and their fortunate brethren. As with the practice of medicine, the primary and overriding requirement is, first, to do no harm. Insofar as the policies of some states impose harms on the nationals of others, a legitimate claim for redress can be made. This is not the occasion to prepare a comprehensive brief on behalf of the world's have-nots against the haves—or, for that matter, the haves against the have-nots—but the points made in the following five subsections convey a sense of the direction that a liberal account of justice across borders will take.

## A. Noncooperation with oppression

Both the state acting in its official capacity and citizens in their roles as private actors are to refrain from lending assistance to foreign oppressors. To facilitate the violation of rights is itself to be a rights-violator. This is true globally as well as locally. Murder and theft do not change their nature when committed across borders. They are strictly impermissible.

As a programmatic statement of liberal dicta, the foregoing is impeccable. However, application of the principle of nonfacilitation quickly becomes murky in a world of states that exercise authority in ways that deviate significantly from the paradigm of liberal democracies operating under an impersonal rule of law. Consider, for example, loans across state borders from rich to poor made either by governmental agencies, quasi-governmental instrumentalities such as the World Bank, or private lenders. On the one hand, resultant debt burdens fall on subject populations, sometimes weighing heavily for generations. Typically without any prior concurrence on their part, their meager income streams are encumbered to satisfy the demands of wealthy foreign note holders. On the other hand, access to capital is a necessary ingredient for lifting a people out of want and into contact with the markets in which wealth is generated. To decline to take on external debt is to acquiesce to continued poverty. What, then, is a conscientious lender to do? There exists no algorithm that yields answers satisfactory for all cases. Still, there are some general guidelines for respecting the interests of vulnerable populations. All else equal, loans that create only voluntarily assumed indebtedness are to be preferred to those that inflate tax burdens. Direct investment by foreign corporations or joint ventures with domestic parties satisfy this criterion unless they come attached to "guarantees" offered by the host state. Money extended directly to sovereign borrowers is more suspect, especially when there is no mechanism for containing it within national borders so that it does not take flight to nest in anonymous Swiss bank accounts. However, improvements in infrastructure—roads, education, health-care facilities—that are required for economic advancement and that will pay for themselves many times over in increased national productivity often can only be supplied through public funds. In such cases, it makes good economic and moral sense for responsible states to borrow and for conscientious dispensers of capital to lend. The problem is to tell these cases apart. Perhaps the fairest and most reliable means for getting situations like this right is to ensure that much or all of the risk of subsequent inability to repay falls on the lender. That way self-interest, if not a robust sense of justice, will lead lenders to do their homework before extending credit.

Similar considerations apply with regard to transnational corporations' access to labor and physical resources. For rulers who find vexingly slow the rate of cash flow into their coffers generated by taxes extracted from an impoverished citizenry, an occasion to secure personal emoluments from wealthy foreign firms in exchange for concessionary grants will be a welcome windfall. Between functionaries of the state and corporate buccaneers, not much may be left for those who do the laboring. But if exploitation of laborers by their own rulers is avoided, the entry of corporations from abroad affords welcome opportunities. Would-be Western well-wishers are wont to denounce as exploitative the low salaries and onerous working conditions that are offered to employees in developing countries, but those workers who find the terms of employment offered by branches of transnational corporations by far their best available opportunity will wish that they could bask yet more deeply in such "exploitation." [19]

Liberal principles of international justice, then, are friendly to cross-border economic transactions insofar as they do not incorporate coercion by local authorities. Transnational firms themselves do not threaten the rights of host populations, because it is almost never the case that businesses are in a position to exert undue pressure on their workers without the complicity of local authorities. If in pursuit of accommodating labor relations, however, businesses accept authorities' offers of truncheons and prison cells so as to deny laborers an option of free exit, then they stand as co-perpetrators of injustice. Ultimately, estimations of where to draw lines with regard to acceptable lending, investment, and employment must avoid the opposed tendencies of utopianism and a cynicism that passes as realism. Transactional partners are rarely economic or moral paragons. Rejecting deals with parties tainted by oppressive, even murderous activities, would mean that even those states perched toward the high end of the spectrum of respect for individual rights would be barred from dealing with themselves! (Consider, for example, the 1993 killing of David Koresh and his followers by federal agents in Waco, Texas; or the systematic British humiliation of Irish prisoners.) Judgments must always be made at the margin: Is the proposed relationship more likely to nudge subject peoples toward decency and prosperity than to tighten the vise of their misery? Where money and power are at stake, honest responses are hard to come by, but, one must hope, not impossible.

---

[19] Denunciations of the degrading nature of working conditions abroad are especially suspect when offered by parties such as labor unions who stand as competitors to these foreign enterprises.

## B. *Revising the public/private aid mix*

Liberal international justice ought to be suspicious of government-to-government aid packages. Typically they come with strings attached. Superpowers shop for allies, and the foreign policy of mid-level states is often in the service of domestic commercial interests. On the recipient side, political elites who control aid distribution may be motivated by private interests that diverge from those of the populations they allegedly serve. States operate in a less ambiguous capacity, however, when they facilitate person-to-person aid between nongovernmental donors and targeted recipients. They are well-positioned to deploy their good offices to persuade rulers of host nations at least not to interfere with such aid arrangements. Simple state noninterference may be all that is needed to make a substantial difference. There is good reason to expect aid offered by private charitable agencies to be more effective and benevolent than that tendered politically. Because nongovernmental agencies are not able to secure funds through coercive extraction, and because they serve a simple agenda of doing some good abroad, they are apt to be more responsive than are state bureaus both to the donors who support their philanthropies and to the intended beneficiaries.

It may be asked whether enough assistance will be forthcoming under general privatization of the international assistance business. The question is ill-defined without some prior specification of what is meant by "enough." Even under the most optimistic forecast, it must be conceded that sums extended by charitable donors will not suffice to put impoverished peoples on a path to prosperity. That is not because individuals acting in a private capacity are less generous than governments, but because the necessary conditions for achieving general well-being are mostly domestic and only secondarily capable of being supplied by external grantors. Even if privatization of aid would result in smaller sums crossing borders, itself a speculative forecast, it is predictable that a much lesser fraction would be diverted to enrich corrupt authorities or be wasted on showy projects that better serve the interests of elites than those of needier segments of the population. Furthermore, private aid would have what from a liberal perspective must be the considerable advantage of being voluntarily tendered rather than coercively extracted. The interests of both givers and recipients count, and these interests are respected by an order of voluntary philanthropic relations.

Although anecdotes can take us only so far in reflecting on principles of international justice, it is worth observing that in response to disasters such as the December 2004 tsunami, individuals and charitable organizations across the world opened their pockets to assist devastated populations. Less spectacular, but no less estimable, are the continuing philanthropies of organizations such as Oxfam and the Bill and Melinda Gates Foundation. Governments and quasi-governmental agencies can genuinely contribute to the

efficacy of those activities by quietly exerting influence on host governments not to block charitable transfers and to desist from siphoning off
funds. They also can assist with transportation, communications, and accumulation of materiel in response to acute crises. But basically the role of
the state should be secondary.[20] Moreover, it is to be expected that as governmental agencies gradually shed their role as leading players within the
aid business, entrepreneurial charities would come up with innovative ways
of occupying the territory ceded to them. "Crowding out" would be
replaced by "crowding in." Critics will contend that the scenario depicted
is rosily optimistic, that the actual accomplishments of an order of privatized aid are apt to fall short of these depictions. These critics may well be
correct. However, it is not as if the practice of state-dominated aid that has
obtained since the end of the Second World War has shown itself to be sig-
nally successful—else it would no longer be needed. Rather than calling
for "more of the same," liberal principles of international assistance endorse
substantial restructuring of the roles of private and public parties, according priority to the former.

## C. Justice in trade

Liberal support for loosening shackles that constrain trade across borders is more crucial than ever. Ready access to foreign markets is not
merely an economic desideratum at the fringes of national economies but
a necessary condition for lifting populations out of poverty. The argument
for free trade has been thoroughly and consistently set out for more than
two centuries. If intellectual merit sufficed to generate policy victories,
protectionism would now be as defunct as the dodo. But impartial theorizing is apt to take a back seat to the play of interests, and those whose
livelihoods depend on buying and selling rarely will oppose on principle
measures that promise to shield them from some degree of competition.
Thus, freeing up trade is not a battle that is won once and for all, but is
rather an endless series of forays, each of which has to be fought anew.
Today the campaign against open markets is waged most noticeably in

---

[20] It might be objected that coercion by the state is needed to overcome what decision
theorists call an "assurance problem." Citizens, it is claimed, might individually have some
desire to act philanthropically, but they will contribute only if they are confident that others
will also contribute. Without some mechanism affording assurance to each citizen of the
similar compliance of the others, the philanthropic preference will go unrealized. Mandated
tax contributions thus not only bring about a valuable result but also give effect to the
predilections people already hold.
  The story, although not impossible, is far-fetched. That many people really do strongly
desire themselves and their compatriots to be taxed more heavily so as to swell foreign-aid
budgets seems to be confirmed neither by opinion polls nor by the observed politics of
national budget-making. Nor is it evident that most people's charitable impulses are so
strongly contingent on the behavior of others. It is an open question whether an order of
privatized international aid would be hobbled by widespread tendencies to free-ride, and it
is best answered by putting the hypothesis to the test.

the media and the streets by "antiglobalization" cadres, an ill-matched assortment from across the political spectrum who unite only on a platform of substituting political for economic parameters in governing production and exchange. One of the banners under which they march, "Fair trade, not free trade," explicitly represents the campaign as one for justice. Liberals will, of course, reject the implied opposition between freedom and fairness. The freedom of willing parties to transact on terms they find mutually agreeable is of the essence of fair dealing. Conversely, imposition of terms by third parties who foist their own interests and ideals on unwilling others is the epitome of injustice. But this is a very old tune that need not be rehearsed here.

However one interprets nuances of fairness and freedom, it is apparent that poor nations suffer from sins against both in the global marketplace. Extensive programs of tariffs, quotas, and subsidies distort markets for those primary commodities, especially agricultural goods, that are mainstays of the fledgling economies of these countries. Not only is it difficult for them to compete against the technological sophistication and efficiency of producers in the United States and Europe, but in addition they must contend with the subsidies these wealthy countries bestow on their own producers. These subsidies lead to underpricing of weaker competitors, which effectively bars them from international markets. The result is that wealthy corporate producers of crops such as cotton earn handsome profits while African workers of the land starve. In the postwar period, the various installments of the General Agreement on Tariffs and Trade (GATT) and its successor, the World Trade Organization (WTO), have enjoyed signal success in lowering trade barriers. The result has been an unprecedented growth of international trade and the prosperity resulting therefrom. Not all parties, however, have benefited at this high level. Too many economies languish. That is not all to be laid at the door of the WTO, but it is presumptive evidence that the job of liberalizing the world market is far from complete.

Because economic activity is positive-sum, all parties are benefited by arrangements that afford them greater scope for undertaking beneficial transactions. Lowering trade barriers is not a "gift" to foreign entrants, but rather advances also the interests of domestic producers and consumers who thereby secure access to desired commercial relations. Therefore, each sovereign entity has self-interested reasons to liberalize markets regardless of what other states do. However, each does better still if those others also eschew protection. This is one reason why the game of trade negotiation often features states refusing to dismantle barriers unless other states reciprocate by offering corresponding relaxations.[21] It is possible, then, especially in a setting where the

---

[21] Another important reason is that while economies as a whole will benefit from increased openness, there will always be some parties disadvantaged by widening the scope of competition. If they are politically potent, they may be able to block agreement.

number of players is great and their interests diverse, that they remain indefinitely blocked from agreeing on measures that benefit everyone, each player holding out for terms that are yet more favorable from its own perspective. This is a fair characterization of recent stumbling at the 2004 WTO meetings in Doha, Qatar, in which rich countries demanded, among other provisions, enhanced protection for intellectual property rights, poor countries more welcoming markets for agricultural exports, never the twain managing to meet. Liberal theorists have no difficulty in characterizing such nonagreement for mutual disadvantage as ludicrously counterproductive and unjust. The theorists' expertise does not, however, extend to deriving tactics calculated to break such impasses. But as the diplomats continue to play their tortuous games, spectators on the sidelines ought to proclaim in a loud voice that while all protectionism perpetrates injustice, insult is added to injury by those barriers that especially disadvantage the poor. If it is impossible to brush away webs of restriction with one sweeping gesture, then first priority should be given to the elimination of those barriers most directly implicated in destitution and despair.

Some social philosophers, Thomas Pogge chief among them, have argued that deformities in international trade structures constitute actionable wrongs inflicted by the rich on the poor, and that these support a call for massive reparations to be made in the form of cash transfers.[22] For several reasons the call is misdirected. First, the timing is backwards. Before demanding of parties that they repair damages caused by their unjust policies, they must be persuaded that those policies are indeed wrong. In a world in which protection still carries (unmerited) respectability, demands for reparations are, at the very least, premature. Second, this is a thinly disguised plea for intergovernmental aid transfers, a less good medicine for the ills of poverty than is a grant of free access to markets. Third and most fundamentally, it confuses the nature of the harms done by the international trade regime. The OECD high-flyers are labeled culprits who unjustly enrich themselves at the expense of the world's poor. This is to buy into the protectionist fable that a country advances itself by erecting barriers to imports. From the early years of liberal theory, this conception has been put to the test and found wanting. What is objectionable about subsidies, quotas, and tariffs is not that these are techniques of hard-dealing via which the rich get richer and the poor get poorer. Rather, they are no less welfare-diminishing domestically than they are internationally. If, for example, cheap foreign textiles are not allowed into the United States, then would-be American consumers are made worse off for the advantage of American clothes manufacturers. If

---

[22] See Thomas Pogge, "'Assisting' the Global Poor," in Deen K. Chatterjee, ed., *The Ethics of Assistance: Morality and the Distant Needy* (Cambridge: Cambridge University Press, 2004), 260–88.

African cotton cannot compete with American cotton because the latter benefits from substantial subsidies, then domestic cotton growers are being unfairly enriched at the expense of all other Americans—and, of course, at the expense of foreign producers. And so on with regard to the myriad gothic adornments of the world trade order. Their primary damage is intranational, not international.

The reason I focus on this point is because it spotlights with special clarity what is distinctive about the liberal understanding—an avowedly *classical liberal* understanding—of international justice advanced in this essay. Using some parties against their will as mere means for the ends of others is wrong wherever it is practiced. Crossing borders does not cleanse the practice. However, domestic forced redistributions that impose costs on some population segments so as to shower benefits on others are enthusiastically cheered by egalitarians of both liberal and antiliberal persuasions. They accord to these redistributions the honorific rubric "social justice." But then when a practice warmly endorsed within states is seen to exacerbate hardships in distant lands, convoluted justificatory scrambling follows. Somehow, what is wrong with the European Union's Common Agricultural Policy has to be spelled out in a manner that does not impugn the EU's commitment to a sweeping range of internal controls and transfers.[23] Without recapitulating the entire social justice debate, starting with the first page of Rawls's *A Theory of Justice*, it is not possible to demonstrate in detail why this is a vain hope. Rawls himself bites the bullet of confining substantial redistribution within national borders, thus disappointing those followers who wish to extend the demands of (re)distributive justice into a seamless cosmopolitan theory.[24] They take the sharp difference between Rawls's theories of domestic and international justice to represent a debilitating inconsistency. Perhaps it does. But a more glaring inconsistency is to defend sacrifices imposed by a national politics of redistribution on some segments of the citizenry in order to benefit others while decrying the same when the victims are foreign nationals. A considerable advantage of the classical liberal theory of justice is that it exhibits greater continuity within and across borders than do any of the rival accounts.

## D. Free movement across borders

Most of the reasons supporting free movements of goods and services across borders also support free movement for individuals. The lines on

---

[23] French opponents of the proposed European Constitution successfully engineered its May 2005 referendum defeat in part by decrying its "extreme Anglo-Saxon liberalism." Despite whatever other grounds on which their appraisal of the proposed constitution was misjudged, they accurately diagnosed the intrinsic opposition between the welfare state's forced redistributions and the fundamental precepts of political and economic liberalism.

[24] See, for example, the authors cited in note 5 above.

a map that separate Mexicans from Americans or the European-Ins from the European-Outs are morally arbitrary, yet on which side one happens to have landed is liable to make an enormous difference for one's life prospects. To be blocked from buying and selling across borders is an unjustifiable restraint on liberty, but so also are general barriers against cross-border employment and residence agreements.[25]

There are two chief reasons why movement of persons across borders can be more problematic than movement of products: security concerns and financial entailments. A widget purchased from abroad is inert; it lies there until put to the service that widgets perform. But immigrants exercise agency. As no one needs to be reminded post–September 11, 2001, some intend harm to the country they have entered. Migrants who are utterly benign in their intentions need food, shelter, and occasional health services. They produce children who require these basic goods and educational services as well. For those who carry along with them a handsome asset portfolio or who are lucratively remunerated, meeting basic needs is not a problem. But the much greater number who are accompanied across borders only by their poverty may be deemed a significant potential drain on resources. As with the potentially hostile, their exclusion is justified on grounds of self-interest.

It is not possible to offer more than a cursory response to these two worries. Against the former, it is conceded that addressing security concerns is a legitimate function of the state, indeed its central function. The necessity of thwarting would-be malefactors, both domestic and external, should condition all state policies. Freedom of movement is a deeply held liberal principle, but it may permissibly be constrained by legitimate security concerns. Nonetheless, and with all due acknowledgment of the grim realities that have intruded into twenty-first century consciousness, it is simply not credible to maintain that the vast bulk of immigration poses any significant security threat. The tens of thousands of Mexicans who each year cross the Rio Grande, either legally or otherwise, do not enter the United States to do it harm. Their motives of self-advancement are transparent. So too for the vast majority of those who seek to work or study in Europe, Australia, and the other wealthy OECD countries. Reasonable persons will differ concerning the nature of immigration controls needed at entry points to address legitimate security concerns, but on even the most conservative reckoning, such measures will not exclude any large number of potential economic entrants.

The financial drain objection cuts more deeply. With a few dishonorable exceptions (e.g., restrictions on Chinese nationals), the United States throughout the nineteenth century and into the first two decades of the

---

[25] I develop a fuller response to the implications of morally arbitrary borders for trade and migration in "Toward a Liberal Theory of National Boundaries," in David Miller and Sohail Hashmi, eds., *Boundaries and Justice* (Princeton, NJ: Princeton University Press, 2001), 55–78.

twentieth was, to its enduring credit, a land that threw open its borders to millions of individuals who wished to commence a new life under new skies. The United States is still one of the world's major recipients of immigration, but with many more restrictions on would-be entrants. What has changed in the interim? Prospects for personal advancement in America have not waned, nor has the ability of the economy to support increased numbers. The U.S. population has not become more insular in its vistas or more viciously nativist in its prejudices. Rather, the transformative process that most strikingly conditions immigration policy in the United States (and other traditional magnets for migrants) is the rise of the welfare state. To be on the lucky side of the border is to be in possession of a brass ring that entitles one to a wide variety of benefits, courtesy of the public treasury. It is no wonder that residents of well-off states in which taxation supports extensive welfare functions are disinclined to welcome impoverished entrants likely to be net subtractors from the pie to be carved up. Professionals and investors, yes; poor, tired, huddled masses, no.

Although some will cast blame on the greed of a grasping, inhospitable bourgeoisie, I do not share that assessment. A desire to possess and augment one's property is both honorable and the engine of economic advance. What is unfortunate is that in combination with the characteristic form of contemporary Western social democracies, this desire harshly damages the prospects of countless individuals who are stymied from relocating to where their lives would go better. I believe that the optimal resolution of this dilemma would be wholesale rolling back of the welfare state. That, of course, is utopian (others will say dystopian!) fantasy—if not forever, then at least for the foreseeable future. However, intermediate means are available for relaxing the firmness of borders while nonetheless maintaining politically popular redistributionist measures. For example, individuals could be allowed to enter at will, but with an express proviso that they and their families would not be permitted to avail themselves of any of the state's welfare services for a stipulated period. Although it is much preferable to current policies of exclusion, such a measure would almost certainly prove to be unsustainable.[26] To observe people sick from hunger and inadequate shelter, who are then denied health services for which they are unable to pay, and who lack the means to provide even basic education for their children, would be intolerable. Of course, such is the plight of vastly greater numbers of individuals living in destitution abroad, people whose prospects would skyrocket if they were allowed to immigrate even under a no-welfare proviso, but not having actually to experience them close-up is wonderful balm to the conscience.

What may under current circumstances be the least bad policy would be to allow entry to all individuals who provide a surety that they are not

---

[26] Nor would it likely pass muster with courts either in the United States or in the European Union.

likely to be a charge on the public.[27] This condition could, for example, be satisfied by posting a bond. The evident problem with this device is that penniless migrants are in no position to comply. However, others of like nationality, religion, or family connection (or charitable agencies) may choose to vouch for and provide surety for entrants. This has the great advantage of substantially privatizing immigration policy decisions. In addition, those immigrants in possession of a bona fide employment offer on terms such that they are thereby enabled to support themselves at a minimally decent level—where minimal decency is understood not as may be conceived by rich Westerners but relative to the standards that obtain in the countries from which the immigrants fled—would be deemed to have provided the requisite surety. Note that this policy is responsive not only to the interests of those desirous of entering the country but also to the rights of would-be employers to enter into mutually advantageous contractual relationships. To keep a tight lid on borders is to restrict the liberties not only of foreigners but also of citizens. Here again, the conclusions of international justice are congruent with those of intranational justice.

I do not deny that there are numerous complications that will have to be addressed in giving effect to these proposals. What happens when an immigrant loses her job or is exploited by a threat of being fired with deportation to follow? For how long a period must someone reside in the country and post a record of acceptable conduct before being accorded the full rights and privileges of residents? And so on. Without denying that these are legitimate concerns, and without having a grab-bag full of remedies on offer, I content myself with noting that in these considerations we are far from the world of ideal theory. The appropriate question to ask with regard to the desirability of any policy proposal is: Compared to what? Rendering borders less inimical to possibilities of human flourishing, if only at the margin, is a worthwhile aspiration of liberal theorizing.

Let me address two related matters before moving on. First, the principle propounded here radically revises current international legal practices that privilege refugees fleeing persecution over "mere" economic migrants. The former have a right against the host nation to be harbored (assuming that they are able to show their fear of persecution to be well-justified), while the latter do not, even if they can prove that they are escaping destitution. This I take to be backwards. Refugees ought indeed be accorded sanctuary, but the basis of their pull on our moral sensibilities is compassion or pity rather than justice in a strict sense. Observe that refugees must be sheltered even if doing so imposes significant costs on

---

[27] I say "not likely" because, for example, a net contributor may become a net subtractor by committing a crime and then consuming resources of the judicial and penal systems. This is true for both citizens and immigrants; in fact, citizens may be more likely to become net subtractors, insofar as one available cost-cutting sentence that can be employed against alien felons is deportation.

the receiver state. Economic migrants who are self-supporting or supported by willing private parties impose no direct costs on unwilling others, and thus their exclusion cannot be justified on grounds of defense of one's property. Why, then, the priority accorded refugees? I believe that the rationale is less a matter of concern for the persecuted than a handy pretext for barring the gates against all others. Is this belief cynical? Yes. Is it more accurate than not? Readers are invited to hazard a response. In saying that, from the perspective of justice, economic migrants possess the more substantial claim, I am not advocating withdrawal of sanctuary from refugees. To shield defenseless victims is admirable. Rather, the contention is that denying means of bettering their lot to those who do not satisfy the lawyers' criteria for being considered refugees is disgraceful.

Second, critics may contend that opening borders does not solve the problems of poor nations, and may indeed exacerbate them by allowing a brain-drain—and a labor-drain, and an ambition-drain—from venues where human as well as physical capital is in short supply. I concede the point. Relaxing border stringency will not erase those yawning inequalities and vast stretches of misery that are generated by the incompetence and brutality of the institutions of dysfunctional states. The problems that beset severely disadvantaged peoples are only slightly softened by the proposal. Unlike Rawls, however, I do not take the primary, let alone exclusive, focus of international justice to be *peoples,* but rather *people.* It is incompatible with basic liberal principles to hold individuals hostage to the collective entities, the "peoples," from which they would separate themselves. Hospitality to migrants is only a small component of international justice, but it is indispensable.

### E. Humanitarian intervention

On any given day, deliberate campaigns of murder and despoliation carried out by the powerful against the powerless generate mounds of corpses and crowds of displaced persons. As this paragraph is being composed, the Darfur region of Sudan is a notorious example. A few years earlier, the examples that would have come to mind were genocidal rampage in Rwanda, "ethnic cleansing" in the Balkans, Maoist slaughter of class enemies, and, paradigmatic for our time and perhaps all time, the Holocaust. If there has been any period of recent history in which these barbarisms have been absent, I am not aware of it. Certainly any theory of international justice has to take cognizance of such crimes against humanity. And yet . . .

Some problems do not admit of solution. Massacre is not one of them. Indeed, in virtually every such case the solution is transparently simple: let the perpetrators desist! The derivative problem is that they do not choose to do so, and to this there may indeed be no solution. More specifically, there may be no solution accessible to well-meaning external parties. What can be done about Darfur? Rephrase the question as: What can the United States/Europe/the United Nations/you-and-I do about Darfur? No doubt there are better and worse responses to each of these question-variations. The dispiriting fact of the matter may be, however, that against these greatest of injustices, no very good response is available to any party able and willing to make a difference. Perhaps sit-ins and public demonstrations are called for, not because they promise to alleviate the distress of those who are suffering, but because the alternative is to lend accommodation to evil by silence.

The best I am able to offer here are platitudes, but because not offering platitudes is offering nothing at all, platitudes it will be. Platitude number one is that those who are in a position effectively (and without imposing undue costs on nonconsenting others) to intervene should do so. This principle has extensive application to officials of those regimes that are superintending the killing, but may have limited scope for all others. The party most capable of addressing the ongoing misery of the North Korean masses is Kim Jong Il. The parties next most capable of taking action are North Korean military officers in a position to stage a coup or an assassination. Perhaps the Chinese government can exercise useful suasion, although even in these post–Tiananmen Square years, their hands are far from clean with regard to the practice of domestic oppression. But beyond these levels, the capacity of others to intervene effectively may be vanishingly small.

Platitude number two is that those unable to rectify the evil ought at least to try not to exacerbate it. Propping up great tyrants is to be avoided, even when those tyrants are useful allies in some international venture. Unfortunately, even this platitude is no better than a prima facie principle. During World War II, it was right and necessary for the Allied powers to lend support to Stalin in the fight against the Axis powers, even though Stalin remains high on the list of World's Greatest Despots. Nonetheless, and with all due acknowledgment of the manifold epistemic hurdles to be surmounted in determining whom to take on as an ally, not every crusade is as crucial for the maintenance of civilization as that against Hitler. There is a very strong presumption in favor of undermining rather than cooperating with tyrants. The leaders of liberal democracies have not always lent to that presumption the weight that it merits.

Platitude number three is that failure to intervene against murderous regimes can carry an exorbitantly high cost, but also that intervention itself can carry an exorbitantly high cost. Which of these is likely to be greater will often be unclear prospectively and even retrospectively. Without wishing to add fuel to contemporary debates, I note that the series of U.S. encounters with Saddam Hussein and Iraq—from initial support in Iraq's war against Iran, through the first Gulf War, the blockade and sanctions, the second Gulf War, and the subsequent reconstruction—has been such that at every stage reasonable persons can and do disagree about policy decisions. Issues of trade policy are (relatively) easy; issues surrounding relations with rogue regimes are excruciatingly difficult.

Platitude number four is that between forcibly intervening and refraining from intervention, there exists a standing presumption in favor of the latter. This may indeed be seen as nonplatitudinous, indeed erroneous, by those of a Wilsonian temperament. For them, the presumption is instead to seize opportunities where one finds them to make the world safe for democracy, or safe for whatever other ideal commands the day. The rationale for the platitude is not that Wilsonians are bound to do more harm than good, although I suspect that this may well be the case. Rather, the presumption against intervention appeals because of a very strong underlying presumption against pursuing valued ends by dragooning the lives and resources of others. The broken bodies of conscripts are as much battlefield fodder when the cause is just as when it is not. All-volunteer armies are funded by nonvoluntary taxation. In a world bearing marked affinities to the Hobbesian state of nature, coercive incursions on citizens are sometimes necessary, but they are to be kept to a minimum. That is why this principle is indeed a platitude within liberalism.

Platitude number five commends to all civilized states the task of seeking to devise fairer and more effective means of maintaining international order. There can be little disagreement with the observation that unilateral interventionary thrusts by superpowers for ostensibly humanitarian ends tend to work out rather less well than advertised in advance by their proponents. There can also be little disagreement with the observation that multilateral humanitarian operations also tend to work out less well than might be desired. And, of course, failures to intervene also may prove disastrous. The technology of international cooperation for humanitarian ends remains primitive. Certainly the United Nations as it is currently structured is a weak reed—although in some circumstances the strongest available. It may be that the various special interests of the several states thwarts all possibility of disinterested cooperation for the good of others. If so, then the need is to contrive some mechanism where, as in economic markets, an invisible hand transforms self-interest into the common good. Perhaps no such mechanism can be invented, but this cannot be known prior to serious, sustained attempts to achieve it.

## V. CONCLUSION

Imagine the world as a board with many squares large and small. On some squares, chips are piled high, while others are almost vacant. The difference in size among piles is objectionable. The problem for a theory of justice can be conceived as devising a mechanism for transferring chips from where they are plentiful to where they are few. The viewpoint taken is external, that of a benevolent and impartial spectator rather than that of a square occupant. The viewpoint is also fundamentally prospective.

Although some attention may be given to the historical record of how the piles grew or shrank, the aim of the exercise is not to evaluate the quality of preceding moves in the game as essayed by the various players, but rather to derive a strategy for moving toward pile equalization.

The checkerboard model is much too simplified to be pinned to any of the sophisticated philosophical theories of international justice that have been advanced over the more than three decades since the appearance of Rawls's *A Theory of Justice*. Nonetheless, both its inclusions and its exclusions provide a useful framework for assessing that literature. Certainly the model cannot be faulted for insisting that the absence in many locales of a minimally sufficient supply of goods constitutes a central issue for political morality, although perhaps it too exclusively assesses the moral imperative under the rubric of justice rather than generosity or compassion. Nor is the model to be faulted for observing that some wealth piles are many times larger than others. That observation is important if for no other reason than to identify these oases of plenty as objects of aspiration and potential emulation. If, however, the model then presumes that some piles are low *because* others are high, and that the well-endowed squares *act unjustly* unless they transfer some quantity of their chips to those that have little, it has taken a step too far. Why penury obtains where it does, which parties are obligated to act to alleviate it, and how that alleviation can be brought about are not data to be brought to the formulation of a theory of justice but rather theorems that are yielded by its construction. Both the externalism and the prospective reasoning of the checkerboard model must be modified by attention to how the occupants of the various squares appraise the trajectories that have landed them on their spots and the reasons they have from these various perspectives to respond to claims that might be lodged against them.

This essay has attempted to supply a framework for such investigations that is recognizably liberal and, thus, that propounds an account of international justice as continuous in the foundational principles it endorses with those of intranational justice. Rawls is frequently held by his critics to have failed to achieve such continuity. They propose to remedy that lapse by instituting a global difference principle or some similarly sweeping structure of cosmopolitan governance. By way of contrast, the account offered here derives from a more traditional liberalism of respect for persons' liberty and property. It contends that the persistence of poverty has much to do with the malformed domestic institutions of dysfunctional states, that hoped-for turnarounds will, therefore, mostly come from internal restructuring (if at all), and that wealthy peoples are obligated to support such efforts but are neither required nor in a position to be their primary engine. As that not-quite-liberal political theorist Deng Xiaoping observed, "To be wealthy is glorious!"—not a mark for recrimination. Acts of commission or omission that deprive others of opportunities to obtain wealth of their own are, however, injustices. Wealthy and powerful states have a duty not to lend assistance to despots who despoil subject populations, as well as duties to support (but not supplant) international philanthropies that directly address the needs of indigent persons as distinguished from their governors, to dismantle barriers to trade and migration, and to seek better international structures for precluding and responding to gross human rights violations.

One part of the program of international justice concerns the duties that peoples owe to each other. But another and arguably more fundamental part concerns obligations owed to individual persons both within and beyond national borders. To a much greater extent than is generally acknowledged, mandated transfers among citizens of a state and politically imposed restrictions on their liberty to transact with nonresidents foist burdens on nonconsenting others. Some of these burdens are local; others extend across the globe, with devastating effects on those least able to bear them. It is myopic to decry the latter while complacently accepting the former. I conclude by suggesting that the version of liberalism most suitable as a theoretical grounding for both internal and external dealings more closely resembles that of Adam Smith than that of John Rawls.

*Philosophy, University of Virginia*

# LIBERALISM AND THE CONSTITUTION

## By Sotirios A. Barber

### I. Introduction

The U.S. Constitution is widely regarded as the preeminent historical expression of philosophical liberalism, a conception of man and society that emerged in seventeenth-century England. If the fundamental assumptions and ultimate aims of liberalism were ever clear, they are no longer, for liberalism has reached a point of internal divisions at multiple levels. Some of today's self-styled liberals argue that reason can approximate objective moral truth, while others profess varieties of moral conventionalism and skepticism. Some liberals argue for a perfectionist state, a state actively concerned with the beliefs and attitudes of its people, while others insist that liberalism's essence is neutrality among conceptions of virtue and the good life. Some liberals worry about the "size" of government, while others worry about the competence of government.

One part of these debates about the nature of liberalism is the nature of rights in a liberal state—specifically whether a properly liberal understanding of government can admit a constitutional obligation to provide positive rights or, as I prefer, welfare rights, like rights to health care and education. I contend here that if the American Constitution qualifies as a liberal constitution, liberal governments can indeed be obligated to secure welfare rights. I support this contention here by reinforcing arguments I have made elsewhere for a welfarist view of the Constitution and by submitting additional arguments against limiting liberalism to protecting negative rights.

### II. Welfare and the Constitution

I begin by sketching a positive view of the Constitution that fits the constitutional text and the leading argument for ratification. Here I consider questions of constitutional meaning from the perspective of citizens who accept the Constitution's authority. I assume what other writers have shown to be the metaphysical and epistemological beliefs of this perspective. I expect most readers of this essay will assume as I do here, and as I have argued elsewhere, that there are, or at least may be, better and worse understandings of what the Constitution means and what it requires in practice, as measured by something other than personal preferences and conventional beliefs.[1] I expect also that most readers will find that my principal moral conclusions, defended at length elsewhere,[2] require little more than deflation of textual and historical excuses for avoiding moral arguments altogether. The excuses I refer to are those favored in recent years by self-styled conservative jurists.[3] The Supreme Court has held twice over the past quarter-century, for example, that governments in America have no federal constitutional duty to provide police protection (logically, a welfare right)[4] against predictable violence.[5] In the most recent case, involving the murder of three children, the Rehnquist Court found no constitutional duty of municipal police to provide protection despite the order of a state court that made police action mandatory. Expose the fraud in the textual and historical arguments for such holdings, and you enlist the intuition that people generally would have little reason to value a constitution that failed to mandate the least of night-watchman services. Defenders of the Rehnquist Court will answer that free-world constitutions aim chiefly at limiting government, not empowering it. This answer, I trust, will conflict with the intuition that it would make no sense to establish a government for the chief purpose of limiting it. By showing (1) that the framers were more interested in empowering government than limiting it, and (2) that the constitutional text establishes an instrument of positive benefits—promising, *inter alia*, to "provide for the common Defense, promote the general Welfare, and secure the Blessings of Liberty"—I can reinforce the sense that the Supreme Court was wrong to declare no constitutional duty to protect helpless children from perfectly predictable violence. If my argument succeeds, a right to police protection could be the camel's nose that the Rehnquist majority feared. A constitutional duty to protect children from predictable violence could establish a presumptive constitutional duty to protect them from undeserved poverty, ignorance, and dependency.[6]

Arguments against this broader duty can take two general forms: a policy of taxing and spending to provide broader benefits is either (1) morally wrong or (2) counterproductive. The second kind of argument is compatible with welfarism, for it preserves the possibility of broader protection, and the authority to provide it, as prudence advises in changing circumstances. The first kind of argument cannot succeed; it is

---

[1] See Sotirios A. Barber, *The Constitution of Judicial Power* (Baltimore, MD: Johns Hopkins University Press, 1994), chaps. 6–7; and Barber, *Welfare and the Constitution* (Princeton, NJ: Princeton University Press, 2003), chaps. 4–5.

[2] Barber, *Welfare and the Constitution*, 8, 13–14, 25–26.

[3] For a review of these writers, see Barber, *The Constitution of Judicial Power*, chap. 4.

[4] Ibid., 12–15; Norman Barry, *Welfare* (Minneapolis: University of Minnesota Press, 1990), 79; Stephen Holmes and Cass Sunstein, *The Cost of Rights* (New York: Norton, 1999), 29–39.

[5] *DeShaney v. Winnebago*, 489 U.S. 189 (1989); *Castle Rock v. Gonzales*, 125 S.Ct. 2796 (2005).

[6] For an acknowledgment of this point by a supporter of the Court's position, see David P. Currie, "Positive and Negative Constitutional Rights," *University of Chicago Law Review* 53 (1986): 877–78.

either unpersuasive or a form of welfarism deficient in self-awareness. It is hardly persuasive that morality (expressed as justice, for example) requires government to protect the unearned opportunity of first pos- sessors and the unearned (because inherited) wealth of their children at the expense of undeservedly disadvantaged children. When I say "at the expense of" the disadvantaged, I mean the tax on the disadvan- taged imposed by the criminal law—that is, the criminal law's denial of the opportunities of the undeservedly poor (and their right in a state of nature) to help themselves to that part of the excess wealth of the affluent that they think they need for their survival. The classical rejoin- der to this point is that protecting first possessors and their progeny creates a store of wealth and a net increase of opportunities that benefit everyone, including the poor. But this rejoinder is, of course, a welfar- ist claim. It contends that institutions that might initially seem unfair actually redound to the well-being of the poor.[7]

Let us assume, however, that we could prove that broader benefits would be morally wrong by some theory of what is right that is concep- tually independent of a welfare claim. In that case, we could still ask why we should prefer the right thing instead of what benefits us, individually and/or collectively. A true conception of morality (separated, *ex hypothesi*, from well-being) might provide *some* justificatory reason for an act or a practice conforming to its requirements, but it would not constitute *suf- ficient reason* for such conduct. Because we can sensibly speak of reasons for acting unjustly, for example, justice alone seems an insufficient reason for acting.[8] Knowledge of what is good, in contrast, can constitute suffi- cient reason for action.[9] Thus, a *practical* argument invoking justice could not work if justice were disconnected from well-being. This leaves no way to avoid welfarist assumptions, and awareness of that fact should enable us to improve the welfarist assumptions we inevitably make.

## III. The Constitutional Text

The surface welfarism of the constitutional text is clear. The preamble of the Constitution contains a list of ends or goods: a more perfect union, justice, domestic tranquility, the common defense, the general welfare,

---

[7] See Richard A. Epstein, *Takings: Private Property and the Power of Eminent Domain* (Cam- bridge, MA: Harvard University Press, 1985). Epstein argues (pp. 11–18) that although state protection for first possessors means lost opportunities to late-comers, protecting first pos- sessors yields more benefits for everyone. In *Welfare and the Constitution* (p. 149), I discuss the welfarist strain in Epstein's thought.

[8] See David O. Brink, *Moral Realism and the Foundation of Ethics* (New York: Cambridge University Press, 1989), 57–62, 240–45.

[9] Knowledge of what is right might constitute sufficient reason if Immanuel Kant is correct (in the first section of *The Groundwork of the Metaphysic of Morals*) that the only unqualified good is a will disposed to do what is right. I do not explore this possibility here because Kant's proposal seems to me a theory of the good.

and the blessings of liberty. The preamble implies that the government whose establishment it announces is an instrument of these ends or goods — that they will be pursued through the actions of this government. This active instrumentalism calls for structuring and empowering governmental institutions, and that is what the Constitution is chiefly about. Article I establishes a legislature, structures it, and authorizes it to take specific kinds of actions. Section 8 lists most of these authorizations. Logically, this famous "enumeration of powers" indicates the kinds of purposes that the government is authorized to pursue and, indirectly, the kind of society it must cultivate if its ends are to be realized and its institutions are to survive.[10] Section 8 thus authorizes Congress to regulate commerce, coin money and regulate the value thereof, enact bankruptcy laws, and so forth. If we group these specified authorizations into associated kinds, construe them with the clause of Article VI that makes federal law supreme over state law, and reflect on what is conspicuously left out (i.e., the pursuit of religious truth and salvation), it appears that the paramount ends of this government and of the nation it represents are national security and prosperity.[11]

In keeping with the preamble's emphasis on substantive ends, Article I of the Constitution emphasizes institutions and powers: the two bodies of Congress and the kinds of things they are authorized to do. Yet Article I also mentions a handful of rights. Section 9 restricts Congress's power to suspend "[t]he privilege . . . of habeas corpus." It also prohibits bills of attainder, ex post facto laws, and titles of nobility. Section 10 imposes these last three restrictions on the states and adds a prohibition against impairing the obligation of contracts. These rights are clearly restrictions on power and, as such, they fit a negative view of the Constitution's principal function: to restrain government. However, Article I lists three additional rights that suggest a different logic. Section 6 extends qualified immunities from arrest to members of Congress during the legislative session and flatly prohibits questioning them "in any other place" (like a police station or a court of law) for "any speech or debate in either house" of Congress. These rights, while negative, are integral to something positive: the lawmaking function. Analogously, Section 8 empowers Congress (obligates Congress, a welfarist should say)[12] "to promote the progress of science and useful arts, by securing for limited times to authors and

---

[10] Sotirios A. Barber, *On What the Constitution Means* (Baltimore, MD: Johns Hopkins University Press, 1984), chap. 4, esp. 88–91, 97–104. For the theory of action on which I rely to connect powers (to act) with purposes (for acting), see Georg Henrik von Wright, *Norm and Action* (London: Routledge and Kegan Paul, 1963), 35–38.

[11] Martin Diamond, "The Federalist," in Leo Strauss and Joseph Cropsey, eds., *History of Political Philosophy* (Chicago: Rand McNally, 1972), 648–50; Walter Berns, "Judicial Review and the Rights and Laws of Nature," in Philip Kurland, Gerhard Casper, and Dennis Hutchinson, eds., *1982 Supreme Court Review* (Chicago: University of Chicago Press, 1983), 58–61, 65.

[12] Barber, *On What the Constitution Means*, 182–85.

inventors the exclusive right to their respective writings and discoveries."
These two provisions are not enough to establish a welfarist view of the
Constitution. They do illustrate, however, ways in which negative rights
can fit within a generally positive, ends-oriented, or welfarist view of the
Constitution—a welfarist view established by the preamble, the history of
the American founding, and the common-sense proposition that it makes
no sense to establish a government for the sake of limiting it in a purely
negative way.

Rights do not appear again until the last three paragraphs of Article III.
Article II structures and empowers the presidency, and Article III establishes the Supreme Court, defines some of its composition and jurisdiction, and empowers (obligates) Congress to determine the rest. The right
to trial by jury is specified at the end of Article III, Section 2, and Section 3
lists restrictions on government's power to charge, try, and punish persons for treason. Two additional rights appear in the Constitution of 1789
(i.e., before the adoption of the first ten amendments in 1791). Article IV,
Section 2 obligates states to grant citizens of other states the "privileges
and immunities" they extend to their own citizens, and the last sentence
of Article VI—the document's last substantive provision before it concludes with the ratification procedures of Article VII—promises that "no
religious test shall ever be required as a qualification to any office of
public trust under the United States."

Though these rights can be interpreted negatively, as restrictions on
government, they can also admit a positive interpretation, as integral to
the pursuit of governmental ends. Jury trials can enhance public support for the judicial process by bringing the sense of the community to
bear on concrete questions of civil and criminal justice. Defining treason narrowly helps to safeguard criticism of the government's foreign
policy. Rights to criticize the government can be interpreted as elements of government's power because, according to the wording of the
preamble, that power is dedicated to the common defense, implicitly as
a real good. *Real goods like this are the only things that the Constitution
authorizes government to pursue.* A real good is captured by knowledge
of that good, not by a mere conception of that good, which can always
be wrong. Where actors are fallible, criticism can expose false conceptions. Because exposing false conceptions is a step in the pursuit of
better conceptions, defined as conceptions closer to the truth, the right
to expose false conceptions is an element of the power to pursue better
conceptions.[13] For another example, consider freedom from religious
tests for office. This freedom can contribute to domestic tranquility, an
end listed in the preamble. It also contributes to the self-critical and
secular reasonableness that is integral to the (true) well-being of fallible

---

[13] Compare Stephen Holmes, *Passions and Constraint: On the Theory of Liberal Democracy*
(Chicago: University of Chicago Press, 1995), 181, 185–86.

actors trying to cope with a natural world whose essential features are not of their making.[14]

Beyond freedom from religious tests and the narrow definition of treason, two additional parts of the original Constitution imply fallibility at all levels: the immunity of members of Congress from prosecution for anything they might say in congressional debate, and the amending provisions of Article V. These freedoms to criticize policy and effect constitutional change make sense only if fallibility is supposed at all levels, including that of the supreme authority — the people of the United States — whose most authoritative expression is declared by Article VI to be the supreme law of the land. By conceiving these original rights (involving patents and copyrights, jury trials, congressional immunity, treason trials, and religious tests) in a welfarist fashion, we can see how to do the same for the apparently negative rights of the Bill of Rights, ratified in 1791. First Amendment rights to publish, petition, and criticize the government are integral to power dedicated to the pursuit of real ends about which the community and its agent-government can always be wrong. Freedom from religious establishments enhances prospects of domestic tranquility and the general welfare, on the theory that well-being requires the freedom and capacity for independent thought about reality, moral and nonmoral. Rights of criminal defendants (to judicially-issued search warrants, representation by counsel, fair trials, etc.) enhance prospects of punishing only the truly guilty, as justice, one of the ends in the preamble, requires. Security for investors and private property on publicly reasonable terms (in clauses that prohibit warrantless seizures and deprivations of property without due process, takings of property for public use without just compensation, and impairments of contractual obligations) seems a good way under foreseeable circumstances to enhance the material well-being of everyone in the community.

Textual warrant for this kind of interpretation occurs in Article V, which terms all properly ratified amendments "part[s] of this Constitution." To render negative liberties "parts" of a positive or welfarist whole — a whole whose welfarist character is established by the preamble, the history of the founding, and common sense — one must conceive negative liberties as elements of the power to serve real goods. Seen as a list of purely negative liberties, the Bill of Rights would make the Constitution either incoherent or pointless. Incoherence would result from giving equal weight to a negative and a positive — the negative logic of the Bill of Rights and the positive or welfarist logic of the Constitution *sans* negative rights. Pointlessness would result from permitting the putatively negative logic of the Bill of Rights to overpower the Constitution's positive logic; for no one can make sense of a constitution's establishing a government solely or chiefly for the sake of limiting it.

---

[14] Barber, *Welfare and the Constitution*, 88–91.

## IV. The Federalist

Anti-welfarists can concede the instrumentalist language of the constitutional text while denying a constitutional obligation in government to
work for everyone's well-being, including that of the least well-off. Anti-
welfarists can claim that the Constitution's ends centrally involve security
for negative liberties, like the paradigm right of private property. I have
anticipated this objection by highlighting the public-regarding way Article I authorizes Congress to secure rights of intellectual property—
patents and copyrights not (merely) for the sake of justice to inventors
and authors but (also) for the sake of progress in the sciences and useful
arts. Later in this essay, I will contend that although ends or goods can be
the objects of negative rights, negative rights should not be conflated with
their objects because negative rights as such cannot be ends; that is, the
goodness or value of rights cannot consist in their negative aspect. First,
however, I must complete my showing that the Constitution is a welfarist
constitution. Because many anti-welfarists find constitutional meaning
more in (their reading of) the framers' intentions than in the constitutional text, I will have to supplement my treatment of the latter with a
defensible version of the former. I claim no more than a defensible version
of the framers' intentions. I claim no knock-down version, for no such
version exists.[15] And even if it did, its normative relevance could be
established only through a moral argument whose very launching would
imply the normative inadequacy of any mere historical fact of the framers' intentions. Assuming *The Federalist* is a defensible source of the framers' intentions, I show here that one does not have to strain to see continuity
between the framers and the New Deal.[16]

---

[15] See Walter F. Murphy, "Constitutional Interpretation: The Art of the Magician, Historian, or Statesman?" *Yale Law Journal* 87 (1978): 1752–71.

[16] I speak here not of Alexander Hamilton, James Madison, and John Jay, but of "Publius."
In adopting their chosen pen name, I assume the unity of *The Federalist* and the separability
of an argument from the private motives of its authors—that is, motives not publicly stated
or implicit in the argument itself. Assuming the unity of *The Federalist* is necessary for
anyone who would treat that work as a source of normative guidance, for an internally
contradictory message cannot function as a norm. A presumption against the undisclosed
motives of an argument would be uncontroversial in most contexts. It is not uncontroversial
here, however, because of the famous split between Hamilton and Madison in the 1790s. I
give a Hamiltonian interpretation to *The Federalist* for two reasons. First, Madison was in fact
a strong nationalist and an ally of Hamilton during the ratification period. Second, *The
Federalist* is, on its face, more of a strong-government and nationalist argument than a
weak-government and states'-rights argument. John Marshall and Joseph Story gave *The
Federalist* a nationalist reading, and I know of no professional student of *The Federalist* who
has hazarded a states'-rights reading of the work as a whole. Modern exponents of states'
rights prefer either to take evidence of the framers' intentions from arguments in the state
ratifying conventions or to ignore the main thrust of *The Federalist* in favor of its defensive
responses to Antifederalist criticisms. The present treatment of *The Federalist* draws on
Barber, *The Constitution of Judicial Power*, chap. 2. My understanding of *The Federalist* has been
heavily influenced by Martin Diamond and Herbert Storing, two pre-Reagan conservatives
widely recognized by two generations of political scientists as leading interpreters of the

The leading complaint of Publius's Antifederalist critics was that the proposed constitution would require state governments to surrender too much power to the national government. This charge has several dimensions, and the complete answer to it must be collected from different parts of *The Federalist*. But the heart of Publius's response appears in the most emotional paragraph of all the Federalist papers, the second paragraph of *Federalist No. 45*. Here Publius urges, in welfarist fashion, that his critics should ask not how the transfer of power will affect the state governments, but "what degree of power" is essential to "the purposes of the federal government." These purposes include, he says, security against foreign danger, peace among the states, and security against "violent and oppressive factions which embitter the blessings of liberty." Union, he adds, "has been shown to be essential" to these purposes — "in a word . . . essential to the happiness of the people of America." This makes it "preposterous" to object to the new government from fear that it "may derogate from the importance of the governments of the individual States." Those who raise states'-rights objections revive in new form the "impious" old-world doctrine that "people were made for kings, not kings for people." They forget that "the public good, the real welfare of the great body of the people, is the supreme object to be pursued, and that no form of government whatever has any other value than as it may be fitted for the attainment of this object" (45:309).

The spirit of the forty-fifth paper dominates *The Federalist*. Its positive message governs the organization of the entire work. Toward the end of the first paper, Publius promises a series of papers that will show: (1) the utility of the union to the nation's "political prosperity"; (2) the insufficiency of the Confederation to preserve the union; (3) the necessity of a government "at least equally energetic with the one proposed"; (4) the conformity of the proposed constitution to republican principles; (5) the "analogy" of the proposed government to the state constitutions; and (6) the "additional security" the Constitution "will afford" to republicanism, "to liberty, and to property" (1:6–7; italics omitted). The first three themes are assertive in nature; they emphasize ends, powers, and the superiority of the new government. They fit within an overall positive view of the Constitution. The last three themes are defensive in nature; they would assure Publius's audience that the new government is not a threat to their personal and political liberties. In Publius's hands, the defensive themes are consonant with the positive themes. This is evident in what he eventually says about the "additional security" to liberty and property and in his argument against a bill of rights.

---

founding. See Diamond, "The Federalist"; and Herbert J. Storing, "The Problem of Big Government," in Robert A. Goldwin, ed., *A Nation of States* (Chicago: Rand McNally, 1961), 65–87, esp. 79–85. References to *The Federalist* are from the edition by Jacob E. Cooke (Middletown, CT: Wesleyan University Press, 1961). In-text references appear in parentheses with the page number following the paper number and a colon; "*Federalist No. 1*, p. 3" will thus read "(1:3)."

In *Federalist No. 85,* the concluding paper, Publius recalls his sixth promise, namely, to elaborate additional securities to liberty, property, and republican principles. Instead of launching a new discussion, however, he claims to have redeemed this promise through all that he has previously shown about the need for a new government. The securities to liberty, property, and republicanism "consist chiefly in the restraints which the preservation of the Union will impose upon local factions . . . in the diminution of the opportunities for foreign intrigue, which the dissolution of the Confederation will invite and facilitate; in the prevention of extensive military establishments, which could not fail to grow out of wars between the States in a disunited situation; in the express guarantee of a republican form of government to each; in the absolute and universal exclusion of titles of nobility; and in the precautions against the repetition of those practices on the part of the State governments which have undermined the foundations of property and credit, have planted mutual distrust in the breasts of all classes of citizens, and have occasioned an almost universal prostration of morals" (85:588). In brief, and with the one exception regarding titles of nobility, the additional security to liberty, property, and republicanism consists in provisions of the new constitution that have augmented national power at the expense of the states. Power and liberty, it seems, are on the same side, or can be if the power is properly structured and the sphere of government sufficiently enlarged. The final paper thus recalls a leading if not the leading message of the first paper: "the vigor of government is essential to the security of liberty; . . . [and] in the contemplation of a sound and well-informed judgment, their interests can never be separated" (1:5–6).

Consonant with this message is Publius's well-known argument against a bill of rights. In *Federalist No. 84,* he says that in the proposed constitution a bill of rights would be unnecessary and dangerous; he says also that it would be "impracticable." A bill of rights is unnecessary because "it would contain various exceptions to powers not granted." Why guarantee a free press, for instance, "[w]hen no power is given by which restrictions [on the press] may be imposed?" Restraining power not given would be dangerous because it "would afford a colorable pretext to claim more [power] than were granted." Restrain a power not given and "men disposed to usurp" can claim "with a semblance of reason" that there is a power there to restrain—a power, say, "to provide proper regulations" of the press. Finally, the "aphorisms" typical of "our State bills of rights . . . would sound much better in a treatise of ethics than in a constitution of government." No one can give something like "liberty of the press . . . any definition which would not leave the utmost latitude for evasion." In the end, its security "must altogether depend on public opinion, and on the general spirit of the people and of the government" (84:579–80).

When Publius says that specifying a right to an act or activity is unnecessary where the Constitution grants no power to regulate that act or activity, he assumes that a right is violated only by acts whose governing purpose is violating the right. This suggests, for example, that if a government aims at victory in war, and restraining or punishing a given publication appears necessary for victory, then the government can restrain the publication without violating the right. From this it would follow that there is no right to freedom of the press, speech, religious exercise, and so forth, to the extent that abridging any of these freedoms appears necessary to some authorized end such as winning a war, creating a national market, or securing equal educational opportunity for oppressed racial and ethnic minorities.[17] This view of ostensibly "protected" rights all but makes them hostage to the perceptions of necessity and value of the political forces that control judicial appointments. Publius suggests as much when he says, in his third argument against a bill of rights, that the spirit of the people and the government will control what rights are taken to mean. Disturbing as this may be to the modern ear, how could it be otherwise in an imperfect world where, as Publius says in *Federalist No. 51*, men are not angels and angels do not govern men? (51:349). No one can make sense of a constitution that provides unqualified exemptions from the power to secure the ends for which it was adopted.[18] Fully defensible constitutional rights must therefore be seen as elements of power, not genuine exemptions from power. Examples would include intellectual property rights justified in terms of—and therefore limited by—"the progress of science and useful arts,"[19] and freedom of speech as a rational response to human fallibility in pursuit of real goods.[20]

Publius's third argument against a bill of rights deserves further comment here. His position is that the security of rights depends ultimately not on the words of the Constitution as applied by judges, but on the nation's political culture. The upshot of this proposition is that a commitment to rights necessitates a perfectionist state, a state that actively influences the beliefs and shapes the character of its people. Again, it could hardly be otherwise. You cannot expect racists to favor any but a racist view of Fourteenth Amendment rights, a view that favors results that belong to a racist view of the world. You cannot expect members of the religious right to respect religious diversity or a scientific outlook. You cannot expect doctrinaire free-marketeers to acknowledge their dependence on the redistributive state or to see their conception of

---

[17] Vestiges of Publius's assumption survive in present-day doctrines of American law like the "secular-regulation rule" in free exercise cases (which holds that incidental effects of generally applicable laws enacted for secular purposes do not offend the freedom of religious exercise) and the rule that government can abridge protected rights if there is "no less drastic means" to realizing "compelling governmental interests."

[18] Holmes and Sunstein, *The Cost of Rights*, 99–101.

[19] Ibid., 115–16; Barber, *Welfare and the Constitution*, 48–50; compare Aristotle's *Politics*, 1263a.

[20] Barber, *Welfare and the Constitution*, 55–56, 121–22; Holmes, *Passions and Constraint*, 185–86.

equal opportunity as fraudulently narrow. Commit yourself to equal protection, freedom of conscience, and equal opportunity, and you commit yourself to educational and economic strategies aimed at weakening racism, dogmatism, and greed. To generalize and to gloss *Federalist No. 1*'s view of liberty and government as on the same side: *people genuinely interested in negative rights will want big government to secure positive rights.* An oath to preserve and defend the Constitution (including the Bill of Rights) turns out to be an oath to promote certain attitudes, beliefs, and conditions—a belief in the soundness of a scientific worldview, for example, along with attitudes like racial inclusivity and religious toleration, and conditions like equal economic, political, and social opportunity.[21]

This active governmental concern for the beliefs and attitudes of the people—this liberal perfectionism—need not mean dogmatism and totalitarianism. If, as Publius says, no form of government whatever has any value other than as it may be fitted for attaining the general welfare, neither does liberalism. If all can err about the true meaning of the general welfare, so can liberals. If a defining feature of liberalism is an appreciation of human fallibility in a natural world of which humankind appears but one of many dependent parts, then liberalism is fallible too. Liberals generally should, and many do, appreciate that their essentially secular view of the good and its pursuit may ultimately be wrong. Liberals should therefore take pains to tolerate nonviolent forms of antiliberalism, from global philosophic skepticism and radical historicism to sectarian dogmatism and dogmatic secularism.[22]

Accordingly, Publius's view of rights is fully integrated into his larger view of government. *The Federalist* opens with a clear welfarist message: The nation needs a new constitution because the old one does not work; it is inadequate to "the existence of the UNION . . . [and] the safety and welfare of . . . [its] parts" (1:3). Publius also mentions "liberty" in addition to safety and welfare, but here he sees liberty as an end *of government*— that is, as a positive good secured through the agency of the coercive authority that government is.[23] He holds that a good constitution will establish a strong and efficient government, because such a government is essential to "the security of liberty." He urges skepticism toward politicians who would separate the interests of liberty and government, for "a dangerous ambition more often lurks behind the specious mask of zeal for the rights of the people than under the forbidden appearance of zeal for the firmness and efficiency of government" (1:5-6). The proposed constitution would establish the requisite government; it is the "safest course for your liberty, your dignity, and your happiness" (1:6).

[21] Barber, *On What the Constitution Means*, 72-77.
[22] See Barber, *Welfare and the Constitution*, 121-23.
[23] For Publius's view on coercion as essential to government and law, see *Federalist No. 15*, 95-96.

The second paper then turns to the first question Publius promised to discuss: "The utility of the UNION to your political prosperity" (1:6; italics omitted.) *Federalist No. 2* introduces a series of seven papers on national security and the need to avoid war among disunited states by identifying the entity whose interests in security and peace are in question; that entity is the nation as a whole. "[T]he people of America," it seems, already exist as a cultural unity ("same ancestors, . . . same language, . . . same religion, . . . same principles of government, . . . [people] very similar in their manners and customs"). Having fought "side by side throughout a long and bloody war," this people has a history of its own. This same people also has a common inheritance "so proper and convenient for a band of brothers," a blessing from "Providence"—namely, "one connected, fertile . . . country, . . . blessed . . . with a variety of soils and productions, and watered with innumerable streams" that form "highways" for "easy communication" and "a chain around its borders, as if to bind it together" (2:8–10). As Publius poses it here and elsewhere (esp. 14:87–89), the question is not whether to unite a country that is already united; the question is whether to divide the country by rejecting the plan for a more perfect union. With the Constitution's defeat and (he assumes) the subsequent dissolution of the union, the question will be whether, on any occasion, any one of the several states will have sufficient reason to help another under attack by a foreign power. Should union be strengthened, an attack on a part will be an attack on the whole (4:22–23). And since Publius assumes an existing cultural union, he refers in these papers not to the shipping and other interests *in* America vis-à-vis the shipping and other interests of European powers, but to the shipping and other interests *of* the nation as a united whole. Notwithstanding the private ownership of the entities that make up the transportation sector, Publius addresses the electorate at large and refers to "our carrying trade," "our commerce," and "our own vessels." He argues that the military and other resources of one united nation can better protect and promote "our carrying trade" vis-à-vis that of other nations (4:19–20). Because he presents power to promote and protect "our carrying trade" as a reason for adopting the Constitution, Publius takes for granted that his readers share the identity he attributes to them.

The ninth paper introduces the best-known paper of the series, *Federalist No. 10*. In the first nine papers, little or nothing occurs that either resembles or supports the suggestion that the legislative function of constitutional government is one of aggregating partial or private interests. These early papers appeal to public-spiritedness in behalf of public purposes; they emphasize power and suggest little about exemptions from power. The emphasis remains positive even when liberty is discussed. Liberty is seen as an end of government, a positive good to be enjoyed under government's protection (1:5–6). Government is therefore a good thing, and the new constitution will make government better by strengthening it. This multilayered emphasis on the positive seems to change in *Federalist No. 10*, where the concern seems to be making government not more efficient, but less efficient, and the common-sense strategy of cultivating public-spiritedness gives way to one of coalition-building (interest aggregation?) among a large number of self-serving interests.

Yet Martin Diamond, whose analysis of *The Federalist* has influenced many political scientists for more than a generation, proved that there is more to *Federalist No. 10* than meets the eye. To appreciate the continuity of this tenth paper with the New Deal, we must attend to Diamond's analysis of the paper. Diamond pointed out that movement from a small to a large country would not guarantee the political pluralism needed for Publius's solution to the problem of majority faction. A large territory with a large population could as easily be polarized along several lines, such as wealth, religion, or, we could add, race.[24] Whether a nation's group structure is pluralist or polarized depends on how people see themselves politically. However, Publius is not entitled to assume that Americans will see themselves chiefly in terms of narrow economic interests and not as Catholics against Protestants, rich against poor, or, we could add, black against white. A related problem is Publius's view of modern government's "principal task," which he identifies as regulating economic conflict (10:59). Economic conflict arises from "the various and unequal distribution of property," which Publius calls "the most common and durable source of faction" (10:59). However, he also recognizes other sources of social division, such as "a zeal for different opinions concerning religion, concerning government, and many other points" (10:58–59). Why not regulate these other kinds of conflict? How can it be enough to leave noneconomic conflicts to the state governments after *Federalist No. 10* recognizes the possibility of sectarian faction and argues that the states are incompetent to control majority factions generally? If the states could control majority religious and ideological factions, why could they not deal with majority economic factions? These problems force us to ask whether Publius's theory is adequate to the full range of social problems that he himself identifies.

We therefore have a choice regarding *The Federalist*: we can either look elsewhere for guidance on constitutional meaning, or we can seek a way to save Publius from his difficulties. The latter effort begins by asking if there are any conditions under which Publius can reasonably assume (1) that the large republic will be pluralist and not polarized and (2) that regulating economic conflict at the national level will ameliorate the country's noneconomic divisions. If we find answers to these questions, we must also ask (3) how the nation will achieve and maintain those conditions. Diamond answered the first two questions, and Herbert Storing, Diamond's friend and colleague, answered the third. Both writers answered

---

[24] Diamond, "The Federalist," 648–49.

from a Hamiltonian reading (that is, a nationalist and strong-government reading) of *The Federalist* and the founding generally. Diamond reflected Hamilton's commercialist view of society and government's mercantilist relationship to economy. Storing reflected Hamilton's emphasis on executive power.

Our first question relates to the conditions under which the large republic will be pluralist and not polarized. The system outlined in *Federalist No. 10* is one in which political interest groups form and reform changing electoral and legislative coalitions that exclude no stable minority for long. Diamond argued that the people who belong in this picture must live in an urban-industrial society (because an agrarian society lacks the large number of economic groups around which to form political interest groups). A people who see their political interests in terms of their economic interests will have to be a more-or-less materialistic people. This quality is the key to answering our second question, regarding how the promotion of a certain economy might ameliorate noneconomic divisions. Materialistic people want government to protect their physical security and promote their material well-being. Even if they care for the salvation of their souls as individuals, they will not insist that the government facilitate or compel the salvation of their neighbors' souls. This makes them appear religiously and ideologically tolerant. These people will also be a democratic people in several ways. They will support equal economic opportunity regardless of class or religion or (we could add) race or gender, lest the society divide along these lines. They will value equal political opportunity for the same reason.[25]

To avoid polarization and the politics of resentment, the typical citizen of this large commercial republic must have evidence that his or her achievements reflect more-or-less what he or she has been willing to work for. This evidence can only take the form of upward (or downward) mobility for people who start poor (or affluent) and a fair distribution of wealth and status across lines of religion and (we could add) race and gender. A poor man who is black must know many blacks who are not poor in order to believe that racism is not a major cause of his poverty. He must see poor people become rich and rich people become poor in order to feel that people generally have what they deserve. Such a society would also have to be a wealthy society, for much wealth would be needed to feed the economic ambition of everyone willing to work and to convince people that the system is basically fair in practice, not just theory. To this Diamond added with caution that perhaps the wealth of this society would have to increase more-or-less indefinitely—that the society had to be committed to ever-expanding personal and national wealth.[26]

---

[25] Martin Diamond, Winston Mills Fisk, and Herbert Garfinkel, *The Democratic Republic* (Chicago: Rand McNally, 1966), 77–80.

[26] Ibid., 80.

Diamond hesitated about this last condition of the large commercial republic. A student of Nietzsche and Tocqueville, he may have been concerned
with what a commitment to economic growth would do to autonomous
individuality and public-spirited citizenship. A Marxist in his youth, he
may have seen that economic growth would eventually mean a global
oligarchy beyond the control of any government, as well as economic
polarization at home (a growing "income gap") caused by capital flight to
cheaper labor markets abroad. He might also have worried about the
violent reaction of anti-Western cultures targeted as sources of raw materials and as markets for Western goods and ideas. Diamond might have
found this last prospect especially threatening to a highly differentiated
and interdependent society that is profoundly dependent on increasingly
complex and vulnerable technologies.

In any case, I do not contend that the elements of the large commercial
republic constitute the ends to which the preamble of the Constitution is
dedicated. I think Diamond was right to hold that the features of the large
commercial republic *are* necessary for the success of the system outlined
in *Federalist No. 10*. And I have argued elsewhere that these features can
constitute working conceptions of ends found in the preamble, such as
justice and the general welfare. The conception of individual well-being
favored by these ends focuses on the possession of the capacities (intellectual, moral, and material) and the opportunity to engage in the lawful
pursuits of the large commercial republic to the end of securing for oneself, if one wants them, such goods as adequate nutrition and housing,
health care, education for one's children, some leisure, and a secure retirement.[27] The general well-being would include, ideally, the well-being of
each responsible member of the community. But these conceptions of the
preamble's ends are *mere* conceptions; they may be false. It is hardly
beyond contention, for example, that well-being must be conceived in
terms of material goods and the faculties and opportunities for acquiring
them, as typically American as these aspirations are. Have people been
better off, and may they again be better off, in settings that define well-
being largely in terms of spiritual goods? Would people be happier, as
current research suggests, with less wealth and economic mobility and
more leisure and stable families, friendships, and communities?[28] Assume
the Constitution is what it says it is, an instrument of things like the
people's welfare, and acknowledge the gap between any conception of
well-being and the real thing, and you may conclude that a truly well-off
people are well-off due to a certain capacity. I mean the intellectual,
psychological, and material wherewithal to do what the founding generation did: assess their problems and fashion new institutions according-

[27] Barber, *Welfare and the Constitution*, 106–17.
[28] See Robert E. Lane, *The Loss of Happiness in Market Democracies* (New Haven, CT: Yale
University Press, 2000), chaps. 5–6.

LIBERALISM AND THE CONSTITUTION

ly.[29] A constitution adequate to real ends will preserve the capacity for constructive social and governmental change. Whether Americans still have this capacity (or ever really did) is something we can debate. I have discussed this problem elsewhere, and I will not say more about it here.[30] I will say, however, that this element of national well-being—the capacity for constructive change—amends our understanding of the ends of government to include some freedoms of speech, press, political association, religious association, and academic inquiry, and all that accompanies these freedoms, including a politics of public reasonableness, the toleration of reasonable diversity, and private property held on reasonable terms. Seen in this light, property and the freedoms of speech, religion, and the rest are not mere limitations on our collective power as a people. They are elements of that power, for without them we cannot pursue *real* as opposed to merely *apparent* goods.

The American Constitution thus embodies an appreciation of *human fallibility* and a recognition of *higher authority* (either God or nature) which is common to both the Christian and pagan branches of the Western tradition. An element of that tradition at least since Homer's time has been pride in a people's ability to acknowledge and provide for the fact that its beliefs and practices may be wrong. The larger community typically becomes aware of that fact through the agency of some unpopular individual such as Socrates, to whom Publius alludes at one point (63:425). And when individuals or minorities brave "the perils of the community's displeasure" and change the public's mind, the community honors them as benefactors (71:482-83). Because Western thought from the beginning has valued truth over convention and has associated truth with the dissenting individual, the individual enjoys a presumptive dignity. American law reflects this presumption in places like the free speech and criminal-defendant provisions of the Bill of Rights and the guarantees of civil freedom, due process, and equal protection in the Civil War amendments.

From *Federalist No. 10* our quick tour turns to *No. 15* and Publius's criticism of the Articles of Confederation. We know in a general way that the Articles were inadequate to the country's needs. If we could learn more of the specifics, we could better appreciate the structure of the proposed government, for we can assume that the latter was designed to avoid the defects of the former. *Federalist No. 15* discusses "the great and radical vice in the structure" of the Articles, which is that the Continental Congress passed laws that applied not directly to individual citizens, but to the several states (15:93). Under the Articles, Congress's laws took the form of requests or *requisitions* to the state legislatures, requisitions for things like their individual share of the money Congress needed to pay

---

[29] Barber, *Welfare and the Constitution*, 113–14, 153–54.

[30] Ibid., chap. 6; see also Jeffrey K. Tulis, "Constitution and Revolution," in Sotirios A. Barber and Robert P. George, eds., *Constitutional Politics: Essays in Constitution Making, Maintenance, and Change* (Princeton, NJ: Princeton University Press, 2001), 116–27.

down the war debt, support ambassadors and embassies abroad, protect settlers on the western borders, and pay the salaries and expenses of legislative and administrative officials at home. Because these requisitions were not backed by credible threats of force in cases of noncompliance, the states failed to respond fully and in a timely fashion, and Congress's aims were frustrated. Behind this structural defect Publius identifies a philosophic mistake: faith that voluntary compliance with law is sufficiently attractive to dispense with effective and credible threats of force against the noncompliant (15:96). This pair of structural-philosophical mistakes deprived the Confederation of what Publius calls "the energy and efficiency of government."

Publius does not emphasize strong government in his most famous paper, *Federalist No. 10*, but the need for strong government is the dominant message of *The Federalist* as a whole. The very first sentence of *Federalist No. 1* calls for a new constitution to correct "the inefficacy of the subsisting Federal Government." Publius accompanies this call with the important claims that "the vigor of government is essential to the security of liberty; that, in the contemplation of a sound and well informed judgment, their interests can never be separated; and that a dangerous ambition more often lurks behind the specious mask of zeal for the rights of the people, than under the forbidden appearance of zeal for the firmness and efficiency of government" (1:5–6). *Federalist No. 15* reminds us of this opening theme and leaves us with two questions: What or who will supply energy in government, and to what ends will this energy be directed? Diamond's theory of *Federalist No. 10* answers the question of ends in terms of the social conditions for the success of the system described in that paper. These social conditions include a growing economy, a people that values equal economic and political opportunity, and a sense in the community that people have more-or-less what they have been willing to work for—in general, the social conditions of the large commercial republic when it is working as it should. We shall see that Herbert Storing answered the question of who will supply the needed energy: The Constitution institutes presidential government because Publius puts the president in the best position to exercise the initiatives of government.

The kind of energy discussed in *Federalist No. 15* and elaborated in the next several papers is a negative energy: energy to enforce the law against people who disobey. Energy of a different kind emerges as Publius turns to the specific *powers* granted to the new government, powers in the sense of authorizations to enact specific kinds of laws (such as regulations of commerce) or to take certain kinds of actions (such as declaring war). At the beginning of *Federalist No. 22*, Publius defends the commerce power of Article I, Section 8 in terms of the benefits to the nation of stable trade and financial dealings with foreign nations and among the states of the union. He goes on to justify "the power of raising armies" in terms of "a vigorous and economical system of [national] defense" (22:135–38). The logic of these references is made explicit in *Federalist No. 23*: *powers are granted for the sake of ends.* In this paper, Publius can barely restrain his impatience with critics who say that the new government will have too much power. He responds that critics must first decide what they want from the new government. If they want that government to provide national defense and facilitate a stable national market and favorable economic and political relations with other nations, then it follows "that that government ought to be clothed with all the powers requisite to the complete execution of its trust." This conclusion, he says, "rests upon axioms as simple as they are universal: The *means* ought to be proportional to the *end*. The persons, from whose agency the attainment of any *end* is expected, ought to possess the *means* by which it is to be attained" (23:147). He says that how much power may be needed is *"impossible to foresee"* because of *"the extent and variety of national exigencies, or the corresponding extent & variety of the means which may be necessary to satisfy them"* (23:146–47; his emphasis). He applies this proposition not only to national defense, where it would be more acceptable to more people, but also "to commerce, and to every other matter to which [the new government's] jurisdiction is permitted to extend" (23:149). So here we find a *positive energy*: energy for making laws and taking actions in pursuit of the desiderata for which the government was instituted.

Publius recognizes that power in government, while essential, is also risky, for power can be abused. His general approach to this problem is not to withhold power from the new government but to arrange the government's "internal structure" in ways that make abuses of power less likely and more easily detected and remedied. When Publius completes his lengthy discussion of "the general mass of power allotted" to the new government, he turns to that government's "internal structure" and the Constitution's "distribution of this mass of power among [the government's] constituent parts." *Federalist No. 47* begins this inquiry by acknowledging that the "accumulation of all powers legislative, executive, and judiciary in the same hands, whether of one, a few, or many, and whether hereditary, self appointed, or elective, may justly be pronounced the very definition of tyranny" (47:324). How to keep the several parts of the government in their prescribed places is now Publius's question. He goes on to reject several answers that depend on some form of citizen or official virtue. He will rely neither on the law-abidingness of elected officials (*Federalist No. 48*) nor on the public's devotion to constitutional boundaries (*Federalist No. 49* and *No. 50*). "[P]ower is of an encroaching nature," he says in *No. 48*, too strong to be restrained by mere "parchment barriers" (48:332). And in *Federalist No. 49*, he notes that although "it seems strictly consonant to the republican theory to recur to the same original authority [i.e., the people's] not only . . . to . . . new-model the powers of government; but also whenever any one of the departments [of government] may commit encroachments on the chartered authorities of the others" (49:339), in the end the people's judgment "could never be expected to turn on the true merits" of a constitutional conflict among the branches of government. Appealing to the people insures that "the *passions* . . . not *the reason*, of the people would sit in judgment," for the people's judgment "would inevitably be connected with the spirit of pre-existing parties . . . springing out of the question itself" (49:342–43).

Publius's solution to the problem of "maintaining in practice the separation [of powers] delineated on paper" is announced in *Federalist No. 51*: "to divide and arrange the several offices [of government] in such a manner that each may be a check on the other." This system of mutual checks is not one in which virtue checks ambition; it is one in which ambition checks ambition. It "consists in giving to those who administer each department, the necessary constitutional means, and personal motives, to resist encroachments of the others." In this way "the private interests of every individual, may be a sentinel over the public rights" (51:349).

This famous theory of checks and balances is widely assumed to express a negative view of government. Its focus is not on the good things facilitated by government, like national security and a stable national market; its concern is the abuse of governmental power and how to prevent it. Checks and balances are thus often linked with other sorts of restraints on national power, like the first nine amendments and the Tenth Amendment's promise that powers not granted to the national government are reserved to the states or to the people, a promise many construe as a grant of "states' rights" against the national government. Publius, however, offers checks and balances in lieu of devices for withholding power from the national government, devices like a bill of rights, a narrow specification of national powers, and explicit and categorical reservations of state powers. Publius's conception of checks and balances is part of a larger constitutional theory whose general thrust is clearly positive, for Publius connects checks and balances to the need for *energetic government*. As Storing observed, Publius has more in mind than "giv[ing] to each department an equal power of self defense." Looking back on the nation's experience with the state governments under the Articles of Confederation, Publius's great fear was the overbearing power of representative legislatures whose thoughtless response to public opinion too often defeated the public's true interests. "The legislative power," he says in *Federalist No. 48*, "is every where extending the sphere of its activity, and drawing all power into its impetuous vortex." Publius cites Jefferson's observation to similar effect and quotes Jefferson's famous remark: "'An *elective despotism*, was not the government we fought for'" (48: 133, 135; his emphasis). So when Publius turns in *Federalist No. 51* to the question of how to divide power among the branches, he says that it will not be sufficient "to give to each department an equal power of self defense . . . [because] . . . in republican government the legislative authority, necessarily predominates." His "remedy for this inconvenience" is essentially to *divide and weaken Congress vis-à-vis the president and strengthen the president vis-à-vis Congress* (51:350). Storing pointed out that this strategy involves a president whose tenure and power, especially in times of crisis, are largely independent of Congress. This independent and unitary power turns out to be "the primary source of energy and direction for the government as a whole."[31] *Federalist No. 1* opens with a plea for strong or energetic government. Weakness is the essential flaw of the confederation that the Constitution is to replace. And when Publius turns his full attention to the question of what constitutes energy in government, he talks about the "ingredients which constitute energy in the executive" (70:472).

We need look no further into Publius's argument to establish that his purposes can be described in positive terms. He wanted goods like national security and national prosperity. When he referred to "liberty" in the abstract, he treated it not only as something to be secured by strong government against third parties (a negative liberty secured by state action against third-party threats), but also as a positive good, a general state of affairs to be achieved and enjoyed, a condition whose possession would mark a people as a free people, an affirmative end of government. His chief institutional concerns were consonant with this substantive orientation. His lengthy exposition and defense of generic *energy* or *power* and specific *grants* or *powers* consumed much more of his attention than the subject of negative rights. This is what you would expect of one concerned with substantive ends provided by or facilitated through government: power and the organization of power—power to pursue substantive goods efficiently and safely.

## V. Publius and the Positive State

Architects of the New Deal shared Publius's view of national power as dedicated to, *and* as constitutionally adequate to, broad ends like national security and the economic well-being of the nation's people. Over the years, scholars of different ideologies have considered the New Deal and the "mixed economy" of the "welfare state" a moderate middle course between the theoretical extremes of pure socialism and laissez-faire and an extension in new circumstances of a Hamiltonian view of constitutional government.[32] Yet this position is often qualified or equivocal. Thus, Morton Frisch, a colleague of Storing and Dia-

[31] Storing, "The Problem of Big Government," 81.

[32] See Diamond, Fisk, and Garfinkel, *The Democratic Republic,* 490–95; Morton J. Frisch, "Franklin Delano Roosevelt," in Morton J. Frisch and Richard G. Stevens, eds., *American Political Thought: The Philosophic Dimensions of American Statesmanship* (New York: Charles Scribner's Sons, 1971), 225–35; Samuel H. Beer, *To Make a Nation: The Rediscovery of American Federalism* (Cambridge, MA: Harvard University Press, 1993), 3–8, 15–21; and Cass R. Sunstein,

mond, holds that the New Deal "was essentially restorative or conservative, rather than constitutive," that it found its "basis in the Madisonian system," and that Franklin D. Roosevelt correctly held that government was obligated "to satisfy those urgent human purposes, which, in essence, gave it its beginning and provide its present justification."[33] Frisch also holds, however, that the New Deal "constituted a profound modification of the traditional American Democracy . . . arrived at through a break with the earlier liberalism." The older liberalism, says Frisch, alluding to the Declaration of Independence without argument and citing neither the Constitution nor *The Federalist,* saw society and economy as more-or-less self-regulatory and government's role as that of securing not the people's welfare or happiness, but the "conditions" for the private pursuit of happiness. Measures like the Social Security Act, the Fair Labor Standards Act, and the Full Employment Act signaled a shift of emphasis from the mere conditions of happiness to the "enjoyment or possession of happiness" as a governmental responsibility to be discharged through "rearranging [the] economy, if necessary, and redistributing its benefits."[34]

James Ceaser, a political scientist influenced by Storing, displays the same ambivalence. In a recent essay, Ceaser cautions his fellow conservatives that their opposition to strong government weakens institutions they need to realize their own vision for the country.[35] Ceaser finds that the Constitution, properly understood, sanctions *unlimited discretion* in the national government in pursuit of essentially three ends: national security, national prosperity, and racial harmony.[36] From the Hamiltonian perspective that he explicitly adopts, Ceaser approves the New Deal's "expansion of federal power to handle some of the new problems posed by the conditions of the twentieth century." "New Deal program[s]," he writes, "were enacted during the most severe economic crisis in American history," and "[p]revious discretionary policy thinking [i.e., Hamiltonian thinking] would surely have provided in this situation for using national powers to their fullest—and perhaps even asking for more." Yet, writes Ceaser, by enacting programs "to ensure welfare and security," the New Deal parted with the tradition. When Roosevelt called for a second bill of rights that included jobs, medical care, retirement security, and education,

---

*The Second Bill of Rights: FDR's Unfinished Revolution and Why We Need It More Than Ever* (New York: Basic Books, 2004), 44, 57–59, 73.

[33] Frisch, "Franklin Delano Roosevelt," 221, 227, 230.

[34] Ibid., 228–31. Frisch ignores the statement in *Federalist No. 10* that regulating economic conflict is the "principal task of modern Legislation" (10:59). He also misses a matter regarding the Declaration of Independence on which I comment below: Jefferson treats the natural rights of life and liberty as "Ends" to be secured by government, effectively rendering them *positive* rights.

[35] James W. Ceaser, "What Kind of Government Do We Have to Fear?" in Arthur M. Melzer, Jerry Weinberger, and M. Richard Zinman, eds., *Politics at the Turn of the Century* (Lanham, MD: Rowman and Littlefield, 2001), 76–101.

[36] Ibid., 77–83.

writes Ceaser, he "turned the [negative rights] language of limited government on its head."[37]

One might resolve the tension in Ceaser's view of the New Deal by construing him as approving the regulatory policies of the New Deal and the Great Society, but not their redistributive policies: pursuing fair labor standards is constitutional, but Social Security is not; banning discrimination in employment is constitutionally authorized, but affirmative action is not. Interpretive repair of Ceaser's position will not take us far, however. He starts with a clear and, in my view, correct understanding of the logic of power as conceived at the founding, an instrumentalist logic that places few restrictions on government's pursuit of nationally authorized ends. He holds, for example, that a government limited only to the end of national defense "can become quite extensive," requiring "high taxes, a national mobilization of manpower, and extensive government economic planning," presumably of the kind the nation saw carried out by the War Industries Board of World War I and the War Production Board of World War II. Ceaser also has a generous view of constitutional ends. Far from limiting national power over the economy to regulating the flow of interstate commerce, Ceaser talks of "*promoting* the flow of commerce *and* economic development, and protecting the security of rights (especially economic rights from the effects of inflationary policies)."[38] He approves Hamilton's protectionist and mercantilist policies as serving "a direct constitutional purpose." He approves national support for scientific research and the nineteenth-century subsidies for western homesteading, land-grant colleges, and railroad expansion. He also believes the Supreme Court erred in the Civil Rights Cases (1883) by crippling Congress's power over the nation's race relations.[39] Add congressional power over the nation's race relations to the broad economic, military, and foreign-affairs powers of which Ceaser approves, and you have the potential for "very extensive" power indeed.

Yet Ceaser draws the line at "affirmative action," which he defines as government's guarantee not of opportunity but of "certain results for designated minority groups." According to Ceaser, to cross this line is to confound two kinds of rights: rights as expressive of (1) "what the 'demanding' individual want[s]" and (2) what one individual owes another "by way of restraint or duty." Rights of the second kind enhance "traditional" guarantees like freedom of speech, private property, and freedom from racial discrimination. The first kind includes "programmatic benefits" from education to "medical care, day care, . . . and so forth"—all at taxpayers' expense. Ceaser thus joins the American right's professed opposition to positive rights. Nonetheless, he urges his fellow conservatives

---

[37] Ibid., 84, 88.
[38] Ibid., 78; my emphasis.
[39] Ibid., 80–81, 90, commenting on the Civil Rights Cases, 109 U.S 3 (1883).

not to overreact by turning against rights generally. Conservatives should
not "compromise the protection of . . . real rights" like speech, property,
and nondiscrimination; nor should they forget the "underpinning [of real
rights] in Nature and the Constitution."[40]

One can excuse Ceaser for neglecting to defend the distinction between
positive and negative rights, for the distinction is familiar and enjoys
surface plausibility. However, Ceaser needs an argument for his suggestion that only negative rights are real, natural, and constitutional. He
must argue for this conclusion if it is to be more than a way of identifying
where he stands in the current debate over the role of government. Yet
Ceaser offers no argument for his statement about real rights; he merely
asserts it. And since this undefended proposition is crucial to his denial
that the New Deal was faithful to the principles of the founding, that
denial is also undefended. The need for argument on Ceaser's part is easy
to see if we think for a moment not about "rights" but about the positive
benefits that, on Ceaser's own account, the American government was
established to pursue, either by provision or by facilitation. If, as Ceaser
himself believes, a Hamiltonian view of constitutional responsibilities is
best, and if, as Ceaser also believes, tax-supported benefits to American
businesses from bond speculators to railroad developers have contributed to constitutional ends, then it is far from obvious why constitutional
ends cannot be served by tax-supported police protection, housing, and
education for all of the nation's children. Because (as far as I am aware)
Ceaser has no answer to this objection, I turn to my colleague Michael
Zuckert, a writer who does have arguments for the anti-welfarist position
he shares with Ceaser.

## VI. On the Origin and Nature of Rights

Zuckert views the debate about the size of government in America as
including a debate over what kinds of rights the American system was
designed to secure.[41] Those who argue for positive rights, like the right to
health care (Zuckert's leading example), support big government because
it takes big government to secure those rights. Those who favor only
negative rights support government that while possibly extensive will
also be in some sense "limited" and not as big as big government.[42]
Zuckert's argument for limited government and negative rights takes the
form of a contrast between John Rawls and John Locke, the former a
philosopher of positive rights and big government, and the latter the
philosopher of limited government and negative rights. Though Zuckert

[40] Ibid., 90, 92.
[41] Michael P. Zuckert, *Launching Liberalism: On Lockean Political Philosophy* (Lawrence:
University Press of Kansas, 2002), 313.
[42] Ibid., 315, 326.

adopts Locke's position as his own, he does not just assume Locke's authority; he offers arguments in Locke's behalf. This enables me to concentrate not on Zuckert's reading of other thinkers, but on Zuckert's view of the subject at hand: rights and the American Constitution. I contend here that whether Zuckert is right or wrong about Locke and Rawls, he must amend his views about rights and the Constitution.

Problems with Zuckert's position appear even before he begins his argument about the origins and the nature of rights and their relationship to constitutional government. Ultimately, he relies on what he believes is the greater intuitive appeal of negative rights over positive rights.[43] This reliance on intuition makes it a matter of some significance when he says at the outset that "most of us are committed" exclusively neither to positive rights nor to negative rights, but "to some mix" of positive and negative rights.[44] Because the distinction between positive and negative rights seems central to Zuckert's view of liberalism, his ambivalence invites speculation. Might he sense that at some level there is no meaningful distinction between negative and positive rights?[45] If common sense commits us to *a* mix of positive and negative rights, what particular mix does it commit us to? Why one mix rather than another? Can the best mix be something other than the one that best serves the general welfare and the common defense? These questions sit unanswered in the background of Zuckert's arguments against a welfarist view of the Constitution. Zuckert offers three such arguments: (1) that property precedes justice in a way that makes justice "rights preservative"; (2) that property in the self is the origin of (external) property and the origin of the priority of property to justice; and (3) that securing negative rights is the purpose or end of liberal government.

I will address each of these arguments in turn. First, however, I must note Zuckert's definitions of different kinds of rights. A negative right, says Zuckert, implies a duty "not to interfere" with some effort or action of some individual or group. A negative right, like a right to property or the freedom of speech, involves a duty to forbear. A positive right, Zuckert says, involves a "duty to supply" something, like health care; positive rights are welfare rights. And a right, says Zuckert, is a claim on someone else either to forbear or to supply something. But rights cannot be just any claims, he says; they must be "justified claims."[46] These definitions occur early in Zuckert's discussion, and I underscore an obvious implication of the third definition. If rights are not just claims but *justified* claims, *there*

---

[43] Ibid., 317, 327–28.
[44] Ibid., 315.
[45] Zuckert holds that rights to life, liberty, and property are natural rights and, by their logic, negative. He recognizes that the right to their protection by the state is a positive right, but he says this positive right is a civil right, not a natural right. Yet he also says that "it is a part of natural justice that one's legal rights be honored" (ibid., 315–16).
[46] Ibid., 314–15.

*can be no recognized right without some prior sense of what makes for a "justified claim."* This implication alone defeats Zuckert's contention (in his first argument) that justice derives from property—i.e., that there is no justice without property, that we start with property (not justice) in a state of nature, that property makes justice possible because justice is giving every-one his due, and that justice is therefore preservative of property rights (*pace* the progressive concept of "social justice").[47] Zuckert attributes this position to Locke and contrasts it with Rawls's view that justice precedes property and that property may therefore be distributed as justice (as fairness) requires.[48] Whatever position Locke holds, however, Zuckert cannot define rights as justified claims, conflate property with property rights, and say that justice is preservative of antecedent property rights. For if rights are *justified* claims and property entails property rights (duties of forbearance by others), then justice precedes property and property is limited to what can be justified in terms other than preserving property.

I turn now to Zuckert's second argument against a welfarist view of the Constitution. Zuckert's view that justice is rights preservative (i.e., prop-erty preservative) incorporates a second position he finds in Locke: that "human beings are self-owners." "On the rock of self-ownership," says Zuckert, "Locke builds his doctrines of natural rights, justice, and limited government." Zuckert treats this "rock of self-ownership" as a nonmoral or scientific fact. His initial description of the "rock" makes it is easy to accept as a scientific fact, apparently a psychological fact. This fact is "a fact witnessed in our most elementary locutions. . . . The center of the self is the 'I,' the pure abstract and empty ego, possessor of its own data of consciousness (*my* feelings, *my* ideas, *my* experiences), yet never lost in them." But Zuckert moves immediately from the self as possessing the data of one's consciousness to the self as possessing one's body as an "instrument of its [the self's] intentional actions." This self-ownership of body and action is "of the nature of a property right." As such, it implies "exclusivity vis-à-vis others," and "logic (although not the practical con-ditions of existence) requires that each self raising such a claim [to exclu-sive direction of one's body] recognize that every other self raises ipso facto the very same claim on the very same ground."[49]

When Zuckert acknowledges that the "practical conditions of exis-tence" may defeat what "logic" requires, he defeats any claim that self-ownership of the body and its actions is a fact on a par with self-ownership of the data of one's consciousness. Putting aside possibilities like hypnosis and mind-altering substances that render a person tempo-rarily "not himself," self-ownership of one's experiences (data of con-sciousness) plausibly holds even for persons held in slavery. The historical

[47] See ibid., 312, 317, 326.
[48] Ibid., 317.
[49] Ibid., 324–26.

fact of slavery proves, however, that self-ownership of body and actions is at best a contingent fact, even of persons whose consciousness is unimpaired. One held as a slave (plausibly) "has his own experiences" as a matter of psychological fact, but the slave does not enjoy his body "as an instrument of [his] intentional actions in relation to [his] broader purposes in life." Stated as a scientific fact, the proposition that all persons own their bodies and their actions is therefore false. If it is a fact, it must be a *moral fact*, not a scientific fact. An unqualified statement of the moral fact would be that *denying self-ownership is wrong*. Adjusted to accommodate uncontroversial treatment of children, impaired adults, and convicted felons, the moral fact would support the prescription that *each socially responsible adult ought to be treated as having property in his or her body, insofar as he or she remains socially responsible.*

What principle, then, might establish a universal right of self-ownership? The traditional answer is some principle of *equality*. The Declaration of Independence proposes that all persons are created equal and equally endowed by their creator with inalienable rights, and thus no person rightly governs another without the other's consent. Zuckert makes a different argument, however, and in view of his anti-welfarism, well he might. For if a principle of equality helps to justify the property of each person in his or her body and actions, and if this self-ownership is the basis of all subsequent property, then we can argue that there can be no just claim to property—and therefore no property—in other persons. We can argue further that there can be no just use of property to reduce persons to a state of virtual property, such as peonage. We can argue with Diamond that when Publius says that "the first object of government is the protection of different and unequal faculties for acquiring property," he means protecting the faculties both of "the little . . . and the much propertied" in ways that make the former "sanguine about their chances" for improving their condition.[50] Depending, as it seems to depend, on a principle of equality, the principle of self-ownership seems compatible with efforts of the welfare state to help the little propertied overcome those of their disadvantages (vis-à-vis the much propertied) that may be undeserved.[51]

Do we need a premise of equality to establish a general principle of self-ownership? When Zuckert argues for universal self-ownership, he starts with the self-ownership of one person—"my" self-ownership, "your" self-ownership, not yet the self-ownership of all. He establishes this self-ownership of one person through introspection and reflection on ordinary locutions such as "my body," "my experiences," etc. Then, as we have seen, he announces that *logic* does the rest: logic requires that each

---

[50] Diamond, "The Federalist," 650.
[51] My application of Diamond's argument depends, of course, on the existence of undeserved disadvantages. However, I take it as uncontroversial that children of poor households have not earned their disadvantages.

self that raises a claim of self-ownership recognize the same claim of all other selves. Logic is not enough, however. "I own my body and actions" simply does not entail "everyone claiming to own his body and actions owns his body and actions." For I may see, and there may be, stark and important differences between me and others. To connect the first proposition and the second, at least one additional premise is needed, and a likely prospect would be the traditional one. I would then say that everyone owns himself just as I do *because we (I and the others of the "we" referred to) are all sufficiently alike in relevant respects.* Self-ownership alone does not imply forbearance; for self-ownership is consistent with liberty in a state of nature, where each has the right to do whatever he might think necessary for his preservation. To justify property as a social institution, self-ownership must be allied with principles of equality and community, and these principles, in turn, structure what the community can recognize and protect as property.

Zuckert's third argument against a welfarist view of the Constitution is that the purpose of liberal government is securing negative rights, not positive rights. Again, Zuckert purports to make Locke's view his own, and, again, I will comment not on Zuckert's understanding of Locke, but on Zuckert's own view of our subject. According to Zuckert, then, individuals leave a state of nature and enter civil society for the sake of securing their natural rights. The liberal state is thus "rights-securing," says Zuckert, and the rights secured are negative rights.[52] I think this position needs refinement and that a more precise account would start with individuals leaving a state of nature to protect not rights but *goods*— goods like speaking your mind, moving about as you please, or enjoying what you have worked for—the goods that make up the *substantive content* of rights. The liberal state does secure rights, but unless *rights* are conflated with *goods* or *ends* (as often happens), "rights-securing" falls short of the state's central function.

The state that is (negative) rights-securing secures more than rights because rights secure more than rights. I do not deny that a right can be negative or, better, that a right can have a negative aspect. If someone possesses or anticipates a good and seeks its enjoyment without interference from other persons, she can sensibly want others to leave her alone. But restraining or excluding others as such is not a good, and only a psychopath would seek pointless restraints on others. The point served by the negative aspect of a right is the right's *object*, the thing one wishes to enjoy without interference, and the object of a right must be a *good*. Life is a good. Liberty is also a good, as is the liberty to pursue responsible conceptions of happiness. The Declaration of Independence says that government is established to secure these things, and from the particulars of its indictment of George III (charged at one point with "abdicat[ing]

---

[52] Zuckert, *Launching Liberalism*, 314.

Government here") the Declaration clearly supposes that these things are to be secured *through governmental power*, not through governmental inaction. The second paragraph of the Declaration does refer to these things as "unalienable rights." However, it also refers to them as "Ends" and as elements of the people's "Safety and Happiness." In doing so, the Declaration conflates rights and ends.

Conflating rights and ends is unobjectionable if the rights referred to are *positive* rights. Positive rights can be conceived as ends of government. Negative rights cannot be ends of government. Consider two kinds of negative rights. Constitutional rights conceived solely as negative rights against government cannot be ends of government because no sane person would establish a government for the sake of limiting it. Negative rights against third parties cannot be ends of government because restraining others is good only when it is instrumental to the preservation of good things like life and liberty. In contrast with negative rights, positive rights conflated with ends can be ends of government because ends are goods and it makes sense to establish a government to secure good things.

The pursuit and enjoyment of these goods, moreover, would ultimately be justified in terms of *public goods*. The private enjoyment of goods would be involved; but because, as Zuckert says, private rights are *justified claims* (i.e., *publicly* justified claims), their active protection by government must ultimately be seen as a strategy for pursuing public goods.[53] Actors who are fully aware of what they are doing would thus leave the state of nature in pursuit of more than their private interests. These actors would abandon self-help and position themselves to draw on the resources of a newly created public authority, an authority whose charter (if, like the Constitution, it is the expression of some "we") and character (as maker of impersonal and generally applicable laws) permit action only for public purposes. The resources of this authority are far from abundant. Using these resources to protect private rights requires sacrifices, sometimes great sacrifices. The private pursuits thus protected therefore must be functional to the common good.[54] Lincoln called these protected pursuits "laudable pursuits," and, as laudable, they are more than merely private.[55] Publius spoke aptly, therefore, when he began his argument for ratification with an appeal to the "patriotism" and "philanthropy" of his readers (1:3) and when he described checks and balances as a "policy of supplying

---

[53] Holmes and Sunstein, *The Cost of Rights*, 61–62, 115–17.

[54] Ibid., 44–48.

[55] Abraham Lincoln, "Message to Congress in Special Session: July 4, 1861," in Roy P. Basler, ed., *Abraham Lincoln: His Speeches and Writings* (New York: Grosset and Dunlap, 1946), 607. Here Lincoln said that "the leading object" of the national government was "to elevate the condition of men; to lift artificial weight from all shoulders; to clear the paths of laudable pursuit for all; to afford all an unfettered start and a fair chance in the race of life."

by opposite and rival interests, the defects of better motives" (51:349) —
motives he claimed to share with the generation to whose patriotism
and philanthropy he appealed (49:341).[56]

## VII. Constitutional Rights

Conceived as rights against government, constitutional rights cannot
be ends of government. Constitutional rights do not have to be conceived solely in negative terms, however. They can be understood in
terms of virtues and civic institutions or practices. Take the freedom of
speech. As a restraint on government and nothing more, it could hardly
be an end for which government was established. But human fallibility
makes the practice of free speech instrumental to the pursuit of goods
(well-being, security, etc.) conceived as real goods, that is, goods about
whose constituents and conditions the government and indeed the entire
community can be wrong. A commitment to these goods is a commitment to a culture of free speech and its constituent institutions, attitudes, and conditions. For it is through diverse opinions in dialectical
progression that we can hope to get closer to the truth about real
goods and how to pursue them. A commitment to this culture, however, requires power to cultivate it and secure it against the forces that
threaten it, including the conformity, softness, and moral skepticism
that (through inadvertence?) have accompanied the progress of liberal
modernity or, if you prefer, the "large commercial republic." Promoting
free speech as an end of government necessitates an active concern for
the education of the nation's people. It might well mean tax-and-spend
programs like the National Endowment for the Arts and the Corpora-
tion for Public Broadcasting. Promoting free speech as an end of a
liberal government should also require withholding public support (like
voucher-eligibility and tax exemptions) from private schools that teach
religious intolerance, cultivate racism, condemn secular reasonableness,
and train children to substitute clerical authority and "Biblical truth"
for self-critical and autonomous thought.[57] Free speech as an end of
government thus means a lot more than free speech against government. But neither implies small government or negative government.
The former requires big government, and the latter makes sense only
in a positive context.

---

[56] Actors who might see their interests as wholly private would still seek more than
wholly private interests if they reflected on the fact that they might be wrong about what
their interests are. The truth about one's interests is approximated only in communities of
reasonably diverse other persons who represent, in speech and conduct, alternative hypoth-
eses of the good life in dialectical progression. The true interests of self-serving actors would
thus be practically inseparable from the interests of such a community. See Barber, *Welfare
and the Constitution*, 109–14.

[57] See ibid., 143–46.

## VIII. Conclusion

A welfarist view of the U.S. Constitution finds support in the text of the Constitution, the argument of *The Federalist*, and the testimony of common sense, or so I have contended here. But arguments against a welfarist view stretch from the metaphysical to the visceral. I have tried to confront these arguments in other works, to which I have referred the reader. Here I have addressed additional arguments to those who say a welfarist view is inconsistent with the liberal view of constitutional rights and rights in general. I close with brief comments about a problem Americans associate with the subject of rights: the threat welfare constitutionalism may pose to democracy.

When one contends, as I do, that the Constitution obligates our federal and state governments to provide things like police protection and public education, one risks unelected federal judges adding new rights to the Constitution and ordering elected legislators to tax and spend for things the voting public does not want (like abortion funding) or thinks it cannot afford (like universal health care).[58] This is the worry of many anti-welfarists, and my response here can only report conclusions that I have defended elsewhere.[59] This response is meant not to persuade but to inform readers that persuasive arguments may exist.

Anti-welfarists worried about threats to democracy should first consider whether arguments from democracy against judicial activism actually depreciate democracy. These arguments often assume that there are no objectively better or worse understandings of (values like) the general welfare. They leave us to wonder how there can be better or worse understandings of (values like) democracy, or why we should value democracy in the first place. Sometimes these arguments imply that the *demos* is incapable of aspiring to improve its performance regarding ends like justice and the general welfare. I say this because a people more concerned with self-improvement than with self-assertion would institutionalize that concern and because honest and competent judges who think for themselves about constitutional meaning would be part of that institution.[60] So if democracy is incompatible with or cannot produce good judges, then democracy cannot institutionalize a concern for real ends like justice and the general welfare. How, in that event, could anyone justify democracy?

Anti-welfarists worried about welfarism's threat to democracy can accept welfarism as an esoteric teaching and still oppose it both as a public philosophy and as a guide for academic inquiry. They can say that even if welfarism is faithful to the Constitution and the founding, things will

---

[58] See Robert H. Bork, "The Impossibility of Finding Welfare Rights in the Constitution," *Washington University Law Quarterly* (1979): 699–701.

[59] See Barber, *The Constitution of Judicial Power*, chaps. 4–5.

[60] Ibid., chap. 2, esp. 27–40.

go better for Americans if everyone professes negative constitutionalism. This seems to be the position of Harvey Mansfield, a widely influential and spirited critic of welfare constitutionalism.[61] He appears to favor negative constitutionalism as a kind of noble lie.[62] Though Mansfield's position is easy to ridicule, he may be right. His strategy reflects Publius's decision to pursue the common good (a welfarist aim) through a system of private incentives, a system that (inadvertently?) weakens public purposefulness and fosters a normative standard of negative rights.[63] The implicit perfectionism of welfare constitutionalism does clash with Publius's belief in *Federalist No. 51* that instead of trying to correct for "the defect of better motives," the nation should pursue a strategy of checking and balancing "opposite and rival interests" (51:349). If Mansfield's crypto-welfarism is right, however, he still has to understand the Constitution from the welfarist perspective of Publius's "better motives"; this means that welfarism remains a correct (albeit now esoteric) teaching, democracy is degraded (the *demos* blind to the public purposefulness of its better self and incapable of genuine reform), and, its public stature notwithstanding, negative constitutionalism is no more than a welfarist strategy. As an account of the Constitution and the founding, negative constitutionalism is *still false*.

Finally, no metaphysical, semantic, or logical necessity connects welfare constitutionalism with enhanced judicial power. FDR did not ask the courts to enact his "Second Bill of Rights"; he wanted Congress to do it. Nor did he think constitutional amendments necessary, for he held, with the Hamiltonian tradition, that Article I already gives Congress power to tax and spend for the general welfare, broadly conceived.[64] Ironically, to complain that welfare constitutionalism means more power for the courts is to affirm the grandest claim of judicial imperialism: that the Constitution speaks solely through the courts. FDR denied this claim, as did Lincoln, and so do most present-day academic exponents of welfare rights.[65]

Academics who have urged recognition of welfare rights over the years do not constitute a unified tradition. They share no common conception of welfare rights or common ground from which to derive and defend

[61] See Harvey Mansfield, "The Formal Constitution: A Comment on Sotirios A. Barber," *The American Journal of Jurisprudence* 42 (1997): 188–89.

[62] See Sotirios A. Barber, "Reply to Professor Mansfield," *The American Journal of Jurisprudence* 42 (1997): 191–94.

[63] See Benjamin R. Barber, "The Compromised Republic: Public Purposelessness in America," in Robert H. Horwitz, ed., *The Moral Foundations of the American Republic* (Charlottesville: University Press of Virginia, 1986), 47–53.

[64] Sunstein, *The Second Bill of Rights*, 44, 55, 61, 64, 69–70, 143–44. On the general welfare clause, see Barber, *Welfare and the Constitution*, 137–42.

[65] See Barber, *Welfare and the Constitution*, 19, 152; see also Frank I. Michelman, "Welfare Rights in a Constitutional Democracy," *Washington University Law Quarterly* 3 (1979) 684–85; Lawrence G. Sager, *Justice in Plain Clothes* (New Haven, CT: Yale University Press, 2004), 86–92; and Sunstein, *The Second Bill of Rights*, 144–47.

such rights.[66] Welfarists may rationally choose the enlargement of judicial power, when contingencies recommend that course. But this possibility cannot tell against welfarism, for anti-welfarists have also sought and continue to seek enlargements of judicial power when it suits their purposes. As I understand welfare constitutionalism as an academic position, it has four or five ambitions. These ambitions reflect the connection, sketched in Section IV above, between true well-being and a constitution-making capacity.[67] None of these ambitions depends uniquely on judicial power. First, academic welfarism should encourage debate over the true normative properties of the Constitution as a whole. Second, it should encourage constitutional theorists to take up the question of what constitutes well-being and what a constitutional regime can do to facilitate its pursuit. Third, academic welfarism should assess the Constitution's adequacy to its ends. And, fourth, it should formulate substantive standards for evaluating public policies, as in my criticism of vouchers for anti-liberal schools (at the end of the previous section). Welfarists so inclined may also promote a true understanding of the Constitution among the nation's political leaders and encourage them to act on that understanding. These ambitions are either mainly theoretical or, in the case of the last mentioned, cultural in scope. They fall short of court-centered concerns in some respects; they exceed court-centered concerns in other respects. If welfarists with these ambitions threaten American democracy, it must be because American democracy cannot handle the truth about the constitution it purports to revere.

*Political Science, University of Notre Dame*

---

*Political Science, University of Notre Dame*

[66] See Barber, *Welfare and the Constitution*, 6–8.
[67] Ibid., 113–14, 153–54.

# ON CONSTITUTIONAL WELFARE LIBERALISM:
## AN OLD-LIBERAL PERSPECTIVE

### By Michael P. Zuckert

### I. Introduction

I have always been especially intrigued by the dishes one can find on some of the more elaborate Chinese menus, dishes like Thousand Year Old Bird's Nest Soup. I must admit I've never been tempted to order this dish: it has never been clear to me whether extreme aging would make a bird's nest more palatable or less. But the delicious hyperbole in that dish's name puts one in mind of the fact that we have had not just an old and a new liberalism, but nearly a thousand liberalisms. It is striking how subject to modification and evolution that now venerable political orientation has been since it first hatched in the seventeenth century.

### II. The Original Liberalism

The original liberalism emerged with John Locke. Its chief features were captured in that marvel of concision, the American Declaration of Independence. Following Thomas Jefferson, we can identify six features of this original liberalism:

1. *Rationalism.* It is a rationalist doctrine in the sense that it looks to reason (public reason in a broad and nontechnical sense) for its bearings. As Locke said, reason must be our "only Star and compass."[1] That statement was made in the context of his refutation of the divine-right-of-kings political thinking of Sir Robert Filmer, who claimed to take his bearings not by reason but by scripture. Locke does not so much dismiss scripture as insist that on matters where reason can speak, scripture must be understood to agree with it. Since Locke considers politics a sphere of human activity within the legitimate scope of reason, that means that for all theoretical purposes scripture may be set aside, although for some practical purposes it must be deployed. The appeal to reason most definitely does not *ipso facto* rule out natural theology, however.

2. *Rights.* Lockean liberalism conceives each individual adult human being to possess rights, rights which derive from nature or God, not from government or society. Locke and the original liberals had a stable list of rights: life, liberty, and property. Jefferson's Declaration of Independence

---

[1] John Locke, *Two Treatises of Government*, ed. Peter Laslett (Cambridge: Cambridge University Press, 1960), I.58.

dropped the reference to property and added to their list the intriguing "pursuit of happiness," itself a Lockean idea, although nowhere identified by Locke as a right.[2] Nonetheless, it would not be much of a stretch for Locke to endorse such a right as a shorthand summation of all the other rights.[3] Locke also spoke of rights as property. He meant to suggest by that usage both the relation between the rights-holder and his or her rights and the relation of others to those rights. The rights or the objects of the rights are the possessions of the rights-holder. To have a right is to have a kind of sovereign power within the (limited) sphere of the right. A rights-holder's claims are also exclusive in the rights-holder. Locke means to reject Thomas Hobbes's odd conclusion that in the state of nature men can have rights to each other's bodies.[4] Locke captured the property character of rights when he called men "self-owners" and affirmed that all men have a property in their own bodies.[5]

3. *Equality.* From his various thoughts about rights, Locke concluded that "all men are created equal," meaning that no one has a natural claim to rule another. In particular, no one has a right to coerce another, unless that other harms or threatens to harm oneself or others. If human beings are self-owners, then it is a violation of right for one to harm or intrude upon the body of another. More broadly, so far as the pursuit of happiness can rightly be posited as a right, it implies that human beings have a right to pursue a shape and style of life that they think promises to lead them toward happiness. Such a right affirms, all things equal, a right to a very comprehensive control of one's own life by and for oneself. If human beings possess such a comprehensive right, it could not be the case that others have a right to rule them by nature, for the possession by another of a right to rule would be incompatible with one's right to shape one's own life.

4. *Ends of government.* Lockean liberalism is, of course, not anarchistic. Governments claim the right to do the very thing—coerce human beings— that Lockean rights theory seems to deny. The Lockean theory takes its point of departure from the problematical character of political authority. Is there any legitimate natural coercive authority whatever? Locke believes there is. We have the right forcefully to resist and punish those who violate our rights. That is the only legitimate coercion, the only coercion consistent with conceiving human beings as bearers of rights and as self-owners. Since there is no governing authority by nature, governments must be understood to be artificial, to be "instituted" by men. This

[2] John Locke, *An Essay Concerning Human Understanding*, ed. Peter Nidditch (Oxford: Oxford University Press, 1990), II.21.62.

[3] Michael P. Zuckert, *Launching Liberalism* (Lawrence: University Press of Kansas, 2002), 224.

[4] Thomas Hobbes, *Leviathan*, ed. Richard Tuck (Cambridge: Cambridge University Press, 1991), chap. 14, p. 91.

[5] Locke, *Two Treatises*, II.27.

is less a statement about history than it is about legitimacy: all legitimate government must be thought of as instituted. But if "instituted," then instituted to what end? Jefferson answers: "[T]o secure these rights, governments are instituted among men." The idea of institution thus leads to a precise notion of the legitimate ends of governance. Government is an entity with limited ends. These limitations do not derive from denying the value of many other ends, but from the fact that these other ends cannot connect up with the sole source of legitimate coercion. Thus, Lockean liberals do not necessarily deny salvation in the one true faith to be a valuable end, but imposition of that end does not attach to the source of legitimate authority. Likewise, Locke does not deny that certain states of character (i.e., the possession of certain virtues) are rationally desirable, but the imposition of these states of character does not attach to the source of coercive authority either. The original liberalism is thus a doctrine of limited government.

5. *Consent and the right of revolution.* Government exists for the sake of securing the rights of the governed and is best understood as the product of their institution. Government must be understood as arising from the consent of the governed in the sense that it is the massed or pooled legitimate coercive power of each that government wields. At the same time, government is or ought to be pervasively responsible to those in whose name and for whose sake it operates. The original liberalism was a bit vague about how deep this responsibility needed to go. At the very least, a body representative of some or all of the property owners in a society must be involved in the laying of taxes, and perhaps in the general making of laws. Likewise, the body of the people retain a right to "alter or abolish" government when they believe it is not living up to its trust. Thus, the so-called right of revolution is a prominent part of the original liberalism.

6. *Constitutionalism.* Locke (and even more his successors) recognized, however, that revolution is a very blunt instrument for enforcing responsible governance. The original liberalism was concerned from the outset, then, with issues of constitutional design, that is, with ways to structure governmental institutions and their interactions so as to maximize their likelihood of governing well. Among other institutions, original liberalism was partial to markets.

The original Lockean liberalism was modified in three important directions in the eighteenth century. While the new liberal emphases were not without potential tension among themselves and with parts of the original Lockeanism, for the most part liberalism emerged from these modifications relatively coherent and harmonious. The first addition to liberalism was Montesquieu's. In his magisterial *Spirit of the Laws,* Montesquieu took the somewhat underdeveloped Lockean emphasis on constitutional institutions and developed it into the sophisticated and powerful theory of separation of powers. He also took to heart

Locke's concern with commerce and developed the implications for liberal polity and economy.[6]

The second modification of the original liberalism was effected by the American founders. They were Lockeans to a man, but they insisted that the only legitimate liberal order was what they called a "wholly republican" order. By that, they meant a representative democracy, which is what we in the twenty-first century most often mean by the term "democracy."[7] Only governance solely by the representatives of "the great body" of the people could be legitimate, they concluded.[8] In this they went beyond both Locke and Montesquieu, who accepted monarchic and aristocratic or oligarchic elements as legitimate or even desirable.

The final modification of liberalism in the eighteenth century reached its peak expression in Adam Smith's demonstration of the role of markets not only in producing wealth, one of the original liberalism's goals, but also in serving liberty.

In a gesture to Ockham's razor, let us refuse to multiply entities; let us gather together these elements of seventeenth- and eighteenth-century liberalism and call this "classical liberalism," or "the old liberalism."

## III. Liberalisms in the Nineteenth Century and Beyond

After the classical synthesis, there were many new and (allegedly) improved forms of liberalism, but for our purposes let us paint in broad strokes and note just two new liberalisms prior to the more recent forms on which we wish to lavish our subsequent attention. Both emerged in the nineteenth century and continued to be developed in the twentieth. One was a liberalism more libertarian in character than the old liberalism. It had, in turn, two wings, which did not always, but certainly could, reasonably well coexist or even cohere in a unified political orientation. Both were characterized by a more doctrinaire or hard-edged direct commitment to liberty than was the case for the old liberalism. The first of these two wings is exemplified in John Stuart Mill's great classic of liberal thought, *On Liberty*, which formulated a hard and fast rule, a "bright and shining line" of political morality across which governments ought not to go in legislating. Mill's line was captured in his well-known "harm principle." The harm principle holds that "the sole end for which mankind are warranted, individually or collectively, in interfering with the liberty of action of any of their number, is self-protection. That the only purpose for which power can be rightfully exercised over any member of a civilized

---

[6] Montesquieu, *The Spirit of the Laws*, ed. Anne M. Cohler, Basia C. Miller, and Harold S. Stone (Cambridge: Cambridge University Press, 1989).

[7] Alexander Hamilton, James Madison, and John Jay, *The Federalist* (Indianapolis: Liberty Press, 2001), No. 10, p. 46.

[8] Ibid., No. 39, p. 194.

community, against his will, is to prevent harm to others."[9] The harm principle was clearly a descendant of the Lockean-Jeffersonian notion that governments were limited in their legitimate undertakings to securing the rights of persons. But neither Locke nor Jefferson ever drew a line in the sand, or anywhere else, for they did not insist that government be strictly limited to direct rights protecting.

Since they wrote before Mill pushed the issue, Locke and Jefferson never formulated very clearly why they did not go so far in a libertarian direction as Mill went. I would put their somewhat understated thought as follows. The legitimate end of government—securing rights—sets an orienting direction for thinking and acting politically but not a bright and shining line. One would not and could not limit governmental action to rights protection and only that, because there is much more to securing rights than securing rights. There are many features of society and individuals that are means to the securing of rights, and these, for Locke and Jefferson, are all things rightly within the ambit of governmental concern. This range of broad means to the end of securing rights I call the "rights infrastructure." To take an example Jefferson much emphasized, a rights-securing polity was one that required a citizen of a certain sort. A citizen had to be able to understand the rudiments of the principles of political right, that is, the basic theory of liberal politics. He had to be literate enough, alert enough, confident enough, and organizationally capable enough to serve as a sentinel of his own liberty vis-à-vis his rulers, who, however necessary they might be to producing a rights-secure world, were also potentially threatening to rights. Moreover, the only rights-secure (and happy) world is one where the citizens are not dependent on their "betters" to organize and conduct their affairs for them. From these and similar insights, Jefferson concluded that it is imperative that the state provide public education of a certain sort, for only that could help produce the kind of citizens needed in a rights-securing republic.[10] It was not his view that individuals had a direct right to a publicly supplied education, but rather that a polity organized around rights would have a legitimate interest in supplying public education. It would be neither a direct requirement of the rights of individuals nor a violation of the limited ends of government for government to supply public education. It was thus rightly within the realm of legislative discretion and control. Thus, although rights may be used as a stringent limitation on govern-

---

[9] John Stuart Mill, *On Liberty* (1859), in A. D. Lindsay, ed., *Utilitarianism, Liberty, and Representative Government* (New York: E. P. Dutton, 1950), 95.

[10] For Jefferson on education, see "A Bill for the More General Diffusion of Knowledge" (1779), in Joyce Appleby and Terrence Ball, eds., *Jefferson: Political Writings* (Cambridge: Cambridge University Press, 1999), 235–43; and Jefferson, *Notes on the State of Virginia*, query XIV, in Harvey Mansfield, ed., *Selected Writings: Jefferson* (Arlington Heights, IL: AHM Publishing Corp., 1979), 43–46.

mental action (as, for example, they are used by Robert Nozick), the early liberals did not so use them.[11]

Mill was convinced that in an age of democracy, both formal and informal pressures for conformity with the majority endangered liberty and individualism. He was unable to rest easy with the rather loose notion of legitimate governmental action promulgated by his old-liberal predecessors. Perhaps (as much as anything) as a preventative measure, Mill thus promulgated his more rigid harm principle.

At the same time, Mill more or less broke with several of the central elements of the old liberalism. Partly following his one-time mentor, Jeremy Bentham, Mill eschewed any appeal to rights (although he was not so doctrinaire about rejecting rights as Bentham had been).[12] Mill accepted the old-liberal idea of public accountability of public authority, and even extended the democratic extension of that theme in his crusade for proportional representation.[13] He gave more weight to democratic representation and control than to separation of powers. This thrust of his work stood in some tension with his fears of majorities on behalf of individuals. His advocacy of proportional representation makes sense on the basis of his confidence that his "harm principle" could be entrenched in public opinion as "the public philosophy," whence it could morally discipline proportionally representative legislatures as they did their work. Moreover, and perhaps more importantly, he believed that proportional representation would be an impediment rather than an empowering of majorities through guaranteeing broader representation of all, minorities as well as majorities. The "winner-take-all" system of Anglo-American politics tended to artificially create or enhance majorities.

Mill was rather ambivalent about that other aspect of liberal institutionalism, the market; for by the end of his career, he came to flirt with socialism.[14] The second wing of libertarian liberalism more than made up for Mill's hesitations, for it developed a commitment to free markets far more doctrinaire than had been the case even for Adam Smith. The laissez-faire liberals were actually quite diverse in their thinking. Some, like David Ricardo and his fellow classical economists, were more narrowly economistic, and held that free markets were always or almost always best economically. Others, like Herbert Spencer, were rights-oriented: they

[11] Robert Nozick, *Anarchy, State, and Utopia* (New York: Basic Books, 1974). In Mill's own application of his harm principle, he was often less stringent than the explicit formulation of the doctrine would seem to require. Thus, for example, he also supported a system of compulsory, but not publicly provided, education. On Mill and education, see E. G. West, "Liberty and Education: John Stuart Mill's Dilemma," *Philosophy* (April 1965): 35–48.

[12] Mill, *On Liberty*, 97.

[13] See John Stuart Mill, *Considerations on Representative Government*, in Lindsay, ed., *Utilitarianism, Liberty, and Representative Government*.

[14] For Mill on socialism, see his "Chapters on Socialism," in Stefan Collini, ed., *J. S. Mill: "On Liberty" and Other Writings* (Cambridge: Cambridge University Press, 1989), 219–80.

held that legislative interference with markets was violative of private property rights, whether economically beneficial or not.[15]

The two wings of libertarian liberalism were products of the early and mid-nineteenth century. The latter parts of that century saw the emergence of another kind of liberalism. Let us call it "welfare liberalism" or "egalitarian liberalism." In one form or another, it is this that gets the name "liberalism" in ordinary political discourse in the United States today. It too is quite diverse—at best a family of liberalisms rather than a clear and distinct doctrine. In retrospect, it is much clearer what welfare liberalism was *against* than just what it was *for*. It arose in explicit and intense opposition to libertarian liberalism, especially the latter's laissez-faire wing. The welfare liberals, such as the Progressives in America or the philosopher T. H. Green in Britain, challenged both the economic efficiency of markets (at least as constituted in the late nineteenth and twentieth centuries) and their justice. The welfare liberals were persuaded that the distribution of goods by markets was not necessarily just and in practice was certainly not so. They were thoroughly committed to the notion that a more egalitarian distribution per se was preferable to the greatly inegalitarian distributions markets tended to produce. Alternatively, they were convinced that the plenty produced in market economies could be allocated in a way that would meet far better the vital needs of a far larger part of the population than was being done.

The welfare liberals shared many of these concerns with some radical critics of the established order, for example, socialists. The welfare liberals tended not to go as far as socialists and call for the socialization of productive property; the welfare liberals, for the most part, were committed to maintaining private property. But they shifted from both the original ("old") liberalism and libertarian liberalism in emphasizing much less the limits of governmental authority, and they developed instead an ideology of strong, active, big government. Governmental interventions were to be of two sorts: regulation of the private sector to produce more efficient results and to curb concentrations of private power; and redistribution of the economic product in a more egalitarian or needs-satisfying direction.

Although welfare liberalism (in America especially) stopped well short of the socialist or Marxist agendas, it did take over or put forward critiques of the substructure of the old liberalism that paralleled critiques by the more radical left. Motivated by a desire to dislodge rights-based property claims, the welfare liberals developed a critique of rights-based thinking that led them to posit rights as social allocations rather than as natural

---

[15] See, e.g., Lionel Robbins, *The Theory of Economic Policy in English Classical Political Economy* (London: Macmillan and Co., 1953); Jacob Viner, "The Intellectual History of Laissez-Faire," *The Journal of Law and Economics* 3 (October 1960), 45–69; and Ellen Frankel Paul, *Moral Revolution and Economic Science: The Demise of Laissez-Faire in Nineteenth-Century British Political Economy* (Westport, CT: Greenwood Press, 1979).

possessions of individuals.[16] Somewhat ironically, however, twentieth-century welfare liberals also came up with ever larger lists of rights to which they held all were entitled, rights of the sort embodied in Franklin D. Roosevelt's call for a "Second Bill of Rights" and, later, in the Universal Declaration of Human Rights.[17] President Roosevelt proposed his "Second Bill of Rights" in 1944, in a now little known speech delivered toward the end of World War II. Roosevelt's proposal, unlike the first Bill of Rights, called not only for protections from government, but also for a set of new rights or protections of citizens by government. Roosevelt called for such things as the recognition of rights to employment, to adequate food, clothing, and shelter, to education, to recreation, and to medical care. The Universal Declaration of Human Rights, adopted in 1948 by the United Nations General Assembly, had an even longer list of rights. Many were the sorts of rights protected by the original American Bill of Rights (e.g., the right not to be arbitrarily deprived of property, the right of free expression), or by the Fourteenth Amendment (protection against discrimination in rights on the basis of race). Others were much more like the new rights of FDR's "Second Bill of Rights" (e.g., a right to rest and leisure, a right to social security). The welfare liberals broke with what they saw as the false and morally suspect individualism of the old liberalism. They thus modified the substructure of liberalism to a fair degree, taking issue with the core idea of rights, and redefining the emphasis on limited government while greatly expanding the notion of the ends of government.[18]

In the American context, welfare liberalism was promoted by the Progressive movement and came to a political peak of sorts in the New Deal and Great Society eras of the twentieth century. Perhaps the theoretical peak of this liberalism was John Rawls's *A Theory of Justice* (1971), a book that attempts to supply a more comprehensive grounding for welfare liberalism than had been theretofore presented.[19] Rawls was particularly eager to show how this variety of liberalism could retain a great concern for liberty as well as for equality and welfare, and thus legitimately belonged to the liberal tradition. In justifying this version of liberalism, he even returned to a Lockean or quasi-Lockean style of philosophy.

Rawls cast his theory in such a way as to reveal continuities with traditional liberal commitments, but the original American welfare liberals, the Progressives, were much less likely to emphasize continuities. Thus, we see one of the founding documents of Progressivism, Charles

---

[16] See, e.g., T. H. Green, *Lectures on the Principles of Political Obligation and Other Writings* (Cambridge: Cambridge University Press, 1986).

[17] See esp. Cass Sunstein, *The Second Bill of Rights: FDR's Unfinished Revolution and Why We Need It More Than Ever* (New York: Basic Books, 2004).

[18] On the various types of liberals, see T. H. Marshall, *Class, Citizenship, and Social Development* (Chicago: University of Chicago Press, 1964).

[19] John Rawls, *A Theory of Justice* (Cambridge, MA: Harvard University Press, 1971).

Beard's *An Economic Interpretation of the Constitution* (1913), mounting a full frontal assault on the old-liberal American founders who established the Constitution.[20] The founders and their Constitution, Beard argued, were enemies of progress and of the kinds of legislation and other reforms the Progressives sought. The founders, Beard said, acted as a class (the wealthy and well-born) to produce a governing structure (the Constitution) that would operate to favor their own interests. The point was to move his countrymen away from their deep attachment to the Constitution, an attachment that was standing in the way of the substantial changes the Progressives believed were needed, changes such as the thorough democratization of the polity and the regulation of the economy.

Although the need to appeal to the American electorate led them to temper their public presentations, the Progressives, and later the New Deal liberals, shared the idea that truth and justice required a break with the American constitutional order and with much of the inherited American political culture.

The late twentieth century saw the emergence of a yet newer form of liberalism, which requires at least brief mention. Like welfare liberalism, it is group-oriented rather than individualist in character; but where the economy, class, and distribution issues characterize welfare liberalism, the newer liberalism is far more centered on issues of culture and identity. Thus the name: "identity liberalism" or "multiculturalism." Identity liberalism is not only associated with the political causes of different elements of the population from those that were at the center of the advocacy of welfare liberalism, but it has also become attached to quite new and different styles of political thinking. Welfare liberalism was associated with the political cause of the working and middle classes, but identity liberalism is connected to the causes of racial and cultural groups (e.g., African Americans, Native Americans) and gender related groups (e.g., women, gays). Identity liberalism makes a more radical break with the preceding liberal traditions in that it is accompanied in many quarters by a call for a break with Enlightenment thinking, that is, a turn away from the kind of rationalism that has, in one form or another, underpinned liberalism ever since Locke.

Identity liberalism is a still-powerful force, but it is also partly responsible for the political waning of liberalism in America today. Eschewing the universalism of earlier liberalisms, targeting itself to discrete and identifiable groups, it has cut itself off from an appeal to the broader electorate; the present weakness of the Democratic Party in the United States has to be traced to a large degree to the success of identity liberalism in influencing the party.

---

[20] Charles Beard, *An Economic Interpretation of the Constitution of the United States* (New York: Macmillan and Co., 1913).

That weakness underlies the appeal of the "new liberalism," with which we shall be most concerned here. This form of liberalism is a species of welfare liberalism. It returns to many of the earlier distributional themes. Thus, Cass Sunstein, one of its leading proponents, wrote a book aiming to revive Roosevelt's vision of a "Second Bill of Rights," centered on economic and welfare entitlements. This new version of welfare liberalism also retains some of the concerns of identity liberalism, such as gay rights, civil rights, and women's rights. From a purely political point of view, one might see this new welfare liberalism as an attempt to broaden the appeal of liberalism for the American public as a whole by committing to an agenda of benefits (e.g., health care) that will be attractive to the middle and working classes.

It differs from the original welfare liberalism in a number of ways. It has absorbed many of the lessons of the post–New Deal world, and thus is much friendlier to markets than the original welfare liberalism was. The twentieth-century worldwide experience of economies that opted for central planning and nonmarket allocations of resources has proved to the satisfaction of almost all reasonable observers that the hopes attached to nonmarket economies were greatly misplaced. The market is not perfect, but it is much more productive and more supportive of liberty than any alternatives. Despite its greater friendliness to markets, the new form of welfare liberalism remains focused on distributional outcomes, for it retains the view of the original welfare liberalism that markets tend not to spread the results of their productive power equitably or reasonably among the population.[21]

Although it made its initial appearance earlier, in the 1960s, this new welfare liberalism is also, in its most current form, very visibly a reaction against the views that more or less triumphed in the Reagan Revolution of the 1980s. In many ways, Ronald Reagan's views and policies were very like libertarian liberalism, and it is not of interest here to explore the differences. It is merely worth noting that, in contemporary discourse, the welfare liberals have managed to capture and hold onto the venerable title "liberal," and with it the claim to be the legitimate heirs of the liberal tradition. The welfare liberals particularly object to the hostility to positive government that surfaced under Reagan. "Government is not the solution," said a famous Reagan slogan, "it is the problem." The welfare liberals would reverse that motto, and, more than that, they insist that the Reaganites did not really believe in or live up to their other motto: "Get government off our backs." The reality, they claim, was a selective use of government to favor the causes and interests dear to the Reaganites.[22] Opposition to government was reserved for opposition to programs and

[21] Sunstein, *Second Bill of Rights,* 203–4.

[22] Ibid., 17–34; Sotirios Barber, *Welfare and the Constitution* (Princeton, NJ: Princeton University Press, 2003), 8–12, 65–68.

policies they disdained. The welfare liberals are thus committed to positive government, and a public philosophy that recognizes government's responsibility for the comprehensive welfare of the people.

What most strikingly distinguishes the current version of welfare liberalism from the older instantiation of that doctrine is the about-face it has made with respect to the inherited elements of the liberal and particularly the American tradition. Instead of presenting themselves, as Beard and the other Progressives did, as hostile to the Constitution, the current welfare liberals present themselves as grounded in the Constitution and in American political culture as it is, as it has been, and as it could be if it lived up to its own foundational commitments. Sotirios Barber, a University of Notre Dame constitutional theorist, and the most profound and thoughtful of the new welfare liberals, presents a theory that maintains that the original Constitution contains or implies the welfare liberalism he advocates.[23] Political theorist Stephen Holmes argues that the liberal tradition from Hobbes onward has had one driving commitment, the relief of insecurity. Over time, "the *sources* of insecurity changed ... but the *value* of security itself remained the same."[24] The welfare state these liberals call for is thus said to be in direct continuity with and a fulfillment of the older liberal tradition as a means of relieving insecurity. In line with this emphasis on continuity, this new welfare liberalism is centered on the Constitution. Therefore, I propose to name it "constitutional welfare liberalism," or CWL.

The first glimmerings of what became CWL appeared in the late 1960s in the hey-day of the Warren Court, when some important legal scholars attempted to develop the idea that the Constitution contained or implied a right to welfare.[25] For a short while, it looked as though the welfare liberals might succeed in having the Supreme Court announce such a right to be in the Constitution.[26] The timing of that original emergence offers one clue to the impetus behind the shift to a Constitution-centered welfare liberalism: if this political program could be attached to the Constitution, there was a chance the courts would adopt it, and that certainly looked easier than running the gauntlet of the political process.

The revival and renewed attractiveness of CWL in the 1990s and beyond is no longer so clearly tied to the hopes that the courts will adopt and then impose this vision, for in the meantime the Supreme Court has become far more conservative and far less likely to adopt any such constitutional doctrine as this. Indeed, one of the *bêtes noires* of the welfare liberals is a

---

[23] Barber, *Welfare and the Constitution*, 63.

[24] Stephen Holmes, *Passions and Constraint: On the Theory of Liberal Democracy* (Chicago: University of Chicago Press, 1995), 257–58; Barber, *Welfare and the Constitution*, 44.

[25] Charles A. Reich, "The New Property," *Yale Law Journal* 73 (1964): 733; Frank Michelman, "On Protecting the Poor through the Fourteenth Amendment," *Harvard Law Review* 83 (1969): 7.

[26] For an account of how that did not happen, see Sunstein, *Second Bill of Rights*, 149–75.

fairly recent Supreme Court case, *DeShaney v. Winnebago County Department of Social Services* (1989), with a majority opinion authored by Chief Justice William H. Rehnquist.[27] In that case, the Court maintained that the states do not have a constitutional obligation to supply even much more ordinary kinds of protection to citizens, such as protections of children from abusive parents, much less the kinds of benefits CWL calls for. The welfare liberals now tend to distinguish levels and kinds of legal/ constitutional obligation. The obligations they find in the Constitution are no longer presented as a part of the Constitution to be judicially enforced. The welfare duties are held to be duties in the Constitution, binding to be sure on public officials, but not in the ordinary case to be adjudicated. Thus, legal scholar Lawrence Sager develops a theory of "constitutional underenforcement";[28] Barber develops a strong distinction between judicially enforceable and nonenforceable duties;[29] and Sunstein develops a distinction between the agencies that are to apply the first Bill of Rights (the courts) and those that are to apply the second Bill of Rights (the political branches).[30]

Thus, CWL is not advocating that judges command Congress to undo the 1996 Welfare Reform Act, which cut back substantially on the welfare commitments of the federal government and promised to "end welfare as we know it." Nor are the partisans of CWL pressing for the courts to take over welfare departments, prisons, schools, and other security- or welfare-providing institutions, as sometimes happened in the headiest days of judicial activism. Not only is CWL more sensitive to the judiciary's limited capacity to step outside the bounds of its normal activities, but CWL is sensitive also to concerns about judicial supremacy and the need to respect democracy and the political institutions of self-government. CWL, as we see it today, is in this respect chastened and far more moderate than the earliest versions of the doctrine.

As constitutional doctrine, CWL fights for a certain interpretation of the Constitution and sets itself firmly against another interpretation, which it tends to identify as the dominant or orthodox view. The constitutional welfare liberals oppose "the negative-liberties model" of the Constitution (to use Barber's terminology) and would replace that with a "benefits model." In brief, the negative-liberties model holds that the Constitution secures negative rights but not positive rights, that its aim is to protect against governmental oppression or tyranny, and that it operates chiefly to restrain the government through practices like judicial review, bills of rights, separation of powers, and federalism. By contrast, the benefits model maintains that the Constitution is not only or even primarily a

[27] *DeShaney v. Winnebago County Department of Social Services*, 489 U.S. 189 (1989).
[28] Lawrence Sager, *Justice in Plain Clothes* (New Haven, CT: Yale University Press, 2004), 84–128.
[29] Barber, *Welfare and the Constitution*, 68–71, 82–86.
[30] Sunstein, *Second Bill of Rights*, 209–30.

negative or restraining instrument but has the actual provision of general welfare as its task, a provision which includes the elements of welfare that we normally think of as part of the "welfare state." In Sunstein's closely related idea, the Constitution is not only to be concerned with the Bill of Rights, a series of provisions to limit government, but also with the Second Bill of Rights, as proposed by FDR, which is concerned roughly with the same set of welfare-state entitlements that Barber identifies with the government's duty to the "general welfare."

## IV. Constitutional Welfare Liberalism: A Critique

At the bottom of CWL are two pieces of complementary analysis, which together constitute the core of the CWL position. One is developed by Holmes and Sunstein, the other by Barber. The two arguments operate functionally very similarly, for they are meant to show that the negative-liberties model is inadequate, and at the same time, to ground the benefits model in the materials of traditional American constitutionalism and liberalism. I will address these arguments in turn.

### A. CWL and negative rights

Holmes and Sunstein, in their book *The Cost of Rights* (1999), develop an argument of the following sort. The American constitutional/liberal tradition affirms rights, which are normally taken to be negative rights. But Holmes and Sunstein deny that the distinction between negative and positive rights makes sense; all rights, they maintain, are, in effect, positive rights, which is why they present their crucial analysis in a chapter called "All Rights Are Positive." Since all rights are positive, the American commitment to rights in fact amounts to a commitment to the benefits model.[31]

Central to their argument is their definition of the two sorts of rights. The distinction between negative and positive rights (as usually drawn) is "perceived to be the same" as the distinction "between liberties and subsidies." Alternatively, "negative rights ban and exclude government; positive ones invite and demand government." Thus, Holmes and Sunstein conclude that negative rights "require the hobbling of public officials"; these rights "typically protect liberty." In contrast, positive rights "require . . . the affirmative intervention" of public officials; these rights "typically promote equality." "Negative rights shelter us from the government, . . . positive rights grant us services by the government."[32]

---

[31] Stephen Holmes and Cass Sunstein, *The Cost of Rights: Why Liberty Depends on Taxes* (New York: W. W. Norton, 1999), 35–48.

[32] Ibid., 39, 40.

Holmes and Sunstein summarize the distinction as the one usually drawn by the labels "immunities" and "entitlements" respectively, but they consider the alleged distinction between these sorts of rights to be a "story book distinction." [33] The distinction is "palpably inadequate." That insight, they believe, is particularly important, for most persons from all positions on the political spectrum generally accept the distinction as meaningful, even if persons at different points on the spectrum value the different kinds of rights differently. "The negative/positive polarity . . . furnishes a common language within which welfare-state liberals and libertarian conservatives can understand each other and trade abuse." [34] Although Holmes and Sunstein are defenders of a welfare liberal position, they are following a different strategy from their fellow liberals: not to value positive rights more highly, but to demonstrate that "upon inspection, the contrast between the two fundamental sorts of rights is more elusive than we might have expected. . . ." [35] More than that, the alleged distinction, they say, "turns out to be based on fundamental confusions, both theoretical and empirical." [36]

The core of their critique of this common distinction is the claim that "[a]ll rights are claims to an affirmative governmental response. All rights, descriptively speaking, amount to entitlements defined and safeguarded by law." [37] This claim, in turn, is supported by the idea that all legal rights involve redress by government (and Holmes and Sunstein treat all rights as legal rights). Rights are "hollow to the extent they are unenforced," and the call for enforcement, even of a right that appears to be negative, is a call for governmental action, that is, a call of the positive-rights sort. "[A]lmost every right implies a correlative duty, and duties are taken seriously only when dereliction is punished by the public power drawing on the public purse. There are no legally enforceable rights in the absence of legally enforceable duties, which is why law can be permissive only by being simultaneously obligatory." [38]

In contrast to the Holmes and Sunstein view, I will present an argument that will ultimately establish three conclusions: (1) that there is a perfectly lucid and valid distinction between negative and positive rights; (2) that Holmes and Sunstein do not understand that distinction correctly; and (3) that their denial of the distinction is based on a fundamental confusion on their part about the logic of rights and rights enforcement.

Let us begin with two closely related features of their analysis. Holmes and Sunstein take for granted that all rights (both putatively negative and

---

[33] Ibid., 40.
[34] Ibid., 42.
[35] Ibid., 43.
[36] Ibid.
[37] Ibid., 44.
[38] Ibid., 43–44.

putatively positive rights) are rights against government.[39] Relatedly, they maintain that the only rights of interest are legal rights. They dismiss (merely) moral rights—that is, rights not recognized and enforceable by positive law—as "hollow," and therefore, apparently, unworthy of consideration. However, it is not true that all rights are rights against government. If we take the famous Lockean triad of natural rights—life, liberty, and property—these are held to pertain to individuals prior to or in the absence of government. These are rights held against agents other than the government; indeed, these are rights against all comers—in the first instance, against other (private) individuals.

Moreover, it is quite misleading to dismiss moral rights so quickly as hollow and unimportant. Consider the claims of nineteenth-century abolitionists. They insisted that the slaves on whose behalf they agitated had the right to be free even though no government recognized or enforced that right. Admittedly, it would be a more valuable right if it were enforced, but it makes no sense to dismiss this rights claim as meaningless. Indeed, it appears central to the logic or function of rights that we can and do raise such claims, for the function of rights claims is precisely to attempt to gain recognition and protection of rights that are not being recognized and protected. To agree with Holmes and Sunstein that there is a tendency for rights claimants to attempt to transform moral rights into legal rights does not imply that one can ignore the reality of moral rights. Indeed, it is clear that moral rights are (often) logically prior to legal rights, for they are the preexisting bases for claims to legal rights.

Holmes and Sunstein limit their analysis to legal rights, but this is simply question-begging. Legal rights are, by definition, rights for the vindication of which one can appeal to government for action of some sort. The limitation of their analysis to legal rights thus produces automatically the conclusion they draw that all rights are positive, that is, that all rights are claims on government.

Clarity on the meaningfulness of speaking of nonlegal moral rights is a prerequisite to getting to the core of the issue: Do Holmes and Sunstein understand the difference between negative and positive rights correctly? I do not believe they do. The true difference between these two kinds of rights is not what Holmes and Sunstein tentatively identify as the commonly held distinction, namely, that negative rights "ban and exclude government," while positive rights "require affirmative intervention" of public officials. The true difference comes out more clearly if one starts where Holmes and Sunstein refuse to, with moral rights, and move from there to legal rights.

It is useful to make a larger distinction within the realms of right and rights. I refer to the distinction between objective and subjective right. The former is captured in a statement such as the following: "It is right that Ellen speak up about matters of public concern." The latter kind of right is captured in the apparently similar proposition: "Ellen has a right to speak up about matters of public concern." These statements sound very similar, but they are saying quite different things. In the case of the first, the objective right, the right expresses a duty for Ellen to speak up. If she fails to do so, she is violating right, that is, the right state of affairs. In the case of the second, the subjective right, Ellen is not violating right if she fails to speak up. She has a right to speak (i.e., a moral permission), but she does not have a duty to do so. Such rights inhere in a subject (the rights-holder) in such a way that the subject has a range of discretion regarding the exercise of the right. A subjective right is a permission to act or not, as the rights-holder chooses. Subjective rights are thus sometimes called "choice rights."

The debate about rights in which Holmes, Sunstein, Barber, and other welfare liberals are engaged is a debate about subjective rights, for it is these rights that are subdivided into negative and positive rights. The welfare liberals have not put their fingers on the real distinction between positive and negative rights, however, and this failure to grasp the distinction correctly is responsible for their strongly worded conclusions that there is no difference at all. It is as though one were saying that the difference between humans and other animals is that humans are two-footed and other animals four-footed, and then, observing that there are plenty of other two-footed animals (e.g., birds), concluding that there is no difference between humans and other animals.

Holmes and Sunstein first go astray in dismissing moral rights and limiting their horizon of discourse to legal rights. They then miss the defining feature of the positive-negative divide. The difference between positive and negative depends on the duty that stands correlative to the right in question. All rights-in-the-proper-sense imply a duty in some other or others as their correlate. But the nature of the duty can vary a good deal. In some cases, a right implies a duty in others only to forbear from interfering with the right the rights-holder possesses or asserts. In other cases, the duty extends farther and encompasses the objects to which the rights-holder's right extends. Simple examples can illustrate the difference. Consider the right to free speech. The rights-holder asserts a claim to be free to speak as he or she chooses. Duty-holders are obliged only not to interfere with the rights-holder's exercise of the right. No one has a duty to provide the rights-holder with a speech to deliver, with a forum in which to deliver it, or even to listen to the speaker. By contrast, the right to the money in your savings account is different. Here the duty-bearer, the bank, has the duty to supply the very thing to which the rights-holder lays claim, namely, the money in the account, when properly applied for, and so on. Contrary to what Holmes, Sunstein, Barber, and others say, this distinction is perfectly intelligible, perfectly lucid, and stable. There is no reason whatever to conclude that "all rights are positive."

Now, of course, the identification of a stable line of classification between types of rights does not yet settle the politically most important question: What kinds of rights do we in fact have? Do we have rights like a right to health care (a positive right), which point to a welfare state, or those like the right to free speech, which do not necessarily do so? Holmes and Sunstein attempt to sidestep that issue by (falsely) declaring it a nonissue on the basis of denying the distinction between types of rights. Their denial is based not only on a failure to grasp the real dividing line between the two kinds of rights, but also on their confusedly throwing into the analysis a quite separate right, which makes the fundamental character of rights and their relation to government and law obscure. So far, I have spoken of rights as moral and not legal rights. In the perspective of the old liberalism, we have a basic right in addition to our other rights: we have a right to protection of our rights by government. This is what the idea of the social contract means to say. Originally, we have rights that are merely moral in character. Human beings being human, the possession of merely moral rights by no means guarantees that one will be able securely to exercise or enjoy one's rights. We need an agency to enforce or secure our rights. That is, in a Lockean framework, the point and purpose of government, and government therefore has a duty to its citizens to supply protection of their rights. A strong echo of this additional right is visible in the Fourteenth Amendment, where a right to (equal) protection of the laws is affirmed.

The right to governmental protection of rights is the positive dimension of rights that Holmes and Sunstein see when they look at rights. Since they limit their survey of the rights universe to legal rights, this additional right, of course, shows up as part of every right they see. Nonetheless, a better way to see this additional right would be as a shadow of the primary rights rather than as an actual component of the primary rights. The example of the right to property can help make all this clear. The right to property as it exists in a civil society is, in itself, a negative right. It is the right to inherit, purchase, lease, sell, hold, and convey real and personal property.[40] The immediate correlative duty involved is that all others must forbear from interfering with the congery of liberties, powers, and objects that go into the property right. Duty-bearers include both private individuals and entities like governments. Thus, the U.S. Constitution contains provisions that say the government may not deprive persons of property without due process of law. That is to say, the government is obliged to recognize persons as property-rights holders and to respect their property. The government may interfere with property only in recognizably valid ways and for recognizably valid purposes. These are

---

[40] This list comes from Section 1 of the Civil Rights Act of 1866 as reprinted in Henry Steele Commager, ed., *Documents of American History*, 7th ed. (New York: Appleton-Century-Crofts, 1963), 464.

public purposes, which citizens can be conceived to have rationally authorized the government to pursue. Thus, the negative right to property by no means immunizes property owners from all governmental involvement or interference with property, but it does demand that government recognize property rights and be able to satisfy certain justificatory conditions when it interferes with those rights.[41]

John's property right, then, implies a duty in government, no less than in Ringo, Paul, and George, not to take from John what is his. John's right to property does not contain the correlate that government must supply him with property. That is a sure sign that this is a negative right, not a positive one. In addition to the negative property right, however, John has the "shadow-right" to the protection of his property by government. I call this a "shadow-right" not because it is in any way insubstantial, but because it shadows, that is, follows from and is in a sense a derivative of the primary right, in this case, the negative right to property. This shadow-right is a right John holds vis-à-vis government, which in this case has a duty to supply that to which John has a right. So if John's property is interfered with or threatened by others, government has a duty to protect it. If his Rolls-Royce is stolen, he can appeal to the authorities to (try to) recover it for him. John's shadow-right to the protection of the laws is thus a positive right. It accompanies but is not the same as the primary rights.

The implication for the Holmes-Sunstein doctrine should be clear: they find the line between positive and negative rights to be blurry or worse, because they fail to distinguish the primary rights from the shadow-rights involved. Perhaps, they might say in reply, the analysis could be drawn more sharply than they have drawn it, but the point remains the same: our negative rights do contain or imply or have as an accompaniment a positive-rights claim, for all negative rights imply positive rights (at least if they are legal rights). This is a far more defensible claim than the one Holmes and Sunstein make.

Even so, the distinction between positive and negative rights does not collapse, because the duties government has continue to differ according to whether the government's duty relates to a positive or a negative right. The right to protection of a negative right is quite different from what is involved in securing a positive right. In both cases, John has a right to call on government, and government has a duty to act. But what government is duty-bound to do is quite different.

If John has a right to, say, his Social Security check, then government has a duty to supply it. If Ringo has a right to free speech, government remains without a duty to supply a speech or to procure for him an

[41] Admittedly, the recent Supreme Court case *Kelo v. New London*, 545 U.S. (2005), throws some of this into question as valid constitutional law by supplying a very loose notion of "public purpose." The analysis nonetheless remains cogent within the framework of Lockean liberalism.

audience for his speech. Its duty is not to interfere with or prevent Ringo from speaking, and to act, by supplying the protection of the laws, to prevent others from interfering with his right to speak (recognizing, of course, all the qualifications that must be made as to "time, manner, place," etc.). In both cases, government must (ought to) do something, but they are quite different somethings. It is just not possible to leap from, say, John's negative right to property (together with his positive right to protection of his property) to a welfare state. Holmes and Sunstein sought a short-cut to their destination, a Northwest Passage of political philosophy. Like the quest for most such short-cuts, theirs does not succeed.

Holmes and Sunstein have another argument on rights that is more far-reaching yet. Not only are all rights positive in the sense that they are not negative, but also, they say, all rights are positive in the sense that they are non-natural. "Rights," they say, "are interests on which we as a community have bestowed special protection, usually because they touch upon 'the public interest'—that is, because they involve either the interests of the collectivity as a whole or the fair treatment of various members of the community. By recognizing, protecting, and financing rights, the collectivity fosters what are widely construed to be the deeper interests of its members." [42] Rights, Holmes and Sunstein are saying, are not natural, inherent possessions of individual human beings but are endowed by "the collectivity," that is, by society. All men are endowed—by their society—with certain alienable rights. Thus they would rewrite the Declaration of Independence.

In so saying, Holmes and Sunstein indicate that they are breaking more with the liberal tradition than they normally present themselves as doing. They bring out the nonliberal character of this aspect of their argument when they gloss it out of Aristotle. Property is best understood as a social institution—the social granting of specific rights and powers to individuals—for the sake of achieving desirable "social purposes," for example, the improvement of "a nation's real estate and capital stock." [43] This more or less reverses the classic liberal understanding and, among other things, stands in significant tension with Holmes and Sunstein's own construal of the liberal tradition and their way of relating CWL to it. If the entire tradition is aimed at alleviating insecurity, or providing security for individuals, it seems that Holmes and Sunstein are committed to some prior notion of an individual claim or right that precedes social allocations of rights and powers and provides a standard for those allocations. Since they do not develop their argument extensively or very deeply, it is difficult to judge how they reconcile the different elements of their own argument, just as it is difficult to assess the merits of their explicit denial of natural rights. As it stands in their text, this denial is

---

[42] Holmes and Sunstein, *Cost of Rights,* 115–16.
[43] Ibid., citing Aristotle.

merely an assertion and thus provides no occasion for assessing whether they can, in fact, self-consistently jettison the very notion of natural rights. I therefore leave this more radical and antiliberal argument aside, for it is not really an argument at all.

## B. CWL and benefits

Sotirios Barber is another Henry Hudson, searching for his own Northwest Passage. In his book *Welfare and the Constitution,* Barber endorses the Holmes-Sunstein analysis of rights, but moves on to develop his own parallel argument in favor of the benefits model of the U.S. Constitution.[44] Where Holmes and Sunstein present their central argument in a chapter titled "All Rights Are Positive," Barber develops his in a chapter called "Every State a Welfare State." He outdoes Holmes and Sunstein in his lack of respect for his opponents' position. "The negative-liberties model," Barber tells us, is "indefensible, if not fraudulent."[45] The negative-liberties model is "pointless"; it "makes no sense."[46]

Holmes and Sunstein take as their point of departure the Constitution as a document of rights affirmations, and they go on to reason from these affirmations. Barber insists that that is far too narrow a way to view the Constitution. The Constitution provides a set of structures, processes, practices, and powers to accomplish things. As he rightly emphasizes, it just makes no sense to conceive of a constitution as having no point other than to prevent governmental action. Why have a government then? The limitation of governmental powers cannot be the sole or even the first thing. The first thing must be the existence and empowerment of government to act in some way; the reservations of powers and restrictions of action in the name of rights and individual liberties make sense only against a background of active, instrumental government.

Contrary to what the negative-liberties partisans and Holmes and Sunstein say, Barber points out that the very text of the American Constitution supports the alternative idea that government exists to do something. It grants powers (e.g., to spend money for the general welfare), and it states the ends of action in its preamble: to form a more perfect union, to provide for the common defense, to promote the general welfare, and so on. These positive empowerments, and, even more decisively, the ends to be achieved through them, must be given first place in thinking about what the Constitution is.

Barber thinks that the founders themselves are in agreement with his insistence on placing higher priority on the ends of action than on the means of action, to say nothing of limitations on the means of action.[47]

---

[44] Barber, *Welfare and the Constitution,* 15, 19, 49, 52.
[45] Ibid., 6.
[46] Ibid., 44, 51, 57.
[47] Ibid., 92–96.

The preamble lists the ends, which are stated as a set of general concepts ("more perfect union," "general welfare") and not in terms of specific conceptions of these goods. The language of the preamble is very vague and general in order to convey the idea that the Constitution is dedicated to these general goals, which in varying circumstances must be interpreted so as to require us to draw on our best moral theories of matters like human well-being, and to reach a wide equilibrium, a maximal "fit" among moral insight, cultural potentialities of this (or any) society, and legal text.

Barber defends his position with much acumen and more than a little ingenuity, but at bottom it rests on the same confusion that underlies the Holmes-Sunstein analysis. We must begin by conceding, even emphasizing, Barber's first big point: constitutions and governments exist to do something. But Barber is quite mistaken to think that this fact refutes the negative-liberties model, for the negative-liberties model affirms that very thing—that governments are established "to secure these [negative] rights."

Barber is also quite mistaken to think that there is no logical line between affirming power to secure negative rights and affirming power to secure positive rights. Surely there is: it is just the logical line that distinguishes negative from positive rights. Barber needs to show that human beings possess positive (natural) rights, but like Holmes and Sunstein he is seeking a short-cut around that difficult task.

He believes that the Constitution affirms positive rights. For example, he says at the beginning of his book: "The American Constitution makes sense (and originally made sense) only in light of general substantive ends like national security, freedom of conscience, domestic tranquility, and the people's economic well-being."[48] All of these do indeed set tasks for government, but all but the last are clearly negative rights or manifestations of the shadow-right of which I have already spoken. National security requires great governmental exertion, but it is in service of the fundamental quartet of negative rights, life, liberty, property, and the pursuit of happiness. The right of conscience is itself a negative right. Domestic tranquility is exactly parallel to national security. Finally, it is not exactly clear what kind of right "economic well-being" is or whether it is a right at all. I do not recall noticing this as a power of government or even as an end in the preamble.

To Barber's list one might add "establishing justice," an end that *is* listed in the preamble. The affirmation that one of the ends of the Constitution is to establish justice is sometimes taken to mean that the American founders went beyond Lockean liberal commitments to premodern conceptions of politics such as we might find in Plato or Aristotle. This, I believe, is a misreading, for the founders understood the natural rights philosophy to specify what justice is and requires. The natural rights

---

[48] Ibid., 1.

philosophy specifies justice in the sense that it expresses what is due or owed to each, or what is the "own" which each possesses by nature. It thereby provides a specification for the general formula for justice—to each what he is due, or to each his own. What is due, or what is most our own, are our rights and the objects of our rights. To establish justice, therefore, is, in the language of the Declaration of Independence, "to secure these rights." The preamble of the Constitution does not, then, commit the national government to anything that goes beyond the negative-liberties model, if properly understood.

In other words, neither Barber's correct observations about empowerments nor his claims about positive preambular rights get him where he wishes to go. There is a perfectly clear account of governmental empowerment and constitutional duty to act that is consistent with, and indeed demanded by, the negative-liberties model; there is a clear line of division that allows us to affirm the negative-liberties model without going on to affirm any and every positive right one might dream up.

I might add that even if constitutional welfare liberals were correct in their views about rights and powers, it would remain true that they pay very insufficient attention to the fact that the Constitution of the United States was established to accomplish only certain limited ends, ends that were not coextensive with the liberal goals set forth in, for example, the Declaration of Independence. The entire political system, state plus federal governments, was to "secure these rights," but the great bulk of rights-securing was to be accomplished by the states. This fact in itself casts grave doubt upon Barber's heavy reliance on the preamble to the Constitution. The large ends of the preamble must be read in such a way as to be consistent with the relegation of most rights-securing to the states. Admittedly, the Fourteenth Amendment made a difference in the federal system, but not such a difference as to transfer the task of securing basic rights to the federal government of the United States.[49]

## V. Conclusion

Let me conclude by attempting to clarify what I think I have accomplished in this essay and what I have not. I have attempted to locate constitutional welfare liberalism as a "new liberalism" within the broad context of the "thousand liberalisms" we have seen emerge since Locke. I have approached this "new liberalism" from the perspective of the

[49] On the original federalism, see Michael P. Zuckert, "Federalism and the Founding: Toward a Reinterpretation of the Constitutional Convention," *Review of Politics* 48 (1986): 166–210. On the change in federalism effected by the Fourteenth Amendment, see Michael P. Zuckert, "Completing the Constitution: The Fourteenth Amendment and Constitutional Rights," *Publius* 22 (1992) 69–91; and Michael P. Zuckert, "Congressional Power under the Fourteenth Amendment—the Original Understanding of Section Five," *Constitutional Commentary* 3 (1986): 123.

original "old liberalism" and have concluded that the new liberalism's attempt to imply that the welfare state, as a matter of right, is the only logical or plausible rendition of a constitutional republic grounded in rights is quite false. The most significant insight I have brought to the analysis is the identification of the shadow-right, a right to the protection of one's primary rights by government. This shadow-right is indeed a positive right, but it does not obliterate the distinction between positive and negative rights as the constitutional welfare liberals argue; nor does it, as a positive right, in itself imply the existence of a plethora of (or of any) other positive rights.

I do not mean to imply that the failure of constitutional welfare liberalism entails the triumph of what Barber calls the negative-liberties model of government, however. I believe that the old-liberal rights theory, fully developed, does imply something beyond the negative-liberties model as depicted in constitutional welfare liberalism. The result of such a full development, I hasten to add, is not so far-reaching as the Barber benefit model, nor so far-reaching as FDR's "Second Bill of Rights." To work out the full implications of rights theory, however, is a large enterprise in itself, and thus cannot be undertaken here as an addendum to a focused analysis of the claims of one version of new liberalism, constitutional welfare liberalism.

*Political Science, University of Notre Dame*

# WHY THE NEW LIBERALISM ISN'T ALL THAT NEW, AND WHY THE OLD LIBERALISM ISN'T WHAT WE THOUGHT IT WAS

By William A. Galston

## I. Introduction

It is conventional to distinguish between an old liberalism, with a robust conception of private property and a limited role for government in the economy, and a new liberalism that permits government to override individual property rights in the pursuit of the general welfare. The New Deal of the 1930s is often taken to mark the dividing line between these two forms of liberal governance in the United States. This essay complicates the conventional narrative in three ways. First, property rights form only one out of several ways in which the scope of government may be limited, and these different dimensions of limited government interact, conceptually and in the history of the United States, to form a more variegated typology of regimes. Second, when we focus on property rights through the magnifying lens of Fifth Amendment takings clause jurisprudence,[1] we find that the movement away from strong property rights begins not with the New Deal but in the late nineteenth century, at what is normally taken to be the peak of constitutional protection for private property. Third, this movement away from strong property rights is justified in the name of the general welfare, often understood as wealth maximization. The much-criticized 2005 Supreme Court decision in *Kelo v. New London* (which I discuss in Section IV below) represents not a break with past doctrine, but rather its logical consequence.

Protecting individual property-holders against expansive state powers of eminent domain would require the Court to overrule more than a century of settled case law and to develop a new conceptual architecture for distinguishing between legitimate and illegitimate takings. Any such effort, however, runs into a structural conundrum: while categorical restraints on state power limit government's ability to promote important public purposes, an explicitly purposive approach renders all limits on governmental power (including individual rights) vulnerable to an aggregative calculus. The tension between deontological and consequentialist moral theories thus is mirrored in competing conceptions of govern-

---

[1] The takings clause of the Fifth Amendment states: "nor shall private property be taken for public use, without just compensation." As we shall see, much depends on the interpretation of the phrase "public use."

ment's purposes and limits. The most plausible response, I argue, is a two-tiered approach: respect for legally established categories in ordinary circumstances, regardless of their aggregate consequences, and consequentialism in circumstances of emergency, when the lives or basic well-being of citizens are at stake. Judged against this template, the consequentialism guiding modern takings clause jurisprudence in ordinary, nonemergency circumstances is hard to justify.

## II. LIBERALISM AS LIMITED GOVERNMENT

From a philosophical and conceptual point of view, liberalism is a doctrine not of the structure of governmental decision making or of the substance of governmental decisions, but rather of the scope of governmental power. Any genuinely liberal theory must offer an account of limits to public power. It is John Stuart Mill's harm principle that makes him a liberal, not his man-as-a-progressive-being account of human flourishing.[2] It is John Rawls's account of individual rights that joins him to the liberal tradition, not his difference principle.[3] "Liberal" democracy joins decision making based on the political equality of all citizens with limits on the legitimate scope of public decisions, however democratically they are made.

I do not want to suggest that liberalism is only about limited government. Historically, it has also involved assertions of basic human equality and efforts to liberate individuals and socioeconomic relations from the oppressive weight of ascribed characteristics and unchosen bonds. On the individual level, this has entailed faith in human agency in circumstances of reasonably equal opportunity; on the socioeconomic level, it has entailed confidence in the efficacy of robust markets and freedom of association.

In trying to parse possible differences between the "old" liberalism and the "new" liberalism, however, the issue we must keep in view is the nature and extent of limits on government. Here disagreements pervade the history of liberal thought and continue to the present day. In the U.S. context, the canonical type of position draws from the theory enunciated in the Declaration of Independence: governmental powers are doubly limited, by rights that individuals cannot alienate and by the parameters of public agreement. The Declaration famously declares that governments "deriv[e] their just powers from the consent of the governed," by which it means that the exercise of governmental power beyond the bounds of that consent is presumptively illegitimate.

As in the broader history of liberalism, the development of limited government in the United States owes much to controversies over relations between church and state. In 1785, James Madison published his

---

[2] John Stuart Mill, *On Liberty*, ed. Currin V. Shields (Indianapolis, IN: Bobbs-Merrill, 1956), chap. 4.

[3] John Rawls, *A Theory of Justice* (Cambridge, MA: Harvard University Press, 1971), section 11.

"Memorial and Remonstrance" against a proposed Virginia statute to publicly fund teachers of Christianity. The language of this influential defense of rights of religion and conscience against state authority is remarkable (and radical) enough to merit extended quotation:

> It is the duty of every man to render to the Creator such homage and such only as he believes to be acceptable to him. This duty is precedent, both in order of time and degree of obligation, to the claims of Civil Society. Before any man can be considered as a member of Civil Society, he must be considered as a subject of the Governour of the Universe: And if a member of Civil Society, who enters into any subordinate Association, must always do it with a reservation of his duty to the General Authority; much more must every man who becomes a member of any particular Civil Society, do it with a saving of his allegiance to the Universal Sovereign. We maintain therefore that in matters of Religion, no man's right is abridged by the institution of Civil Society and that Religion is wholly exempt from its cognizance.[4]

Madison's efforts to secure religious authority against state power continued at the national level during the early constitutional period. Indeed, two of the amendments that Madison drafted for inclusion in the Bill of Rights, one of which would have been binding on the states, made explicit reference to "rights of conscience." The idea of a robust right of conscience as protection against otherwise legitimate state acts has reemerged episodically throughout the history of U.S. jurisprudence, most notably in cases involving Jehovah's Witnesses and conscientious objectors to military service.[5] In the latter case, the Supreme Court has deliberately expanded the scope of conscience beyond formal religion to include deep, identity-shaping beliefs that play a role in individuals' lives equivalent to that of faith for the devout. So understood, rights of religious conscience may be regarded as the kernel around which broader notions of rights of autonomy and privacy gradually developed.

### III. Two Kinds of Limits on Government, Four Public Philosophies

Since the onset of corporate industrialization in the decades following the Civil War, the debate over limits to governmental power has taken the

---

[4] James Madison, "Memorial and Remonstrance Against Religious Assessments," paragraph 1, available online at http://religiousfreedom.lib.virginia.edu (accessed March 16, 2006).
[5] The leading case involving Jehovah's Witnesses is *West Virginia v. Barnette*, 319 U.S. 624 (1943), in which the Supreme Court held that school-age Witnesses could not be compelled to salute and pledge allegiance to the flag as a condition of attending public school. The most significant cases expanding conscientious objection beyond the bounds of traditional religion are *United States v. Seeger*, 380 U.S. 163 (1965), and *Welsh v. United States*, 398 U.S. 333 (1970).

form of an interplay between two baskets of rights, which I will call *property rights* and *privacy rights* (the latter are sometimes referred to as rights of autonomy or personal security). This dyad generates four ideal-typical alternatives, each of which finds a rough analogue in American politics and jurisprudence. Strong property rights coupled with weak privacy rights yield *mainstream conservatism*. Strong property rights and strong privacy rights yield *classical liberalism* (also called libertarianism). Weak property rights and weak privacy rights yield *Progressivism*, which shaped the thought and policies of the early New Deal. Finally, weak property rights combined with strong privacy rights are the hallmark of *contemporary liberalism*. Each of these ideal-types embodies a form of philosophical liberalism—that is, an element or elements of limited government—a fact obscured by contemporary political terminology.

Of these four tendencies, which have done so much to shape U.S. politics since the 1890s, the Progressivism that originated in the late nine-teenth century and bestrode the landscape like a colossus during the 1930s and 1940s is arguably the weakest today. The two dominant group-ings, mainstream conservatism and contemporary liberalism, contend with one another across the full range of property and privacy issues. For their part, a small but hardy band of libertarians makes common cause with conservatives on issues involving property rights, such as regulation and the interpretation of the takings clause of the Fifth Amendment, and joins with liberals on issues involving privacy rights—those often thought to be threatened by the USA PATRIOT Act, for example.[6]

These categories help illuminate changing patterns of U.S. Supreme Court decisions. Beginning in the 1890s, the Court deployed a broad construction of property rights against the states while leaving political and civil liberties under the aegis of the states' power—a jurisprudential strategy that reached its peak in the famous (for some, infamous) 1905 decision in *Lochner v. New York*, which struck down New York State's efforts to limit the number of hours employers could require their employ-ees to work.[7] Legal commentators and dissenting justices began asking how these two tendencies could be reconciled.

In 1920, for example, the case of *Gilbert v. Minnesota* came before the Supreme Court.[8] Gilbert, a pacifist, had criticized American participation in World War I. He was convicted under a state statute prohibiting advo-cacy or teaching that interfered with or discouraged enlistment in the mil-itary. While the Court's majority declined to extend Fourteenth Amendment liberty guarantees to Gilbert, Justice Louis Brandeis dissented. He wrote:

---

[6] This act, passed in late 2001 in the wake of the September 11 terrorist attacks on the United States, significantly expanded the power of the U.S. government to discover terrorist activities and deter future attacks. The enhanced ability of the government to gather infor-mation about individuals raised fears about invasion of privacy and abridgement of civil liberties.

[7] *Lochner v. New York*, 198 U.S. 45 (1905).

[8] *Gilbert v. Minnesota*, 254 U.S. 325 (1920).

I have difficulty believing that the liberty guaranteed by The Constitution, which has been held to protect [a wide property right], does
not include liberty to teach, either in the privacy of the home or
publicly, the doctrine of pacifism. . . . I cannot believe that the liberty
guaranteed by the Fourteenth Amendment includes only liberty to
acquire and to enjoy property.[9]

Over time, the Court's unwillingness to abandon its doctrine of broad
economic rights helped create the basis for a broader understanding of
constitutionally protected and enforceable liberties. Consider the controversy sparked by a Nebraska law which, reflecting the nativist passions
of the World War I era, prohibited instruction in any modern language
other than English. Acting under this statute, a trial court convicted a
teacher in a Lutheran parochial school for teaching a Bible class in German. In *Meyer v. Nebraska* (1923), the Supreme Court struck down this law
as a violation of the Fourteenth Amendment's liberty guarantee.[10] Writing for a seven-member majority, Justice James Clark McReynolds declared:
"That the State may do much, go very far, indeed, in order to improve the
quality of its citizens, physically, mentally, and morally, is clear; but the
individual has certain fundamental rights which must be respected. A
desirable end cannot be promoted by prohibited means."[11]

Two years later, in *Pierce v. Society of Sisters*, the Supreme Court rejected
the right of a public authority (in this case, the state of Oregon) to require
all parents within its jurisdiction to send their children to public schools.
In justifying its stance, the Court declared: "The fundamental theory of
liberty upon which all governments in this Union repose excludes any
general power of the State to standardize its children by forcing them to
accept instruction from public school teachers only. The child is not the
mere creature of the State; those who nurture him and direct his destiny
have the right, coupled with the high duty, to recognize and prepare him
for additional obligations."[12] This does not mean, of course, that family
activities are immune from political regulation. The *Pierce* Court explicitly
recognized a substantial degree of legitimate governmental regulation of
the family, including its educational decisions. For example, the Court's
understanding of the fundamental theory of liberty on which it relied
allowed the state to require "that all children of proper age attend *some*
school."[13]

It is not far-fetched to think of the 1920s as a brief quasi-libertarian
moment (perhaps the only one) in the history of U.S. constitutional jurisprudence, a period in which key Supreme Court decisions affirmed both
strong property rights and a range of immunities against governmental

---

[9] Id. at 343 (Brandeis, J., dissenting).
[10] *Meyer v. Nebraska*, 262 U.S. 390 (1923).
[11] Id. at 401.
[12] *Pierce v. Society of Sisters*, 268 U.S. 510 (1925), at 535.
[13] Id. at 534; emphasis mine.

intrusion into personal and family life. The theory of liberty enunciated in *Meyer* and *Pierce* pointed in both directions simultaneously. Some who understood these consequences rejected the underlying principle. For example, while still a law professor, the ardent Progressive Felix Frankfurter inveighed against *Pierce* when the decision was first handed down, on the grounds that a Court that deployed fundamental principles of liberty against state regulation of education could deploy comparable principles against state regulation of the economy. If you like *Pierce*, Frankfurter's reasoning went, you must accept *Lochner*. For Frankfurter and other Progressives, that was a cost that outweighed the gains.[14]

Progressives did not have to wait long to turn the tables. The radical social critic Randolph Bourne once remarked that "war is the health of the state." The Progressivism that reached its apogee in the decade following Franklin D. Roosevelt's accession to the presidency in 1933 perfectly illustrates Bourne's point. The Great Depression, the only peacetime equivalent of war in American history, flowed directly into the real thing. The same Supreme Court that sustained the constitutionality of the New Deal's economic legislation[15] gave its blessing to the internment of Japanese Americans.[16] In light of the New Deal's disregard of both property rights and civil liberties, one may wonder whether it qualifies as "liberal" at all. Taking a broader view, however, one might justify FDR's program as a response to a national emergency—the deliberate impairment of some traditional liberties in the name of preserving the constitutional system of liberty as a whole. In similarly threatening circumstances, Abraham Lincoln defended his suspension of habeas corpus in 1861 with the argument that this extreme measure was needed to save the Constitution. Should all the laws but one go unexecuted, he asked, just to honor the requirements

---

[14] Felix Frankfurter, "Can the Supreme Court Guarantee Toleration?" *The New Republic* 43 (June 17, 1925): 85.

[15] During the early years of the New Deal, the Court struck down basic building blocks of the Roosevelt administration's economic recovery efforts. In *A. L. A. Schechter Poultry Corp. v. United States*, 295 U.S. 495 (1935), the Court invalidated significant portions of the National Industrial Recovery Act. In *United States v. Butler*, 297 U.S. 1 (1936), the Court set aside the Agricultural Adjustment Act of 1933. In *Carter v. Carter Coal Co.*, 298 U.S. 238 (1936), the Court struck down the Bituminous Coal Conservation Act of 1935. And in *Railroad Retirement Board v. Alton R.R.*, 295 U.S. 330 (1935), a closely divided Court held that this legislation exceeded Congress's constitutional power to regulate interstate commerce. These efforts angered the Roosevelt administration, which responded by proposing a Court "reorganization" plan, which would have allowed the president to nominate a number of new justices without waiting for the death or retirement of sitting justices. Perhaps in response to this threat, a slim majority of the Court began upholding New Deal legislation that rested on a more expansive reading of the commerce clause. The lead cases of this new judicial era include *NLRB v. Jones & Laughlin Steel Corp.*, 301 U.S. 1 (1937), which put the stamp of constitutionality on the National Labor Relations Act of 1935; *United States v. Darby*, 312 U.S. 100 (1941), which upheld the Fair Labor Standards Act of 1938; *United States v. Wrightwood Dairy Co.*, 315 U.S. 110 (1942), which sustained the Agricultural Marketing Agreement Act of 1937; and *Wickard v. Filburn*, 317 U.S. 111 (1942), which upheld the Agricultural Adjustment Act of 1938, thereby sustaining the kinds of measures struck down six years earlier in *Butler*.

[16] *Korematsu v. United States*, 323 U.S. 214 (1944) is the most important and best known of the three Supreme Court decisions on this issue.

of the one? If only a stable constitutional regime can sustain the rule of law, including the Great Writ, then is it not self-defeating to adhere to the writ at the cost of endangering the survival of constitutional government?

Pushed to an extreme, this argument converges with the Vietnam-era claim that it was "necessary to destroy this village in order to save it." Nonetheless, a serious philosophical issue lurks beneath the history: Should we understand the rights that limit government as inviolable regardless of circumstances, or rather as aspects of an overall system of goods and values that public power seeks to enhance? (This issue is what Robert Nozick had in mind when he distinguished between rights as side-constraints and a utilitarianism of rights.)[17] The former view of rights has the advantage of drawing a bright line that eliminates abuses of discretionary power, the sort of reasoning that led Justice Hugo Black to insist that when the Constitution says that Congress shall make "no law," it means just that—no law whatever.[18] It has the disadvantage of preventing legislatures and courts from assessing the overall social costs of holding that line.

This is an important disadvantage, I would argue, because of the pluralist nature of value. On this account, genuine goods are heterogeneous, lacking either a common measure of value or a once-and-for-all internal ordering. There may be good reasons to prefer certain goods to others in specific circumstances; there may be strong presumptions in favor of certain goods that only the weightiest considerations can rebut; but there are no goods that dominate all others in every circumstance, come what may. Societal decisions represent an endless series of contestable judgments about the most sensible and sustainable balance to be struck among values that compete with one another, at least in the real world.

Because constitutions have the same underlying moral structure as social life, similar considerations apply. Every constitution establishes a sphere of plural goods and values containing latent tensions that invariably emerge in the course of application to specific circumstances. This is a principal source of hard cases, which no theory of constitutional interpretation can eliminate. If judging were a matter of measurement, a sufficiently well-programmed machine could do it. But it isn't. It is more than a tautology to insist that judging involves the exercise of judgment, as distinct from calculation. Moreover, judging is not just what judges do; it is what legislatures and executives, after due deliberation, must do as well.[19]

---

[17] Robert Nozick, *Anarchy, State, and Utopia* (New York: Basic Books, 1974), 28–30.

[18] While Black never incorporated precisely this sentence into a Court decision, he repeated "'No law' means 'no law'" many times during oral arguments and elsewhere. See Michael C. Dorf, "The Supreme Court's Cell Phone Decision: An Unusual Balancing Act by the Court," May 30, 2001, at http://findlaw.com.

[19] For elaborations on these sketchy thoughts, see my *Liberal Pluralism* (New York: Cambridge University Press, 2002) and *The Practice of Liberal Pluralism* (New York: Cambridge University Press, 2004).

Fortunately, judging does not take place in a vacuum. Constitutions contain not just values, institutions, and rules, but also public purposes that frame and motivate everything else. It is not often enough remarked that the U.S. Constitution is an explicitly purposive document. Its preamble could have read simply, "We the People of the United States do ordain and establish this Constitution for the United States of America." This would have been a straightforward enunciation of the basic republican principle of legitimate government. But of course the preamble says more than that: after its authors declare their identity and before they specify their deed, they insert the crucial words "in Order to," following which they declare what goods the document values most highly and what purposes it is intended to promote.

Although necessarily general in phrasing, this enumeration is nonetheless meaningful, both for what it affirms and for what it excludes.[20] "Domestic Tranquility" affirms the importance of social continuity and order, by implication ruling out Thomas Jefferson's preference for periodic revolutions to lift the dead hand of the past. The reference to the "Blessings of Liberty" made emphatically clear not only the high value of that good, but also the norm that order was not to be achieved through oppression. Most notably, the goods enumerated in the preamble are this-worldly and for the most part tangible. There is no mention of promoting religion, let alone a specific religion; there is not even a mention of fostering morality. The drafters of the Constitution probably believed that without religion and morality, the regime the document sought to establish would fail; the president of the constitutional convention, soon to be the first president of the United States, certainly believed that. Nonetheless, while the Constitution relied on certain civic virtues, it established no institutions to promote them. That task, the founders believed, was someone else's business.

## IV. The Preamble, Rights of Property, and the Takings Clause

Constitutional purposes turn out to be relevant to constitutional interpretation, often in surprising ways. Consider the ongoing debate over the reach of the Fifth Amendment's takings clause, which states that "private property [shall not] be taken for public use, without just compensation." Note the implicit political theory behind the clause, which runs roughly as follows: There is such a thing as the "public," as distinct from the ensemble of private property owners, and this public has some claims that rank higher than the claims flowing from ownership, however uncon-

---

[20] The preamble enumerates the following as key purposes of the U.S. Constitution: forming a more perfect union; establishing justice; ensuring domestic tranquility; providing for the common defense; promoting the general welfare; and securing the blessings of liberty for ourselves and posterity.

tested and long-standing those claims may be. Under certain conditions (specified in practice by applying the terms "public use" and "just compensation" to particular circumstances), even a government that possesses limited powers and is dedicated to principles of liberty may legitimately act on behalf of the public to override rights of private ownership. It is in respecting the bounds set by those conditions, rather than by giving absolute respect to the boundaries established by individual holdings, that government remains within the limits of its power and avoids oppressive acts.

For purist libertarians, this kind of theory is unacceptable, and the policies flowing from it are illegitimate. The Cato Institute's Sheldon Richman characterizes the takings clause as "one of the few parts of the Bill of Rights that authorizes the government to violate individual liberty," and he insists that "a true property rights movement should not stop short of calling for eradication of the takings clause, . . . the root of all evil in this matter."[21] While mainstream conservatives are not willing to go that far, they do seek to limit takings by restricting what counts as a genuinely "public use." This is an inherently challenging task, and the Supreme Court has not made it any easier.

In *Kelo v. New London*, a decision handed down in June 2005,[22] the Court ruled in favor of the city of New London, which had designed a plan to revitalize its downtown and waterfront areas. The plan sought to capitalize on the impending arrival of a new research facility to be built by the pharmaceutical company Pfizer by developing the ninety acres adjacent to the proposed new facility with a new waterfront hotel and conference center, a river walk, a new U.S. Coast Guard museum, a renovated marina, and 90,000 square feet of research and development office space. In the process, the plan would displace a number of homeowners, many of whose houses had been in their families for generations.

As plaintiffs, the homeowners alleged that implementing the plan would violate the "public use" requirement of the Fifth Amendment, as made applicable to the states through incorporation into the due process clause of the Fourteenth Amendment. While the Supreme Court had long held that non-blighted property could be taken in the process of urban renewal to revitalize a blighted area, the plaintiffs argued that taking non-blighted property for the generic purpose of economic development and increasing tax revenues went well beyond previous holdings and breached the bounds of public use.

A five-member Court majority disagreed. Writing for the majority, Justice John Paul Stevens observed that the facts of this case placed it in a gray zone between two well-established poles. On the one hand, the Constitution clearly forbids government from forcibly transferring prop-

---

[21] Sheldon Richman, "Takings: The Evils of Eminent Domain," July 2005, accessed at http://fff.org/freedom.
[22] *Kelo v. New London*, 125 S.Ct. 2655 (2005).

erty from individual A to individual B without A's consent. On the other hand, the Constitution just as clearly permits government to take private property for use by the general public (public roads and parks, for example) and for private entities, such as railroads, that are prepared to operate as common carriers, open to all. Still, in prior cases the Court had broadened the concept of public use beyond general access to include public *purposes*. New London's development plan was acceptable because it served such a purpose—namely, economic revitalization of a struggling city. Promoting economic development, Stevens noted, was a "traditional and long accepted function of government," and there was no principled way of distinguishing it from other functions that the Court had already deemed to meet the test of public use. In the past, moreover, the Court had deferred to legislative judgments about policies needed to carry out these purposes in specific contexts, and the majority saw no need to start second-guessing local authorities now.

Writing for the four dissenters, Justice Sandra Day O'Connor conceded that in previous decisions the Court had indeed allowed takings that serve a public purpose "even if the property is destined for subsequent private use."[23] In *Kelo*, however, the majority had expanded the meaning of public use so far as to deprive it of limiting force by holding that the sovereign authority may take property currently in ordinary, innocuous use and give it over to other uses by other private parties, so long as there is some overall public benefit: "if predicted (or even guaranteed) positive side-effects are enough to render transfer from one private party to another constitutional, then the words 'for public use' do not realistically exclude *any* taking, and thus do not exert any constraint on the eminent domain power."[24] To be sure, the majority's position still excludes flatly irrational takings, ones that lower the productivity of the property taken or that impose net burdens on the public. But this weak residual limitation will be of little comfort to property owners who are newly exposed to the possibility that public authorities may take their property if they can identify a higher-valued private use that increases tax revenues. Under this doctrine, Justice O'Connor concludes, "The specter of condemnation hangs over all property. Nothing is to prevent the State from replacing any Motel 6 with a Ritz-Carlton, any home with a shopping mall, or any farm with a factory."[25]

In a separate dissent, Justice Clarence Thomas agreed with O'Connor but (characteristically) radicalized her argument. The majority's opinion, he argued, has the effect of effacing the distinction between the Fifth Amendment's takings clause and the preamble's general welfare clause: the majority's logic suggests that if a taking promotes the general welfare, it is presumptively legitimate, in effect eliminating the criterion of public

---

[23] Id. at 2673 (O'Connor, J., dissenting).
[24] Id. at 2675.
[25] Id. at 2676.

use as a limitation on governmental power. The root of the error, Thomas claimed, lies in broadening the concept of "public use" beyond "use by the public" (such as public buildings and public conveyances) to include public purposes. Once the Court made that move, it began sliding down a slippery slope, at the bottom of which lies *Kelo*'s public benefit test.

For our purposes, the key point of Thomas's dissent is his historical reconstruction of how the Supreme Court came to stray from the straight and narrow constitutional path. The two key steps were, first, broadening "public use" to include public purposes, and second, deferring to the legislature's definition of public purposes and its determination that specific policies would promote them. It turns out that the Court made these missteps in two cases decided in the same year—*1896*, near the height of the era of strong judicially protected property rights![26] The Court built on these cases during the latter half of the twentieth century to create the precedents on which it relied in *Kelo*. To return takings clause jurisprudence to what he argued was its original intent, Justice Thomas was compelled to advocate overruling a line of cases stretching back more than a century.

The spokesman for the Supreme Court in both the 1896 cases that Thomas rejects was Justice Rufus Peckham, who was to achieve notoriety a decade later as the author of the majority opinion in *Lochner*. In broadening the public use clause, Justice Peckham reasoned that to adhere to the narrower construction would be to forbid takings for the purpose of constructing an irrigation ditch, which would have meant that no general system of irrigation could proceed. This would be an unacceptable outcome, Peckham argued, and thus the reading of the Constitution that required it could not stand.[27] Justice Thomas's response goes to the heart of the matter: Peckham's claim is "no statement of constitutional principle," because it is a mistake to assume that the Constitution requires, or even permits, a course of action that many believe represents the most advantageous course of action. The results-oriented jurisprudence of the late nineteenth century was no more acceptable than is the comparable interpretive strategy of the early twenty-first century. The takings clause is one thing, the states' police powers[28] another, the general welfare clause yet another: the takings clause is narrower than police powers and constrains the kinds of results-oriented activities toward which the general welfare clause points. The takings clause is one of the many features of

---

[26] The two crucial cases were *Fallbrook Irrigation District v. Bradley*, 164 U.S. 112 (1896), and *United States v. Gettysburg Electric R. Co.*, 160 U.S. 668 (1896). *Fallbrook* broadened the standard for valid takings from "public use" to public purpose, while *Gettysburg* allowed legislatures to define the scope of valid public uses.

[27] *Fallbrook Irrigation District v. Bradley*, at 160–62.

[28] In common law, police powers are regarded as inherent in sovereignty and relate to the safety, health, well-being, and morals of the public. For systematic discussions, see Richard A. Epstein, *Takings: Private Property and the Power of Eminent Domain* (Cambridge, MA: Harvard University Press, 1985), chap. 9; and Ellen Frankel Paul, *Property Rights and Eminent Domain* (New Brunswick, NJ: Transaction Books, 1987), 103–14.

the Constitution that seek to minimize the possibility of tyranny; it does not seek to maximize anything. To the extent that outcomes matter, Justice Thomas emphatically agreed with Justice O'Connor that the expansive reading of the takings clause was most likely to maximize the influence of powerful forces, corporate as well as governmental, at the expense of relatively powerless poor and minority citizens.

Justice Thomas's dissent forces us to ask whether any interpretation of an explicitly purposive document can be indifferent to that interpretation's results. The noted University of Chicago law professor Richard Epstein argues that it cannot. His thesis is that there is a distinction between rules of individual conduct, which are presumptively nonconsequentialist, and rules of social organization, which are emphatically consequentialist. Thus, he asserts: "The traditional natural law justifications for freedom are not sufficient to sustain the case for individual liberty or for limited government. We are, as it were, all consequentialists now."[29]

Epstein deploys this proposition against nonconsequentialist (or, as he puts it, "deductivist") libertarian defenses of inviolable private property and in defense of the state's power of eminent domain. The deductivist position, he argues, does not take into account the possibility that individual holdouts can thwart successful cooperation that increases aggregate welfare and benefits all. The cooperation of ninety-nine out of a hundred private landowners along a proposed railroad route will not suffice. Some authority above the individual contractors must bring the recalcitrant landowner into line. The state that compels the sale must offer the landowner just compensation, which Epstein defines as the highest value of the land in any alternative use whose value is not dependent on the railroad that is about to be built: "The public, including those whose property is condemned, gain the benefit of the railroad, but if compensation is correctly calculated—a big *if*—no individual suffers financial deprivation in the process. State coercion is used to create the win/win situations found in private contracts."[30]

In the course of working through a series of examples involving taxation as well as eminent domain, Epstein arrives at a general proposition about social philosophy. "The central challenge to any political theory," he asserts, is to "devise a set of institutions that first allows and then controls the use of coercion against individual citizens for their own benefit.... The traditional deductive form of libertarianism allows for state force to protect against aggression and fraud. The more complex version recognizes that state power is also appropriate to overcome holdout problems by the limited use of force. This two-tier inquiry clearly legitimates some forms of government action, but by the same token it

---

[29] Richard A. Epstein et al., "Coercion vs. Consent: A *Reason* Debate on How to Think about Liberty," March 2004; accessed at reasononline, http://www.reason.com/0403/fe.ra.coercion.shtml.

[30] Ibid.

makes the case *against* state intervention stronger in those settings where *none* of these justifications are available."[31] But doesn't this two-tier approach sacrifice liberty to other values of lower rank (at least from the classical-liberal perspective)? Not at all, Epstein replies: "Our limited use of coercion is done with the paradoxical intention of expanding the scope of individual freedom."[32]

To an unsympathetic reader, this unexpected echo of Jean-Jacques Rousseau's dictum that human beings must sometimes be forced to be free may prove disconcerting. As we saw earlier, however, it rests on a serious philosophical proposition, not easily dismissed. If liberty is a human good, then we can ask whether it has a quantitative dimension and, if so, how that dimension is structured. It seems plausible to say that an individual can be not only free or unfree, but also more or less free: Martha Stewart in home detention is not as free as her unconvicted fellow citizens, but she is freer than she was in federal prison. (In the language of social science, freedom is a continuous rather than a dichotomous variable.) It is similarly plausible to say that a society can be more or less free, depending on the decisions it makes and the circumstances in which it is placed. A "system of liberty" is an aggregate, measured across dimensions and individuals. If so, it is conceptually possible to say that public authorities can act to maximize liberty, even at the cost of restricting the liberty of some individuals. In Epstein's railroad example, the state would be understood as acting to enhance the liberty of the ninety-nine willing sellers to enter into an arrangement that would benefit both them and the future users of the railroad, a gain in liberty that far outweighs the loss for the holdout who is compelled to sell against his will.

There is an obvious objection to this approach. If individual rights are, by definition, protections designed to withstand the force of majoritarian and aggregative claims, then Epstein's consequentialism of liberty leads straight to the conclusion that rights in the strict sense do not exist (except perhaps for each individual's right to be treated equally in the consequentialist calculus). Indeed, the logic of Epstein's position on its face is that while nonconsequentialist norms help structure morality at the individual level, they are not adequate at the societal level. *Fiat justitia et pereat mundus*[33] is not tolerable as a principle of social justice; a constitution is (famously) not a suicide pact. Even in less extreme circumstances, norms that are designed to safeguard individuals but that impose large costs on the liberty or welfare of others will come under intense pressure. At some point, for example, rules of evidence designed to minimize the possibility that the innocent will ever be convicted may become so stringent as to allow large numbers of criminals who would otherwise be incarcerated to continue terrorizing their communities. A reasonable conception of social

---

[31] Ibid.
[32] Ibid.
[33] "Let justice be done, though the world perish."

morality will not foreclose the possibility of loosening these rules of evidence to promote the ability of members of the public to enjoy their lives, property, and liberty with a greater measure of certainty and security.

Nonconsequentialist defenders of liberty will stumble, of course, at the threshold of Epstein's argument. But it is also possible to criticize it in consequentialist terms. Legal scholar Randy Barnett, for example, acknowledges that without some version of Epstein's approach, the problems that the principle of individual consent poses for social coordination may be insoluble. Nonetheless, he fears, the cure is worse than the disease, because it opens the door to unjust uses of coercive power. For example, "the consequence of rent-seeking—of interest groups using the coercion of the state to acquire unearned benefits for themselves—matters as much as the consequence of failing to build a road. Ask the residents of Poletown, whose Detroit neighborhood was destroyed by eminent domain to build a General Motors assembly plant." [34] The problem, Barnett concludes, is that once we start down Epstein's consequentialist road, it is hard to see how we can stop short of the conclusion the *Kelo* majority reached. [35]

An intriguing question lurks just beneath the surface of Barnett's challenge—namely, how much of a deviation from New Deal jurisprudence does Epstein's position represent? My answer: Not as much as parties to the dispute imagine. Like the New Deal era Supreme Court, Epstein employs a results-oriented theory in the service of the general welfare. To be sure, his understanding of the general welfare differs from that of the New Dealers. Nonetheless, Epstein and the New Dealers are as one in their opposition to the kind of formalism that dominated American law schools in the early decades of the twentieth century. [36]

Cass Sunstein distinguishes between "judicial maximalism," which seeks coherent theoretical foundations to ground individual decisions and connect them with one another, and "judicial minimalism," which stays closer to the surface, renders decisions on a case-by-case basis, and makes no effort to find a single unifying theory. [37] Justices Antonin Scalia and Clarence Thomas are maximalists; former justice Sandra Day O'Connor was

[34] For a persuasive critique of this policy and of the decision of the Michigan Supreme Court upholding it (*Poletown Neighborhood Council v. City of Detroit*, 304 N.W.2d 455 [Mich. 1981]), see Paul, *Property Rights and Eminent Domain*, 32–37. It is notable that the Michigan Supreme Court recently overturned *Poletown* in a case that pivoted on a more restrictive interpretation of the "public use" doctrine. See *Wayne County v. Hathcock*, 684 N.W.2d 765 (Mich. 2004).

[35] Randy Barnett, response to Epstein's remarks, in "Coercion vs. Consent." My account is an interpretative paraphrase, because Barnett offered his rejoinder more than a year before *Kelo* was decided. However, I do not believe that I have deviated from either the logic or the spirit of Barnett's position.

[36] Despite the notoriety of the *Lochner* decision, during those decades the courts were less inclined than were law professors to defer to legal categories at the expense of real-world results, as the history of takings jurisprudence indicates.

[37] Cass Sunstein, *One Case at a Time: Judicial Minimalism on the Supreme Court* (Cambridge, MA: Harvard University Press, 1999).

a minimalist. Within this framework, Epstein falls in the same category as Ronald Dworkin: both are unabashed maximalists who offer competing theories about the general principles courts should use to reach their conclusions.[38] It is even the case that their disparate theories have something in common: neither represents a straightforward defense of the natural rights tradition that suffuses the Declaration of Independence and constituted the *lingua franca* of early American jurisprudence.

It is conventional, and not entirely misleading, to describe thinkers like Dworkin as "egalitarian" and those like Epstein as "libertarian." It is certainly true that Dworkin speaks more about equality than Epstein does, and that Epstein returns the favor with regard to liberty. Nonetheless, Epstein subscribes to the egalitarian premise "everyone to count for one, no one for more than one" just as firmly as Dworkin. And like Epstein, Dworkin is more than willing to use aggregative consequentialism to reach policy conclusions. Thus, Dworkin has no trouble arguing that as long as the interests of every student are given equal weight, no one has a right to complain if the criterion of general social benefit leads legislatures and courts to approve race-sensitive admissions policies.[39]

If the usual bright lines blur under scrutiny, do any clear distinctions between egalitarians and libertarians remain? Although further reflection may turn up counterarguments or counterexamples, two distinctions seem promising. Both libertarians and quasi-libertarians of the Epstein variety reject distributive patterns as acceptable components of the general good or welfare that takings of private property may promote, while at least some egalitarians would permit the inclusion of such patterns in the general welfare. Thus, those in or near the libertarian camp reject the holding of at least one of the two key cases on which the *Kelo* majority relied — *Hawaii Housing Authority v. Midkiff* (1984),[40] in which the Supreme Court upheld a taking that sought to reduce an extreme concentration of land ownership on the island of Oahu.[41]

Second, and more fundamentally, a distinction remains between consequentialist and nonconsequentialist social philosophies (and legal understandings). There is such a thing as a jurisprudence of rules justified on nonconsequentialist grounds. As the case of Justice Thomas shows, Epstein

---

[38] Epstein, *Takings*; Ronald M. Dworkin, *Taking Rights Seriously* (Cambridge, MA: Harvard University Press, 1978).

[39] Dworkin, *Taking Rights Seriously,* chap. 9. Underscoring my point that these scholars have more in common than is often thought, Epstein also finds a way to support affirmative action. See Richard A. Epstein, "A Rational Basis for Affirmative Action: A Shaky but Classical Liberal Defense," *Michigan Law Review* 100 (2002): 2036–61.

[40] *Hawaii Housing Authority v. Midkiff*, 467 U.S. 229 (1984). For Epstein's negative judgment on this case, see *Takings*, 110, 161, and 162. The other key case on which the *Kelo* majority relied is *Berman v. Parker*, 348 U.S. 26 (1954).

[41] It might be argued, and sustained by the facts, that certain extreme concentrations of land ownership interfere with the appropriate functioning of markets and may be remedied on those grounds.

is wrong: we are *not* "all consequentialists now."[42] When Thomas rejects takings based on public purposes rather than public use as inconsistent with the original intent of the Fifth Amendment, he is not making a consequentialist argument. In principle, he must acknowledge the possibility that policies forbidden by the discernible intention of constitutional language may be more desirable than those it permits. While this state of affairs is unfortunate, and in extreme cases may warrant constitutional revision, it does not *ipso facto* warrant an interpretive strategy that departs from original intent.

## V. Conclusion: Consequentialism, Nonconsequentialism, and Emergency Powers

Nonconsequentialist jurisprudence looks backward, not forward, to origins rather than outcomes. Its central concern is with legitimacy rather than desirability, with the authorization of the law rather than its impact. The question Epstein rightly raises is whether a jurisprudence of this sort can indefinitely resist the pressure of circumstances. When the New Deal Court in effect read the commerce clause in the light of the general welfare clause, it may well have exceeded the limits of what previous generations would have accepted as a legitimate strategy of interpretation. Nevertheless, the Court's actions were part of a broader strategy to preserve constitutional democracy against the totalitarian tide that overwhelmed so much of Europe during the 1930s. If there had been a populist-fascist revolution in the United States, as many observers feared, we would really have ended up with a "constitution in exile."[43]

This example, and others I have mentioned, points to a possible *via media*: a jurisprudence of rules for normal circumstances and a jurisprudence of consequences for extreme cases. Absent the supreme emergency

---

[42] Nor should we be. From a pluralist standpoint, the "general welfare" is one thing, the "blessings of liberty" another, and there is no guarantee that they will coincide in specific cases. In the long run, laws of property may be justified as promoting the aggregate good of citizens, but in the short term and in individual cases, there is no reason to suppose that this will always be so—any more than individual acts of protected speech invariably promote the general welfare. In most circumstances, the protections of private property are attributes of individual liberty and should be understood as such, not as part of an aggregative calculus. Epstein's approach in chapter 9 of *Takings* tacitly rejects this proposition and seems to endorse the proposition that just compensation (as he defines it) suffices to justify a proposed taking in circumstances in which that taking would create an overall resource benefit. This begs the question of why we should define "public use" in a consequentialist manner, as aggregate benefit, rather than categorically.

[43] This phrase, originated by federal appeals court judge Douglas Ginsburg in 1995, is shorthand for the proposition that the New Deal's expansive interpretation of federal power (and in particular its interpretation of the commerce clause) represented the subversion by stealth of the Constitution, the original meaning of which must now be restored through rectificatory jurisprudence. Many originalists argue that this concept is a straw man employed by few conservatives; liberals cite works by leading conservatives such as Randy Barnett and Richard Epstein to justify their continuing use of the term.

of the Civil War, it would not be necessary even to discuss whether President Lincoln was justified in suspending habeas corpus. While the presumption is in favor of the rule, law, or constitutional provision laid down, circumstances can conspire to rebut that presumption.

The difficulty is that there is ultimately no way to immunize the determination of when an emergency exists from the vagaries of political leaders' discretionary judgments. Lincoln's foes accused him of being a tyrant; John Wilkes Booth shot him with the words *sic semper tyrannis* on his lips. While a tyrant would have acted as Lincoln did, Lincoln was no tyrant. But at the moment that settled law is set aside, no bright-line rule can distinguish between them.

We will never know whether the government of the United States would have won the Civil War, preserved the union, and abolished slavery if, rather than acting on his own authority, Lincoln had followed what most scholars believe is the letter of the Constitution and asked Congress to suspend habeas corpus. Nor can we know today whether the war against al-Qaeda could be as effectively prosecuted in the absence of President George W. Bush's decision to evade the provisions of the 1978 Foreign Intelligence Surveillance Act and on his own authority order the National Security Agency to monitor overseas calls to U.S. citizens. One thing is clear: a self-confidently affirmative answer oversimplifies the awesome decisions that political leaders occasionally face.

I conclude that we cannot understand the rights that limit government as inviolable regardless of circumstances; rather, they are aspects of an overall system of goods and values that public power seeks to enhance. Nozick's choice between rights as side-constraints and a consequentialism of rights must be resolved in favor of the latter. A constitution is not a suicide pact, and *fiat justitia et pereat mundus* is not a maxim by which a responsible leader can operate.

Nevertheless, the considerations that require consequentialism also limit its scope. An emergency is one thing, a desire to attain more rather than less of a social good is quite another. The city of New London would hardly have faced a threat to its existence or even its well-being if it had elected to honor rather than override the property claims of some citizens who had the misfortune to be living in the path of economic development. It is hard to avoid the conclusion that the Supreme Court has expanded the concept of public use beyond reasonable bounds, to a point where it can no longer play an independent role in protecting individuals against whatever government may seek to do in the name of the general welfare. By granting almost automatic deference to legislative determinations, the Court is abdicating its core responsibility to protect individual liberty.

*Public Policy, The Brookings Institution*

# FEDERALISM AND THE OLD AND NEW LIBERALISMS

By Jacob T. Levy

The name of federalism has been given to an association of governments which preserved their mutual independence, and were kept together merely by external political links. This institution is especially pernicious. On the one hand federal states claim over the individuals or portions of their territory a jurisdiction which they should not have; while on the other hand they pretend to maintain, in relation to municipal power, an independence which should not exist. Thus federalism is compatible both with internal despotism and external anarchy. —Benjamin Constant[1]

## I. Federalism, Liberalism, and Freedom

I have previously argued that liberalism has historically contained and will continue to contain both rationalist and pluralist strands, the former emphasizing the potential threat to freedom posed by intermediate institutions and communities, and the latter stressing the freedom from the central state guaranteed by such institutions and communities. I have also argued that the difference between these two strands crosscuts rather than tracks the difference between welfare liberalism and classical or market liberalism.[2] Indeed, welfare liberalism and classical liberalism—the "new" and "old" liberalisms of this volume's title—face the rationalist-pluralist trade-off in fundamentally the same ways and for the same reasons, sharing a commitment both to freedom from the dictates of the central state and to freedom from local despotisms; and in this both liberalisms differ from other ideologies and philosophical systems. Neither conservatism nor socialism nor democratic theory confronts this tension in that same way; each can more easily plump for the central or the local *simpliciter*. I have suggested that this helps us to see the commonalities and continuities between classical liberalism and welfare liberalism, to see them as belonging to a common intellectual genus, notwithstanding the partisans of each who occasionally try to read the other out of the liberal tradition.

---

[1] Benjamin Constant, "On Municipal Power, Local Authorities, and a New Kind of Federalism," in *Principles of Politics Applicable to All Representative Governments,* in Constant, *Political Writings,* ed. and trans. Biancamaria Fontana (Cambridge: Cambridge University Press, 1988), 253–54.

[2] Jacob T. Levy, "Liberalism's Divide After Socialism, and Before," *Social Philosophy and Policy* 20, no. 1 (2003): 278–97.

Insofar as the trade-off between federalism and central-state government is a particular case of the pluralist-rationalist trade-off, it follows, of course, that questions about federalism and centralism will also fail to track questions about classical liberalism and welfare liberalism. One purpose of this essay is to make that claim more concrete.

Another is to test the claim against what many classical liberals would take to be a hard case: the history of federalism in the United States. The shift from classical to welfare liberalism as a public philosophy in the United States—indeed, the shift from one to the other as the generally understood meaning of the word "liberalism"—was more or less contemporaneous with an increasing centralization of power in the American federal system. I mean to suggest that these trends have less to do with each other than it appears at first blush, less than many have assumed. The relationship between federalism and the classical liberal understanding of freedom in eighteenth- and nineteenth-century American liberal and constitutional thought was one of general institutional approximation, not one in which federalism was constitutive of freedom. The centralization of power in the American constitutional system is not one unified development. It began, not as an aspect of the development of welfare liberalism, but as an aspect of a general trend in the United States and elsewhere against liberal constitutionalism generally. Later in the twentieth century, the authority of the states was further restricted, but primarily in ways that do not divide welfare and classical liberals.

## II. FEDERALISM AND THE FOUNDING

Federalism is the accidental innovation of the American constitutional system. Other novel aspects of that system were intentionally developed and intensively discussed and theorized: these include a distinctive sort of separation of powers in which the executive and legislature were each, separately, dependent on the same electorate; written constitutions (at the state and then federal levels) adopted by special conventions summoned for that purpose, rather than by legislatures; and bicameralism without a separation into estates. One arguably novel aspect of the system as it eventually developed, the permanent party system, was theoretically *rejected* and developed more or less in spite of the intentions of the framers.[3]

Federalism was neither intentionally chosen nor rejected. Confederation of one sort or another was widely understood as necessary and inevitable. Thirteen independent polities could not have won the Revolutionary War, but their abolition and consolidation into a single polity

---

[3] Each political party was itself a deliberate creation, of course, but each party's creators initially understood themselves as creating a temporary institution in response to the development of the other. No one set out to create a system of a plurality of permanent parties contesting elections.

was unthinkable. And use was made of the (thin) available resources in political theory concerning confederated republics, notably the brief discussion of them in *The Spirit of the Laws*, the great work of the French political theorist Montesquieu (1689–1755).[4] For the most part, however, the federal system evolved as the unintended result of a series of compromises and power struggles, both among the states and between the states and the center.[5] These compromises and contests began in the Constitutional Convention held in Philadelphia in 1787, with the so-called Great Compromise creating one legislative house representing the people and one representing the states on the basis of equality. The U.S. Constitution, as written, included some elements of James Madison's initial proposal, the so-called Virginia Plan, but not one element that he considered crucial for the system's success: a congressional veto over state legislation. The question of whether states could judge federal legislation unconstitutional and nullify it or interpose themselves between federal authority and the citizenry was to arise within a few years of ratification and was finally to be decided only by force of arms decades later in the Civil War.

It is only in retrospect that we have developed theories about federalism as a complete, complex system. (I will consider these theories in the next section.) All of this is perhaps unsurprising when we remember that it was not yet clear, and would not be clear until after the Civil War, that the United States was effectively a single state with internal administrative divisions. At the time of the American founding, the Holy Roman Empire (962–1806 C.E.) was the only apparent example in the world of a large confederation, and it was only *a* state in complicated and attenuated ways, being made up of (as we would say today) sovereign armed states with international personalities of their own. Europe itself had been imagined as a federation or confederation by eighteenth-century philosophers, which meant only that the nascent international legal order and shared community of morals and commerce might be strengthened so as to eliminate interstate war; it did not mean a dissolution of the states.[6] This suggests that the bare concept of federation did not mean to eighteenth-century minds what it means to ours, namely, one internationally-sovereign state that happened to have a distinctive kind of purely domestic constitutional organization. Instead, "federation" (or "confederation") could denote a range of systems that blurred the domestic-international distinc-

---

[4] See Montesquieu, *The Spirit of the Laws* (1748), ed. and trans. Anne Cohler et al. (Cambridge: Cambridge University Press, 1989), part II, book 9, chaps. 1–3, pp. 131–33.

[5] For the history of these struggles, see Forrest McDonald, *States' Rights and the Union: Imperium in Imperio, 1776–1876* (Lawrence: University Press of Kansas, 2000).

[6] This idea dates back to Abbé Saint-Pierre, *A Project for Settling an Everlasting Peace in Europe* (London: J. Watts, 1714). The theme was later taken up by Jean-Jacques Rousseau in commentaries on Saint-Pierre in the 1750s, and then most famously by the German philosopher Immanuel Kant; see Kant, "Perpetual Peace: A Philosophical Sketch" (1795), in Kant, *Political Writings*, ed. H. S. Reiss (Cambridge: Cambridge University Press, 1991), 93–130.

tion. Moreover, while there is endless dispute over how the founding generation of Americans viewed the relationship among the colonies-*cum*-states, and about the relative priority (in time and in importance) of the thirteen polities and of the union, it seems clear that the relationship was at least to some degree an international one, and the founding to at least some degree a treaty-and-alliance-like development.[7] The fears about interstate war expressed throughout the 1780s and prominently in *The Federalist* were not, or were not simply, hyperbole.

Thus, for example, the idea of competitive federalism, of federalism enhancing freedom because it introduces exit-based competitive pressures on each state to liberalize its laws, long post-dates the founding. In a 1791 essay against the consolidation of the states into a single government, Madison focused all his attention on the possibility that consolidation would dangerously increase executive power, and none at all on any competition between the states.[8] The mechanisms by which the founding generation imagined that federalism might enhance liberty were much blunter. The states would check the center, the states would check each other, and the center would check the states in ways that relied on a general balancing of power (with the possibility of armed force lurking in the background), not on any smoothly or automatically operating incentives.

The first such mechanism, by which states would check the center—as laid out in *Federalist Nos. 25, 45,* and *46*—relied on the greater loyalty that citizens would tend to feel to their states than to the federal center. This would tend to check any move to despotism by the center, *in extremis* through armed resistance. "Publius" (meaning Alexander Hamilton for *Federalist No. 25,* James Madison for *No. 45* and *No. 46*) maintained that a standing army at the center would be less dangerous to republican liberty than the alternative, standing armies in the several states, because "in any contest between the foederal [*sic*] head and one of its members, the people will be most apt to unite with their local government":

> [T]he liberty of the people would be less safe in this state of things [with the states maintaining standing armies], than in that which left the national forces in the hands of the national government. As far as an army be considered a dangerous weapon of power, it had better be in those hands, of which the people are most likely to be jealous, than in those of whom they are least likely to be jealous. For it is a truth which the experience of all ages has attested, that *the people are*

---

[7] See David C. Hendrickson, *Peace Pact: The Lost World of the American Founding* (Lawrence: University Press of Kansas, 2003).

[8] *The Papers of James Madison,* ed. William T. Hutchinson et al. (Charlottesville: University of Virginia Press, 1962), vol. 14, pp. 137–39.

*always in the most danger, when the means of injuring their rights are in
the possession of those of whom they entertain the least suspicion.*[9]

The reasons for this suspicion and jealousy, this natural likelihood that
the "first and most natural attachment of the people will be to the governments of their respective States," are so plentiful as to place the prediction "beyond doubt." People are more likely to have neighbors, friends,
and family in state than in federal offices or employment. They are more
likely to have reasonable hopes of such offices or employment themselves. State governments will attend to immediately-felt local needs,
whereas the federal government's primary business will seem far-off and
relatively unimportant. State politics will simply be more familiar and
comprehensible. For these reasons, "the popular bias may well be expected
most strongly to incline" toward the states.[10]

This inclination, this salutary suspicion and jealousy, will tend to prevent the buildup of any armed forces that exceed the federation's genuine
needs for external defense. Such a buildup cannot take place all at once,
and the people and the states (electing the House and the Senate, respectively) would certainly interrupt the process before it could be completed.
Even if the buildup did take place, however, the greater attachment of the
people to their states than to the federal center would allow the states to
defend themselves successfully:

> Let a regular army, fully equal to the resources of the country, be
> formed; and let it be entirely at the devotion of the federal govern-
> ment; still it would not be going too far to say, that the State gov-
> ernments, with the people on their side, would be able to repel the
> danger. . . . Besides the advantage of being armed, which the Amer-
> icans possess over the people of almost every other nation, the exis-
> tence of subordinate governments, to which the people are attached,
> and by which the militia officers are appointed, forms a barrier against
> the enterprises of ambition, more insurmountable than any which a
> simple government of any form can admit of.[11]

Madison emphasized elsewhere that the constitutional system itself
would not mechanically protect liberty, and that its protection depended
on the willingness of the people to act:

> In bestowing the eulogies due to the partitions and internal checks of
> power, it ought not the less to be remembered, that they are neither

---

[9] *Federalist No. 25*, in James Madison, Alexander Hamilton, and John Jay (collectively as
Publius), *The Federalist, with the letters of Brutus*, ed. Terence Ball (Cambridge: Cambridge
University Press, 2003), 116; emphasis added. *The Federalist* was originally published in 1788.
[10] *Federalist No. 46*, 229.
[11] Ibid., 231.

the sole nor the chief palladium of constitutional liberty. The people, who are the authors of this blessing, must also be its guardians. Their eyes must ever be ready to mark, their voice to pronounce, and their arm to repel or repair, aggressions on the authority of their constitutions. . . .[12]

Although Madison in the late 1780s did not expect or hope that this combination of state and popular resistance to the center would often be needed, a decade later he coauthored the Virginia Resolution, leading the Virginia legislature to declare the censorship rules of the 1798 federal Alien and Sedition Acts unconstitutional, aiming to rally popular opinion and the other states against the restrictions.

In addition to the states' checking the center through popularly supported resistance, Madison noted a second mechanism whereby the compound federal system could protect freedom: "in a confederal system, if one of its members happens to stray into pernicious measures, it will be reclaimed by the frowns and the good examples of the others, before the evil example will have infected the others." He repeated this idea on occasion from *The Federalist* through the end of his career, with regular attribution of it to Montesquieu, who wrote: "If a sedition occurs in one of the members of the confederation, the others can pacify it. If some abuses are introduced somewhere, they are corrected by the healthy parts." [13]

Notice that, here, it is not the *federal* government whose frowns and good examples would correct the domestic evils of any one state. But neither Montesquieu nor Madison offered any intra-constitutional mechanism by which the states might affect each other's internal conduct. The idea seems to have been that, in certain extreme cases such as one state's falling to a would-be monarch or military despot, the other states could be relied on to respond extra-constitutionally, militarily if need be.

Montesquieu also held that "the federal government should be composed of states of the same nature, above all of republican states," not of a mixture of republics and monarchies as in the Holy Roman Empire.[14]

---

[12] James Madison, "Government of the United States," February 4, 1792, in *Letters and Other Writings of James Madison*, vol. 1 (Philadelphia: Lippincott, 1865), 473–74. Note both "arm to repel or repair," suggesting the possibility of resistance, and "their constitutions," plural, suggesting that the state constitutions are proper objects of protection.

[13] Montesquieu, *The Spirit of the Laws*, II.9.1, p. 132.

[14] Ibid., II.9.2, p. 132. The American founding generation generally misinterpreted Montesquieu's view of federal republics. They took him to be straightforwardly an advocate of that form of government. In fact, while he thought it a better form of republicanism than a republic in a large unitary state, Montesquieu was not fundamentally a partisan of republicanism, not even of confederal republicanism. The English commercial constitutional monarchy, not the Dutch commercial or the Swiss agrarian confederal republics, excited his greatest admiration. I discuss Montesquieu's critique of republicanism as anachronistic in my essay "Beyond Publius: Montesquieu, Liberal Republicanism, and the Small-Republic Thesis," *History of Political Thought* 27, no. 1 (2006): 50–90.

And the Constitution was to "guarantee" this, in its only clause committing the federal government to the defense of freedom within the states in
any general way. The so-called republican guarantee clause[15] completes
our survey of federalism and freedom, by introducing a third mechanism,
a *federal* check on *states*. The great expounder of the Constitution and
nineteenth-century Supreme Court Justice Joseph Story explained the
republican guarantee clause as follows:

> Without a guaranty, the assistance to be derived from the national
> government in repelling domestic dangers, which might threaten the
> existence of state constitutions, could not be demanded, as a right,
> from the national government. Usurpation might raise its standard,
> and trample upon the liberties of the people, while the national gov-
> ernment could legally do nothing more, than behold the encroach-
> ments with indignation and regret. A successful faction might erect a
> tyranny on the ruins of order and law; while no succour could be
> constitutionally afforded by the Union to the friends and supporters
> of the government.[16]

This is a sharp reminder of how different the constitutional order seemed
in the decades before the Civil War. Note the astonishing thought that,
without the clause, the national government would be legally powerless
to intervene even though a state faced usurpation, tyranny, the trampling
of liberties, and the ruin of law and order! And the debates in the Constitutional Convention reflected the same assumption. Of all the delegates
recorded as discussing the clause, only John Rutledge of South Carolina
expressed the idea that "Congress had the authority if they had the means
to co-operate with any State in subduing a rebellion. It was & would be
in the nature of the thing." No one supported Rutledge in thinking the
clause superfluous. Five other delegates all championed the clause as
necessary to authorize such action:

> At this rate an enterprising Citizen might erect the standard of Mon-
> archy in a particular State, might gather together partizans from all
> quarters, might extend his views from State to State, and threaten to
> establish a tyranny over the whole and the General Government be
> compelled to remain an inactive witness to its own destruction.[17]

---

[15] U.S. Constitution, Article IV, Section 4: "The United States shall guarantee to every
State in this Union a Republican Form of Government, and shall protect each of them
against Invasion; and on Application of the Legislature, or of the Executive (when the
Legislature cannot be convened) against domestic Violence."

[16] Joseph Story, *Commentaries on the U.S. Constitution* (Cambridge: Brown, Shattuck, and
Co., 1833), vol. 3, chap. 41, sec. 1808.

[17] James Madison, *Notes of Debates: In the Federal Convention of 1787* (Columbus: Ohio State
University Press, 1984), Wednesday, July 18, 1787, p. 281.

Conspicuously absent from that picture, to a contemporary eye, are the federal courts. The would-be monarch might induce his state legislature to grant him a title of nobility, which could in principle authorize federal court review even under the unamended Constitution. (So would a state's suspension of habeas corpus.)[18] However, no one seems to have thought that the federal courts could act as the primary federal guarantors of freedom as such within the several states. The "General Government's" action would be congressional and presidential. Beyond the kinds of extreme abuses that would fall under the guarantee clause, Madison noted that the federal government was relatively powerless to protect freedom within the states:

> If the act of a particular state ... be generally popular in that State, and should not too grossly violate the oaths of the State officers [then the] opposition of the Foederal [sic] Government, or the interposition of Foederal officers, would but inflame the zeal of all parties on the side of the State, and the evil could not be prevented or repaired, if at all, without the employment of means which must always be resorted to with reluctance and difficulty.[19]

Thus, the ways that the founding generation conceived of federalism as enhancing liberty were not, or not simply, those that became familiar to later generations, who thought about federalism as a single, complex but unified, purely domestic constitutional order. The states could protect liberty against the center by commanding sufficient loyalty to call forth resistance—if necessary, armed resistance—even against the center's professional army. The states could monitor each other's internal actions, disapproving them with "frowns." The center could protect freedom within the states by removing whole domains of legislative authority from the latter, and by enforcing republicanism if necessary, but not with a general federal supervision over state laws (as Madison wanted) nor by detailed federal court review of state laws. (For many decades after the founding, most judicial review of the era was intrastate—state courts reviewing state legislation.)

To this must be added the *Federalist No. 10* analysis of factions in the extended republic: individual states might endanger local minorities by coming under the sway of a passionate and interested local majority faction, but such factions would be difficult to assemble in the extended republic. It is curious, however, to note the mismatch between this argument and the actual institutional design at hand. *Federalist No. 10* is an argument in favor of large republics, not federal ones. It offers no reason

---

[18] The bans on states granting titles of nobility or suspending habeas corpus are both found in Article I, Section 10.
[19] *Federalist No. 46*, 231.

to *ever* prefer state over federal jurisdiction. A federal government of a few enumerated powers sitting atop thirteen state governments of general jurisdiction does not seem like the proper remedy for the ills diagnosed in *Federalist No. 10*. The specific denial to the states of a few of the powers most easily abused by local majorities—the power to print paper money or to abridge contracts[20]—improves the match between analysis and institutions a bit, but not overwhelmingly. The argument about faction pushes in the direction of a *unitary* extended republic in order to protect the liberty of local minorities. It is not an argument about *federalism* and freedom at all.

In short, the constitutional federal order, even combined with the political thought about federalism in the founding generation and the immediately following decades, does not amount to a streamlined system seamlessly operating to protect or promote individual liberty. Neither competitive federalism automatically checking the states through a market-like mechanism, nor a legal order allowing federal courts to guard individual liberty against the states and to monitor the enumeration of federal powers, is much in evidence. What we find instead is a number of powerful governments given more or less blunt tools with which to affect one another, with some reason for hope that they will generally do so in directions favorable to liberty because the people in some broad sense are likely to want liberty. There is no *equation* of the safeguarding of freedom with state authority, federal authority, judicial authority, or the balance of these attained by the federal order as a whole.

To some degree, this is true of all good political theory about institutional design; it shows an understanding that institutions at best approximate justice, and it does not conflate generally good procedures with morally desirable particular outcomes. The American founders, however, treated at least some questions of institutional design as more nearly identical with questions of justice. Federalism might have been a good idea all things considered, but (for example) the separation of powers was an absolute moral necessity. Also indispensable was an independent judiciary that had the sole authority to issue criminal convictions because habeas corpus was guaranteed against the executive, and because bills of attainder (and ex post facto laws, of which bills of attainder are a subset) were prohibited to the legislature. The political thought of the founding era is filled with references to the separation of powers as being at least partly *constitutive* of liberty, quite unlike the way that federalism was discussed.

## III. Federalism in Practice

The absence of any systematic theory of federalism's contribution to freedom in the early decades of American constitutionalism might be

---

[20] U.S. Constitution, Article I, Section 10.

taken to be a matter of blindness to what was close at hand. Perhaps American federalism in practice *did* create a system that worked consistently and necessarily for the promotion and protection of freedom. We should pause to consider contemporary accounts of liberalism and federalism to see whether they are sound and whether they describe federalism as it came to exist in the United States over the eighteenth and nineteenth centuries; this will affect how we view the departures from that system in the twentieth century.

The most fully worked-out theory of federalism's benefits for freedom is the theory of competitive federalism, summarized by James M. Buchanan[21] and refined, developed, and tested by public choice economists and scholars in the neo-institutionalist school of political science.[22]

In general, competitive federalism as an ideal fits poorly with federalism as it actually exists in the world, however.[23] Federalism generates competition insofar as exit from provinces (or states, in the U.S. case) is feasible, and insofar as there is a suitable range of other provinces to enter into so that one's preferred policy option is available. In order to generate competitive *pressure* on the provinces to reform, moreover, there must be some connection between the exit of those dissatisfied by existing policies and the incentives faced by public officials. Finally, in order for competition to generally increase *freedom,* those whose (potential) mobility affects officials' incentives must act on the basis of preferences *for freedom.*

These conditions are fairly well met for businesses that are major local sources of employment or tax revenue, but that are nonetheless fairly mobile across jurisdictional boundaries and are interested in moving primarily to avoid high taxes or onerous regulations. Nevertheless, for natural persons and for policy domains besides taxation and business regulation, these conditions are typically met badly if at all.

Consider the following facts: The states or provinces that make up federations tend to be very large. The average population size in states or provinces of major modern democratic federations—the United States, Canada, Germany, Spain, Australia, and so on—is in the mid-single-digits of millions. The number of provinces in a federation is typically in the

---

[21] James M. Buchanan, "Federalism and Individual Sovereignty," in *Federalism, Liberty, and the Law: The Collected Works of James M. Buchanan,* vol. 18 (Indianapolis: Liberty Fund, 2001).

[22] Barry Weingast, "The Economic Role of Political Institutions: Market-Preserving Federalism and Economic Development," *Journal of Law, Economics, and Organization* 11 (1995): 1–31; Yingyi Qian and Barry Weingast, "Federalism as a Commitment to Preserve Market Incentives," *Journal of Economic Perspectives* 11, no. 4 (1997): 83–92. See also the discussion in Jenna Bednar, William Eskridge, and John Ferejohn, "A Political Theory of Federalism," in *Constitutional Culture and Democratic Rule,* ed. John Ferejohn, Jack N. Rakove, and Jonathan Riley (New York: Cambridge University Press, 2001); and see also Albert Breton, "Towards a Theory of Competitive Federalism," *European Journal of Political Economy* 3 (1987): 263–329; and Albert Breton, *Competitive Government* (Cambridge: Cambridge University Press, 1996).

[23] The discussion in the following paragraphs is developed more fully in my essay "Federalism, Liberalism, and the Separation of Loyalties" (in submission).

low-to-mid double digits. This simultaneously makes exit from provinces costly—much costlier than moving across the street or to a neighboring city—and restricts the number of provinces that are providing policy packages. Insofar as persons and businesses are would-be policy consumers, they face an oligopoly of policy providers; or, conversely, insofar as residents and tax bases are the goods that states/provinces try to purchase with their policies, the provinces are oligopsonistic buyers. "Entry" into the policy-provision market by new provinces is typically constitutionally difficult or impossible. And provinces offer their laws and policies as a package, almost all of the time, meaning that even policy-consumers with realistic possibilities of exit can probably only choose on the basis of one or two policy topics, immunizing the rest from competitive pressures. The combination of a fixed and small number of providers and high costs of exit makes it very difficult to get significant competitive pressure out of a federal system.

Furthermore, provinces in really-existing federalism are very often tightly linked with an ethnic, cultural, or language group. This imposes substantial costs on those who would exit the province; there may be no other place they can go where their language is the local language or where they feel identified with the local culture. To put it another way, the ethnocultural aspects of the policy package offered by provinces are often weighted very heavily, so heavily as to greatly reduce any competitive pressures on the provinces with respect to any other policy domains. Indeed, Buchanan notes that "federalized structures allow for some partial mapping of politics with tribal identities. At the very least, federalized structures reduce the extent to which tribal identities must be grossly transcended."[24] Buchanan takes this to be a virtue, because it reduces the taxing demands on our extended moral sympathies imposed by the Hayekian "great society" or extended order. Nonetheless, just to the extent that this is true, exit is weakened as a general feature of federalism, and the competitive federalism that Buchanan is generally concerned to defend is ineffective. Moreover, just to the extent that this is true, the local polities run the risk of becoming oppressively homogenous—of being dominated by an unjust majority faction, as Madison feared.

The federalism of the American Constitution and early republic did not approximate the ideal federalist order imagined by competitive-federalism theory. It did not even approximate it as well as contemporary American federalism does. Transportation costs and times have fallen tremendously; both persons and businesses or capital can exit states much more easily today than they could two hundred years ago. The loyalty to states, their approximation of "tribal identities," has dwindled to almost nothing in most parts of the United States. There are regional or sectional loyalties, but these do not impede exit and competition in the same way; and

[24] Buchanan, "Federalism and Individual Sovereignty," 85.

loyalty to the nation-state as a primary identity is much more powerful than those regional ties, much more powerful than could have been imagined in the eighteenth century. During the founding era, references to exit from one state to another (as opposed to exit from one state to the frontier) as an important constitutional fact were almost nonexistent.[25]

Much closer to the views of the founders are understandings of federalism that depend on political rather than market-like mechanisms. One understanding rests on the thought that more-local governments are easier for the electorate to control effectively, and less prone to the agency problems that allow public officials to pursue their own ambitions and agendas unchecked. If the electorate tends to wish to preserve liberty—as always, a premise that American political thought is somewhat ambivalent about—and if the states are more directly responsive to the electorate's wishes, then the prerogatives of the states in a compound system will tend to protect liberty. This idea, which centers on democratic voice rather than on individual exit, does not require radical versions of states' rights, much less opposition to the existence of any center at all. It can accompany recognition that certain goods (e.g., continental defense) must be or are better provided by a federal union. The idea is reflexively skeptical of the center in the compound system, however, and tends to insist on narrow understandings of central authority. This account, unlike competitive federalism, bears a recognizable relationship to the political thought of the founding era and the following two generations.

Two related and crucial sets of antebellum disputes about federalism did involve exit, of course: the treatment of fugitive slaves—the subject of the 1850 Fugitive Slave Act—and the treatment of slaves who accompanied their masters into free territory, the subject of the 1857 case *Dred Scott v. Sandford*.[26] Until the 1850s, the existence of a plurality of jurisdictions, some of them without legal slavery, did informally contribute to freedom via exit. They did not do so in a way that much resembles the standard image of competitive federalism. Free states typically did not understand themselves to benefit from an influx of free blacks and, indeed, took steps

---

[25] A few authors have suggested otherwise: Competitive federalism as a theory is attributed to the Antifederalists by Norman Barry, "Constitutionalism, Federalism, and the European Union," *Economic Affairs* 24, no. 1 (2004): 11–16; to the Federalist founders by Michael Greve, *Real Federalism: Why It Matters, How It Can Happen* (Washington, DC: American Enterprise Institute, 1999), and Buchanan, "Federalism and Individual Sovereignty"; and to the pre–New Deal "original constitution" by John O. McGinnis, "Presidential Review as Constitutional Restoration," *Duke Law Journal* 51 (2001): 901–61. Compare Alex Tabarrok: "In many ways, the competitive federalism vision is the closest to that of the Founders—because it treats federalism as a way of sustaining liberty just as are the other checks and balances in the U.S. system." Alex Tabarrok, "Arguments for Federalism," Lecture at the Hastings Law School, University of California, San Francisco, September 20, 2001, http://www.independent.org/issues/article.asp?id=485. I take this to be received wisdom of a sort among contemporary libertarians, and I mean to challenge its accuracy, however much I sympathize with the normative upshot.

[26] *Dred Scott v. Sandford*, 60 U.S. 393 (1857).

to prevent this. Nonetheless, the escape of slaves from slavery was a cost to slaveholders and slave states, and they successfully sought to end the jurisdictional competition. It seems to me that federalism's facilitation of exit from slavery was very far from being seen as a particular case of a general feature of federalism. It was anomalous, and was defended by abolitionists but not by moderate northerners, even though the latter were both critical of slavery and, as Whigs and heirs of Whigs, generally supportive of states' rights.

This brings us, at last, to the central difficulties with any claim that the federalism of the early American republic operated in practice to advance liberal freedom in anything other than a rough and ready way. These difficulties are evident in the increasing convergence, over the course of the first half of the nineteenth century, between the cause of states' authority and the cause of slavery; the inescapable fact that slavery was finally eradicated only by a tremendous increase in the effective capacity and the constitutional authority of the central government, leaving the federal system transformed; and the postwar struggle between southern state governments determined to recreate racial tyranny, and a central government that, consistently for a little while and intermittently thereafter, tried to stop them. The antebellum constitutional order cannot be defended on liberal grounds in any detailed way; and the postbellum Constitution was superior precisely insofar as it shifted authority to Washington, D.C. That Reconstruction ultimately failed and was replaced with Jim Crow does not alter this conclusion, as this failure was understood as a partial restoration of the status quo ante in the federal system.

Federalism can either directly impede central-state enforcement of rights against provincial governments, by reserving the relevant authority to the provinces or denying it to the center; or indirectly do so, by sufficiently weakening the central state's political autonomy, political capacity, or institutional strength so that it cannot effectively take the needed actions. The system of approximations and balances before the Civil War tended in the former direction; the central government arguably lacked the constitutional authority to ban slavery within the states (and, according to the *Dred Scott* Court, lacked the authority even to ban it in territories).[27] The system after the Civil War was a failure not of de jure authority but

---

[27] I say "arguably" here to bracket the dispute over whether a truer interpretation of the antebellum Constitution than that offered by the Supreme Court would have revealed the Constitution to be either neutral between slavery and abolition or affirmatively pro-abolition. Some abolitionists held that the Constitution was a pro-slavery document, a "pact with the devil," and therefore morally void; others said that slavery could be critiqued and abolished from within the constitutional framework. One might want to distinguish between two senses of "de jure" authority, that which is recognized by positive law and that which is ultimately legally correct, if the legal system is a constitutional one in which the short-term positive law may coherently be criticized as unconstitutional and therefore illegal. The dispute over slavery concerned whether the Constitution legitimized or prohibited slavery only in the second sense of "de jure."

of effective political capacity. Of course, these are also the same means by which federalism can restrict the center from *violating* rights—the enumeration of powers and the Tenth Amendment[28] exercising direct legal restraint, the fostering of *Federalist No. 46*–style loyalty to the states and suspicion of the center exercising indirect political restraint. My point here is only that both mechanisms were in evidence in the failure to liberalize the *herrenvolk* democracies of the South;[29] and thus neither type of federalist approximation of justice can be thought to have approximated it so closely as to render any departures from it suspect on liberal grounds.

I should note that by "liberal grounds" I mean nothing that distinguishes between market liberalism and welfare liberalism in the slightest. It has been argued that conceptions of freedom have always been developed in contrast to the reality of slavery; in any event, that was certainly true in the United States.[30] Liberal freedom—negative liberty, individual liberty, the "liberty of the moderns"[31]—faces its starkest opposite in human slavery, a fact that has been central to the development of American ideas of freedom. American liberal constitutionalism has also been deeply concerned with institutional questions, with understanding what political arrangements could most effectively protect and promote freedom over the long term. But the institutional questions are about means, whereas slavery is a denial of the end. The rhetoric of freedom that has been used by defenders of slavery and Jim Crow has always been designed to obscure this, focusing attention on the means of federalism and constrained central power and away from the ends at stake.

## IV. Approximation

A liberal federalism needs to be concerned with a number of actors simultaneously, each of which has more than one possible normative valence: the central state, state governments, and private persons and institutions. Private persons and institutions are the primary holders of the rights that liberalism seeks to protect; but they can also be the threats

---

[28] "The powers not delegated to the United States by the Constitution, nor prohibited by it to the States, are reserved to the States respectively, or to the people."

[29] For the concept and the phrase of *herrenvolk* or master-race democracy, widely applied to both apartheid South Africa and the Jim Crow South, see Pierre van den Berghe, *Race and Racism* (New York: Wiley, 1967).

[30] On the general case, see Orlando Patterson, *Freedom, Volume 1: Freedom in the Making of Western Culture* (New York: Basic Books, 1991); on the American case, see Judith Shklar, *American Citizenship* (Cambridge, MA: Harvard University Press, 1991), and Judith Shklar, "Positive Liberty, Negative Liberty in the United States," in Shklar, *Redeeming American Political Thought*, ed. Stanley Hoffmann and Dennis F. Thompson (Chicago: University of Chicago Press, 1998).

[31] Benjamin Constant, "The Liberty of the Ancients Compared with That of the Moderns," in Constant, *Political Writings*, ed. Biancamaria Fontana (Cambridge: Cambridge University Press, 1988), 308–28.

to each other's freedoms, the problem that justifies the turn to government in the first place. State governments should be in the business of restraining those threats, but will sometimes instead authorize or reinforce them, as in the case of a system of slavery in which private persons are made the masters and owners of other persons by law, and in which the "rights" of the masters are enforced using the power of the state's legal system. State governments also may check expansions of central authority, whether those expansions are detrimental to liberty (the Alien and Sedition Acts) or otherwise (Reconstruction). The central government, in turn, may directly act to threaten freedom, may empower either private actors or state governments to do so, or may intervene *against* either private actors or state governments to prevent them from violating rights.

No one of these actors always seeks to protect or promote freedom, and none of them always seeks to restrict it, either. Balancing them against each other in the hope of approximating a just degree of freedom as the outcome must be an imprecise enterprise, no matter how detailed the constitutional texts and doctrines specifying which has what power. If, as Madison thought, the states might sometimes be the enforcers of the Constitution, then they will necessarily have some amount of autonomous political weight that might also be thrown around in less desirable ways. If the federal government is to have the authority to prevent private actors from harming or enslaving one another, then it will necessarily have some political capacity to infringe on private actor's rights. Constitutions are not self-enforcing, and grants of power are not easily contained by initial purposes. Even judicial review cannot transform these basic facts of political life. What arrangement of power and authority will generate the most just political outcomes is a contingent matter; sometimes one actor will pose the greatest threat to freedom, sometimes another. We should expect variation over time as well as across different federations.

To acknowledge this variability is not to deny the existence of a general link between federalism and freedom. Buchanan suggests "that a coherent classical liberal must be generally supportive of federal political structures, because any division of authority must, necessarily, tend to limit the potential range of political coercion." [32] I think that is roughly correct. I doubt that "necessarily"; federalism might, in principle, simply subject people to an additional layer of injustice and domination. Nonetheless, as a matter of fact, the different levels of government do tend to check one another in desirable ways. That the balance of authority is a matter of approximation, and that no particular balance can just be identified with freedom or justice, does not mean that the balance does not matter; at the extreme, wholly unitary states are less likely to be respectful of freedom than states with some real element of federalism. But Buchanan is right not to say anything much more precise than "generally supportive" and

---

[32] Buchanan, "Federalism and Individual Sovereignty," 79.

"tend to." Liberals (classical or otherwise) need not automatically support just any given federalist status quo against any given changes to it. Shifting authority at the margin to the center does not automatically increase "the potential range of political coercion."

## V. Federalism and Liberalism Over Time

If federalism's contribution to freedom is, or as a matter of American public philosophy was generally conceived to be, a matter of approximation and general balancing tendencies, then reallocations of authority and competences to the center cannot be understood as necessarily diminishing liberty. Moreover, if twentieth-century liberalism was generally sympathetic to reallocations in the direction of the center, that is not even prima facie proof of a decisive break between it and earlier American liberalisms. And with more fine-grained analysis we will see that the first stage of the centralization in the American constitutional order had relatively little to do with liberalism of any sort, while the second stage improved the federation's approximation of freedom in ways that welfare liberals and market liberals alike can endorse.

Over the decades from, say, 1910 to 1950, a number of broad fundamental changes took place in American constitutional practice and theory, and in American public philosophy and policy. The economy came under increasing regulation, and that regulation was increasingly central rather than state-level. Authority shifted away from the courts and Congress to the presidency, especially during wartime and the Great Depression. The federal government increasingly abridged individual liberties and restricted civil freedom (e.g., universal conscription and suppression of antidraft and antiwar speech, the Red Scare, the internment of Japanese-Americans during World War II, the federalization of Jim Crow under Woodrow Wilson, and so on). Eventually, the federal courts would increasingly become the guarantors of a variety of liberties against both the federal and the state governments; but that came later, and there was little movement in that direction until after the end of World War II.

More or less simultaneously, "liberalism" came to denote a much more redistributive and regulatory stance than it once had. The political and philosophical position formerly known as liberalism dwindled so dramatically that social critic Albert Jay Nock could romanticize the few remaining adherents as "the Remnant." [33]

Some have been tempted to equate these trends, identifying all of the changes in the constitutional order with the intellectual shift from classical to welfare liberalism. This seems to me untenable.

---

[33] Albert Jay Nock, "Isaiah's Job," in Nock, *Free Speech and Plain Language* (New York: William Morrow, 1937).

American political history cannot be understood in isolation. Over the decades from the 1910s to the 1940s, the Liberal Party in Britain imploded; liberal parties in continental European democracies were pretty thoroughly squeezed between, at best, social and Christian democratic parties, or at worst, communist and fascist ones. The legacy of liberal constitutionalism and the rule of law came under sustained assault during the long crisis of the Depression and the two world wars, never emerging unscathed and sometimes not emerging at all.

Franklin Roosevelt propounded a constitutional theory in which the president could enter into international agreements without the consent of Congress, in which much authority previously understood as legislative was concentrated in the administrative apparatus of the executive branch, and in which the elected branches, governing with a broad electoral mandate, could legislate more or less unconstrained by a judiciary enforcing a written constitution. Roosevelt also, of course, abrogated the very strong long-standing norm against presidents seeking third (much less fourth) terms in office, a norm grounded in a fear of the centralization and entrenchment of power in the presidency. Such is the character of executive branches; in times of crisis or emergency, they are impatient with norms and formalities and restraints, feeling the urgent need for action. But the "crisis of parliamentary democracy,"[34] the perceived incompatibility of the rule of law and formal procedures with the circumstances of emergency, the pressure on constitutional systems to vest power in one man when catastrophe loomed—none of this was unique to the United States. In examining the meaning and significance of the intellectual shift from classical to welfare liberalism in the United States, and of the centralization of power within the American federal order, we should try to control for the general trends in the world at the time. We should certainly not simply equate welfare liberalism with the presidencies of, for example, Woodrow Wilson and Franklin Roosevelt. These were less market-oriented than earlier American practice, but they were also less liberal by any meaning of that word, just as governing orders around the world were generally less liberal in the period from the 1910s to the 1940s than they had been for the fifty years before that.

What is relatively distinctive about the American case is that the constitutional system recognizably survived these decades; it was transformed and perhaps weakened but never completely ruptured either by internal collapse or by external conquest. If this was also true of the other English-speaking democracies (Britain, Canada, Australia, New Zealand) and of Switzerland, it was not true much of anywhere else.

The distinctiveness of the American case is all the more striking when one remembers that Britain and New Zealand had no written constitu-

---

[34] Carl Schmitt, *The Crisis of Parliamentary Democracy* (1923), trans. Ellen Kennedy (Cambridge, MA: MIT Press, 1986).

tions at all, and that they and Canada and Australia operated under Westminster systems that divided authority and power much less than the American system. None of the four had a judicially enforceable bill of rights; only Australia had robust bicameralism; and, of course, none had an independently elected executive who might face an uncooperative legislature. These features of the American constitutional order came under real pressure during the long crisis.

But none of these features was actually abolished. Supreme Court Justice Harlan Stone, in the 1938 *Carolene Products* case,[35] established the rationale for late-twentieth-century judicial activism in defense of non-economic liberties just a year after the Supreme Court's surrender on economic questions in the face of Roosevelt's open threat to the Court's independence.[36] The potential of Stone's theory was not to be made use of for some time—*Korematsu* lay in the near future, *Brown* in the far future, and Stone's idea was rarely cited before 1950.[37] Still, the Court's willingness to stake a claim for its institutional prerogatives so soon after the climb-down of 1937 is striking. So too is the Court's willingness to directly oppose presidential emergency powers during wartime in the 1952 Steel Seizure case.[38]

Moreover, the corporatist, presidentialist, anti-constitutionalist views of the Roosevelt administration did not unambiguously carry the day even in economic policy. As the legal historian William Forbath has shown, the survival of common-law legal liberalism, of federalism, and of constitutional formalities restrained the ambitions of the New Deal reformers by comparison with the latter's British social democratic counterparts. Forbath suggests that

> the institutional contours of this new American state were deeply influenced by the ambivalent and lawyerly brand of American liberalism that [was] . . . poised between progressive commitments to

[35] *United States v. Carolene Products,* 304 U.S. 144 (1938); Justice Stone, concurring, 152.

[36] The so-called "switch in time that saved nine," the Supreme Court's newfound willingness to uphold rather than strike down New Deal legislation under the shadow of Roosevelt's proposal to increase the number of justices so as to "pack the court" with his own appointees, took place in *West Coast Hotel Co. v. Parrish,* 300 U.S. 379 (1937). Whether the switching justices were actually motivated by Roosevelt's threat is an issue of historical dispute that does not much matter for the point at hand.

[37] *Korematsu v. United States,* 323 U.S. 214 (1944), upheld the wartime mass internment of Japanese and Japanese-American civilians and is now seen as one of the low points for judicial protection of minorities and civil liberties. *Brown v. Board of Education,* 347 U.S. 483 (1954), the flagship case of the judicial protection of minorities against state governments, declared racial segregation of public schools unconstitutional.

[38] *Youngstown Sheet and Tube Co. v. Sawyer,* 343 U.S. 579 (1952), prevented President Harry Truman's attempted seizure of the steel industry during the Korean War—checking presidential powers and reasserting the importance of the separation of powers even during wartime, and incidentally protecting the property rights of large corporations—not at all what would have been expected from the quiescent Supreme Court Roosevelt had hoped for.

social reform, social provision, and administrative state-building, on one hand, and older, classical liberal commitments to limited and decentralized, dual federalist government and the primacy of courts and common law and traditional legal and constitutional niceties, on the other. If New Dealers had been able to design the state and American public social insurance according to their specifications, its institutions . . . would have looked dramatically different—and far more like England's.[39]

And if that lawyerly liberalism could survive the long crisis and even exercise some restraint on the reactions to that crisis, it could reemerge after World War II as the core of a new approach to federal-state relations that, unlike the New Deal, centralized power for liberal reasons.

## VI. Conclusion

The long failure of American federalism to protect freedom in the slaveholding and Jim Crow South did not meet its end during the rule of the Progressive centralizer Woodrow Wilson. Indeed, Wilson's disdain for constitutionalism, the American-style separation of powers, and federalism was joined with a disdain for civil liberties and for civil rights, and he imported southern Jim Crow restrictions into *federal* law. Nor did federalism's failure meet its end during Franklin Roosevelt's era of centralization. The end did not truly begin until the "lawyerly liberals" fully committed to federal court intervention within the states. Beginning in the 1950s, the federal judiciary gradually took on the task of vigorously enforcing the Fourteenth Amendment's requirement of equal protection of the laws against the legally entrenched racial caste system. The judiciary also assumed the task of protecting individual liberties against state governments, by "incorporating" the protections of the Bill of Rights (originally aimed mainly at the federal government) into the Fourteenth Amendment's prohibition on state infringements of life, liberty, or property without due process of law.

This was a further transformation of the federal-state balance beyond, but largely unrelated to, the New Deal revolution in constitutional jurisprudence. The latter, it should be remembered, not only freed *Congress* to engage in widespread economic regulation; it did the same for the states. The New Deal did centralize power; but it also simply increased government power relative to the market, whether that power was exercised centrally or locally.

The jurisprudence of incorporation and of equal protection was quite different: it was begun by different actors at different times for different

[39] William E. Forbath, "The Long Life of Liberal America: Law and State-Building in the U.S. and U.K.," *Law and History Review* 24 (2006): 179–92.

reasons. Given that the republican guarantee clause of the Constitution[40] had long since become a dead letter, this jurisprudence marked a novel commitment to avoiding the sort of federalism that, as the French classical liberal Benjamin Constant complained in the passage with which I began this essay, was compatible with "internal despotism."

The classical liberal legal theorist Randy Barnett, among others, has argued that the jurisprudence of the *Carolene Products* era was constitutionally misgrounded—because it accepted the expansion of government power as a background assumption—but not constitutionally *un*grounded, because the Civil War amendments really had transformed the federation's constitutional order and mandated federal court rejection of state laws that violated individual liberty.[41]

It is not costless to freedom-enhancing federalism to accept ongoing judicial review of state legislation, even when that review is in the service of protecting freedom (which we cannot assume it always is). The federal courts may well strike down laws that would have contributed to the feeling of local distinctiveness that could generate state-level loyalty and thus generate *Federalist No. 46*–style effects. This might generate a short-term backlash that intensifies state loyalty, but the long-term effect is likely to be a kind of homogenization that makes the states insufficiently different from one another to be worth much genuine emotional attachment. If a federation is successfully making use of those attachments and loyalties as checks on central power, and if there is reason to think that the central power would behave more illiberally than the component provinces if unchecked, then there might be good liberal-federalist reasons for limiting such judicially imposed homogenization. But these are contingent and empirical conditions that did not hold in the United States by the mid-twentieth century. State loyalty had long since ceased to be an effective check on any central-state action *except* those actions aimed at weakening the states' internal despotisms. Under such circumstances, the call for a "new kind of federalism," in Constant's words, a kind that deployed the power of the center to protect freedom against intrusions by the states, was a compelling call to all liberals who understood federalism as a means, and freedom as the end.

With this sketch of the constitutional history of American federalism seen through liberal lenses, I hope to begin to dislodge a standard historical story that equates American centralization with a turn from classical liberalism to welfare liberalism. It seems to me that welfare liberals are poorly served when they imagine that centralization has always been to their liking and that greater authority for states has always been some-

---

[40] See note 15 above.

[41] Randy Barnett, *Restoring the Lost Constitution* (Princeton, NJ: Princeton University Press, 2004); compare chapter 9 on *Carolene Products* with chapter 8 on the privileges or immunities clause. The Civil War amendments are, of course, the Thirteenth, Fourteenth, and Fifteenth amendments to the Constitution, passed in 1865, 1868, and 1870, respectively.

thing they ought to resist. They have sometimes read early-twentieth-century centralization, which was tied up with views that had little sympathy for liberal constitutionalism at all, in light of the later centralization that threw down Jim Crow. Some classical liberals, however, have been even more poorly served when they have fallen prey to the equation of federalism and liberalism. They have misread the Civil War, Jim Crow, and the legacies of both by generalizing from the constitutional disputes of 1937. They have mistaken a history of brutal internal despotisms being gradually overcome for a history of freedom being stolen away.

Federalism, the accidental innovation, turns out to have been a tremendously important one. To return to a passage from James M. Buchanan quoted above, it does seem to me that liberals—not only classical liberals, but all liberals, committed as they are to individual freedom—should be "generally supportive of federal political structures."[42] Yet all liberals, including classical liberals, should be sure not to mistake the means for the end. If federalism is a structure that tends to encourage liberal politics, it does so only by approximation. Approximations can sometimes be quite poor ones; and they are, appropriately, subject to revision.

*Political Science, McGill University*

---

[42] Buchanan, "Federalism and Individual Sovereignty," 79.

# INDEX